1982

Models for Behavior

Models for Behavior

Stochastic Processes in Psychology

Thomas D. Wickens
University of California, Los Angeles

W. H. Freeman and Company
San Francisco

To Carol and Wick

Project Editor: Pearl C. Vapnek
Designer: Sharon Helen Smith
Production Coordinator: Linda Jupiter
Illustration Coordinator: Richard Quiñones
Compositor: Bi-Comp, Inc.
Printer and Binder: The Maple-Vail Book Manufacturing Group

Library of Congress Cataloging in Publication Data

Wickens, Thomas D., 1942–
    Models for behavior.

    (A Series of books in psychology)
    Bibliography: p.
    Includes index.
    1. Psychology—Mathematical models.   2. Markov
processes.   I. Title.   II. Series.
BF39.W525   150′.724   81-17349
ISBN 0-7167-1352-7   AACR2
ISBN 0-7167-1353-5 (pbk.)

1 2 3 4 5 6 7 8 9 0   MP   0 8 9 8 7 6 5 4 3 2

Contents

Glossary of Symbols   xi

Preface   xiii

1   Theories and Markov Models   1

    1.1   An Example: The All-or-None Model   1

    1.2   Theories and Models   6

    1.3   Markov Models   9

        *The State Space / Transitions Between States /
        The Markov Property*

    1.4   Overview of This Book   16

2   Representation of Psychological Processes as Markov Models   18

    2.1   Markov Models   19

    2.2   Simple Models of Learning   24

        *The All-or-None Association Model / All-or-None Learning
        on Errors / The Linear Model / The Random-Trials-
        Increment Model*

    2.3   Two-Stage Learning Models   32

        *An Intermediate State / The Long-and-Short Model /
        Multiple Transition Operators*

2.4   *Choice Models   39*

> *Single Choices / Sequences of Choices /*
> *Probability Learning*

2.5   *Random Walks   46*

3   Algebraic Analysis of Finite Markov Chains   51

3.1   *State Probabilities   52*

3.2   *Response Probabilities   58*

3.3   *The Number of Errors   60*

3.4   *Sequential Response Probabilities   65*

3.5   *Item Variability   68*

4   Matrix Methods   77

4.1   *Representation and State Probabilities   78*

4.2   *Transitions Among Sets of States   82*

> *State Sets as Responses / Likelihoods of Response*
> *Strings / The Fundamental Matrix*

4.3   *Distributions of Some Summary Statistics   92*

> *The Number of Errors / The Trial of Last Error /*
> *Latency of Responses*

4.4   *Selection of Items Taking Particular Paths   98*

> *Likelihoods Again / The Backward Learning Curve /*
> *The Backward Latency Curve*

5   Estimation of Parameters   108

5.1   *The Estimation Problem   109*

5.2   *Method-of-Moments Estimators   113*

5.3   *Maximum-Likelihood Estimators   116*

5.4   *Minimum Chi-Square Estimators   123*

5.5   *Finding Numerical Extrema   126*

6 **Statistical Testing** **135**

6.1 *Goodness-of-Fit Tests* *137*

6.2 *Tests of Parameters and Comparison of Models* *141*

6.3 *Examples of Likelihood-Ratio Testing* *145*

7 **Identification of Models and Parameters** **151**

7.1 *Unidentifiable Parameters and Equivalent Models* *152*

7.2 *Vector-Space Representation* *158*

7.3 *Treatment of Identifiability Problems* *162*

      Equivalence Classes of Models / Parametric Restrictions / Analysis in a Broader Domain

8 **Markov Chains Without Absorbing States** **171**

8.1 *Classification of Markov States and Chains* *172*

8.2 *State Probabilities* *176*

      Transient States / Ergodic States and Chains / Periodic States

8.3 *Renewal Properties of a Finite Markov Chain* *185*

      Recurrence Probabilities / Recurrence of Transient States / Expected Return Times / Matrix Formulation

9 **Markov Chains with Unbounded State Spaces** **199**

9.1 *Random Walks* *200*

      State Probabilities / Asymptotic Behavior / State Types and Recurrence Probabilities

9.2 *A Queuing Example* *206*

9.3 *Learning Models* *208*

9.4 *Generating Functions* *211*

      Properties of Generating Functions / Difference Equations and State Probabilities / The RTI Model / Recurrence Probabilities

10   **Continuous-Time Markov Processes   226**

   10.1   *The Poisson Process   227*

            *Definition of a Poisson Process / The State Distribution /
            Waiting Times / Erlang Processes*

   10.2   *Birth Processes with State-Dependent Rates   238*

            Yule Processes / Death Processes

   10.3   *Processes with Arrivals and Departures   246*

            *A Simple Queue / State Proportional Rates /
            Multiple-Step Transitions*

A   **Summary of Probability Theory   254**

   A.1   *Fundamental Definitions   254*

   A.2   *Random Variables   256*

            Expected Values

   A.3   *Some Discrete Distributions   261*

            *The Geometric Distribution / Sums of Geometric Series /
            The Binomial Distribution / The Negative Binomial
            Distribution / The Poisson Distribution*

   A.4   *Some Continuous Distributions   271*

            *Distributions from Statistics: The Chi-Square
            and the Normal / The Exponential Distribution /
            The Gamma Distribution / The Beta Distribution*

B   **Difference Equations   280**

   B.1   *Homogeneous Difference Equations   282*

   B.2   *Nonhomogeneous Difference Equations   285*

   B.3   *Simultaneous Difference Equations   288*

C   **Introduction to Linear Algebra   291**

   C.1   *Basic Definitions   292*

   C.2   *Fundamental Operations   294*

C.3   *Matrix Inversion   299*

C.4   *Partitioned Matrices   303*

C.5   *Vector Spaces, Bases, and Transformations   304*

C.6   *Eigenvalues and Eigenvectors   308*

D   **Some Concepts from Calculus   314**

D.1   *The Derivative   315*

         Finding Extrema of Functions / Finding Derivatives

D.2   *Integration   321*

         *Integrals as Weighted Combinations / The Relation
         of the Integral to the Derivative / Calculation of Integrals*

D.3   *Differential Equations   327*

E   **The Greek Alphabet   329**

F   **Chi-Square and Normal Distributions   330**

Solutions to Problems   331

References   343

Index   347

Glossary of Symbols

This glossary defines some quantities and conventions that are used throughout the book. Page number(s) indicates a definition; for further citation, refer to the index.

a, b, c, ... Row vectors 292

A, B, C, ... Matrices 293

a' Subvector of absorption probabilities 85

$\alpha, \beta, \gamma,$ ... Parameters 26

$\hat{\alpha}, \hat{\beta}, \hat{\gamma},$ ... Parameter estimates 109

b, b' Probability of no errors following a response 63, 90

$B(a,b)$ Beta function 277

C, E Correct responses, errors 27

χ^2 Chi-square test statistic 124, 136

Δt Small interval of time 229

E_t The event of an error on trial t 58

$f_i^{(t)}$ Probability of first return to S_i on tth trial 187

f_i Probability of eventual return to S_i 191

$\Gamma(r)$ Gamma function 275

$L(\omega)$ Likelihood function 117

L Trial of last error 75

$\mathcal{L}_t$ Latency on trial t 97

λ Eigenvalue 308

N Fundamental matrix, $(\mathbf{I} - \mathbf{Q})^{-1}$ 91

$o(x)$ Any function that goes to 0 faster than its argument 231

1' Column vector of 1's 90

$\boldsymbol{\omega}$ Vector of parameters 109

$\hat{\omega}$	Vector of parameter estimates	109
Ω	Space of permissible parameter values	109
ω^*, Ω^*	Parameter estimates and parameter space for restricted model 143	
$\mathcal{M}, \mathcal{M}^*$	Unrestricted and restricted models	142
$\{p_i\}$	The series $p_0, p_1, \ldots$	212
$p_{ii}^{(k)}$	k-step transition probability, $P(S_{i,t+k}\|S_{i,t})$	187 .
$\mathbf{p}_t$	Response-probability vector on trial t	79
$P(z)$	Generating function for $\{p_i\}$	212
$\mathbf{Q}$	Submatrix of transient states	85
$R_1, R_2, \ldots$	Responses (in general)	21
$\mathbf{r}, \mathbf{R}$	Response mapping and matrix	21, 79
$S_0, S_1, \ldots$	States (in general)	13, 21
$S_{i,t}$	The event that a process is in state S_i at discrete trial t 13, 22	
$S_i(t)$	The event that a process is in state S_i at continuous time t 228	
$\mathbf{s}_t$	State-probability vector at time t	78
$\mathbf{s}_\infty$	Asymptotic state-probability distribution	179
T	Total number of errors	61
$\mathbf{T}$	Transition mapping and matrix	21, 78
$\mathbf{T}^{(k)}$	k-step transition matrix	81
$[t, t+\Delta t)$	Interval from time t (inclusive) to $t+\Delta t$ (exclusive) 229	
$\mathbf{W}_X$	Response-selection matrix	99

Preface

This book describes a variety of stochastic processes that can be used to construct models of psychological phenomena. It emphasizes the processes themselves and the mathematical methods used to analyze them. Thus, a reader may discover here something about how to represent psychological theory as a Markov process, and, in more detail, how to make a particular calculation or to derive a statistic, but will find less about the psychological theories that make the models important.

Why this particular orientation? Fundamentally, I believe that there is an important, although often underdeveloped, role for quantitative models in psychological theory. Theories expressed only as verbal statements are often hard to work with and are not readily subject to exact tests. Mathematical models are a valuable way to provide the more exact representation necessary for testing. Even when a psychologist's goal is not the construction of a general theory, a simple model process summarizes data better than do average performance statistics. As the field of psychology develops more rigor and exactness, I believe that quantitative models will play an increasingly central role.

However, these quantitative models cannot be written unless the relevant mathematical methods are familiar. This requires a good sourcebook. Over the years I have encountered a number of students who recognized the value of a mathematical model for their work, but who lacked the tools to create it. Unfortunately, there is no good place to send these students to learn the techniques. Research articles, quite appropriately, are devoted to the substance of the model they are presenting. Textbooks in mathematical psychology are better, but by necessity must choose between limiting coverage and presupposing too much mathematical skill. Mathematical sources, although often excellent, are not oriented to the psychologist reader and are frequently too advanced. A book for psychologists that treats the mathematical methods at an intermediate level of difficulty is needed.

Although this book contains mathematical techniques for psychologists, it is not a survey of mathematical psychology. I have made no attempt to review the field nor to do much more than present models because they are good examples of a particular stochastic process. There are two reasons for this. The first, and most simple, is space: to include the methods, their motivation within psychology, and a review of their uses would make a single book both difficult to use and expensive. At a deeper level, I have always felt that "mathematical psychology" is an awkward designation for a field. Content better defines an area of psychology than does methodology. Mathematical methods may be useful to the study of human learning, of perception, or of clinical psychology, but the value of these models lies in their relationship to the complete field. The particular places where mathematical methods have proved valuable should not be the central focus of a survey, but should form part of a general review anchored in the content area. A book on modeling techniques is not the place for this review.

Thus the present book. I hope that it presents a sufficiently wide range of techniques to give useful ideas, while remaining simple and complete enough so that a reader without extensive mathematical background can use it. Although the material is not of uniform difficulty (some of the harder sections are indicated by a vertical rule in the margin), a student with a good background in intermediate psychological statistics should be able to follow most of it. Of course, no one becomes proficient with mathematical modeling without having worked to apply the models in practice; so some things will probably remain obscure after a first or second reading. Working the problems provided here should help, but the reader must not become discouraged. I hope this book will also provide a reference for someone who is trying to read a technical article on some quantitative model, and perhaps help that person to develop and use a new model.

In writing this book, I have received much help and assistance. Many friends have discussed various points with me or have read chapters. In particular, Jill Larkin helped me to formulate a number of my ideas as I was starting to write, Eric Holman served as a source or a sounding board for many of my thoughts, John Cotton taught a class from an early draft and returned many comments on it, and Richard Millward submitted that draft to a careful, critical, but encouraging reading. I also thank Geoffery Keppel and Florence Wong at the Institute of Human Learning of the University of California, Berkeley, for providing space at the Institute for me both during and after a sabbatical leave. Finally, many students, my own and others', at the University of California in Berkeley, Los Angeles, and Santa Barbara, have struggled with and commented on various drafts of the text. To all of these people, and to others who have encouraged me, my thanks. Without any of them, the book would be less than it is; as it falls short of what it might be, it reflects myself alone.

October 1981   *Thomas D. Wickens*

Chapter 1

Theories and Markov Models

Psychological theories can be expressed in many different languages. Conventional verbal statements best explain certain theories, while others gain from more formal representation. Some theories benefit from a physiological expression, and others are most clearly revealed as a computer program. Another possibility is a mathematical representation. This can be valuable not only because mathematical expressions give a clear and unambiguous formulation of the theory, but also because the mathematics allow the implications of the theory to be developed in a rigorous manner. If the theory describes changes in the state of the subject, it is often profitable to express it in the language of probability theory. This book concerns representations of this type, and particularly the most useful of the probabilistic processes, the Markov process.

1.1 An Example: The All-or-None Model

A very simple all-or-none model of learning is presented in this section. It serves to introduce the principles by which psychological theories are written as probabilistic processes. Although this model is the simplest nontrivial model of learning, it embodies most of the important ideas used in more complex models. It will be used extensively as an example throughout this book.

Consider a subject learning a list of paired-associate items, constructed by pairing some members of a large set of potential stimuli (e.g., nonsense syllables) with responses drawn, with replacement, from a small set of alternatives (the digits 1 through 5, say). The subject's goal is to learn what response goes with each stimulus, so that, when presented with the stimulus, the appropriate response can be produced. On each trial the stimulus member of a pair is shown to the subject, who answers by choosing one of the responses. Following this response, the correct pair appears, providing both feedback and a chance to study the pair. This completes a trial. On the next trial another pair, possibly different from the first, is presented. The experiment continues in this way until all pairs are learned or until the time available for the experiment is exhausted. The data that are collected include the sequence of stimuli that are presented, the subject's responses, and possibly such additional information as latencies or confidence ratings.

The theorist's job is to construct an explanation, or *model,* for the subject's behavior in the learning task. Suppose that this model is approached from an association point of view. Consider learning as the formation of associations, and suppose that these associations are quantum linkages, which are either there in full or completely absent. The model should describe how associations between the stimulus member of a pair and the response are formed. Obviously, the development of a complete, general theory of association learning is a major task and goes well beyond the data of any single experiment. There is no need for such a complete theory in order to construct the model here. A simplified picture is enough. The model must embody the basic idea that the learning of the item is the formation of an association, but the model can do this as part of a relatively restricted picture. The complications of the general theory of associative learning are ignored, while its essential aspects are preserved.

To create this model, suppose that three simplifications are made. First, the learning of each pair, or *item,* is treated as being independent of the learning of the other pairs. This independence lets each item be modeled in isolation. From the complete sequence of trials, those trials on which a given item is presented are extracted. The model describes what happens on these trials only, and another item would be represented by a separate application of the model. Second, each item is represented by a single quantum association. At any time, the stimulus member of a pair is associated with at most one response. This association has an all-or-none character, so that it is either completely present or completely absent. A pair is known or not, without intermediate possibility. Finally, responses other than the correct one are lumped together, so that each response is classified as either correct or in error. No attempt is made to describe which incorrect response is made, only that it is not correct.

With these simplifications, a model of association learning, known as the *all-or-none model* can be written. This model is formalized in a series of very specific assumptions or axioms:

> *Assumption 1.* The subject's knowledge about an item is represented by one of two states: either nothing whatsoever is known about the item and it is in the *guessing state,* or it is completely learned and is in the *learned state.*
>
> *Assumption 2.* Initially, all items are in the guessing state.
>
> *Assumption 3. a.* An item can change from the guessing state to the learned state whenever feedback is given. The probability of this transition is constant, depending neither on the trial number nor on the past history of the pair.
> *b.* An item in the learned state says there indefinitely.
>
> *Assumption 4. a.* When presented with the stimulus member of an item that is in the guessing state, the subject responds by choosing randomly among the full set of potential response alternatives.
> *b.* When presented with an item in the learned state, a correct response is always made.

Each of these four assumptions concerns one part of the subject's behavior. The first describes what the subject can know about a pair, that is, how the subject's knowledge is represented. The second indicates the subject's state when the experiment begins. The third describes how learning occurs, that is, how the state changes. The final assumption relates the subject's internal state of knowledge to an overt response.

It is not enough for the model to describe a psychological process; it must do so with sufficient completeness to tie it to data. In fact, these four assumptions not only describe a specific mathematical process, but make precise predictions about how paired-associate data should look. Many of these predictions are treated in detail in Chapters 3 and 4. Although the mathematical derivation of these predictions is an essential part of working with the model, some of the predictions can be anticipated less formally. Consider the way in which errors on successive presentations are related. The fourth assumption states that errors are made only when the subject is in the guessing state. Thus, if an error is observed on the tth presentation of an item, that item cannot yet have been learned. There is only one guessing state, and this must be the state of the item regardless of whether the error occurs on the first, the tenth, or the fiftieth presentation. The information gained by observing this error can be applied to predict what happens on the next presentation. Because the item is known to be in the guessing state, the only way for the next presentation to also be an error is for the subject to fail to learn from the feedback on presentation t, then to make a wrong guess. In terms of probabilities,

$$
\begin{aligned}
P(\text{error on presentation } t + 1 &\text{ given an error on presentation } t) \\
= P(\text{error given the item} &\text{ is in the guessing state}) \qquad (1.1) \\
&\times P(\text{item not learned after feedback})
\end{aligned}
$$

None of these probabilities depend on t, so that the conditional error probability in Equation 1.1 is a constant. The constancy of this quantity over presentations is a strong prediction of the all-or-none model and can be tested by examining data from a paired-associate experiment.

At this point—or perhaps before—some objections to the model come to mind. The four assumptions are surely not altogether realistic. Many things may be wrong. Some objections center on the underlying theory. Associations may not be quantum, or at least associations of intermediate strength may occur, and so the all-or-none nature of Assumptions 1 and 4a is wrong. Other objections involve the way that the associations are applied. Even if associations are only there or not, it may still be impossible for a single association to completely represent the connection between stimulus and response (Assumption 1 again). Furthermore, the items probably are not independent of each other (Assumption 3a). A third group of objections concerns the description of the task. If easy items are learned first, then the pairs that remain after a number of trials are more difficult and harder to learn (a violation of Assumption 3a). Numerous other objections can be raised. Almost certainly, some of them are correct.

The goal in raising these objections is not to prove the model wrong. To do so is not very exciting. If one wanted only to disprove the model, one could easily reject Assumption 3b (no forgetting) by retesting the subject a few weeks after learning. Undoubtably, most of the items would no longer be remembered. But this would be a trivial rejection. The value of the model to psychological theorizing comes in other ways. The extent to which the model is correct gives information about which assumptions are reasonable; and even when the model is wrong, the way in which it fails tells how the theory might be changed.

Consider the two objections to Assumption 3: the dependence of items and the learning of easy items first. Both imply that the probability of an error on presentation $t + 1$ given an error on presentation t is not a constant. However, they have opposite implications about the

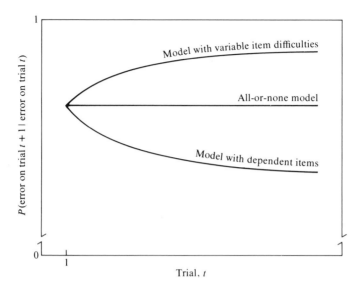

Figure 1.1   The effect of two different violations of Assumption 3 on the conditional error probability in the all-or-none model.

way in which this probability changes. Suppose that the items are not independent because one unlearned item tends to interfere with another. Then the items still unlearned at the end of the session would appear easier because most of the other items had been learned and could no longer interfere. This affects the second term of the product in Equation 1.1. The probability of being in the learned state on presentation $t + 1$ given the guessing state on presentation t would go up with t, and accordingly the conditional probability of an error would decrease. Alternatively, if easy items are learned at the beginning and harder items remain at the end, then the first term in Equation 1.1 is changed and the probability of an error given an error increases. These implications are summarized in Figure 1.1. The lines representing the two violations are quite different. A look at data would help to discriminate between them. Thus, even if the original model fails to predict the conditional error probability correctly, more can be said about the process. This information would be difficult to obtain without the explicit analysis provided by the model.

If the model is observed to fail in one of the ways shown in Figure 1.1, it can be modified to take the new processes into consideration. This produces a more complex model, but one that may fit the data better and lead to further psychological insights. Modifications of these sorts are considered later in this book. However, changing the model is not without hazard. Much of the usefulness of the model lies in the fact that it is simple and easy to work with, rather than in its generality. It is easier to add complexity to a model than to see how the processes can be represented simply. Parsimony in the description, while not always a virtue in itself, is important to keep in mind. If the all-or-none model were able to explain 70% of the behavior in an experiment, it would be of far more use than a model that explained 75% of the behavior but was twice as complex.

1.2   Theories and Models

The principles exemplified by the all-or-none model in the preceding section apply to many models in psychology and to all that are discussed in this book. For this reason, it is worth recapitulating more abstractly what is involved in constructing a model. Most research in experimental psychology has as its ultimate goal the construction of a general therory about psychological processes. These general theories are much larger than can be encompassed by any single experiment or even by a series of them. For example, the all-or-none model is based on association theory. One may believe that the mind acts according to principles of a network of associations; yet no single experiment is going to establish or disprove this belief. However, some evidence is provided by how well the all-or-none model fares.

The development of a general theory is a slow process, which proceeds more often by accretion than by sudden decisive changes. Even in the rare cases where a new theoretical position is proposed, it is based on—often as a reaction to—a body of older theory that has been laboriously worked out. One experiment supports a theory, another suggests how the theory might be changed, and a third extends it to a new domain. Each step is tested by comparing the predictions of the theory (or better, predictions from several competing theories) to data. As a result of the comparison, the standing of one theory is advanced, while another is found in need of modification.

A serious problem in constructing a theory is finding a proper balance between generality and specificity. A truly general theory must say something about a wide range of situations and individuals. But it is nearly impossible for the theory to be this generally applicable, yet specific enough to make unambiguous predictions. A completely specified general theory would contain so much detail that it would be hopeless to try to clarify all of it at once. The breadth of the theory, which is one of its most important aspects, is incompatible with great specificity. At some point, a unified theory that contains too much detail founders in a mass of special cases and inconsistencies. Anyone who has examined any theoretical controversy in psychology has observed the difficulties involved in pinning down exactly what a general theory does and does not predict.

A complementary difficulty concerns making predictions with sufficient precision. If a theory only weakly specifies details, its predictions are vague and difficult to test exactly. It is often unclear what supports a theory and what does not. This vagueness frequently appears in experiments designed to test theories by looking at the mean scores for several conditions. Suppose that for a two-group experiment, a theory predicts that group A has a larger mean than group B. Statistically, this theoretical prediction is tested as the hypothesis $\mu_A = \mu_B$, with rejection of equality in the appropriate direction taken as support for the theory. Yet surely not all values of μ_A and μ_B for which $\mu_A > \mu_B$ are equally in accord with the theory. The results of an experiment may be such as to reject $\mu_A = \mu_B$, but be even less consistent with the theory than the rejected hypothesis. The evidence from such an experiment is particularly thin when, as is too often the case, the event $\mu_A = \mu_B$ is not predicted by any interesting or plausible theory. A better test can be made if the theory predicts more exact values of μ_A and μ_B.

The two needs are in conflict. On the one hand, detail is necessary to make exact, testable, and useful predictions; on the other, this detail is impossible to achieve with consistency. One solution is to separate the generality from the detail. There is a general theory that remains broad, and there are more precise representations of its parts that include greater levels of detail. Limiting the scope of the specific forms of the theory lets the exact predictions that are necessary for a good experimental test be made. At the same time, since the limited theories are derived from the more general one, they are saved from being purely ad hoc. The global theory ties the narrower ones together and shows how their implications link.

In this book the term *model* is used to denote these limited theories. The important characteristic of a model is that it is concrete enough and clear enough so that its properties are well defined and its predictions are exact. Hence, it is subject to exact testing. A model is smaller and more restricted in scope than the general theory from which it derives, but makes up for this in precision. Of course, the restricted nature of a model limits its applicability to the situation for which it was defined, but this is a fair price for its exactness.

A model is usually tied not only to a particular psychological phenomenon but also to a particular experimental task. It is intended to describe behavior in one specific situation, not in others. Thus, the all-or-none model presented above applies only to a rather simple version of paired-associate learning, not to other tasks. Yet, if it were satisfactory, it would lend support to the associationist theory. The link to other situations comes through the general theory, which generates other, related models for other tasks. If a model proves satisfactory for a given task, it provides support for the antecedent general theory. On the other hand, if a model is unsatisfactory because data disagree with its predictions, then doubt is cast on the original theory. However, the general theory is not disproved thereby, for one can always question the way that the theory is represented in the model. No general theory is so narrow that it falls because a model that it suggests is wrong. The general theory is supported or rejected only as a collection of models derived from it are predominantly supported or rejected. The larger the collection of satisfactory models that arise from a theory, the more support the theory receives. If such a collection of models cannot be found or if they do not form a consistent pattern from situation to situation, the theory is weakened and may need to be abandoned.†

Because of its precision, one must interpret the rejection of a model with caution. Models make exact predictions, so it seems most natural to test them as null hypotheses against less definite alternatives. In such a situation, rejecting the model is the most definitive conclusion that can be made. However, in order to derive a tractable model from a general theory, it is always necessary to simplify some of the assumptions; so the model is always wrong in some details. With a sufficiently large group of subjects, it is always possible to reject a particular model. Even if a model fit one set of data exactly, another set could be found where it fails.

Once a distinction is made between general theories and models, the failure of a model is not a problem. The value of the model is as the expression of a theory, not as a complete description of behavior. The model only represents the theory in a particular situation and to a particular degree of accuracy, so the fact that there are situations where it fails is a commonplace. Hence, the simple statistical testing of a model at a conventional significance level is of little interest in itself. A more useful approach is to look at the way in which a model fits or fails to fit and to compare one model to other models derived from different general theories.

The logic of these tests is quite similar to that of conventional statistical testing. In conventional tests, the data are also represented by models from which consequences are derived and hypotheses tested. For example, consider a two-group t-test. For this test, a model of independent, normally distributed observations is adopted. However,

---

† A good example of the use of probabilistic models in the pursuit of a more general theory is the series of investigations reported by Greeno, James, DaPolito, and Polson (1978).

this model is not directly tested—it would be no surprise if the normal-distribution assumption could be found to fail in some particular, such as because it says that the potential range of scores extends infinitely in either direction. Rather, two alternative models are considered: one in which the group means are equal, the other in which they differ. A comparison of these models is tested by the *t*-statistic.

In spite of this similarity, the conventional statistical models differ from the models in this book in that they are models of data and not of psychological process. The statistical models describe what the data look like, but not how they came about. The methods presented below attempt a further step, interpreting the data through a description of the mechanisms that underlie them. This more elaborate basis gives the models greater power to test psychological theory.

The process-oriented nature of these models makes them useful for data analysis, even when tests of the process itself are not of interest. The quantities on which the model depends may reflect characteristics of the behavior under study with more accuracy than does any overt response. One of the clearest examples of this is the use of signal detection theory (e.g., Green and Swets, 1966; McNicol, 1971) to separate the sensitivity of an observer to detect a stimulus from the bias of the observer to respond by saying "yes or "no." A derived sensitivity measure (known as d') better measures the ability to detect the stimulus than do more overt measures such as the probability of a correct response. In the context of learning models, the probability with which items pass from the guessing state to the learned state in the all-or-none model is a good measure of learning rate, while such quantities as the error probability are contaminated by guessing. It is better to base a comparison of whether two groups differ in learning rate on this transition probability, particularly when the groups also differ in their rate of guessing. Such a test has value, even when the details of the all-or-none model are not correct.

1.3   Markov Models

This book discusses models that are formulated as mathematical entities known as *stochastic processes*. These are processes based on probabilistic descriptions (*stochastic* means "governed by the laws of probability"). Not all stochastic processes are treated, only what are known as *denumerable-state Markov processes*. The denumerable-state Markov processes do not exhaust the mathematical forms that have been used for psychological models, but they encompass a large proportion of them.

As their name indicates, the denumerable-state Markov processes are characterized by three properties:

1. *Denumerable states.* The state of the process at any time is specified by one of a discrete set of alternatives, that is, by a member of a denumerable set of states.

2. *Probabilistic transitions.* The way in which the state changes is described by a probabilistic mechanism.

3. *The Markov property.* The state of the processes at time $t > T$ depends only on the state at time T. In particular, how the process gets to a particular state is not important. All information about the past is embodied in the current state.

These three assumptions are considered in more detail in the remainder of this section. A formal definition of a Markov model appears in Chapter 2.

The State Space

In the all-or-none paired-associate model, the state of each item is represented by one of two possibilities, the *guessing state* or the *learned state,* and the change of state from guessing to learned defines learning. This is one example of the representation common to all the models considered in this book. With respect to the process being modeled, the subject is characterized as being in exactly one of a set of states at any point of time. This set of states is called the *state space* of the model. Changes, such as learning, are represented by transitions from one state to another. States are usually denoted by letters, most abstractly S_1, S_2, S_3, and so forth, but more mnemonically where possible. The two states of the all-or-none model are indicated by G and L, for example.

A large part of the work in defining a useful model lies in finding an appropriate state space. The trick is to select a sufficiently large state space to allow interesting properties to appear, but not one that is so complex as to be unworkable. Small state spaces often make a good model, and it is rather surprising to see the complexity of behavior that is predicted by very simple processes. However, large state spaces are not necessarily bad, particularly when the relationships among the states are simple.

The most critical part of constructing a model is properly defining the state space. Quite frequently, models that initially appear messy and intractable become very simple when changes are made in the state space. Several examples appear later in this chapter and throughout Chapter 2.

An idea of the different representations that are possible can be obtained by looking at some alternate state spaces for the all-or-none model. Part of the simplicity of this model comes from the fact that it is formulated at the level of a single item rather than of the full list of items. Any interactions between items are neglected. A more complicated state space is needed if these interactions are to be considered. For example, suppose that the list consists of n items and that the rate of learning for any particular item, call it item X, depends on the number of items that are yet to be learned. An appropriate state space for item X now requires $n + 1$ states:

Item X and all other items are yet unlearned.
Item X and $n - 2$ other items are yet unlearned.
Item X and $n - 3$ other items are yet unlearned.

$$\vdots$$

Item X alone is yet unlearned.
Item X has been learned.

If the interactions among particular items are important, it might be necessary to work with the state space for the whole experiment, by keeping track of the state of all the n items at once. Each item has two states, so altogether 2^n states are needed, one for each possible combination of learned and unlearned items. Obviously, the complexity of the models increases greatly in the larger spaces, although less than it may seem at first if the relationships among states remain simple in the larger state spaces. Note that the model in all three cases still has a finite state space and learning is still all-or-none.

Which of these three state spaces one decides to use depends on the level of detail at which one wishes to work. The full space of 2^n states gives the most detail, allowing interactions between particular items to be modeled. For most purposes, this is excessively complex. In the sort of simplification that characterizes the construction of models, the differences between individual associations are ignored. If the number of other unlearned items determines the rate of learning, as in one of the models leading to Figure 1.1, the intermediate-sized state space is necessary. For other purposes, the two states suffice.

The state space of a model need not be finite. For example, suppose one postulates that the probability of learning an item (in an all-or-none manner) changes as a function of the number of trials the item has been studied. This model needs a separate state to represent an unlearned item on each trial of the experiment. Since the number of trials is potentially unbounded, the state space of the model is infinite, although, of course, only a finite number of states is needed to represent any finite body of data.

Although infinite in size, the state space in the last example is still countable and discrete (i.e., the states can still be numbered 1, 2, 3, ...). There is no mathematical reason why the state space could not be any set, including sets that are uncountably infinite. In particular, it is possible to construct models in which the state space is the set of points on a line. Processes of this sort are called *diffusion processes,* since they can be used as a model of the physical diffusion of a particle through space. However, recent psychological theory has tended to emphasize relatively sharp changes in the subject's state—the formation of an association, the change of view brought about by feedback, the occurrence of an insightful answer to a problem. These are easy to represent as changes within a discrete state set. Because of this, and because of their mathematical difficulty, diffusion processes have found little use in psychological models and so are not covered in this book.

Transitions Between States

Once the state space is defined, the next step is to decide how the process moves from state to state. First, one must define how time is to be measured. Although time is, of course, a continuous variable, it is often much simpler to think of the process as operating in discrete time. Frequently, this is a reflection of the experimental design. For example, many experiments are organized as a series of trials. With such experiments, it is usually more helpful to index events by the discrete trial number than by continuous clock time. For example, in the paired-associate experiment described above, only the state of an item at the start of the test phase of a trial is important. Both the response and the effect of feedback are completely determined by the state. So successive tests of an item are counted as one unit, in spite of the fact that the elapsed time between two presentations may be quite variable. The time measure takes only the integral values: 1, 2, 3, ... Most models in this book use this sort of quantized time. Some continuous-time models appear in Chapter 10.

However time is measured, the course of the process is represented by the sequence of states it occupies. The point of a model is to describe changes, so the rules by which one state leads to another are fundamental. These rules give the next state of the process as a function of some combination of information about the history of the process. The past history of a process is entirely embodied in the sequence of states leading up to the current state, so the model's future behavior is determined by this sequence. The transition rules describe exactly how future states depend on this history. In stochastic models, no attempt is made to write exact, deterministic rules of transition. Instead, the rules are given in probabilistic form. In other words, for a process now at time t_1, the model determines a probability distribution over the state space at a later time $t_2 > t_1$, but does not determine exactly which state occurs at t_2. For most models this probability distribution depends at least on the state at t_1. In the all-or-none learning model, the probability of being in the guessing state, say on trial 10, is different if on trial 9 the subject had been guessing than if the item had been learned. Thus, the probability distribution is in some way conditional on the history of the process.

At this point it is worth developing some notation. Suppose that the state space is the finite or countably infinite set $\{S_1, S_2, S_3, \ldots\}$ and that the process operates in discrete time. Let $S_{i,t}$ indicate the event that the process is in state S_i on trial t. In particular, suppose that the process starts in state S_i on trial 1, moves to S_j on trial 2, and so on. Then defining the transition mechanism of the model involves giving the probabilities of being in each state on the initial trial,

$$P(S_{i,1}) \qquad i = 1, 2, \ldots$$

and the probabilities of being in each subsequent state, conditional on the past history of the process,

$$P(S_{j,2}|S_{i,1}) \qquad i, j = 1, 2, \ldots$$
$$P(S_{k,3}|S_{j,2} \wedge S_{i,1}) \qquad i, j, k = 1, 2, \ldots$$

and so forth. More generally, for any sequence of states $i_1, i_2, \ldots, i_t$, the probabilities

$$P(S_{j,t+1}|S_{i_t,t} \wedge S_{i_{t-1},t-1} \wedge \ldots \wedge S_{i_1,1}) \qquad j = 1, 2, \ldots \qquad (1.2)$$

are required. These probabilities are provided by Assumption 3 of the all-or-none model, although without the formalism.

Obviously, the choice of state space is important to the way that the probabilities are defined. In order to get a consistent definition, the state space must be adequate. Things cannot go on that systematically modify the value of Equation 1.2, but are not included in the state space. From any state and with the same history, the probability of each future state should always be the same. When the transition probabilities are not constant, processes that should be included in the model must have been omitted. When this happens, it is usually necessary to redefine the state space to resolve the difficulty, often by enlarging it. Thus, expanding the state space of the all-or-none model in the examples of the preceding section allows models to be written that are too complicated to have stable transition probabilities in the original state space.

The use of probabilistic rules to describe the transitions is important; in fact, it is the defining characteristic of a stochastic process. The decision to use a probabilistic model rather than a deterministic one is sometimes interpreted as a statement about the implied nature of psychological processes. The use of Equation 1.2, such an argument would say, indicates that psychological events must be, in the end, uncertain. This is not really true, for the probabilistic aspects are mainly a convenience. The stochastic properties of a model are closely related to its simplified nature and to the fact that it does not capture every part of a process in detail. Global understanding and a full analysis of details are the province of more general theories. The use of probabilities lets one construct a model that concentrates on certain parts of the behavior and ignores others. One may believe that the behavior in question is completely deterministic; yet one still may not be able to write a model that is precise for an individual subject, general enough to apply to any subject, and short enough to be tractable. Practical knowledge is not adequate to remove all uncertainty from behavior. Psychological theories are never sufficiently exhaustive for one to be able to write a precise deterministic model, nor is one's knowledge about a subject sufficiently detailed. The use of probability in the model is a way to get around this ignorance. Subsequent, more sophisticated models may remove some of the probabilistic aspects, but they will retain others.

The probabilistic character of a stochastic model also serves to describe parts of the task that are truly random. Generally these are aspects of the experimental design involving randomization. Material is often chosen for presentation according to some random schedule, and this is easily accommodated in the probabilistic part of the model.

One effect of using a stochastic model is that the predictions of the model apply to populations of subjects or of items, but not to individuals. Except for the exclusion of a few impossible transitions, it is not possible for a stochastic model to predict unequivocally the future of a particular subject. Only the state distribution for a population of subjects is determined. Hence, tests of models are based on large collections of data, not on what a particular individual does. In a sense, this imprecision at the individual level is the price one pays for being able to ignore fine details and keep the model simple. In fact, the practical restrictions caused by using a probabilistic model are little different from the restrictions imposed by normal statistical testing, in which a probabilistic model is placed on the data rather than on the process. In either case, a reasonably large collection of independent observations is needed before tests can be made.

The Markov Property

A model constructed by explicitly specifying all the conditional probabilities called for by Equation 1.2 would contain so many parameters
as to be all but impossible to write. As written, the probability of a
particular state on trial $t + 1$ depends on the entire history of the process from trial 1 through t. This makes the model prohibitively complex; among other things, it would surely be impossible to get realistic
estimates of all these probabilities from a reasonable-sized body of
data. Some sort of simplification must be made. The usual solution is to
construct the model in which the future of the process is independent of
all past states except for the one the process currently occupies. Thus,
for the discrete-time model, Equation 1.2 is simplified to

$$P(S_{j,t+1}|S_{i,t} \wedge S_{i_{t-1},t-1} \wedge \ldots \wedge S_{i_1,1}) = P(S_{j,t+1}|S_{i,t}) \qquad (1.3)$$

This is known as the *Markov property* (after the Russian mathematician
A. A. Markov, 1856–1922), and stochastic processes for which it holds
are called *Markov processes*. Where the time is discrete, as in Equation
1.3, the process is known as a *Markov chain,* or, if the state space is
finite, a *finite Markov chain.*

For a process in continuous time, Equation 1.3 must be changed
somewhat. With continuous time, it is not possible to list the states at
every past time. Nevertheless, the Markov property remains essentially the same. The independence of history holds for any choice of
times when the process is observed. For any $t_1 < t_2 < \ldots < t_{k+1}$, and
states $S_{i_1}, S_{i_2}, \ldots, S_{i_{k+1}}$ at these times, the Markov property states that

$$P(S_{i_{k+1},t_{k+1}}|S_{i_k,t_k} \wedge \ldots \wedge S_{i_1,t_1}) = P(S_{i_{k+1},t_{k+1}}|S_{i_k,t_k}) \qquad (1.4)$$

In words, no matter when it is examined, the future of the process
depends on its past history only through the current state. Equation 1.4
is more general than Equation 1.3, and it includes Equation 1.3 as a
special case.

Ignoring the events on trials prior to the most recent is less of a
restriction on a model than it might seem. The idea that the current
state of an organism determines what it does next is consistent with the
type of deterministic thinking that lies behind most psychological theories. Although the past determines where the subject is now, it is the
subject's current state that determines future activity. If it were possible to know the subject completely at a moment of time, that information would be sufficient to predict the subject's future behavior. If one
is unable to make such a prediction, the fault lies in having inadequate
information about the current state or in having an inadequate rep-

resentation of that state, rather than in needing to refer to the past. The Markov property expresses this idea as a mathematical statement.

Where the Markov property seems to fail, the model can usually be reformulated to make it hold. Once again, the trick is to define the state space properly. Any information that is needed for the response must be represented in the state. An example shows this. Suppose that a model has been proposed with three states, A, B, and C, and that the transitions out of state B depend on whether the process has ever been in state C in the past. For example, in a learning model, suppose that state B represents items whose association is unknown, state A represents items that are permanently learned, and state C represents items learned only temporarily. It may be easier to relearn an unknown item (passing from B to A) if it has been temporarily learned in the past (has been in C) than if it has never been known. Knowing whether the process has been in C does not require access to the entire past history. It is necessary only to expand the state space by splitting state B into two states that differ only in whether the process has passed through C. The state space now contains four states, A, B_c, B_{nc}, and C. State B_c indicates that the process has been in state C at some time in the past, while B_{nc} indicates that it has never been there. The process starts in B_{nc}; then, after reaching C, it moves into B_c or A and never returns to B_{nc}. Different transition probabilities can exist leaving B_c and B_{nc}, which solves the original problem. Doubling state B allows the process to "remember" the passage through C. Without violating the Markov principle, very elaborate characteristics of the history can be retained in the states.

1.4   Overview of This Book

This book discusses various types of Markov processes that can be used as models of psychological processes. As the discussion in the preceding sections shows, the way that the state space of the model and the transitions among the states are defined is of fundamental importance. In Chapter 2, a number of models are described, illustrating how state spaces and transition probabilities can capture a psychological theory.

The major emphasis of this book is on the way in which predictions about behavior are made from the Markov models. Examples drawn from the models in Chapter 2 are used to illustrate the analysis procedures. The next five chapters, 3–7, discuss one type of Markov process: finite Markov chains in discrete time containing states in which the process eventually comes to rest. These models are characteristically finite: both their state spaces and the number of trials on which transitions take place are finite.

Within this series, Chapters 3 and 4 look at the basic derivation of predictions, first without, then with, the use of matrix algebra. Of course, these predictions are useful only when comparisons to data are possible, either to match the model to data or to test it. The statistical problems involved in these operations are discussed in the next two chapters. Chapter 5 considers how numerical quantities are estimated; and Chapter 6, how hypotheses about models are tested. Although these chapters take their examples only from the finite, absorbing Markov chains, their methods are more general and can apply to the processes discussed in the later chapters as well.

Unfortunately, it is not always the case that models that appear dissimilar make different predictions. When different models predict the same behavior, they do not differentiate between the general theories that lie behind them. For similar reasons, it is frequently not possible to estimate all the numerical quantities that seem to be present in a model. Questions of this sort—when models make the same predictions and what to do about it—are the topic of Chapter 7.

The restrictions on the variety of models imposed in Chapters 3–7 are removed in the last three chapters. Chapter 8 drops the need for a state in which the process comes to rest, so that the process can continue to change state forever. In Chapter 9, infinite state spaces are considered. The methods of analysis in each of these cases are very similar to the methods of the earlier chapters, but expanded in one way or another. Finally, in Chapter 10, the discrete-time requirement is relaxed and Markov processes in continuous time are considered.

Throughout these chapters, results from probability theory, linear algebra, and calculus are needed. Some users of this book may find parts of these fields to be unfamiliar. For them, reviews of these topics, as well as of the solution to difference equations, are provided in a series of four appendices. These sections can be read before starting with Chapters 3 (Appendix A, probability theory, and Appendix B, difference equations), 4 (Appendix C, linear algebra), and 5 or 10 (Appendix D, calculus), although many readers will be anxious to get to the Markov models and so will prefer to turn to the appendices only as needed.

Certain sections of the text and certain problems have been marked with a vertical rule in the margin. These contain material that is either more technical, involves more difficult mathematics, is some what off the track of the chapter, or that for other reasons can be skipped on first reading. Unmarked material in later chapters does not require earlier marked material.

Chapter 2

Representation of Psychological Processes as Markov Models

The first step in creating a Markov model of a psychological theory is to define the state space of the Markov process and the way that the subject moves from state to state. In many respects, this step is the hardest one. Often many attempts are necessary to find a way to describe a psychological theory in a fairly simple set of states without losing its essential aspects. This chapter introduces the construction of models. Unfortunately, within the confines of the chapter, it is impossible to do more than illustrate how models are defined. Indeed, within a book of any length, it would not be possible to give explicit rules for how to write a successful model. In the end, the creation of a good model lies in the skill of the researcher. Because of this, and because the technical methods of mathematical analysis are easier to define (but often more disturbing to the student), it is easy to ignore the construction of the model altogether and start immediately with the calculation. This would bypass an important part of the modeling process. So the examples here illustrate some of what lies behind the formal models.

In this chapter a number of psychological theories are translated into the state spaces and transition probabilities of Markov models. The models are chosen to be simple and relatively clear examples. They are reasonable approximations to complicated processes and can serve as building blocks in the construction of larger theories. Throughout the chapter, no calculations are made. The mathematical methods whereby the models are analyzed occupy the remainder of the book.

This chapter is not a survey of the applications of mathematical models to psychology, however. The principal goal of this book is to present the techniques for analyzing models, so the selection of examples is limited. Although the models represent areas of psychology where appreciable use has been made of Markov models, they are more complete as examples than as descriptions of theorizing in any area. Simpler or clearer models have often been selected in preference to current ones. Other texts (e.g., Coombs, Dawes, and Tversky, 1970; Lamming, 1973; Restle and Greeno, 1970) provide more extended surveys. Many of the models derive from a general theory known as *stimulus sampling theory,* largely formalized by W. K. Estes and his associates (see the collection of papers reprinted in Neimark and Estes, 1967).

2.1 Markov Models

Before starting with the examples, the ground rules for the models must be established. Accordingly, this section presents an abstract definition of a Markov model. In the remainder of the chapter, this mathematical definition is filled out into a variety of psychological models.

The natural application of finite Markov chains to psychological theory is as models of changes in the subject's cognitive state. The elements of the state space correspond to the subject's states of knowledge about the task, and the transition mechanism shows the way these knowledge states change. Application would be easy if it were possible to observe the subject's state directly. One would need only to tally the types of states, then count the transition frequencies to estimate the probabilities of going from one state to another. However, the cognitive states postulated by most contemporary theories cannot be observed directly (if they could, much of psychology would be made trivial). Even in a case as simple as the all-or-none paired-associate model of Chapter 1, the two states, guessing and learned, are not directly observable.

What can be observed is the subject's sequence of responses. If the model is to be tested against data, it is these that must ultimately be modeled. This suggests that it might make more sense to model the responses directly, instead of the unobservable internal states. However, this procedure fails with regard to both the mathematics and the theory. First, responses are usually not Markovian. For example, suppose that one treated the correct and error responses in a paired-associate task as the states of a stochastic process. If these states were

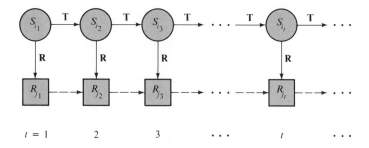

Figure 2.1 The sequence of states in a Markov model. The response process (dashed arrows) is induced from the Markov process on the knowledge states by the response mapping (solid arrows).

Markovian, the conditional probability of a correct response on trial $t + 1$ given a correct response on trial t would be independent of the past history of the process. Yet surely the probability of a correct response depends on more than this. A run of five correct responses gives fairly good evidence of learning and is likely to be followed by another correct response, while the final correct response in the sequence "error, error, error, error, correct" could well be a lucky guess and is much more likely to be followed by an error. The Markov property (Equation 1.3) does not hold for the responses.

This might suggest that the Markov property should be abandoned, even at the cost of greater mathematical complexity. A model that cannot describe data is not of much interest even if it is simple. But a second difficulty warns that this is not the direction to proceed. Current cognitive theories do not deal only with responses, but also with the underlying knowledge states of the subject. For example, when one describes a piece of information as being in "short-term memory" or in "long-term memory," one is making a distinction that is not directly reflected in a response. Presumably, information remembered in either way yields the same correct response. What differs (in the theory) is what happens to the information and how it interacts with other information. Thus, the representation of knowledge is more complex than the responses. Modeling only the responses precludes the expression of many important theories.

The solution to this minor dilemma is to use a Markov process as the model of the subject's internal states and to let the responses be functions of these states. The internal knowledge states can be Markovian, even though the response states are not. Two sets of states and two stochastic processes are involved. A space of unobservable states, which in this book is called the *knowledge-state space* (or often just the

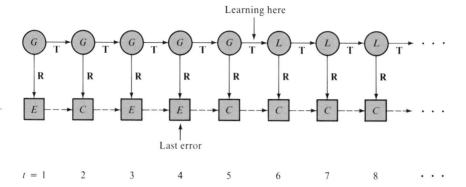

Figure 2.2   State sequence for all-or-none model generating the responses *E, C, E, E, C, C, C, C, ...* The subject learns after the fifth trial.

state space), is defined together with a Markov process on it. This process is mapped onto the observable *response-state space,* inducing the second stochastic process. The response sequence produced in this way need not be Markovian. The function that carries the knowledge states to the responses is called the *response operator* or *response mapping.* Depending on the model, this mapping may be probabilistic.

The situation is illustrated in general in Figure 2.1 and (anticipating somewhat the next section) for a specific example of the all-or-none model in Figure 2.2. The states of the general knowledge-state space are denoted by $S_1, S_2, \ldots, S_n$, and the response states by $R_1, R_2, \ldots, R_m$. For the particular example, a more mnemonic choice of state label is possible. States G (guessing) and L (learned) constitute the knowledge-state space of the all-or-none model, while states C (correct) and E (error) are responses. Suppose a subject starts in state S_{i_1} at time $t = 1$ (in discrete time) and passes from there to S_{i_2} at time $t = 2$, then to S_{i_3}, and so forth. This sequence is shown in the series of states at the top of Figure 2.1. The transformation **T**, called the *transition operator,* takes one underlying knowledge state and changes it to the next. With the state space $\{S_1, S_2, \ldots, S_n\}$, it forms a Markov chain. In Figure 2.2, this is illustrated by the particular sequence $G, G, G, G, G, L, L, L, \ldots$, indicating that for that particular item the subject spent the first five trials guessing, then learned. The transformation **R**, which turns an underlying knowledge state into a response, is the response mapping, linking the knowledge states with the response states. In Figure 2.1 this is shown generating the sequence $R_{j_1}, R_{j_2}, \ldots$; in the particular example of Figure 2.2, a sequence $E, C, E, E, C, C, C, C, \ldots$, is produced. The dashed arrows in the figures show the non-Markovian stochastic process implicitly defined over the response-state space.

This collection of entities constitutes a *Markov model,* as the term is used here: a knowledge-state space, $\{S_1, S_2, \ldots, S_n\}$; a transition operator, T; a response-state space, $\{R_1, R_2, \ldots, R_m\}$; and a response operator that connects the two spaces, $\mathbf{R}$.

The transition operator of the knowledge-state process is Markovian and so can be described by the probability that one state follows another. As in Chapter 1, let $S_{i,t}$ indicate that the process is in state S_i on trial t. More specifically, for the all-or-none model, G_3 indicates that the item is in the guessing state on trial 3. Then the *transition probability* of passage from S_i on trial t to S_j on the next trial is $P(S_{j,t+1}|S_{i,t})$. These probabilities are conveniently written in a square array:

State on trial $t + 1$

		S_1	S_2	...	S_n	
	S_1	$P(S_{1,t+1}|S_{1,t})$	$P(S_{2,t+1}|S_{1,t})$	...	$P(S_{n,t+1}|S_{1,t})$	(2.1)
State on	S_2	$P(S_{1,t+1}|S_{2,t})$	$P(S_{2,t+1}|S_{2,t})$	...	$P(S_{n,t+1}|S_{2,t})$	
trial t	$\vdots$	$\vdots$	$\vdots$		$\vdots$	
	S_n	$P(S_{1,t+1}|S_{n,t})$	$P(S_{2,t+1}|S_{n,t})$	...	$P(S_{n,t+1}|S_{n,t})$	

The rows correspond to the source state on trial t; and the columns, to the resultant state on trial $t + 1$. This array is called the *transition matrix* of the chain. The mathematical properties of the transition matrix as a matrix become important in Chapter 4.

A similar *response matrix* lays out the array of probabilities for the response mapping:

Response

		R_1	R_2	...	R_m	
	S_1	$P(R_1|S_{1,t})$	$P(R_2|S_{1,t})$	...	$P(R_m|S_{1,t})$	(2.2)
State on	S_2	$P(R_1|S_{2,t})$	$P(R_2|S_{2,t})$	...	$P(R_m|S_{2,t})$	
trial t	$\vdots$	$\vdots$	$\vdots$	$\vdots$	$\vdots$	
	S_n	$P(R_1|S_{n,t})$	$P(R_2|S_{n,t})$	...	$P(R_m|S_{n,t})$	

Where only two responses are involved, as with correct responses and errors,

$$P(R_1|S_{i,t}) = 1 - P(R_2|S_{i,t})$$

and it suffices to report only one column of this matrix.

Most psychological models simplify this representation in one important respect. The transition probabilities describe the underlying psychological processes by showing how the knowledge states change. These processes themselves usually do not change from trial to trial. Thus, the transition matrix is independent of t and

$$P(S_{j,t+1}|S_{i,t}) = P(S_{j,u+1}|S_{i,u})$$

for any trial numbers t and u. If this is the case, the time subscript can be omitted and the probabilities written as $P(S_j|S_i)$. A process in which the transition probabilities do not change with time is said to be *homogeneous* or *stationary* (there is some variation in terminology). Psychological models are so often stationary that the fact is seldom noted. On the contrary, it is more common to refer to models with changing transition probabilities as *nonstationary* or *nonhomogeneous* than for a homogeneous model to be identified as such. The same principles apply to the response mapping in Matrix 2.2. The homogeneity of a model is a property of the model, not of the theory it represents. One model of a particular theory may be homogeneous, while another model of the same theory is not. It is often possible to change a nonhomogeneous model to a homogeneous one by redefining the state space.

In order to completely define a Markov chain, more than just the transition probabilities must be given. The state where the process starts is also needed. A precise selection of one and only one starting state, as in the all-or-none example, is not necessary. In keeping with the probabilistic nature of Markov processes, it is enough to give an initial probability distribution across the knowledge-state space, that is, to give the probabilities

$$P(S_{1,1}), \ P(S_{2,1}), \ P(S_{3,1}), \ \ldots , \ P(S_{n,1}) \tag{2.3}$$

These probabilities are known as the *initial-state vector* (or simply the *initial vector*) of the model. As with the transition matrix, the vector properties of the initial vector are treated in Chapter 4.

Specifying the probabilities in Equations 2.1, 2.2, and 2.3 completes the definition of a Markov model. From the initial vector and the transition matrix, the future of the Markov process can be determined, at least at a probabilistic level. For any trial, the probability distribution across the states, or *state vector,* is found. Applying the response mapping to this produces the response probability distribution for that trial. Other quantities, such as the frequencies with which states are entered or returned to can also be determined. These often represent psychological characteristics of the theory as important as the response probabilities.

2.2   Simple Models of Learning

One of the major applications of Markov models to psychology is in the area of learning. Of the many different learning paradigms to which models have been applied, probably the most common one is the paired-associate task. In part this is because the paired-associate task lends itself to a simple analysis. Accordingly, many of the models in this section apply initially to paired-associate data.†

In a paired-associate experiment, subjects are presented with a series of stimulus–response pairs to be learned. The subject must learn to give the response member of the pair when presented with the stimulus member. For the purpose of exposition here, the stimulus member may be thought of as drawn from a set of nonsense syllables; the response member, from a small set of integers. Such a pair is NOF–3. On each trial of the anticipation form of the paired-associate procedure, the stimulus member of a pair (NOF) is presented alone and the subject attempts to recall the response (3). Following the response, feedback is given as to the correct pairing. This provides a new opportunity to learn the pair and completes the trial. On the next trial, a different pair is presented for test and study.

In most experiments, many different pairs (or items) are learned simultaneously, each pair being presented at various spacings with various numbers of other items between presentations. A typical sequence of trials is shown in Figure 2.3. Ultimately, a theory must deal with the interrelationships in the learning of all these items. However, as in the example of Chapter 1, it is a good first approximation to treat each pair in isolation. Thus, a sequence consisting of trials 2, 6, and so forth, in the experiment of Figure 2.3 can be extracted to look at the item JIV–5. The word *trial* is commonly used to refer both to the trial of the experiment and to the trial for a particular item, so that trial 6 of the experiment is also trial 2 for the item JIV–5. The models in this chapter largely deal with the sequence of trials for a particular item.

The All-or-None Association Model

The all-or-none model introduced in Chapter 1 is the first and most basic example of a paired-associate model. Although it is undoubtedly oversimplified as a realistic model of learning, it nevertheless embodies the basic principle of learning. Thus, it can serve as an initial approxi-

---

† For a good discussion of the representation of learning by simple state transitions, see Greeno (1974).

Trial

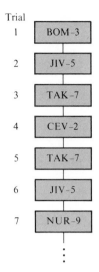

1   BOM-3

2   JIV-5

3   TAK-7

4   CEV-2

5   TAK-7

6   JIV-5

7   NUR-9

Figure 2.3   A sequence of trials from a paired-associate experiment.

mation to a more complicated model or as one component of such a model. As an example, it illustrates most of the principles of more involved models. It is simple enough to minimize the amount of algebraic manipulation, but still complex enough to show clearly how techniques are applied. It will also turn out that the algebraic methods used to analyze the all-or-none model in Chapter 3 closely parallel the general matrix methods of Chapter 4, which are applicable to any model.

The logic behind the all-or-none model has already been described in Chapter 1 and expressed as four assumptions. These assumptions are readily formalized in the notation of a Markov chain. The model describes the acquisition of a single item, and its states represent the knowledge of that item. Clearly, the guessing and learned states are the underlying knowledge states of the process; and correct responses and errors, the two response states. The first three assumptions define a homogeneous two-state Markov chain over the knowledge-state space:

Assumption 1. The knowledge-state process has two states, denoted by G and L.

Assumption 2. The initial state probabilities are

$$P(G_1) = 1 \qquad \text{and} \qquad P(L_1) = 0 \qquad (2.4)$$

Assumption 3. The transition probabilities from state L are

$$P(L_{t+1}|L_t) = 1 \qquad \text{and} \qquad P(G_{t+1}|L_t) = 0$$

and those from G are

$$P(L_{t+1}|G_t) = \alpha \quad \text{and} \quad P(G_{t+1}|G_t) = 1 - \alpha$$

for some parameter α, $0 \leq \alpha \leq 1$. More compactly, the transition matrix is

State on trial $t + 1$

		L	G
State on	L	1	0
trial t	G	α	$1 - \alpha$

(2.5)

The quantity α is an unknown *parameter* of the model, that is, a quantity that needs to be specified in order to be able to make numerical predictions. It represents the probability that the feedback on a trial is effective in causing an item to be learned, so it is called the *learning rate*. Even with a detailed analysis of the particular experiment that is being modeled, it is usually impossible to assign a value to α by a priori analysis. It must be estimated from data. Methods for making this estimate are treated in Chapter 5. In this book, Greek letters† are used to symbolize parameters that require estimation from data, keeping Latin letters for other quantities such as constants derived from the procedure or intermediate results.

A diagrammatic representation of the transitions is often quite helpful. For the all-or-none model, this diagram is fairly trivial (see Figure 2.4). Conventionally in a state-transition diagram, the states are represented as nodes and potential transitions among them by arrows. Paths from a state to itself are indicated, except for states from which there is no exit. Each path is labeled with the probability that it is chosen. Note that this state diagram is not the same thing as the diagrams in Figures 2.1 and 2.2, where the sequence over a series of trials was illustrated.

State L has the property that, once an item has reached it, no further changes are possible. Such a state is known as an *absorbing state*. State G, on the other hand, is not permanent. Eventually, with probability 1, the process departs from it and (being caught in L) never returns. Such states are called *transient states*. Most models of learning have at least one absorbing state and one or more transient states. The distinction

---

† Many different Greek letters are used in this book, so it pays to get their names straight. A table of the Greek alphabet is included as Appendix E.

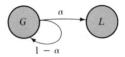

Figure 2.4   State-transition diagram for the all-or-none model.

between transient and absorbing states is amplified further in Chapter 8.

These three assumptions define a Markov chain, but they do not complete the learning model, for they do not describe the response process. The fourth assumption does this:

Assumption 4. The response-state space consists of the states C and E. The response mapping is

$$\text{Response}$$

State	C	E
L	1	0
G	g	$1 - g$

(2.6)

where g is the probability of a correct guess,

$$g = \frac{1}{\text{number of response alternatives}}$$

Like α, the symbol g represents a numerical quantity, but it has a somewhat different status. It is easily given a value by an analysis of the experimental paradigm and need not be estimated from data. The word "parameter" is not generally used for quantities of this type.

All-or-none models of the type described here were developed in the Markov context by Bower (1961). A discussion of them can be found in any survey of mathematical psychology.

All-or-None Learning on Errors

The version of the all-or-none model just presented does not take into account any feedback about the subject's response. Learning is as likely to occur if the response is correct as if it is in error. While this independence of feedback might be appropriate for a simple paired-associate task, there are other cases where it is clearly not realistic. Suppose that an experiment is run in which there is a rule by which the stimuli can be classified. For example, if the stimuli are geometric figures, red figures may have one response, blue ones another. The subject's task in this *concept-identification experiment* is to learn the correct response to a stimulus, but to do this by discovering the rule so that novel stimuli can also be correctly classified. One way for the subject to discover the rule is by a win–stay/lose–shift hypothesis-testing strategy. At any given time, the subject holds a hypothesis about the rule and uses it to make responses. If that hypothesis, be it ultimately right or wrong, happens to yield a correct response, the subject sticks with the hypothesis. If it yields an error, the subject abandons it and tries a new hypothesis. If the correct rule is color, for example, a rule based on the size of the stimulus yields correct responses only by chance and is changed as soon as it causes an error. "Learning" is all-or-none in nature and takes place when the correct rule is chosen.

The all-or-none model, as embodied in the four assumptions above, does not properly represent this situation. In order to adequately describe the subject's actions, the feedback must be able to influence the transition probabilities, so that transitions to L take place only after errors. To let this happen, the knowledge of the outcome is incorporated into the knowledge-state space by breaking the guessing state G into two states, GC and GE. These represent the subject's knowledge following both the response and the feedback: in GE a guess has been made and called an error; in GC a guess has been made and called correct. The state L is unchanged.

Transitions among these states are shown in Figure 2.5. At first, the process passes between states GC and GE, going to GC with probability g and to GE with probability $1 - g$. Transitions into L take place only from GE (i.e., following an error) and occur at a learning rate denoted by the parameter β. This defines the transition matrix

	L	GC	GE	
L	1	0	0	(2.7)
GC	0	g	$1 - g$	
GE	β	$(1 - \beta)g$	$(1 - \beta)(1 - g)$	

Initially, the subject guesses, so starts in one of the G states. The chance of this initial guess being correct is g; the initial state probabilities are

$$P(L_1) = 0 \qquad P(GC_1) = g \qquad P(GE_1) = 1 - g$$

The incorporation of the feedback into the knowledge states

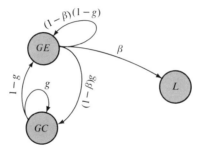

Figure 2.5   State-transition diagram for an all-or-none model in which learning only follows errors.

simplifies the response probabilities and makes them nonprobabilistic. Correct responses result from states L and GC, while errors result from state GE, all responses taking place with probability 1. The nonprobabilistic aspect of this response mapping is useful in its own right, as will be seen in Chapter 4.

Hypothesis-testing models of this type were developed by Bower and Trabasso (1964) and Restle (1962). A more complete discussion, including several related models, is given by Millward and Wickens (1974).

The Linear Model

The learning process can be viewed as the gradual accumulation of information, rather than the formation of a discrete association. In such a view, each successive study of a paired-associate item increases the chance that the item will be responded to correctly on the next trial, but there is no single sharp jump. In the simplest model of this type, known as the *linear model*, the item passes regularly through a series of states, moving one state further after each presentation, as the probability of a correct response increases.

Formally, let S_i be the state of the item following i study opportunities. The process starts in S_0 and advances to a new state on each trial (see Figure 2.6). The transition probabilities are

$$P(S_{j,t+1}|S_{i,t}) = \begin{cases} 1 & j = i + 1 \\ 0 & \text{otherwise} \end{cases} \qquad (2.8)$$

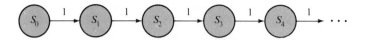

Figure 2.6   State-transition diagram for the linear model.

or, in tabular form,

	S_0	S_1	S_2	S_3	...
S_0	0	1	0	0	...
S_1	0	0	1	0	...
S_2	0	0	0	1	...
:	:	:	:	:	

(2.9)

Although this process is not very interesting probabilistically, it introduces two important new properties. First, its state space is not finite, but infinite. Although in any real experiment an item has only a finite number of presentations, there is no good way to set a limit on this number. In such cases it is easier to define a potentially infinite state space. The second difference between this model and those presented earlier is the lack of an absorbing state. The process never comes to rest in a single state of Matrix 2.9, but continues to advance.

This knowledge-state process is not probabilistic and is only trivially a Markov chain. But responses must be attached to its states, and the probabilistic aspect is introduced in the response mapping. Suppose that the probability of an error while in S_i is e_i. Clearly, all the e_i cannot be free parameters, for there would never be enough observations to estimate them and to test the model. Instead, let $e_0 = \epsilon$, and let each change of state shrink the probability of an error to a proportion θ of its prior value:

$$e_i = \theta e_{i-1} \tag{2.10}$$

As is demonstrated in the next chapter or by using the methods of Appendix B, this implies that

$$e_i = \epsilon \theta^i \tag{2.11}$$

The linear model has an important history in mathematical learning theory (see Bush and Mosteller, 1955; Bush and Sternberg, 1959; or any mathematical psychology text). The linear model has often been contrasted with the all-or-none model, for each represents something of an extreme of its type.

The infinite state space just described is not the only way to formalize the linear model. It can also be thought of as a one-state Markov chain with a nonhomogeneous response mapping. With only one state, there are no transitions in the Markov-chain portion of the model. To that one state is attached a response mapping that reflects the probabilities of Equation 2.11:

$$P(C_t) = 1 - \epsilon\theta^t \qquad P(E_t) = \epsilon\theta^t \qquad (2.12)$$

This version of the linear model is no different in its predictions from the infinite-state version. Which way one thinks of the model depends on whether one is more comfortable with a response process indexed by states, as in Equation 2.11, or by trials, as in Equations 2.12. In one case an infinite state space is necessary; in the other, homogeneity is abandoned. The larger theory from which the model is derived determines which view is simpler, for in the mathematics there is no difference between the choices.

The Random-Trials-Increment Model

In the linear model, every presentation of an item is effective, in the sense that every trial leads to some learning and some increase in the probability of a correct response. This is not necessarily a realistic assumption. Quite reasonably, some useless presentations occur, on which the subject learns nothing. This suggests combining the response mapping of the linear model with a probabilistic transition mechanism.

One way to construct such a model is to use something like the all-or-none model as a building block to govern the transitions upward. Let α be the probability that an advancement through the state space takes place. Then the transition probabilities of the linear model (Equations 2.8 and 2.9) become

$$P(S_{j,t+1}|S_{i,t}) = \begin{cases} 1 - \alpha & j = i \\ \alpha & j = i + 1 \\ 0 & \text{otherwise} \end{cases} \qquad (2.13)$$

and

	S_0	S_1	S_2	S_3	$\ldots$
S_0	$1 - \alpha$	α	0	0	$\ldots$
S_1	0	$1 - \alpha$	α	0	$\ldots$
S_2	0	0	$1 - \alpha$	α	$\ldots$
S_3	0	0	0	$1 - \alpha$	$\ldots$
$\vdots$	$\vdots$	$\vdots$	$\vdots$	$\vdots$	$\vdots$

(2.14)

The response mapping is the same as that of the linear model, given by Equation 2.11. The resulting model is known as the *random-trials-increment (RTI) model* (Norman, 1964) because the probability of a correct response is incremented on randomly occurring trials.

The RTI model contains the linear model as a special case when $\alpha = 1$. It also subsumes the all-or-none model when $\theta = 0$, for then the probability of an error falls from its initial value to 0 after the first transition. All transitions after the first are not reflected in changes in the response probabilities, so are invisible in the data. The model can then be reformulated with S_0 and S_1 playing the role of the guessing and learned states of the all-or-none model. This position as a generalization of both the all-or-none model and the linear model is a useful property of the RTI model. For one thing, when the model is fit to a set of data, the sizes of α and θ indicate whether the all-or-none or gradual properties are emphasized in a set of data. For another, tests of the hypotheses $\alpha = 1$ and $\theta = 0$ let the linear and the all-or-none models be compared. In fact, the original motivation for construction of the RTI model was this generalization of the two simpler models.

2.3   Two-Stage Learning Models

Both the linear model and the RTI model are considerable retreats from the simplicity of the single association embodied in the all-or-none model. Some such retreat is necessary, for the all-or-none model is frequently not supported by data. Often there is evidence for performance that is better than chance guessing, yet not perfect. This suggests that partial learning states should be added to the model. However, it is not necessary to go as far as the linear model or the RTI model. A single state interposed between G and L is often sufficient. This section examines such models. In many of these models, associations remain all-or-none in nature, but with a more complex structure for the learning process.

An Intermediate State

When a second state of learning is inserted between the two states of the all-or-none model, the result is a model commonly known as the *two-stage model* (or sometimes the *two-element model*). There are three knowledge states: a guessing state G, an intermediate state I, and a learned state L. The process passes from G to L perhaps via I. There are several psychological processes the state I could represent, but before discussing them, consider a general form of the two-stage model.

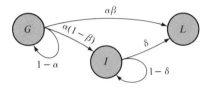

Figure 2.7 State-transition diagram for a two-stage model.

As with the all-or-none model, items start out in the no-knowledge state G, where only guessing takes place. Whenever an item in G is presented, there is a chance that some learning occurs: let exit from G take place with probability α (see Figure 2.7). The difference between the two-stage model and the all-or-none model comes in what happens next. With probability β, an item that leaves G is completely learned and goes into the learned state L. (Of course, neither α nor β is the same as it was in the all-or-none model; parameter letters are reused in different models.) With probability $1 - \beta$, an item leaving G does not enter L, but ends in the intermediate state I. Thus, for example,

$$P(I|G) = P(\text{go to } I|\text{leave } G)P(\text{leave } G) = (1 - \beta)\alpha$$

In the version of the two-stage model treated here, once an item has entered I, it never returns to G, but either stays there or progresses to state L. If the probability of progression to L is δ, then the probability of remaining in I is $1 - \delta$. When the item reaches state L, representing final learning, it is absorbed and no further transitions are made. Summarizing these probabilities, the transition matrix of the chain is

$$
\begin{array}{c|ccc}
 & L & I & G \\
\hline
L & 1 & 0 & 0 \\
I & \delta & 1 - \delta & 0 \\
G & \alpha\beta & \alpha(1 - \beta) & 1 - \alpha
\end{array}
\tag{2.15}
$$

Next, consider the starting configuration. Rather than starting all items in one state, as was done above for the all-or-none, linear, and RTI models, a more general initial vector can be used. Let

$$P(L_1) = \sigma$$

$$P(I_1) = (1 - \sigma)\tau \tag{2.16}$$

and

$$P(G_1) = (1 - \sigma)(1 - \tau) \tag{2.17}$$

be initial conditions, where σ and τ are unknown parameters. In this way, any configuration of starting states is possible. In many situations, it may be possible to partially determine the parameters σ and τ from a priori information; for example, if all the items are unknown to start with, then $\sigma = \tau = 0$. In other cases, one or both parameters must be estimated.

The response mapping remains to be specified. Clearly, in the guessing state, the probability of a correct response is g, as it was for the all-or-none model. The value to assign to $P(C|I)$ depends on the interpretation of the intermediate state. In many interesting cases, the responses in I are not simple guesses. Hence, to be general, the probability of a correct response is left free here, denoted by π.

Many different theories give rise to the two-stage model. Three of these are described in the next few paragraphs, and some others in Problems 2.6 and 2.7. Although the general theories underlying the three models are different, they lead to the same formal model and so make the same predictions. This emphasizes a point already made in Chapter 1: the fact that a model fits the data is no proof that the theory behind the model is correct. Acceptance of a general theory must rest on more than the agreement of one of its predictions with data. Issues of consistency, simplicity, and breadth—beyond the scope of this book—are important. The situation is further complicated by the fact that the equivalence of two models is not always obvious. Models that appear different may be mathematically identical. This issue is quite important and is the topic of Chapter 7.

One interpretation of the intermediate state is as a state of partial learning. Suppose that the task is such that selection of the correct response requires information about two different aspects of the response. The set of response alternatives, for example, may be divided into several classes; in particular, the set $\{1, 2, 3, a, b, c\}$ contains both numbers and letters. Entry into L means that both the class of the response and its particular value within the class have been learned; while state I indicates that the class of the response has been learned, but the value is still unknown. Whether the response probability, π, in the intermediate state differs from g depends on whether knowledge of the class of the response lets the subject eliminate enough alternatives to increase the chance of a correct guess. Even when $\pi = g$, the two-stage model's predictions differ from those of the all-or-none model because the passage through I retards learning.

A second interpretation of the two-stage model is as a picture of short- and long-term memory. An item in state G is one that has not been learned yet in any sense, while an item in state L has been placed in some form of long-term memory store, where it will not be forgotten, at least for the duration of the experiment. Between these states, items are retained in a short-term store in which they may eventually be learned or may be forgotten again. This is state I. There is still a chance of forgetting in this state, so the probability of an error is not zero. However, because the item is retained for some time, the probability of a correct response is greater than g. A version of this model is presented in greater detail in the next section.

Finally, the model can be interpreted in terms of the way in which the items are coded (Greeno, 1967, 1968, 1974). Suppose that there are many ways to encode an item: most totally inadequate, a few adequate to last for the duration of the experiment, and some that are adequate for a few trials but eventually fail. The model's states correspond to which of these encodings is currently employed. In state G the item is inadequately encoded and performance is no better than chance, in state L an adequate encoding has been adopted, and in state I one of intermediate worth is held. The intermediate encoding produces correct responses for a while, but eventually fails. Because of these correct responses, $g < \pi < 1$. In some circumstances this interpretation is most natural if the changes of encoding are brought about by errors within a hypothesis-testing framework. The subject keeps an encoding in force until it fails. This requires a modification of the two-stage model to allow state changes only following errors (see Problem 2.5).

The Long-and-Short Model

The interpretations of the two-stage model in the last three paragraphs are quite brief. Obviously, the psychological bases are more complex than presented here. The models originally developed out of the theory, rather than the other way around. To show this development in more detail, a version of the two-stage model based on a more elaborate analysis of long-term/short-term memory stores is presented in this section. The model is closely based on a model proposed by Atkinson and Crothers (1964).

Once again suppose that items start out in a state of no knowledge, denoted G, in which only guessing takes place, and once again suppose that, whenever an item is presented, departure from the state takes place with probability α (see Figure 2.8). This event is interpreted as the initial encoding of the item, which brings it into the subject's short-term store. This encoding is indicated by passage to the small hexagonal node labeled $\mathscr{E}$ in the state-transition diagram. However, before the next trial, several things can happen so that, when next observed, the item may not still be in this encoded state. One possibility is that the item is transferred into long-term or permanent memory. Represent this by the state L, and let β denote the probability of the transfer. With

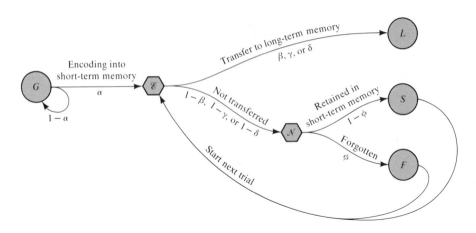

Figure 2.8   State-transition diagram for the long-and-short model. The hexagonal nodes are intermediate steps in the analysis of the model, but are not knowledge states of the Markov chain.

probability $1 - \beta$, the item stays in short-term store (indicated by the hexagonal node $\mathcal{N}$). If not transferred to L, an item in this state may be forgotten before the next test; let the probability of this be ϕ. Thus, two additional states are needed: F for items forgotten from short-term store and S for items still retained. In summary, the transition probabilities for an item starting in state G are

$$P(G|G) = 1 - \alpha$$
$$P(L|G) = \alpha\beta$$
$$P(S|G) = \alpha(1 - \beta)(1 - \phi)$$

and

$$P(F|G) = \alpha(1 - \beta)\phi$$

These sum to 1, as they must.

Once an item has been encoded and has left state G, it will not return; so all transitions into G have probability 0. State L, which represents permanent storage, is absorbing, so without outward transitions. If the item is in either state S or state F, it has been encoded and is subject to transitions very similar to those following departure from G. In effect, it starts each trial from the hexagonal node $\mathcal{E}$ in Figure 2.8. Presentation of a forgotten item (in state F) brings it back to the short-term encoded state, with a chance of transfer to L or of further forgetting. To allow for the possibility that the initial encoding may interact with the transfer to long-term memory or the recovery from F, parameters γ and δ can be used to represent long-term encoding instead of β. Except for this change, and for the omission of the α term, the transition probabilities look like those of the transitions from G; for example,

$$P(S|S) = (1 - \gamma)(1 - \phi) \qquad P(S|F) = (1 - \delta)(1 - \phi)$$

and so forth.

The response mapping depends on what is retained in the various states. Suppose retention is all-or-none, so that items are either known or guessed. Then the response carries states S and L to a correct response, but maps states F and G to a correct response only with probability g.

The model is summarized in the transition matrix and response mapping:

	L	S	F	G	$P(\text{correct}|\text{state})$
L	1	0	0	0	1
S	γ	$(1 - \gamma)(1 - \phi)$	$(1 - \gamma)\phi$	0	1
F	δ	$(1 - \delta)(1 - \phi)$	$(1 - \delta)\phi$	0	g
G	$\alpha\beta$	$\alpha(1 - \beta)(1 - \phi)$	$\alpha(1 - \beta)\phi$	$1 - \alpha$	g

$$(2.18)$$

This also illustrates how Markov states are used to provide "memory" within a model. Although the response properties of states G and F are the same—in both states the current response is not known—their transition probabilities are different. The distinction between the states allows one element of the history of the process to be remembered: state F distinguishes forgotten items, which have been in state S, from items in state G, which have never been encoded.

The transition matrix of the long-and-short model in Matrix 2.18 does not look like the matrix of the two-stage model in Matrix 2.15. However, the states can be grouped into three sets, $\{G\}$, $\{S, F\}$, and $\{L\}$, with the process passing from the first set to the last, but never backward. This grouping parallels the three states of the two-stage model. The parallel is quite fundamental: in fact (as will be discussed in Chapter 7), the two models make identical predictions. Models with either Matrix 2.15 or Matrix 2.18 fit data equally well. The long-and-short model, with more states and more parameters than the two-stage model, is more elaborate than computation alone requires. In fact, some of the parameters of Matrix 2.18 cannot be estimated. However, if the psychological theory that underlies the long-and-short model is of primary interest, it is the model of Matrix 2.18 that one wants to test. Even in this case, the model in the form of Matrix 2.15 is useful as a computational aid.

Multiple Transition Operators

In the construction of a Markov model, there is no necessity to apply the same transition operator at every instance when the state may change. If several different operations take place in the course of the experiment, it may be best to represent them by different transition operators. Depending on what happens, one or another operator applies. The composite process is the combination of several simpler operators.

This notion has been used to represent both acquisition and interference in a learning model (Calfee and Atkinson, 1965). The models for the paired-associate task that have been described so far have followed a single item and have neglected what happens to other items. Of course, subjects learn more than one pair in an experiment, and between any two presentations of one pair, other pairs are presented. The situation was illustrated in Figure 2.3, which showed three different pairs presented between the two presentations of the pair JIV–5. These presentations create interference and can lead to forgetting of what had been learned about the JIV–5 association on trial 2. A more complete model of the process requires learning operators that apply when an item is studied and forgetting operators that apply when any other item is presented.

Consider a two-stage model in which the intermediate state represents a less durable encoding of the response. When the item is presented for study, the normal transition operator, Matrix 2.15, applies:

$$
\begin{array}{c|ccc}
 & L & I & G \\
\hline
L & 1 & 0 & 0 \\
I & \delta & 1-\delta & 0 \\
G & \alpha\beta & \alpha(1-\beta) & 1-\alpha
\end{array}
\tag{2.19}
$$

So far, this is nothing new. Now consider the presentation of an interfering item. The interference has no effect if the item is in L or G, for items in L are permanently learned and there is nothing to forget about an item in G. But if the item is in I, it can be forgotten, that is, transferred back to the guessing state. This operation is described by a second transition operator:

$$
\begin{array}{c|ccc}
 & L & I & G \\
\hline
L & 1 & 0 & 0 \\
I & 0 & \zeta & 1-\zeta \\
G & 0 & 0 & 1
\end{array}
\qquad (2.20)
$$

where ζ is the probability that the interference does not cause forgetting. Consider the pair JIV–5 in Figure 2.3. The operator in Matrix 2.19 applies on trials 2 and 6, and the operator in Matrix 2.20 on trials 3, 4, 5, and so forth. The net effect is more complicated than that expressed by either of the simple operators alone.

Procedures of this sort are of value when a model for a fairly complicated process is being constructed. Even if the overall process is complex, it is often possible to break it down into several stages, each of which can be represented by a simple operator. By methods to be covered in Chapter 4 (actually, just ordinary matrix multiplication), the simple operators are combined into a transition operator for the full process. It is much easier to understand and to modify a complicated model that is expressed in this fashion.†

2.4   Choice Models

Consider a person (or an animal) faced with a choice between two alternatives. The person ponders for some period of time, then selects one of the alternatives. Data from such a situation are characterized by the choice that is made and by the time it takes to make the choice. A successful model should make predictions for both of these.

Single Choices

The simplest possible model is for a single choice between two alternatives, say A and B. At a minimum, three states are needed to describe the situation: an initial state of uncertainty, U, and two decision states, A and B, that express the choice that is made. A single transition takes place that brings the process from U into one of the two decision states. The time space for this model could be either continuous or discrete. It seems most natural to construct the transition mechanism to operate in

---

† Where the particular transition operator that is applied depends on an external stimulus, the model becomes a *stochastic automaton* or a *stochastic machine*. Such entities are studied as part of computation theory (see, e.g., Paz, 1971).

continuous time. This way latencies could take any possible value. However, it is somewhat easier to see what is happening with a model constructed in discrete time. In this chapter, models are presented that operate in discrete time, while models in continuous time are developed in Chapter 10. In fact, the choice between continuous and discrete time is of less importance than it first seems, for the predictions of continuous-time models are almost identical to their discrete-time counterparts.

The immediate problem with a discrete-time model is to decide what a time step or "trial" means in this context. The grain of a discrete-trials model must be imposed either by the experimental situation or by the theory. Plausible alternatives here include letting a trial refer to a very short interval of time, defining a trial sequence based on some hypothetical internal event generated by the subject (a "look" at the alternatives), or constructing an experiment that enforces a temporal grain on the subject's actions. The first two of these are approximations for continuous time; the last is based on a discontinuity that is more fundamental.

The transitions among the three states are simple. The only thing that can happen is for the process to move from U to A or B. Using the same transition mechanism as in the all-or-none learning model, let the subject remain in indecision on each trial with probability $1 - \delta$ and decide with probability δ. When transition takes place, let it be to alternative A with probability α and to alternative B with probability $1 - \alpha$. The transition matrix for the resulting process is

$$
\begin{array}{c|ccc}
 & A & B & U \\
\hline
A & 1 & 0 & 0 \\
B & 0 & 1 & 0 \\
U & \delta\alpha & \delta(1 - \alpha) & 1 - \delta \\
\end{array}
\qquad (2.21)
$$

Defining the response process of the model is trivial, for the three states map directly onto observable states of indecision or choice.

A model like Matrix 2.21 lacks subtlety. As will be seen in Chapter 3 (Problem 3.2c), a consequence of this is that the time until the choice is made has a geometric distribution, which is often quite unrealistic. A better model is obtained if some internal processing is added. As with the learning models, an additional state can be interposed between the initial and the final state. Consider a choice model in which, before a final choice is made, the subject moves from the initial indecision state into a state in which one of the alternatives is seriously considered. From this state either a decision is made or the subject returns to the uncommitted state. The intermediate states represent conditions in

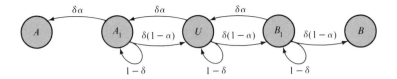

Figure 2.9   State-transition diagram for a two-alternative choice model with intermediate states.

which the subject approaches, but does not yet make, a choice. For example, these are the "vicarious trial-and-error" (*VTE*) states of Tolman's learning theory (e.g., Tolman, 1939; see the choice models discussed by Aktinson, Bower, and Crothers, 1965, from which the present model is adapted). The model now contains five states in the knowledge-state process: an uncertain state, U; approach states for the two decisions, denoted A_1 and B_1; and the final decision states, A and B (see Figure 2.9). On any trial let a state change take place with probability δ, and let this be toward choice A with probability α and toward B with probability $1 - \alpha$. Rearranging the matrix a bit, the transitions are

$$
\begin{array}{c|ccccc}
 & A & A_1 & U & B_1 & B \\
\hline
A & 1 & 0 & 0 & 0 & 0 \\
A_1 & \delta\alpha & 1 - \delta & \delta(1 - \alpha) & 0 & 0 \\
U & 0 & \delta\alpha & 1 - \delta & \delta(1 - \alpha) & 0 \\
B_1 & 0 & 0 & \delta\alpha & 1 - \delta & \delta(1 - \alpha) \\
B & 0 & 0 & 0 & 0 & 1
\end{array}
\qquad (2.22)
$$

The response mapping carries A_1, U, and B_1 onto a no-decision state and A and B to the corresponding decision states.

Clearly, the principle by which Matrix 2.21 is expanded to Matrix 2.22 can be used to interpose any number of states between the two alternatives. The choice of the appropriate number may be dictated by a theory of internal events or left as a free parameter. For the moment, Matrix 2.22 is sufficient.

Sequences of Choices

If one were not interested in the latencies, the internal processing is irrelevant and the model in Matrix 2.22 is identical to that in Matrix 2.21. This is not very interesting unless a series of choices is involved.

Suppose that on each of a series of trials, a subject selects one of two alternatives, A or B. If alternative A is selected with probability α and the choices are independent, this is represented by the Markov chain

$$
\begin{array}{c|cc}
 & A & B \\
\hline
A & \alpha & 1-\alpha \\
B & \alpha & 1-\alpha
\end{array}
\tag{2.23}
$$

Each new choice is a trial in this chain. There is no absorbing state, for there is no terminal response. After each choice the subject goes on to the next trial. The result is, in effect, a series of identical Bernoulli events.

One point of starting with such a simple model is that it is easily modified. Suppose that instead of parameterizing by $P(A)$, the model is constructed so that κ is the probability that the subject makes a different response from the response on the previous trial. Then the transition matrix of the process is

$$
\begin{array}{c|cc}
 & A & B \\
\hline
A & 1-\kappa & \kappa \\
B & \kappa & 1-\kappa
\end{array}
\tag{2.24}
$$

The behavior of this chain depends on the value of κ. When κ is near 0, the sequence of responses contains long runs of the same response. When κ is near 1, the choices tend to alternate.

Evidence for a more complicated structure comes from the fact that sequences of choices do not have a simple Bernoulli structure. Thus, they are not independent. Dependencies among the responses are introduced by expanding the state space. Suppose that the probability of changing the choice is κ when the current choice is different from the previous choice and λ when it is the same. To express this dependence, four states and a mapping to carry them onto the responses are required. Using familiar principles and notation, one writes the model as

$$
\begin{array}{c|cccc|c}
 & A_2 & A_1 & B_1 & B_2 & P(\text{choose } A \mid \text{state}) \\
\hline
A_2 & 1-\lambda & 0 & \lambda & 0 & 1 \\
A_1 & 1-\kappa & 0 & \kappa & 0 & 1 \\
B_1 & 0 & \kappa & 0 & 1-\kappa & 0 \\
B_2 & 0 & \lambda & 0 & 1-\lambda & 0
\end{array}
\tag{2.25}
$$

If $\lambda = \kappa$, the states of Matrix 2.25 collapse to those of Matrix 2.24; while if $\kappa = 0$, the model predicts perfect double alteration, $A, A, B, B,$ $A, A, B, B, \ldots$. The ideas behind this model can readily be extended to treat dependencies over larger numbers of trials.

Probability Learning

One experimental paradigm to which the models for sequences of choices apply is known as *probability learning*. In this task, the subject is asked to predict which of two (or more) events will take place on a series of trials. The sequence of events on a typical trial goes as follows: First some sort of warning indicator (usually a light) appears, notifying the subject that a response is to be made. The subject makes a prediction among the possible alternatives (typically by pressing a button). Once this is done, the "correct" event is indicated (a light again). This completes the trial. Although the experiment could employ any number of events and responses, the probability-learning models are best illustrated in the simplest and most common case of two events, E_1 and E_2, and two responses, R_1 and R_2.

In the basic probability-learning task, the events that the subject attempts to predict are random Bernoulli events, independent from trial to trial, with $P(E_1) = \pi$ and $P(E_2) = 1 - \pi$. The subject's responses reflect, therefore, the action of a pattern of inconsistent reinforcement. In practice, what commonly happens (Estes, 1964; Myers, 1976) is that the subject eventually adopts a pattern of responding in which $P(R_1)$ approximates π. This is in spite of the fact that more correct responses are made by consistently selecting the most frequent event.

One model for behavior in this situation[†] can be constructed in the same way as the choice sequence models. Starting with an all-or-none picture, the model consists of two states (R_1 and R_2) and, on each choice, the subject makes a prediction appropriate to the current state. The reinforcement event determines the transitions between these states via a mechanism such as the one proposed in Matrix 2.23 or Matrix 2.24. However, these operators are too simple, for their particular form surely depends on the feedback. Suppose that a win–stay/ lose–shift strategy applies: when the subject has made a "correct" prediction, the same prediction is made again on the next trial; while if a prediction is "incorrect," then the response is switched with probability σ. In effect, a single "element" is associated to the most recent

---

[†] There are other models that are not covered in this discussion (see Millward, 1971; Myers, 1970).

event, although the association process is not perfectly efficient. Two operators represent this process. They differ only in the direction of the change of state that takes place. After E_1, the operator

$$
\begin{array}{c|cc}
 & R_1 & R_2 \\
\hline
R_1 & 1 & 0 \\
R_2 & \sigma & 1 - \sigma
\end{array}
\tag{2.26}
$$

can change the state from R_2 to R_1; while after E_2, the opposite change applies:

$$
\begin{array}{c|cc}
 & R_1 & R_2 \\
\hline
R_1 & 1 - \sigma & \sigma \\
R_2 & 0 & 1
\end{array}
\tag{2.27}
$$

The analysis of this model is in some ways simplified by redefinition of the state space so that both the response and the subsequent event are modeled in a single operator. Whereas Matrices 2.26 and 2.27 are models for the subject, what is created now is a model for the complete experiment, including both the subject and the experimenter's presentation schedule. Four states are needed, pairing a response and an event. Denote by $R_i E_j$ the state in which the subject makes response R_i and the experimenter follows this with event E_j. The transition from this state to the state on the next trial depends on two things: first, the changes in the subject's state, as given by Matrix 2.26 or Matrix 2.27, and second, the random event of the next trial, which is a Bernoulli event with probability π. Combining these gives

$$
\begin{array}{c|cccc}
 & R_1E_1 & R_2E_1 & R_1E_2 & R_2E_2 \\
\hline
R_1E_1 & \pi & 0 & 1 - \pi & 0 \\
R_2E_1 & \sigma\pi & (1 - \sigma)\pi & \sigma(1 - \pi) & (1 - \sigma)(1 - \pi) \\
R_1E_2 & (1 - \sigma)\pi & \sigma\pi & (1 - \sigma)(1 - \pi) & \sigma(1 - \pi) \\
R_2E_2 & 0 & \pi & 0 & 1 - \pi
\end{array}
\tag{2.28}
$$

The combination of subject and experimenter processes is reflected in the structure of the transition matrix. The 2×2 submatrices connecting pairs of states with the same event look like Matrix 2.26 or Matrix 2.27, but multiplied by π or $1 - \pi$.

The model just developed, being essentially all-or-none in nature, is often too simple. Trials are independent and only a single association determines the response. More complex models are formed by treating two or more associations. The simplest of these has two associations, rather in the same way that the two-stage model extends the all-or-none model. Suppose that one of the two associations is chosen on each trial to determine the response. Modeling the subject only (without the events) requires four states:

A_{11}: both associations are to E_1.

A_{12}: one association is to E_1, one is to E_2, and the association to E_1 is chosen to determine the response.

A_{21}: one association is to E_1, one is to E_2, and the association to E_2 is chosen to determine the response.

A_{22}: both associations are to E_2.

As only the chosen association participates in the response, R_1 is made from A_{11} and A_{12}, and R_2 is made from the other two states. The transition mechanism of this model depends on the way that an association is chosen to dictate the response and the way that associations are formed or broken. Suppose that the choice is random, either of the two associations being selected with probability $\frac{1}{2}$. Further, suppose that only the chosen association can be changed (the unselected association remains the same) and that the action of this change is the same as that described by Matrices 2.26 and 2.27. Then the new transition operators are

$$
\begin{array}{c|cccc}
 & A_{11} & A_{12} & A_{21} & A_{22} \\
\hline
A_{11} & 1 & 0 & 0 & 0 \\
A_{12} & 0 & \frac{1}{2} & \frac{1}{2} & 0 \\
A_{21} & \sigma & (1-\sigma)/2 & (1-\sigma)/2 & 0 \\
A_{22} & 0 & \sigma/2 & \sigma/2 & 1-\sigma
\end{array}
\tag{2.29}
$$

following E_1 and

$$
\begin{array}{c|cccc}
 & A_{11} & A_{12} & A_{21} & A_{22} \\
\hline
A_{11} & 1-\sigma & \sigma/2 & \sigma/2 & 0 \\
A_{12} & 0 & (1-\sigma)/2 & (1-\sigma)/2 & \sigma \\
A_{21} & 0 & \frac{1}{2} & \frac{1}{2} & 0 \\
A_{22} & 0 & 0 & 0 & 1
\end{array}
\tag{2.30}
$$

following E_2. These operators apply with probability π and $1-\pi$, respectively. Obviously, this scheme can be extended to a larger number of associations. Just as with the two-stage model, there are many interpretations for models of this type.

2.5   Random Walks

Many of the models above, including some forms of the two-stage model, the choice model in Matrix 2.22, and the RTI model in Matrices 2.13 and 2.14, are examples of an important class of Markov chains known as *random walks*. Random walks are defined on an ordered series of states with transitions that obey two rules. First, on each trial the process can move (if at all) to an adjacent state, but never further than that. Second, the transition probabilities are the same for any state, except perhaps at the end of the series of states. In effect, the process makes a series of steps in randomly determined directions. Because random walks are simple and relatively well analyzed, they are good bases for psychological models.

There are several varieties of random walk. Consider first a model similar to Matrix 2.22, with *absorbing barriers* at either end. The transition matrix of a random walk of this type with five states, numbered from S_0 to S_4, is

	S_0	S_1	S_2	S_3	S_4
S_0	1	0	0	0	0
S_1	$\gamma(1 - \eta)$	$1 - \gamma$	$\gamma\eta$	0	0
S_2	0	$\gamma(1 - \eta)$	$1 - \gamma$	$\gamma\eta$	0
S_3	0	0	$\gamma(1 - \eta)$	$1 - \gamma$	$\gamma\eta$
S_4	0	0	0	0	1

$$(2.31)$$

The parameter γ is the probability that a step in one direction or the other occurs on a given trial, and η is the probability that that step is toward the right.

One or both ends of the random walk can be made into *reflecting barriers,* rather than absorbing barriers. When the process reaches such a barrier, it is (probabilistically) turned back on itself. Modifying Matrix 2.31 in this way gives

	S_0	S_1	S_2	S_3	S_4
S_0	$1 - \gamma\eta$	$\gamma\eta$	0	0	0
S_1	$\gamma(1 - \eta)$	$1 - \gamma$	$\gamma\eta$	0	0
S_2	0	$\gamma(1 - \eta)$	$1 - \gamma$	$\gamma\eta$	0
S_3	0	0	$\gamma(1 - \eta)$	$1 - \gamma$	$\gamma\eta$
S_4	0	0	0	$\gamma(1 - \eta)$	$1 - \gamma(1 - \eta)$

$$(2.32)$$

A process with these transition probabilities continues to operate forever, without coming to rest in any single state.

The random walks in Matrices 2.31 and 2.32 are on finite state spaces. Now suppose that the model in Matrix 2.32 contains a very large number of states, so that the highest-numbered state is essentially out of reach. Wherever the process is, there are always more states available. For practical calculations, one could write this model as a very large finite Markov chain with an upper limit so large that one never runs into it. However, it is tidier to think of the process as one with an infinite state space. The state space is the sequence S_0, S_1, S_2, S_3, ... The state probabilities obey the same random-walk rules as for the finite chains. These probabilities can be expressed in a number of ways. Directly, they are

$$P(S_{j,t+1}) = \begin{cases} (1 - \gamma\eta)P(S_{0,t}) + \gamma(1 - \eta)P(S_{1,t}) & j = 0 \\ \gamma\eta\, P(S_{j-1,t}) + (1 - \gamma)P(S_{j,t}) + \gamma(1 - \eta)P(S_{j+1,t}) & j > 0 \end{cases}$$
$$(2.33)$$

As an unbounded transition matrix, they are written

	S_0	S_1	S_2	S_3	...
S_0	$1 - \gamma\eta$	$\gamma\eta$	0	0	...
S_1	$\gamma(1 - \eta)$	$1 - \gamma$	$\gamma\eta$	0	...
S_2	0	$\gamma(1 - \eta)$	$1 - \gamma$	$\gamma\eta$	...
S_3	0	0	$\gamma(1 - \eta)$	$1 - \gamma$	...
S_4	0	0	0	$\gamma(1 - \eta)$	...
$\vdots$	$\vdots$	$\vdots$	$\vdots$	$\vdots$	

$$(2.34)$$

Another form of representation that is sometimes useful is to show where the process goes from each state:

$$P(S_{j,t+1}|S_{0,t}) = \begin{cases} 1 - \gamma\eta & j = 0 \\ \gamma\eta & j = 1 \end{cases} \tag{2.35}$$

$$P(S_{j,t+1}|S_{i,t}) = \begin{cases} \gamma(1 - \eta) & j = i - 1 \\ 1 - \gamma & j = i \\ \gamma\eta & j = i + 1, i > 0 \end{cases} \tag{2.36}$$

Equation 2.33 expresses the columns of Matrix 2.34, while Equations 2.35 and 2.36 extract the rows. The forms are equivalent; whichever is most simple or most useful in a particular situation is best.

Problems

2.1. Modify the all-or-none model to allow the possibility of an occasional error, with probability ϵ, from the learned state.

2.2. Modify the all-or-none model to allow the subject to forget a learned item with probability δ, passing from L back to G.

2.3. Suppose that a problem has two possible solutions, X and Y, either of which suffices to solve the problem, and that the subject learns them in an all-or-none manner. For example, a subject learning to classify stimuli may be able to make the classification on the basis of either the color or the shape of the stimulus (see Trabasso and Bower, 1968). With respect to each of the two solutions, the subject starts in a guessing state and on each trial, with probability α, passes to any one of two (or more) learned states. Define state spaces and transition and response probabilities for this model under two sets of assumptions about the way in which the solution methods are chosen.

    a. Suppose that when learning takes place, it is with one and only one of the solution methods. Solution X is used with probability ξ, and solution Y with probability $1 - \xi$.

    b. Suppose that the two solution methods are acquired independently with probabilities ξ for X and ψ for Y. On a trial for which learning takes place, there is a chance that either of the two solutions or both are found.

2.4. Suppose that in a concept-identification task there are a total of N possible hypotheses that the subject can hold and that these are divided into three classes as follows: (1) n_c are correct hypotheses for which $P(C) = 1.0$; (2) n_i are incorrect hypotheses for which $P(C) = g$; and (3) $n_p = N - n_c - n_i$ are partially relevant hypotheses for which $P(C) = \pi$, with $g < \pi < 1$. Suppose that hypotheses are chosen randomly with replacement from among the full set of N following an error. Write an initial vector and transition matrix for this chain.

2.5. Following the reasoning used with the all-or-none model in Matrix 2.7, construct the hypothesis-testing form of the two-stage model that is implied by the encoding interpretation of the model. Assume that once the subject has adopted an encoding of intermediate value, a useless encoding is never selected again.

2.6. One interpretation of the two-stage model is that there are two associations that must be formed in order to surely make correct responses (whence, this model is sometimes called the *two-*

element model). In the intermediate state one of these associations is known and the other is not.

    a. Suppose that on each trial each of the two associations can be formed with probability λ and that the formation of each association is independent of the other one. Write the transition matrix for this model. The result will be similar to Matrix 2.15, but with fewer parameters.

    b. Suppose that the two associations are learned by mutually exclusive events, so that only one can be formed on a trial. Again, write the simplified matrix.

2.7. Another two-stage model of learning involves the assumption that there are two ways for the subject to view the paired-associate item (again, call them *elements*), either of which can be associated with the correct answer in an all-or-none fashion. On each trial one of the two elements is selected at random. What happens in the remainder of the trial depends only on the selected element. Suppose that the properties of each single element are those of an all-or-none model. If the selected element is associated to the correct response, then a correct response is made; if it is not associated, the subject guesses and there is a chance that a new association is formed for that element. The result is a model that is similar to the two-stage model. In the initial state neither element is associated, the subject guesses, and whichever element is chosen may be learned. In the intermediate state one element is associated and one is not. In the final state both elements are associated. Including the selection of viewpoint in the transitions, it might appear that the transition probabilities are those of the ordinary two-stage model, Matrix 2.15, with $\alpha = \beta = 2\delta$ and $P(E|I) = P(E|U)/2$. However, this does not take into account the association between the probability of learning and the response in the intermediate state; choosing the associated element, for example, leads to a correct response, but cannot result in learning. Modify the model by changing the state space to take this into account.

2.8. Adapt the choice models of Matrices 2.21 and 2.22 to choices among three alternatives.

2.9. For the two-element probability-learning model, combine the transition operators for E_1 and E_2 events in Matrices 2.29 and 2.30 into a single operator that includes the event.

2.10. The probability-learning models in this chapter do not take into account the tendency of a subject to avoid making long runs of the same response. Following the first of a string of E_1 events, the subject may be almost sure to pick R_1; but in the midst of a long string of E_1 events, the subject is likely to occasionally make an R_2 response. Introduce additional states into Matrices 2.26 and 2.27, entered after several E_i, events, from which R_j responses, $j \neq i$, are most likely.

2.11. Suppose that the experimenter modifies the procedure for generating events in a probability-learning task, so that the event depends on the subject's prediction (Yellot, 1969). Let $P(E_1|R_1) = \delta_1$ and $P(E_1|R_2) = \delta_2$. Thus if δ_1 is large and δ_2 is small, the subject is correct most of the time; while if δ_1 is small and δ_2 is large, the subject is usually wrong. Adjust the models of Matrix 2.28 and Problem 2.9 to accommodate this procedure.

2.12. Which of the models in Problem 2.6 is a random walk?

2.13. Write the matrix for a four-state random walk with an absorbing barrier on the left and a reflecting barrier on the right.

Chapter 3

Algebraic Analysis
of Finite Markov Chains

The definition of a Markov model given in Chapter 2 is rich enough to completely determine the model's properties. So the behavior of a subject who operates according to a model can be predicted from a mathematical analysis of the model. This chapter and the next describe the way that predictions from finite Markov models are made. The current chapter considers the most direct way to analyze a model, by applying the rules of simple probability theory. This (usually) requires only elementary mathematics and gives explicit algebraic proofs and exact formulas. Many of the papers on psychological applications of Markov chains use this sort of algebraic analysis.

In order to simplify the calculation, not all types of Markov models are treated in the next few chapters. The models in Chapters 3–7 are subject to two restrictions (which are relaxed in Chapters 8–10). The first restriction concerns the choice of state space and time space. The models studied here are *finite Markov chains,* that is, processes with a finite set for the state space and discrete counts for time. The all-or-none and two-stage models of learning, described in the preceding chapter, are examples of this type of model, as are the simple choice models in Matrices 2.21 and 2.22. The linear and RTI models are excluded.

The second restriction concerns the type of states the chain contains.† When some Markov states are entered, the probability of staying in them is 1. Once the process enters one of these *absorbing states,* it is trapped there and never leaves. The state L in the all-or-none model is an example. Another type of state, called a *transient state,* is eventually left and never reentered. In the all-or-none model, state G is transient. The chains considered in Chapters 3–7 always contain at least one absorbing state, and all other states are transient. This means that the process runs its course in a finite number of trials and then stops changing. Although finite-state, the sequence-of-choices and probability-learning models in Section 2.4 do not have this property, for they lack absorbing states.

As the number of states gets larger, algebraic proofs become cumbersome and often are particular to the model being examined. Considerable skill and cleverness are needed to work with them, as well as a great deal of patience and tolerance for algebraic manipulation. Fortunately, more general methods are possible. Markov chains are linear systems, so all the mechanics of linear algebra and matrix theory can be brought to bear. This provides immense simplification. Matrix methods can be applied and, avoiding the ingenious algebraic proofs, a computer can be programmed to make predictions directly. Models analyzed in this way are easier and faster to use. The matrix methods also help to keep the computation organized if one wishes to obtain explicit solutions. Chapter 4 examines the linear-algebraic formulation of the finite Markov models.

3.1   State Probabilities

The most basic property of any Markov model is the probability of being in a particular state on a particular trial. This is found by directly applying the transition probabilities to the state probabilities for the previous trial. Clearly, the starting point for this is the state on the initial trial.

The steps are particularly obvious for the all-or-none model, as defined in Section 2.2 (Equations 2.4, 2.5, and 2.6). By Equation 2.4 in Assumption 2, on the first trial

$$P(G_1) = 1 \tag{3.1}$$

and

$$P(L_1) = 1 - P(G_1) = 0$$

---

† More formal definitions of the state types are given in Chapter 7.

On the second trial, the only way to still be in G is to have stayed there after the first trial. Putting this in terms of probabilities gives

$$P(G_2) = P(G|G)P(G_1)$$
$$= (1 - \alpha)(1) = 1 - \alpha$$

and

$$P(L_2) = 1 - P(G_2)$$
$$= 1 - (1 - \alpha) = \alpha$$

Concentrating on the guessing state, the steps continue:

$$P(G_3) = (1 - \alpha)P(G_2) = (1 - \alpha)^2$$
$$P(G_4) = (1 - \alpha)P(G_3) = (1 - \alpha)^3$$

and so forth. In this way $P(G_t)$ can be found for any t, but a general formula would be more useful. The pattern that has developed is quite obvious and suggests that

$$P(G_t) = (1 - \alpha)^{t-1} \tag{3.2}$$

A guess at a formula is not enough to show it is right, so Equation 3.2 must be verified by some other means. A proof by induction is the best way. Such a proof requires two steps: first, to show that Equation 3.2 holds for the smallest value of t to which it applies; second, to demonstrate that if it holds for $t = T$, then it will also hold for $t = T + 1$.

1. When $t = 1$, Equation 3.2 reduces to Equation 3.1, which is an axiom of the model, and so correct.
2. From the definition of the process,

$$P(G_{T+1}) = (1 - \alpha)P(G_T) \tag{3.3}$$

Now the value of $P(G_t)$ is substituted from Equation 3.2 with $t = T$:

$$P(G_{T+1}) = (1 - \alpha)(1 - \alpha)^{T-1} = (1 - \alpha)^T$$

This is Equation 3.2 with $t = T + 1$.

This completes the proof. For simple models, guessing a solution based on the first few terms, then proving the result by induction is often a good way to deal with simple problems of this sort. Equation 3.3 is a difference equation in $P(G_t)$, so it could also be solved by the methods of Appendix B.

Equation 3.2 is an example of an *exponential function,* that is, one in which the argument appears as the exponent of a constant. More generally, BA^t is an exponential function. It can also be written as Be^{Ct}, where $C = \log_e A$. Exponential functions appear frequently in the analysis of Markov models.

There are only two states in the all-or-none model, and so

$$P(L_t) = 1 - P(G_t)$$
$$= 1 - (1 - \alpha)^{t-1} \qquad (3.4)$$

This result could also have been obtained by direct calculation, but not as easily. Using the law of total probability (Equation A.4) and the transition probabilities gives

$$P(L_t) = P(L|G)P(G_{t-1}) + P(L|L)P(L_{t-1})$$
$$= \alpha P(G_{t-1}) + P(L_{t-1})$$

Because both $P(G_{t-1})$ and $P(L_{t-1})$ appear, this equation is more complicated than Equation 3.3 and is best solved as one of a pair of simultaneous difference equations (see Section B.3). It is much easier to get $P(L_t)$ by subtraction, as in Equation 3.4. Part of the trick in any derivation is to pick the simplest of the many possible solution methods.

The special nature of the states of the all-or-none model obscures the principle whereby the state probabilities were found. The fact that items never return after leaving the guessing state makes things simple. Normally, transitions among all of the states have to be considered. The state probabilities are obtained by applying the law of total probability in the form

$$P(S_{j,t}) = \sum_{i=1}^{n} P(S_j|S_i)P(S_{i,t-1}) \qquad (3.5)$$

The general method is necessary to get the state probabilities of the two-stage model. Substituting transition probabilities from Matrix 2.15 into Equation 3.5 yields three equations:

$$P(G_t) = P(G|L)P(L_{t-1}) + P(G|I)P(I_{t-1}) + P(G|G)P(G_{t-1})$$
$$= (1 - \alpha)P(G_{t-1}) \qquad (3.6)$$

$$P(I_t) = (1 - \delta)P(I_{t-1}) + \alpha(1 - \beta)P(G_{t-1}) \qquad (3.7)$$

$$P(L_t) = P(L_{t-1}) + \delta P(I_{t-1}) + \alpha\beta P(G_{t-1})$$

These must be solved. There is no problem with $P(G_t)$. Equation 3.6 is the same as Equation 3.3 for the all-or-none model. The solution is the same except for the fact that the initial value, given by Equation 2.17, is $P(G_1) = (1 - \sigma)(1 - \tau)$. Hence,

$$P(G_t) = (1 - \sigma)(1 - \tau)(1 - \alpha)^{t-1} \qquad (3.8)$$

State I is a little more complicated. Substituting Equation 3.8 into Equation 3.7 forms the difference equation

$$P(I_t) = (1 - \delta)P(I_{t-1}) + \alpha(1 - \beta)(1 - \sigma)(1 - \tau)(1 - \alpha)^{t-2} \quad (3.9)$$

Like Equation B.12 in Appendix B, Equation 3.9 is a nonhomogeneous first-degree difference equation with an exponential term on the right-hand side. Its solution parallels that of Equation B.12 and so is only briefly sketched here. If $\alpha \neq \delta$, the solution breaks into homogeneous and particular parts. The homogeneous form of Equation 3.9 has solution $A(1 - \delta)^{t-1}$, and a particular solution to the general equation is $B(1 - \alpha)^{t-1}$, where A and B are constants. Substitution of the particular solution into Equation 3.9 allows B to be found. The general solution is the sum of the homogeneous solution and the particular solution, and using the initial condition $P(I_1) = (1 - \sigma)\tau$ from Equation 2.16 to get the value of A gives

$$P(I_t) = (1 - \sigma) \left\{ \left[\tau - (1 - \tau) \frac{\alpha(1 - \beta)}{\delta - \alpha} \right] (1 - \delta)^{t-1} \right.$$
$$\left. + (1 - \tau) \frac{\alpha(1 - \beta)}{\delta - \alpha} (1 - \alpha)^{t-1} \right\} \qquad (3.10)$$

This function is a linear combination of exponential terms. Such a form characterizes the state probabilities of any finite Markov chain (unless some of the parameters are equal), for such are the solutions to sets of linear difference equations.

Finally, the probability of state L is found by subtraction:

$$P(L_t) = 1 - P(I_t) - P(G_t)$$

There is little point in substituting Equations 3.8 and 3.10 into this to get a final formula.

The ascending nature of the two-stage model allowed the state probabilities to be found one at a time. The same is not true for the random-walk choice model given in Matrix 2.22. Two states, A and B, are absorbing, but the other three states, A_1, U, and B_1, all communicate with each other. No one of these three probabilities can be found without finding the others. They form a system of equations:

$$P(A_{1,t}) = (1 - \delta)P(A_{1,t-1}) \quad + \delta\alpha P(U_{t-1})$$

$$P(U_t) = \delta(1 - \alpha)P(A_{1,t-1}) + (1 - \delta)P(U_{t-1}) \quad + \delta\alpha P(B_{1,t-1})$$

$$P(B_{1,t}) = \qquad\qquad\qquad \delta(1 - \alpha)P(U_{t-1}) + (1 - \delta)P(B_{1,t-1})$$

These can be solved as a system of simultaneous difference equations, using the methods of Section B.3, but the result is not very convenient. The auxiliary equation is a cubic, so has three roots.[†] A bit of algebra shows the roots to be

$$1 - \delta \qquad \text{and} \qquad 1 - \delta[1 \pm \sqrt{2\alpha(1 - \alpha)}]$$

The solution to the difference equation is a sum of three exponentials: as long as α is neither 0 nor 1, the state probabilities have the form

$$A(1 - \delta)^t + B\{1 - \delta[1 + \sqrt{2\alpha(1 - \alpha)}]\}^t$$
$$+ C\{1 - \delta[1 - \sqrt{2\alpha(1 - \alpha)}]\}^t$$

for appropriate A, B, and C. The initial conditions let the constants be determined, but the results are algebraically messy. Unless specific information about the form of the state probabilities is needed, it is easier to use the numerical methods that are discussed in Chapter 4. Hence, further discussion of this model is deferred.

A geometric picture of the state and response probabilities is sometimes useful.[‡] The two state probabilities for the all-or-none model,

$$P(L_t) = 1 - (1 - \alpha)^{t-1} \qquad \text{and} \qquad P(G_t) = (1 - \alpha)^{t-1}$$

can be plotted as a point in two-dimensional space. Denoting this point by s_t, the sequence of points $s_1, s_2, s_3, \ldots$, form a sequence in the space

---

[†] Alternatively, the roots are eigenvalues of the transition matrix—see Section C.6. This sometimes provides an easier way to find them.

[‡] This section, as other sections marked with a vertical rule in the margin, can be omitted without loss of later material.

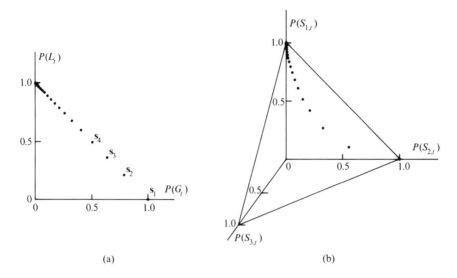

Figure 3.1 State probabilities for a two- and a three-state model plotted as points in space.

(see Figure 3.1a). Because $P(L_t) + P(G_t) = 1$, these points lie on the straight line between [0, 1] and [1, 0]. Where three states are involved, a plot in three-dimensional space is necessary (Figure 3.1b); but because the probabilities all sum to 1, the points fall on a plane. This geometric picture generalizes to as many states and dimensions as desired, although visualization becomes harder with more than four states. An analogous representation holds for the response probabilities.

Viewed in this way, the transition operator maps the space into itself. In fact, the spaces of permissible points are vector spaces, the line and plane in Figure 3.1 being of dimension 1 and 2, respectively. So the transition operator is a mapping of a vector space into itself, as discussed in Sections C.5 and C.6. The response mapping carries a point in one vector space to a point in another. This representation is useful in the more advanced treatment of Markov models, for transformations of vector spaces have been well studied. In this book, the vector-space properties are most important in Chapters 4 and 7.

This geometric view of the model forces attention on the probability distribution of states—the points s_t in Figure 3.1—rather than on what happens to an individual subject or item. Indeed, what happens to an individual is not represented in Figure 3.1 at all. Although this may seem a limitation, in practice it is not serious. Any analysis and testing of a Markov model (as of any probability model) are based on data from a collection of items and not on one item alone. Except in a few special cases, one individual alone does not give sufficient information either to estimate parameters or to test the fit of a probabilistic model. Thus, there is little loss in treating populations rather than individuals. Indeed, a satisfactory treatment of Markov models can be based entirely on the distributions, without any recourse to the individual.

3.2 Response Probabilities

For most models, the state probabilities are not directly observable in data. In order to obtain predictions that can be compared with data, the response mapping must be applied. The simplest observable quantities are probability distributions over the response-state space. To apply the response mapping to the state probabilities, the law of total probability is used again. For response R_j,

$$P(R_{j,t}) = \sum_{i=1}^{n} P(R_j|S_i)P(S_{i,t}) \qquad (3.11)$$

For the all-or-none model the response mapping was given in Chapter 2 by Assumption 4 (Equation 2.6). There are two types of responses: correct responses and errors. It suffices to calculate the probability of either one of these. Consider the event of an error on trial t, which will be denoted E_t, and is, of course, the *learning curve*. Applying Equation 3.11 gives

$$P(E_t) = P(E|G)P(G_t) + P(E|L)P(L_t)$$
$$= (1 - g) \times (1 - \alpha)^{t-1} + 0 \times [1 - (1 - \alpha)^{t-1}]$$
$$= (1 - g)(1 - \alpha)^{t-1} \qquad (3.12)$$

This learning curve is plotted in Figure 3.2 for several choices of α and g. Which of these curves is applicable to a particular experiment depends on the value of g and of α.

The learning curve for the two-stage model is found in the same way. Ignoring states in which errors are impossible gives

$$P(E_t) = P(E|I)P(I_t) + P(E|G)P(G_t)$$
$$= (1 - \pi)P(I_t) + (1 - g)P(G_t) \qquad (3.13)$$

Substitution for the state probabilities from Equations 3.8 and 3.10 gives an explicit formula, but one that is complex enough not to provide

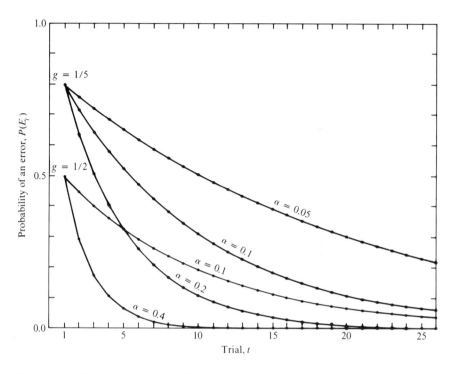

Figure 3.2   Representative learning curves for the all-or-none model.

much further insight. Both state probabilities are exponential functions involving $(1 - \alpha)^{t-1}$ and $(1 - \delta)^{t-1}$, so $P(E_t)$ also has this form. With two exponentials rather than one, the shape of $P(E_t)$ is governed by two rates of decrease. These rates are apparent in the examples plotted in Figure 3.3, in which the total area under the curves (which equals the expected total number of errors) is the same. In the bottom curve, with $\alpha = 0.8$ and $\delta = 0.02$, for example, items rapidly leave G, but linger in the intermediate state. When $g = \pi$, somewhat S-shaped curves are found. If $g > \pi$, curves that rise in the middle can even be obtained.

In practice, when several Markov learning models are compared, there is rarely much difference between the best-fitting learning curves. The nature of the state probabilities means that the error probabilities are sums of exponentials. Many experiments produce learning curves that are quite close to simple exponentials in form, and so most models predict them well. Thus, to find that the learning curve is fit by a model gives little support for that model. Distinguishing among models requires more subtle statistics.

Fitting learning curves to a set of data may be useful at a purely

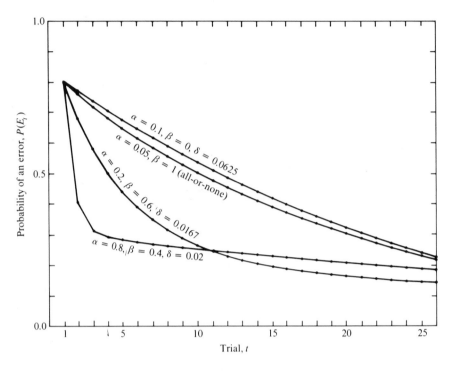

Figure 3.3   Representative learning curves for the two-stage model. For all curves $\sigma = \tau = 0$ (the process starts in G), $\pi = 0.5$, and $g = 0.2$. In addition, the mean number of errors to solution equals 16 for all curves (see Section 3.3 and Problem 3.7).

descriptive level, even when model testing is not an issue. The value of the learning-rate parameter extracts one characteristic from the data in a form less contaminated by other characteristics. For example, the error probability for the all-or-none model depends on both the initial level of errors (the value of g) and the rate at which acquisition takes place (the parameter α). So the value of α is a more pure measure of the speed of acquisition than the simple probability of a correct response. Likewise, the difference between g and π in the two-stage model gives descriptive information about the nature of the intermediate state. Methods for obtaining these parameter estimates (which are also needed for model testing) are discussed in Chapter 5.

3.3   *The Number of Errors*

If the learning curve does not strongly separate models, there are many statistics that give better tests. Which to use in a particular situation depends on the salient characteristics of the model in question. The best choice is a statistic that is closely related to some distinctive property of the model. The statistics can be roughly divided into two classes: those that describe the distribution of some summary random variable and those that express the dependence of two events. In this section, a summary variable is examined; the next treats sequential properties of the responses.

The summary variable treated in this section is the total number of passages through a particular response state. For learning models, the total number of errors made in learning an item is an example. Clearly, this is a random variable, for even with a population of identical items, some items are learned more readily than others. Let this random variable, the number of errors made before learning, be denoted by T. Complete information about T is carried in its distribution. From the distribution, the mean, standard deviation, and other moments of T can be found. The calculation of these quantities is illustrated here using the all-or-none model.

It is important to note that, because errors are made only from transient states, the value of T is always finite. This makes the distribution proper and means that its moments are usually finite. If correct responses are counted instead of errors, this is not the case unless a limit is put on the number of trials in the experiment.

In many situations, the full distribution of T is not required, only its expectation (or first moment or mean), $E(T)$. This can be found without deriving the distribution of T. In essence, the trick is to sum the errors over trials. To see why this works, go from an event notation to a numerical notation. Let X_t be a random variable indicating whether an error takes place,

$$X_t = \begin{cases} 0 & \text{if trial } t \text{ is correct} \\ 1 & \text{if trial } t \text{ is in error} \end{cases}$$

Descriptively, this adds nothing over the E_t notation, but, as numbers, the X_t can be combined. In particular, the total number of errors is just the sum of the X_t:

$$T = \sum_{t=1}^{\infty} X_t \tag{3.14}$$

Running this sum to infinity may seem a bit strange since no real experiment continues that long. But because no errors are made after entry to L, the number of nonzero terms in Equation 3.14 is finite. In effect, the infinite limit means "until learning takes place." If the experiment is stopped before all items have been learned, a finite limit could be put on Equation 3.14. This makes a few changes in the derivations below, but only in detail, not in principle (see Problem 3.8).

The X_t are Bernoulli random variables, although they are neither independent nor identically distributed. The probability of an error, that is, that $X_t = 1$, is $P(E_t)$. Furthermore,

$$E(X_t) = 0 \times P(X_t = 0) + 1 \times P(X_t = 1)$$
$$= P(X_t = 1)$$

The expectation of any sum of random variables is the sum of the expectations (see Equation A.18), so

$$E(T) = \sum_{t=1}^{\infty} E(X_t) \tag{3.15}$$

$$= \sum_{t=1}^{\infty} P(X_t = 1)$$

$$= \sum_{t=1}^{\infty} (1 - g)(1 - \alpha)^{t-1}$$

$$= (1 - g) \sum_{t=1}^{\infty} (1 - \alpha)^{t-1}$$

after substituting $P(E_t)$ for the all-or-none model from Equation 3.12. Methods for evaluating sums of geometric series of this sort are given following the discussion of the geometric distribution in Section A.3. Using Equation A.28, when $x = 1 - \alpha$, gives

$$\sum_{t=1}^{\infty} x^{i-1} = \frac{1}{1 - x} = \frac{1}{\alpha}$$

Thus,

$$E(T) = \frac{1 - g}{\alpha} \tag{3.16}$$

The same technique can be applied to find $E(T)$ for any model for which $P(E_t)$ is known. Indeed, the expectation of any variable that can be written as the sum of trial-wise increments is found this way.

An equation comparable to Equation 3.15 does not exist for the variance. The variance of a sum of random variables does not equal the sum of variances unless the variables are independent, which the X_t are not. To find the variance, one needs the distribution of T. This distribution is also of considerable interest in its own right. For the all-or-none model, the derivation is not very difficult, requiring mainly a careful analysis of the state transitions.

The case where no errors are made is a little different from positive T and must be treated separately. The event $T = 0$ breaks into two parts. First, the subject must guess correctly on the initial trial; then, following the correct guess, learning must take place without further errors. So $P(T = 0)$ is the product

$$P(T = 0) = P(\text{correct guess})P(\text{no more errors}|\text{correct guess})$$

The first of these probabilities is simply g; the second is more difficult and is important enough to warrant a special symbol. Let b be the probability that no errors follow a response in state G, so that

$$P(T = 0) = gb \qquad (3.17)$$

This event can come about either by passing directly from state G to state L or by staying in state G, then guessing correctly, and then making no further errors. Expressing this sentence in terms of probabilities gives

$$b = \alpha + (1 - \alpha)gb$$

This is a recursive relationship in b (it gives b in terms of itself) that can be solved to give

$$b = \frac{\alpha}{1 - (1 - \alpha)g} \qquad (3.18)$$

A second way to find b is given in Problem 3.5a.

The quantity b is also involved in the probabilities of the remaining values of T. The event $T \neq 0$, which has the probability $1 - P(T = 0)$ or $1 - gb$, is the event that at least one error is made. For $T = 1$, the first error is followed only by correct responses, an event whose probability is b. Thus,

$$P(T = 1) = P(T \neq 0)P(T = 1|T \neq 0)$$
$$= (1 - gb)b \qquad (3.19)$$

(or see Problem 3.5b). For exactly two errors, an initial error must be made (probability $1 - gb$), then the subject must not make no more errors (a double negative [!], having probability $1 - b$), then no more errors must be made (probability b). Putting these together gives

$$P(T = 2) = (1 - gb)(1 - b)b$$

The same pattern extends to larger numbers of errors, by repeating the $1 - b$ term. Combining this result with Equation 3.17 gives

$$P(T = k) = \begin{cases} gb & k = 0 \\ (1 - gb)b(1 - b)^{k-1} & k > 0 \end{cases} \qquad (3.20)$$

It is a good idea to check any fresh derivation of a distribution to see that it sums to 1. A little algebra shows that this is the case for Equation 3.20. A second check is given by the expectation, whose value was found in Equation 3.16. Starting with the basic definition of $E(T)$, then employing Equation A.30 to evaluate the sum gives

$$E(T) = \sum_{k=0}^{\infty} kP(T = k)$$

$$= 0 \times gb + \sum_{k=1}^{\infty} k(1 - gb)b(1 - b)^{k-1}$$

$$= (1 - gb)b \sum_{k=1}^{\infty} k(1 - b)^{k-1}$$

$$= (1 - gb)b \frac{1}{b^2} = \frac{1 - gb}{b}$$

Substituting the value of b from Equation 3.18 into this gives

$$E(T) = \frac{1 - \dfrac{\alpha g}{1 - (1 - \alpha)g}}{\dfrac{\alpha}{1 - (1 - \alpha)g}} = \frac{1 - g}{\alpha}$$

This agrees with Equation 3.16.

With the distribution of T in hand, the variance is easily calculated. First, the second central moment of T is found, using the sum in Equation A.31:

$$E(T^2) = \sum_{k=1}^{\infty} k^2(1 - gb)b(1 - b)^{k-1}$$

$$= (1 - gb)b \sum_{k=1}^{\infty} k^2(1 - b)^{k-1}$$

$$= \frac{(1 - gb)(2 - b)}{b^2}$$

Then, by Equation A.19,

$$\begin{aligned}
\text{var}(T) &= E(T^2) - [E(T)]^2 \\
&= \frac{(1 - gb)(2 - b)}{b^2} - \left(\frac{1 - gb}{b}\right)^2 \\
&= \frac{(1 - gb)[1 - (1 - g)b]}{b^2} \\
&= \frac{(1 - g)[(1 - \alpha)(1 - g) + \alpha g]}{\alpha^2}
\end{aligned} \qquad (3.21)$$

For the all-or-none model, many other statistics can be calculated in this way—the trial of last error, the number of errors before the first correct response, and so on. These can be found in other papers or texts. In particular, many statistics are discussed in Bower's original paper on the all-or-none model (1961) and in the text by Atkinson, Bower, and Crothers (1965).

Similar methods can be used to get the same quantities in the two-stage model, although the manipulations are a bit more complex (see Problems 3.7 and 3.12). As the models get larger, the algebra becomes involved and many ad hoc tricks are required. For this reason, distributions for the two-stage model are not covered until the problem can be solved in general with the matrix procedures of Chapter 4 (but see Atkinson and Crothers, 1964, for calculations based on the long-and-short model).

3.4   Sequential Response Probabilities

The second class of statistic that is frequently useful for comparing models reflects the relationship between events on different trials. The most common examples of such statistics are joint or conditional probabilities of two events. Very often the most fundamental characteristics of a model are expressed in the way that responses depend on earlier events. Then, the sequential characteristics give the strongest test of the model, and their breakdown, when the model fails, gives the best idea of what is wrong with it.

One obvious sequential characteristic is the conditional probability of a particular response on one trial given a response on another. In the case of learning models, the probability of an error on trial $t + 1$ given an error on trial t is commonly used. For the all-or-none model, $P(E_{t+1}|E_t)$ is particularly simple. The fact that an error can be made only in state G means that conditionalizing on an error is equivalent to starting the process in G. Thus, following the same argument that was made less formally in Chapter 1 gives

$$P(E_{t+1}|E_t) = P(E_{t+1}|G_t)$$
$$= P(E_{t+1}|G_{t+1})P(G_{t+1}|G_t)$$
$$= (1 - g)(1 - \alpha) \qquad (3.22)$$

which is independent of t. This property, called the *stationarity* of the conditional error probability, deeply characterizes the all-or-none model. Most learning models do not show this stationarity.

The derivation in the last paragraph is quite simple, but, like the derivation of the state probabilities, deceptively so, for it depends on the special properties of the all-or-none model. When more than one error state is involved, an error does not uniquely determine the state. One cannot work directly with the conditional probabilities, but must begin by calculating the joint probability of consecutive errors, $P(E_{t+1} \wedge E_t)$, then divide by $P(E_t)$ to obtain

$$P(E_{t+1}|E_t) = \frac{P(E_{t+1} \wedge E_t)}{P(E_t)} \qquad (3.23)$$

(see Equation A.2). The joint probability is found by applying the law of total probability, expanding over the states on both trials:

$$P(E_{t+1} \wedge E_t) = \sum_{j=1}^{n} \sum_{i=1}^{n} P(E_{t+1} \wedge S_{j,t+1} \wedge E_t \wedge S_{i,t}) \qquad (3.24)$$

The individual terms in this sum are constructed from the state probabilities, the transition matrix, and the response mapping.

Consider the two-stage model. It has three states, so there are nine terms in Equation 3.24. However, the sum need be taken only over states in which errors are possible, so state L can be omitted. This leaves

$$P(E_{t+1} \wedge E_t) = P(E_{t+1} \wedge I_{t+1} \wedge E_t \wedge I_t) + P(E_{t+1} \wedge G_{t+1} \wedge E_t \wedge I_t)$$
$$+ P(E_{t+1} \wedge I_{t+1} \wedge E_t \wedge G_t)$$
$$+ P(E_{t+1} \wedge G_{t+1} \wedge E_t \wedge G_t) \qquad (3.25)$$

Each of these probabilities is found by expanding the joint probabilities, then simplifying them. For example, consider the third term.

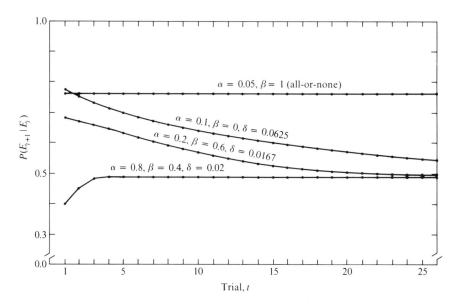

Figure 3.4   Conditional error probability, $P(E_{t+1}|E_t)$, of the two-stage model for the parameter sets used in Figure 3.3.

Using the definition of conditional probability three times gives

$P(E_{t+1} \wedge I_{t+1} \wedge E_t \wedge G_t)$
$$= P(E_{t+1}|I_{t+1} \wedge E_t \wedge G_t)P(I_{t+1} \wedge E_t \wedge G_t)$$
$$= P(E_{t+1}|I_{t+1} \wedge E_t \wedge G_t)P(I_{t+1}|E_t \wedge G_t)P(E_t \wedge G_t)$$
$$= P(E_{t+1}|I_{t+1} \wedge E_t \wedge G_t)P(I_{t+1}|E_t \wedge G_t)P(E_t|G_t)P(G_t)$$

By the Markov property, only the conditionalization on the most recent state is necessary; and because the model is homogeneous, the dependence on t can be dropped from all but the last term. Thus,

$P(E_{t+1} \wedge I_{t+1} \wedge E_t \wedge G_t) = P(E|I)P(I|G)P(E|G)P(G_t)$
$$= (1 - \pi)\alpha(1 - \beta)(1 - g)(1 - \sigma)(1 - \tau)(1 - \alpha)^{t-1}$$

Summing this and three similar terms (one of them is 0) in Equation 3.25 gives the numerator of Equation 3.23. The denominator, $P(E_t)$, is given by Equation 3.13, and so $P(E_{t+1}|E_t)$ is found. There is no point in writing this as a single equation, for it is neither simple nor very illuminating. Computation, however, is straightforward, and examples are readily plotted (see Figure 3.4). Unlike the all-or-none model, the two-stage model is not stationary.

The sequential properties of a model are also reflected in the complete distribution of joint sequential response probabilities. For sequences of two trials in a learning model, the probabilities

$$P(C_{t+1} \wedge C_t) \qquad P(E_{t+1} \wedge C_t) \qquad P(C_{t+1} \wedge E_t) \qquad P(E_{t+1} \wedge E_t)$$

constitute such a set; for three trials, the set contains eight probabilities. These *sequential statistics* are calculated in the same manner as Equation 3.25 (see Problems 3.16 and 3.17). Derivations are straightforward, although considerable care must be taken to keep the terms in good order. The sequential statistics exhaust the response possibilities, and so form a complete probability distribution summing to 1. As such, they can be compared with data using a chi-square test. This provides a way to test the model and to estimate parameters, topics that are considered in Chapters 5 and 6.

3.5   Item Variability

For exact predictions, such as the stationarity of $P(E_{t+1}|E_t)$ in the all-or-none model, to hold, the model must fit quite accurately. Any perturbation of the all-or-none property causes stationarity to fail, making the statistic useful for testing the model. However, as noted in Chapter 1, one reason why stationarity may fail is a lack of homogeneity among the items. If α is not the same for all subjects and items, easy items tend to be learned early and the items still unlearned on later trials are harder, on the average. Although $P(E_{t+1}|E_t)$ may equal $(1 - g)(1 - \alpha)$ for every item, the changing population of items means that α is smaller at the end, and so the average value of $P(E_{t+1}|E_t)$ increases with t.

The problem of nonhomogeneous material is a very serious one for model testing. Almost no body of material of psychological interest is completely homogeneous. Predictions of any characteristic that depends on more than one trial are subject to this bias. One indication of the prevalence of nonhomogeneous items is the fact that models often underpredict the variance of random variables such as the total number of errors. Parameters are usually estimated in ways that make the means of these statistics come out correctly, and so differences among items are reflected in larger variances. The result is to make the model appear to fit less well than it actually does.

A second consequence of item nonhomogeneity affects particularly conditional probabilities. The conditionalizing event acts to select a subset of items for consideration. When the selected items are different from the population at large, considerable bias may appear. For example, a conditionalization on errors selects more hard then easy items from a set of varying difficulty, and the learning rate of this set is slower than the average. The nature of the selection bias depends in detail on the particular quantities involved.

One can try to get around the nonhomogeneity problem in various ways. Some methods involve modification of the experimental design. These include selection of homogeneous items, blocking of items by difficulty, and post hoc comparison between equivalent sets of items. Another approach is to include item variability explicitly as an assumption of the tested model. The second approach is considered in this section (see also Offir, 1972). The basic idea is to treat the parameters of the model as random variables rather than as fixed quantities, to give them a distribution over items, and to calculate expectations of statistics over this distribution.

Consider the problem of nonhomogeneous learning rates in the all-or-none model. In the absence of any extensive theory of item difficulty, there is no theoretical reason to choose a particular form for the distribution of α. The distribution should be over the interval [0, 1] and should be adjustable to fit a range of shapes, means, and variances. The beta distribution (discussed in Section A.4) fits these criteria and is computationally compatible with the Markov process equations. The density for the beta distribution, given in Equation A.55, is written here with parameters γ and δ to avoid confusion with the α of the all-or-none model:

$$f(\alpha) = \frac{1}{B(\gamma,\delta)} \alpha^{\gamma-1}(1 - \alpha)^{\delta-1} \tag{3.26}$$

The mean learning rate for this distribution (see Equation A.57) is

$$\mu_\alpha = E(\alpha) = \frac{\gamma}{\gamma + \delta}$$

With nonhomogeneous items, the shape of the learning curve is changed. As found above in Equation 3.12, the probability of an error on trial t applies only to items of fixed difficulty. Subscripting this to indicate the reliance on α:

$$P_\alpha(E_t) = (1 - g)(1 - \alpha)^{t-1} \tag{3.27}$$

To get the unconditional $P(E_t)$, the value of $P_\alpha(E_t)$ is weighted by the likelihood that α is chosen, $f(\alpha)$, and the product integrated over the range of α (see Figure 3.5). The beta distribution is continuous, so an

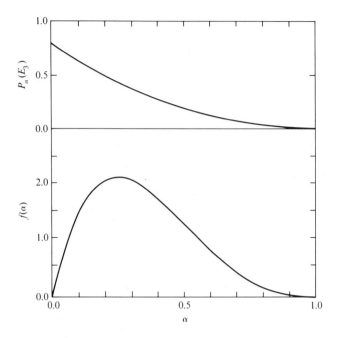

Figure 3.5   Error probability and difficulty density (Equations 3.26 and 3.27), drawn for $\gamma = 2$, $\delta = 4$, $t = 3$, and $g = 0.2$.

integral results (see Section D.2 and Equation D.20):

$$P(E_t) = \int_0^1 P_\alpha(E_t)f(\alpha)\,d\alpha$$

$$= \int_0^1 [(1 - g)(1 - \alpha)^{t-1}] \left[\frac{1}{B(\gamma,\delta)}\,\alpha^{\gamma-1}(1 - \alpha)^{\delta-1} \right] d\alpha$$

$$= \frac{1 - g}{B(\gamma,\delta)} \int_0^1 \alpha^{\gamma-1}(1 - \alpha)^{\delta+t-2}\,d\alpha$$

Except for the constant term, this integral looks like a beta function (Equation A.56) with parameters γ and $\delta + t - 1$. Thus,

$$P(E_t) = \frac{(1 - g)B(\gamma,\delta + t - 1)}{B(\gamma,\delta)}$$

The beta function can be expressed as gamma functions (Equation A.59):

$$B(a,b) = \frac{\Gamma(a)\Gamma(b)}{\Gamma(a + b)}$$

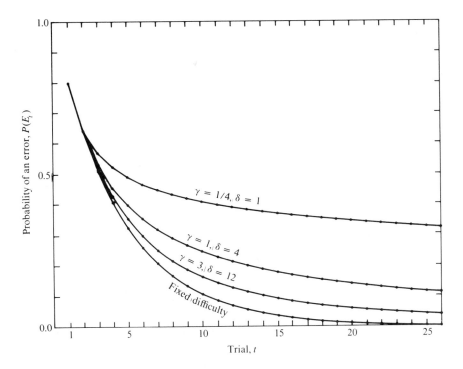

Figure 3.6 Learning curves for the all-or-none model with several distributions of learning rates having $\mu_\alpha = 0.2$, and with homogeneous items of the same mean difficulty. In all cases $g = 0.2$.

which allows $P(E_t)$ to be written as

$$P(E_t) = (1 - g) \frac{\Gamma(\gamma + \delta)\Gamma(\delta + t - 1)}{\Gamma(\delta)\Gamma(\gamma + \delta + t - 1)} \qquad (3.28)$$

For small t, this function falls off at a rate similar to that of the homogeneous-item learning curve, Equation 3.12, with $\alpha = \mu_\alpha$, but drops more and more slowly as t gets large. Learning curves for homogeneous items and a variety of nonhomogeneous items, all with the same mean difficulty, are plotted in Figure 3.6.

To find the conditional probability, $P(E_{t+1}|E_t)$, one cannot simply average values of $P_\alpha(E_{t+1}|E_t)$. As with any conditional probability, the joint probability must be found first, then divided by $P(E_t)$. The joint probability for a particular α is found in the same way as any other sequential statistic:

$$P_\alpha(E_{t+1} \wedge E_t) = P(E|G)P_\alpha(G|G)P(E|G)P_\alpha(G_t)$$
$$= (1 - g)^2(1 - \alpha)^t$$

Integrating over the distribution of α:

$$P(E_{t+1} \wedge E_t) = \int_0^1 P_\alpha(E_{t+1} \wedge E_t) f(\alpha)\, d\alpha$$

$$= \frac{(1-g)^2}{B(\gamma,\delta)} \int_0^1 (1-\alpha)^t \alpha^{\gamma-1} (1-\alpha)^{\delta-1}\, d\alpha$$

$$= \frac{(1-g)^2 B(\gamma,\delta+t)}{B(\gamma,\delta)}$$

$$= (1-g)^2\, \frac{\Gamma(\gamma+\delta)\Gamma(\delta+t)}{\Gamma(\delta)\Gamma(\gamma+\delta+t)}$$

Combining this with $P(E_t)$ from Equation 3.28 gives

$$P(E_{t+1}|E_t) = \frac{P(E_{t+1} \wedge E_t)}{P(E_t)}$$

$$= (1-g)\, \frac{\Gamma(\delta+t)\Gamma(\gamma+\delta+t-1)}{\Gamma(\gamma+\delta+t)\Gamma(\delta+t-1)}$$

$$= (1-g)\, \frac{\delta+t-1}{\gamma+\delta+t-1} \tag{3.29}$$

The last step uses the fact that $\Gamma(x+1)/\Gamma(x) = x$ (see Equation A.51).

Equation 3.29 behaves as one might expect. When $t = 1$, all items are present and

$$P(E_2|E_1) = \frac{(1-g)\delta}{\gamma+\delta} = (1-g)(1-\mu_\alpha)$$

This is essentially the same as the unconditional Equation 3.22. As t gets very large, Equation 3.29 approaches $1 - g$ as the pool of items is reduced to a few that are almost impossible to learn. Values of $P(E_{t+1}|E_t)$ from Equation 3.29 corresponding to the parameters in Figure 3.6 are shown in Figure 3.7.

When γ and δ are very large, the distribution of items is tightly clustered about μ_α. The distribution in Figure 3.5 is essentially a spike. In this case the value of $P(E_{t+1}|E_t)$ does not change much from its initial value of $(1-g)(1-\mu_\alpha)$ until t becomes quite large. As very few items remain unlearned at that point, nonhomogeneity effects are hard to detect. Thus, as would be expected, a tight distribution of similar items is as good as a homogeneous set.

Many distributions and their central moments are found by directly integrating over α. For example, the expected number of errors, $E(T)$, for a nonhomogeneous distribution is found by starting with the value

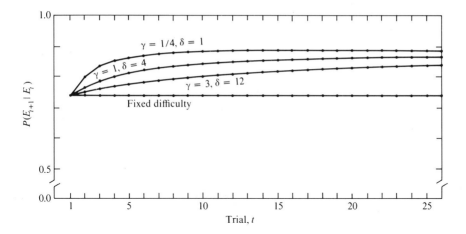

Figure 3.7 Conditional error probability, $P(E_{t+1}|E_t)$, in the all-or-none model for the same distributions of learning rates shown in Figure 3.6.

for a particular α (from Equation 3.16):

$$E_\alpha(T) = \frac{1 - g}{\alpha}$$

then integrating:

$$E(T) = \int_0^1 E_\alpha(T)f(\alpha)\,d\alpha$$

$$= \int_0^1 \frac{1 - g}{\alpha}\,\frac{1}{B(\gamma,\delta)}\,\alpha^{\gamma-1}(1 - \alpha)^{\delta-1}\,d\alpha$$

$$= (1 - g)\,\frac{B(\gamma - 1,\delta)}{B(\gamma,\delta)}$$

$$= (1 - g)\,\frac{\gamma + \delta - 1}{\gamma - 1} \tag{3.30}$$

(except when $\gamma = 1$, for which a different result is obtained). Once again, when there is little variability among the items—when both γ and δ are large—the result is quite similar to $E(T)$ for the homogeneous case.

Any raw moment of T can be found by integrating $E_\alpha(T^k)$ with $f(\alpha)$ to give $E(T^k)$. Integration cannot be used directly to get centered moments such as $\mathrm{var}(T)$, since $\mathrm{var}_\alpha(T)$ is centered about a different value of $E_\alpha(T)$ for each α. The variance can be found from $E(T)$ and $E(T^2)$, however (see Problem 3.20). A similar analysis can be applied to the expectation of other random variables.

Problems

3.1. Simulate five items from the all-or-none model with $\alpha = 0.1$ and $g = 0.2$. Use a random-number table or other random device to provide the necessary stochastic events.

3.2. Consider the three-state version of the two-alternative choice model (Equation 2.21).
   a. What are the state probabilities?
   b. In the limit as $t \to \infty$, what values do the state probabilities take? What do these limits represent?
   c. Suppose that the "trials" in this model represent short intervals of time. The difference $P(U_t) - P(U_{t+1})$ is the probability of leaving U and responding during the tth interval, that is, of a response latency of t units. Find the distribution of latencies and plot them.

3.3. Find the probability of a correct response on trial $t + 1$ given an error on trial t for
   a. The all-or-none model.
   b. The two-stage model (leave the state probabilities unsubstituted).

3.4. What is the probability of a correct response on trial $t + 1$ given a correct response on trial t for the all-or-none model? Why does this result differ substantially from Problem 3.3a?

3.5. Consider the all-or-none paired-associate model.
   a. The probability of no errors, found in Equations 3.17 and 3.18, can be obtained in a different way. Write explicitly the first terms of an infinite series expressing the following statement: "To make no errors, the subject guesses correctly, then either goes from G to L or else stays in G and guesses correctly, then either goes from G to L or else stays in G and guesses correctly, then either .... " Evaluate the sum implied by this statement and show that Equation 3.17 is obtained.
   b. The probability of exactly one error is the sum of the probabilities of the sequences $ECCC \ldots$, $CECCC \ldots$, $CCECCC \ldots$, and so forth. Find each of these probabilities, extrapolate the results to a general formula, and show that they sum to Equation 3.19.

3.6. What is the expected time until a choice in the two-choice model of Matrix 2.21 and Problem 3.2c?

3.7. Show that the expected number of errors for the two-stage model is

$$E(T) = (1 - \sigma) \left\{ (1 - \tau) \frac{1 - g}{\alpha} + [1 - \beta(1 - \tau)] \frac{1 - \pi}{\delta} \right\}$$

3.8. Suppose that a paired-associate experiment is run in which items are presented for m trials, where m is small enough so that not all items are learned. Find $E(T)$ for the all-or-none model. Show that the result converges to Equation 3.16 when m is large.

3.9. Let L be the trial on which the last error is made (define $L = 0$ when no errors are made). For $L = k$ in the all-or-none model, the subject must (1) be in G on trial k, (2) make an error, and (3) make no further errors. Express these events in probabilities and find the distribution of L. Show that the result sums to 1 and find $E(L)$.

3.10. Suppose that a proportion σ of the items in the all-or-none model start in state L. Find
 a. $P(T = 0)$
 b. $E(T)$
 c. $E(L)$

3.11. Consider the hypothesis-testing version of the all-or-none model (Equation 2.7) and let $P(L_1) = \tau$. Find
 a. The state probabilities.
 b. The learning curve.
 c. The expected total number of errors, $E(T)$.
 d. The distribution of the total number of errors, T.
 e. The distribution of the trial of last error, L.
 f. $P(E_{t+1}|E_t)$

3.12. Find the distribution of the trial of last error, L, for the two-stage model. Do not substitute the state probabilities.

3.13. For the all-or-none model, find the distribution and the mean of the following statistics:
 a. The number of errors before the first success, F.
 b. The length of the first run of errors, R.

3.14. The specialization of the two-stage model in Problem 2.6b has fewer parameters than the general two-stage model. For simplicity, let $P(G_1) = 1$. Derive expressions for the state probabilities. Why are these not simply specializations of the results in Section 3.1 (Equations 3.8 and 3.10)?

3.15. Find the state probabilities for the transient states for the model in Problem 2.7. Find the learning curve. Assume the process always starts in G.

3.16. Derive formulas for the complete set of sequential statistics on trials t and $t + 1$, that is, $P(R_{j,t+1} \wedge R_{i,t})$ for R_i, $R_j = C$ or E. Use
   a. The all-or-none model.
   b. The two-stage model.

3.17. Find the probabilities of the three-trial sequential statistics for the all-or-none model (i.e., on trials t, $t + 1$, and $t + 2$), using the initial probabilities $P(L_1) = \sigma$, $P(G_1) = 1 - \sigma$.

3.18. The probability-learning models in Chapter 2 are based on principles of association similar to those of the all-or-none or two-stage model. Probability-learning models analogous to the linear models can also be formed. Denote the state on trial t by the number p_t, $0 \leq p_t \leq 1$, indicating that $P(R_{1,t}) = p_t$. After each trial, change the state according to the linear operators

$$p_{t+1} = \begin{cases} (1 - \theta)p_t + \theta & \text{if } E_1 \\ (1 - \theta)p_t & \text{if } E_2 \end{cases}$$

(cf. Equation 2.10).
   a. What happens to p_t following a very long string of E_1 events? of E_2 events?
   b. Show by computing p_{t+2} that the effects of different events do not commute, that is, that the effect of E_1E_2 is not the same as that of E_2E_1.
   c. Suppose that $P(E_1) = \pi$, independent of the response. The noncommutativity of the operators makes it difficult to find the state distribution. The means are easier to find. Let $\mu_t = E(p_t)$. By the linearity of the expectation,

$$E(p_{t+1}) = \pi E(p_{t+1}|E_1) + (1 - \pi)E(p_{t+1}|E_2)$$

   Use this relationship to find a difference equation for μ_t. Solve this equation. What is the asymptotic value of μ_t as t becomes large?

3.19. Find the probability of a correct response on trial $t + 1$ given an error on trial t for the all-or-none model both with and without variable item difficulty. What happens to the probability for the variable-difficulty model when $t = 1$ and when t is very large.

3.20. Find var(T) for the all-or-none model with variable item difficulty.

Chapter 4

Matrix Methods

The algebraic methods developed in the last chapter are satisfactory so long as the model is fairly simple. However, very soon one runs into computational difficulties. Even for three-state models (such as the two-stage model), calculation of such quantities as the distribution of total errors is very messy. To be successful, an algebraic analysis must capitalize on any zeros or parameter symmetries in the transition matrix. If the Markov models are to have much practical use, more general procedures for doing the calculations are needed. With them, computation can be performed more or less automatically and much of the work passed off to computer routines.

Matrix algebra (summarized in Appendix C) provides exactly what is needed. The calculations required to analyze a Markov chain are almost all linear combinations, and so are easily expressed in matrix form. This has several advantages. The matrix representation lets the state probabilities, distributions of events, and so forth, be stated as relatively compact formulas that are general for any Markov model, regardless of its size. Furthermore, viewing the models in terms of linear transformations makes some general properties apparent that are not obvious when the models are analyzed with individual probabilities.

In essence, what happens when calculations are put in matrix form is quite simple. Probabilities for sets of states are summarized as single vectors or matrices. In matrix notation, these vectors and matrices act in ways that are quite similar to the individual states of the all-or-none model, when analyzed using algebraic notation. This parallel should be noted throughout the chapter.

4.1   *Representation and State Probabilities*

The most fundamental result is that matrix multiplication describes both the change in state probability from one trial to the next and the mapping from states to responses. To start with, the state probabilities are expressed as a row vector, denoted here by s subscripted with the trial number:

$$s_t = [P(S_{1,t}), P(S_{2,t}), \ldots, P(S_{n,t})]$$

The transition probabilities form a matrix:

$$\mathbf{T} = \begin{bmatrix} P(S_1|S_1) & P(S_2|S_1) & \ldots & P(S_n|S_1) \\ P(S_1|S_2) & P(S_2|S_2) & \ldots & P(S_n|S_2) \\ \vdots & \vdots & & \vdots \\ P(S_1|S_n) & P(S_2|S_n) & \ldots & P(S_n|S_n) \end{bmatrix} \tag{4.1}$$

using the same organization in which they were tabulated in Chapter 2. For example, as formulated in Section 2.2 (Equations 2.4 and 2.5), the all-or-none model has the initial vector

$$s_1 = [0, 1] \tag{4.2}$$

and the transition matrix

$$\mathbf{T} = \begin{bmatrix} 1 & 0 \\ \alpha & 1 - \alpha \end{bmatrix} \tag{4.3}$$

The multiplication of s_t by $\mathbf{T}$ gives s_{t+1}, for, by definition (see Equation C.7),

$$s_t\mathbf{T} = \left[\sum_{i=1}^{n} P(S_1|S_i)P(S_{i,t}), \sum_{i=1}^{n} P(S_2|S_i)P(S_{i,t}), \ldots, \sum_{i=1}^{n} P(S_n|S_i)P(S_{i,t}) \right]$$

$$= [P(S_{1,t+1}), P(S_{2,t+1}), \ldots, P(S_{n,t+1})]$$

$$= s_{t+1}$$

This is a matrix difference equation and is analogous to the difference equation obtained for state G in the all-or-none model, Equation 3.3. The same argument that was used to solve that simple difference equation applies here and gives a similar solution:

$$\mathbf{s}_t = \mathbf{s}_1 \mathbf{T}^{t-1} \tag{4.4}$$

Equation 4.4 is a direct way to get the state probabilities on any trial.

The response mapping, from state probabilities to response probabilities, is also linear and thus can also be represented by matrix multiplication. Where only one response is predicted, a vector is all that is necessary. If correct responses are of interest, then

$$P(C_t) = \sum_{i=1}^{n} P(C|S_i)P(S_{i,t}) = \mathbf{s}_t \mathbf{r}' \tag{4.5}$$

where

$$\mathbf{r} = [P(C|S_1),\ P(C|S_2),\ \dots\ ,\ P(C|S_n)]$$

Combining this with Equation 4.4 gives

$$P(C_t) = \mathbf{s}_1 \mathbf{T}^{t-1} \mathbf{r}' \tag{4.6}$$

Equation 4.6 allows the probability of a particular response to be determined. More generally, to obtain the distribution across the full response-state space,

$$\mathbf{p}_t = [P(R_{1,t}),\ P(R_{2,t}),\ \dots\ ,\ P(R_{m,t})]$$

the column vector $\mathbf{r}'$ in Equations 4.5 and 4.6 is replaced by a matrix whose columns contain the conditional response probabilities for a particular response. If

$$\mathbf{R} = \begin{bmatrix} P(R_1|S_1) & P(R_2|S_1) & \dots & P(R_m|S_1) \\ P(R_1|S_2) & P(R_2|S_2) & \dots & P(R_m|S_2) \\ \vdots & \vdots & & \vdots \\ P(R_1|S_n) & P(R_2|S_n) & \dots & P(R_m|S_n) \end{bmatrix} \tag{4.7}$$

then

$$\mathbf{p}_t = \mathbf{s}_t \mathbf{R} = \mathbf{s}_1 \mathbf{T}^{t-1} \mathbf{R} \tag{4.8}$$

Equations 4.5 and 4.6 are special cases of Equation 4.8 with $m = 1$.

Completing the all-or-none example, the response probabilities from Matrix 2.6 give the matrix

$$\mathbf{R} = \begin{bmatrix} 1 & 0 \\ g & 1 - g \end{bmatrix} \tag{4.9}$$

Where only the correct response probability is wanted,

$$\mathbf{r} = [1, g]$$

For some applications, the state of the process is needed only at regularly spaced intervals, say every k trials. For example, one might be interested in the state of the chain on odd-numbered trials, in which case $k = 2$. Looking at the process in this way is like forming a new stochastic process in which every step is equivalent to two steps of the old chain. Suppose k is 2. The process is still a Markov chain, for the distribution of states on trial $t + 2$ depends (through the unrecorded trial $t + 1$) on the state distribution on trial t, but not on earlier trials. Thus, the two-step probabilities can be written as conditional probabilities, $P(S_{j,t+2}|S_{i,t})$, and these form a new transition matrix, which will be denoted $\mathbf{T}^{(2)}$. The symbol $^{(2)}$ here is not an exponent, but an identifying superscript.

The matrix $\mathbf{T}^{(2)}$ is easily expressed in terms of $\mathbf{T}$. Consider the transition from states S_i on trial t to state S_j on trial $t + 2$. This transition can be made by going from S_i to any state, S_h, on trial $t + 1$, then from S_h to S_j on the next trial. In terms of probabilities, this is

$$P(S_{j,t+2}|S_{i,t}) = \sum_{h=1}^{n} P(S_j|S_h) P(S_h|S_i) \tag{4.10}$$

The sum in Equation 4.10 is over the intermediate states on trial $t + 1$.[†]
This is nothing more than one term from the matrix product $\mathbf{T}^2$. Hence,

---

† More generally, one can sum over any intermediate trial in a series: for any $l < k$,

$$P(S_{j,t+k}|S_{i,t}) = \sum_{h=1}^{n} P(S_{j,t+k}|S_{h,t+l}) P(S_{h,t+l}|S_{i,t})$$

This equation is a special case of what are known as the *Chapman–Kolmogorov equations*.

the matrix of two-step transitions is the square of the original transition matrix:

$$\mathbf{T}^{(2)} = \mathbf{T}^2$$

In general, for any k,

$$\mathbf{T}^{(k)} = \mathbf{T}^k \tag{4.11}$$

This means that no special theory is required to deal with multiple steps: one simply defines a new transition matrix and uses all the same formulas.

The same rules apply to matrices of different types. Matrix multiplication allows operators represented by different transition matrices to be combined, as long as they are over the same state space. Consider, for example, the two-stage model with both acquisition and interference operators given at the end of Section 2.3. The two matrices (Equations 2.19 and 2.20) are

$$\mathbf{A} = \begin{bmatrix} 1 & 0 & 0 \\ \delta & 1 - \delta & 0 \\ \alpha\beta & \alpha(1 - \beta) & 1 - \alpha \end{bmatrix} \qquad \mathbf{F} = \begin{bmatrix} 1 & 0 & 0 \\ 0 & \zeta & 1 - \zeta \\ 0 & 0 & 1 \end{bmatrix}$$

If k interfering trials fall between two presentations of the item in question, the composite effect is given by the matrix

$$\mathbf{T}_k = \mathbf{A}\mathbf{F}^k \tag{4.12}$$

In this case it is easy to complete this algebraically. A few multiplications show that

$$\mathbf{F}^k = \begin{bmatrix} 1 & 0 & 0 \\ 0 & \zeta^k & 1 - \zeta^k \\ 0 & 0 & 1 \end{bmatrix}$$

So Equation 4.12 is

$$\mathbf{T}_k = \begin{bmatrix} 1 & 0 & 0 \\ \delta & (1 - \delta)\zeta^k & (1 - \delta)(1 - \zeta^k) \\ \alpha\beta & \alpha(1 - \beta)\zeta^k & 1 - \alpha\beta - \alpha(1 - \beta)\zeta^k \end{bmatrix}$$

Where the matrix corresponding to $\mathbf{F}$ is more complex, it is easier to leave the result as Equation 4.12.

The Markov process is sometimes written with the transition matrix applied on the left of s_t rather than on the right. The forms are equivalent, except that all terms are the transpose of the version given here. Applying the rule for transposing products (Equation C.12) to the equations for computing the state and response probabilities gives

$$s'_t = T's'_{t-1}$$

$$p'_t = R's'_t$$

Of course, if one were using this form, one would have defined everything as the transpose of the convention adopted here, so no primes would appear. There is no fundamental difference between the two representations; they are simply conventions based on the way that the transition matrix is written. The form used here is most common in the psychological literature, but the right-to-left form is often found, particularly in other branches of applied mathematics.

Computationally, when many different powers of T are needed or when t is very large, it is useful to write T in diagonal form, using its eigenvectors and eigenvalues (see Section C.6 and Equation C.35). Then Equation 4.4 becomes

$$s_t = s_1 E^{-1} \Lambda^{t-1} E \qquad (4.13)$$

where Λ is the diagonal matrix of eigenvalues and E contains the eigenvectors as rows. Raising a diagonal matrix to a power is just a matter of raising the elements to that power and is easy to do. The simplicity of this calculation can more than pay for the time spent finding the eigenvectors. Even when a computer is used and the amount of computation is no problem, Equation 4.13 causes less rounding error than does Equation 4.4, so is more accurate.

4.2 Transitions Among Sets of States

Much of the power of matrix methods with Markov chains arises from the fact that vectors giving state probabilities of a set of states can be manipulated in a manner very similar to the algebraic analysis of the probability of an individual state. The matrix equations that result are independent of the number of states in the set. Computational algorithms can then be constructed in a very systematic manner. Much of the material in this chapter derives from methods presented by Kemeny and Snell (1960) and adapted to psychological models by Bernbach (1966), Millward (1969), and Polson (1972).

State Sets as Responses

The overt responses provide the appropriate way to define sets of states for this analysis. For learning models, the most important property is whether the response emitted is correct or not. In what follows, quantities are calculated that are related to correct responses and to errors in learning models. However, the methods are general and apply to any type of model and response division.

To define the set of states associated with a response, the model must be such that each state leads to one and only one response. In other words, the response mapping must not be probabilistic. Unfortunately, as the models were defined above, this was not usually the case. In the simple all-or-none model, for example, processes in state G produce both correct responses and errors. To eliminate this probabilistic aspect, the state space is redefined by splitting any state in which both correct responses and errors are made into a state for errors and a state for correct responses.

Splitting the states is similar to the way in which the states of the all-or-none model are divided when feedback is introduced (see Equation 2.7 in Section 2.2). In fact, the operation is even simpler, for the probabilities of departing from one of the new states does not depend on the response. Each old state divides into as many new states as there are responses that can be made from that state. The probability of entering one of the new states equals the probability of entering the old state multiplied by the probability of the response in the original state. In the case of the all-or-none model, this means multiplying the probability of entering error states by $1 - g$ and of entering correct states by g. This changes the matrix of the all-or-none model from Equation 4.3 into

$$
\begin{array}{c|ccc}
 & L & GC & GE \\
\hline
L & 1 & 0 & 0 \\
GC & \alpha & (1 - \alpha)g & (1 - \alpha)(1 - g) \\
GE & \alpha & (1 - \alpha)g & (1 - \alpha)(1 - g)
\end{array}
\tag{4.14}
$$

The initial vector is similarly expanded. The initial response is a guess, so proportions g and $1 - g$ of the subjects originally in G now start in each of the guessing states. This changes Equation 4.2 to

$$
s_1 = [0, g, 1 - g]
$$

The probability of a correct response is simple: zero in state GE and one in the other two states.

The two-stage model is expanded in the same way. Both states I and G lead to correct and error responses, so both are split. Partitioning gives the five-state Markov chain

	L	IC	IE	GC	GE
L	1	0	0	0	0
IC	δ	$(1 - \delta)\pi$	$(1 - \delta)(1 - \pi)$	0	0
IE	δ	$(1 - \delta)\pi$	$(1 - \delta)(1 - \pi)$	0	0
GC	$\alpha\beta$	$\alpha(1 - \beta)\pi$	$\alpha(1 - \beta)(1 - \pi)$	$(1 - \alpha)g$	$(1 - \alpha)(1 - g)$
GE	$\alpha\beta$	$\alpha(1 - \beta)\pi$	$\alpha(1 - \beta)(1 - \pi)$	$(1 - \alpha)g$	$(1 - \alpha)(1 - g)$

$$(4.15)$$

The initial vector is

$$\mathbf{s}_1 = [\sigma, (1 - \sigma)\tau\pi, (1 - \sigma)\tau(1 - \pi), (1 - \sigma)(1 - \tau)g,$$
$$(1 - \sigma)(1 - \tau)(1 - g)]$$

and the response vector for correct responses is

$$\mathbf{r} = [1, 1, 0, 1, 0]$$

The states of this chain divide into three subsets: absorbing states, transient correct states, and transient error states. It is visually convenient, although not necessary, to reorder the states so that states from the same class are together. Thus, Matrix 4.15 becomes

	L	IC	GC	IE	GE
L	1	0	0	0	0
IC	δ	$(1 - \delta)\pi$	0	$(1 - \delta)(1 - \pi)$	0
GC	$\alpha\beta$	$\alpha(1 - \beta)\pi$	$(1 - \alpha)g$	$\alpha(1 - \beta)(1 - \pi)$	$(1 - \alpha)(1 - g)$
IE	δ	$(1 - \delta)\pi$	0	$(1 - \delta)(1 - \pi)$	0
GE	$\alpha\beta$	$\alpha(1 - \beta)\pi$	$(1 - \alpha)g$	$\alpha(1 - \beta)(1 - \pi)$	$(1 - \alpha)(1 - g)$

$$(4.16)$$

The initial and response vectors are also reordered.

The reorganization into classes partitions the transition matrix into submatrices, each of which contains the transition probabilities between the states of two of the classes. In what follows, the letter $\mathbf{Q}$, subscripted by the responses, indicates a submatrix of transitions between transient states. So $\mathbf{Q}_{ec}$ contains the probabilities of going from an error state to a correct-response state. When there is only one absorbing state, transition probabilities into it form a column vector, which is denoted by $\mathbf{a}'$, appropriately subscripted. Thus, the full transition matrix is

$$\mathbf{T} = \begin{bmatrix} 1 & \mathbf{0} & \mathbf{0} \\ \mathbf{a}'_c & \mathbf{Q}_{cc} & \mathbf{Q}_{ce} \\ \mathbf{a}'_e & \mathbf{Q}_{ec} & \mathbf{Q}_{ee} \end{bmatrix} \tag{4.17}$$

where 0 indicates a vectors of 0's of the appropriate size. For example, in the two-stage model,

$$\mathbf{Q}_{ec} = \begin{bmatrix} (1 - \delta)\pi & 0 \\ \alpha(1 - \beta)\pi & (1 - \alpha)g \end{bmatrix}$$

In a corresponding manner, the state vector is also partitioned into three parts associated with the three sets:

$$s_t = [s_{t,a}, s_{t,c}, s_{t,e}]$$

If the blocks of Matrix 4.17 contained scalars rather than submatrices, the matrix would be very similar to that of the all-or-none model in Matrix 4.14. In fact, the submatrices are used to make calculations in almost exactly the same way that the scalars are used in the all-or-none model. For example, the probability of passage from state GC to GE is a single number in the all-or-none matrix, while in general the probabilities of passage between any correct state and any error state is $\mathbf{Q}_{ce}$. In the all-or-none model the probability of a two-step transition from state GE to GC is

$$P(GC_{t+2}|GE_t) = P(GC|GE)P(GE|GE) + P(GC|GC)P(GC|GE) \tag{4.18}$$

(see Equation 4.10). Applying the rules for multiplying partitioned matrices (Equation C.25), the corresponding matrix quantity,

$$\mathbf{Q}_{ec}^{(2)} = \mathbf{Q}_{ee}\mathbf{Q}_{ec} + \mathbf{Q}_{ec}\mathbf{Q}_{cc} \tag{4.19}$$

operates in exactly the same way. The important point is that Equation 4.18 acts on individual probabilities, while Equation 4.19 expresses the same thing for sets. The only apparent difference between the two equations is that the conditionalizing event in a probability is written on the right side, so that the products in Equation 4.18 work from right to left; while the matrix equation is written from left to right. If Equation 4.19 seems confusing, it may be helpful to multiply out an example detail, say for the two-stage model, to see how the individual probabilities go together.

The subscripts in Equation 4.19 should be noted. They express the dimensions of the submatrices (e.g., Q_{ec} has as many rows as error states and as many columns as correct-response states); hence they must be consistent with the dimensions in the matrix operations. When two matrices are multiplied, the right-hand subscript of the left-hand matrix must be the same as the left-hand subscript of the right-hand matrix. When two products are summed, the two left-hand subscripts must be the same, as must also be the two right-hand subscripts. These facts serve as a useful check on the consistency of matrix formulas.

Splitting the states to obtain an unambiguous relation between state and response is not entirely a simplification. Although it has the effect of concentrating all the stochastic aspects of the process into the transition matrix, it does so at the cost of expanding the size of the matrix. The original model consists of a Markov chain and a probabilistic mapping from the states of the chain to responses. Expanding the matrix puts the response mapping into the Markov chain, but does not change the underlying transition operation by doing so. The analysis of the situation is helped considerably by the interpretation of a Markov model as a transformation of a vector space, as introduced at the end of Section 3.1. When viewed in this way, the expanded transition matrix, although larger, does not operate in a larger space.

For the case of the all-or-none model, a picture of the original model is shown in Figure 4.1a. The process starts in s_1 and moves on successive trials up toward the point [0, 1]. When the model is expanded to include the response states, this two-dimensional picture is embedded in the three-dimensional space, as in Figure 4.1b, but the basic transition mechanism does not change. To avoid confusion between the pictures, let $\tilde{s}_t$, $\hat{T}$, and so forth denote the expanded model for the remainder of this section. The process starts from its initial state $\tilde{s}_1$ and progresses directly toward the point [1, 0, 0]. Although the space is larger, the process is no more complex.

Changing from one space to the other is nothing more than a change of basis, which is accomplished by a matrix multiplication. The states of the original model, s_t, are split by multiplication on the right by a rectangular matrix P:

$$\tilde{s}_t = s_t P \tag{4.20}$$

Each row of P corresponds to a state in the original matrix, each column to a state of the expanded model, and p_{ij} is the proportion of the original S_i that becomes the $\tilde{S}_j$. For the all-or-none model, this matrix is

$$P = \begin{bmatrix} 1 & 0 & 0 \\ 0 & g & 1-g \end{bmatrix} \tag{4.21}$$

Thus, the basis vectors [1, 0] and [0, 1] that spanned the space of state-probability vectors in the original model become [1, 0, 0] and [0, g, 1 − g] as expressed in the space of the expanded model.

In the expanded basis, the transition operator **T** is represented by a larger matrix $\tilde{\mathbf{T}}$. This new matrix is derived from **T** by

$$\tilde{\mathbf{T}} = \mathbf{QTP} \qquad (4.22)$$

where **Q** is chosen so that it takes the states of the expanded matrix back to those of the original version. Because going from the original model to the expanded version and then back doesn't change anything, this means that **PQ** = **I** (i.e., **Q** is a right inverse of **P**). For the all-or-none example,

$$\mathbf{Q} = \begin{bmatrix} 1 & 0 \\ 0 & 1 \\ 0 & 1 \end{bmatrix} \qquad (4.23)$$

and

$$\tilde{\mathbf{T}} = \begin{bmatrix} 1 & 0 \\ 0 & 1 \\ 0 & 1 \end{bmatrix} \begin{bmatrix} 1 & 0 \\ \alpha & 1 - \alpha \end{bmatrix} \begin{bmatrix} 1 & 0 & 0 \\ 0 & g & 1 - g \end{bmatrix}$$

$$= \begin{bmatrix} 1 & 0 & 0 \\ \alpha & (1 - \alpha)g & (1 - \alpha)(1 - g) \\ \alpha & (1 - \alpha)g & (1 - \alpha)(1 - g) \end{bmatrix}$$

giving Matrix 4.14, as it should. The expanded matrix represents the same transformation under the basis change, so its rank is no greater than that of the original matrix. Thus, $\tilde{\mathbf{T}}$ is singular.

It is worth verifying that the expanded model gives the same answers as the original model. Because of the inverse relationship of **P** and **Q**,

$$\tilde{\mathbf{s}}_t \tilde{\mathbf{T}} = (\mathbf{s}_t \mathbf{P})(\mathbf{QTP})$$

$$= \mathbf{s}_t (\mathbf{PQ})\mathbf{TP} = \mathbf{s}_t \mathbf{ITP}$$

$$= \mathbf{s}_t \mathbf{TP} = \mathbf{s}_{t+1} \mathbf{P} = \tilde{\mathbf{s}}_{t+1}$$

Thus, the transformed model takes one state vector to the vector on the next trial. Geometrically, because $\tilde{\mathbf{s}}_{t+1}$ is the transformed version of $\mathbf{s}_{t+1}$, the process has never left the straight line in Figure 4.1b.

The change of basis works in the opposite direction as well. Multiplying Equation 4.22 by **P** on the left and **Q** on the right gives

$$\mathbf{P}\tilde{\mathbf{T}}\mathbf{Q} = \mathbf{PQTPQ} = \mathbf{ITI} = \mathbf{T} \qquad (4.24)$$

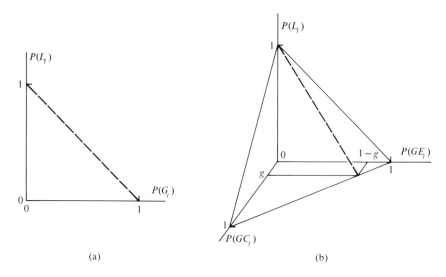

Figure 4.1 Geometry of the change to a model with a nonprobabilistic response mapping. In both spaces, state vectors s_t lie only on the dashed lines.

Likewise,

$$\tilde{s}_t = \tilde{s}_t Q \qquad (4.25)$$

Because it constitutes only a basis change, the transformation to the expanded model adds no new information to the model, only reexpresses it. So it is possible to write all the functions in this chapter with the reduced model. The representation is sometimes less transparent, but the answer is the same. For example, in the remainder of this chapter, it is often necessary to find the joint probability of a particular state and a response. The expanded representation makes it easy to go backward across the response mapping from a response to a state: when an error is made, the process must be in an error state and the joint probability of the error and any other state is 0. When the reduced form of the matrices is used, the same thing can be done, but the restriction of states is probabilistic, not absolute. In the all-or-none model, an error eliminates all items currently in state L and a proportion g of the items in state G (those for which a correct response takes place). A more complete example of probabilistic restriction appears later.

Likelihoods of Response Strings

The probability of obtaining a particular string of responses is a quantity of considerable importance. It is known as the *likelihood* of the string and is both interesting in its own right and useful in the estimation of parameters (see Chapter 5). The partitioning of **T** by states begins to pay off here, for the likelihood of a particular sequence of responses is easy to express in terms of the **Q** submatrices.

To keep the notation simple, it is easiest to see how likelihoods are found by looking at an example. Consider the response sequence

$$E_1C_2C_3E_4C_5C_6 \ldots$$

ending with a string of correct responses. The probability of this string is found by tracing the transitions between sets of states corresponding to the responses, so that the process is in an error state on trial 1, a correct state on trials 2 and 3, and so forth. The probability of starting in one of the error states, thus making a first error, is given by the error portion of the initial state vector, $s_{1,e}$. This assures E_1. Multiplying this vector by $\mathbf{Q}_{ec}$ gives a vector of length c containing the joint probabilities of starting in an error state and, on the next trial, being in each of the transient correct-response states. Expressing this in terms of the state probabilities, using the two-stage model as an example, gives

$$s_{1,e} = [P(IE_1), P(GE_1)]$$

$$\mathbf{Q}_{ec} = \begin{bmatrix} P(IC|IE) & P(GC|IE) \\ P(IC|GE) & P(GC|GE) \end{bmatrix}$$

and so

$$s_{1,e}\mathbf{Q}_{ec} = [P(IC|IE)P(IE_1) + P(IC|GE)P(GE_1),$$
$$P(GC|IE)P(IE_1) + P(GC|GE)P(GE_1)]$$
$$= [P(IC_2 \wedge E_1), P(GC_2 \wedge E_1)]$$

Clearly, the matrix form, $s_{1,e}\mathbf{Q}_{ec}$, is simpler and more general.

Responses on the third and fourth trials are included in the same way, giving

$$s_{1,e}\mathbf{Q}_{ec}\mathbf{Q}_{cc}\mathbf{Q}_{ce}$$

Mnemonically, think of entering the set of states specified in the rows, or first subscript, and departing through the columns, or second subscript. Making sure that the matrix on the right is entered through the same set of states by which the matrix on the left departs assures that the number of rows and number of columns agree, to permit multiplication. For example, $\mathbf{Q}_{ec}$ can be followed by either $\mathbf{Q}_{cc}$ or $\mathbf{Q}_{ce}$, but not by $\mathbf{Q}_{ec}$ or $\mathbf{Q}_{ee}$.

At this point, the result is a row vector containing the probabilities of being in each of the error states following the sequence $E_1 C_2 C_3$. If only the probability of the string through the fourth response is desired, these probabilities are summed by multiplying them on the right by a column vector of 1's:

$$P(E_1 \wedge C_2 \wedge C_3 \wedge E_4) = s_{1,e} \mathbf{Q}_{ec} \mathbf{Q}_{cc} \mathbf{Q}_{ce} \mathbf{1}'_e \qquad (4.26)$$

The subscript e on $\mathbf{1}'_e$ indicates the size of the vector. For many purposes this summation completes the calculation.

If the string continues with a sequence of correct responses following trial 4, a vector other than $\mathbf{1}'_e$ is needed to represent that fact. This vector plays a role analogous to the probability of no errors following a response used to find the distribution of T for the all-or-none model (the quantity b given by Equation 3.18). The entries of this vector are the probabilities that no further errors follow each of the error states. Let $\mathbf{b}'_e$ be this vector (the subscript e associates it with the transient error states, and the prime indicates that it is a column vector). Finding $\mathbf{b}'_e$ is similar to finding Equation 3.18. For the trial following an error to be correct, one of two things must happen: either the process passes directly into the absorbing state, or else it goes to one of the transient correct-response states. Probabilities for the first of these events are given in $\mathbf{a}_e$, for the second in $\mathbf{Q}_{ec}$. If passage is to the absorbing state, there can be no further errors. Otherwise, if the process passes to the transient correct state set, an additional factor is required to assure that an error state is never reentered. The appropriate quantity is a vector $\mathbf{b}'_c$ containing the probabilities of no further errors following each transient correct-response state. In a formula, the argument is

$$\mathbf{b}'_e = \mathbf{a}'_e + \mathbf{Q}_{ec} \mathbf{b}'_c \qquad (4.27)$$

An analogous equation expresses $\mathbf{b}'_c$ in terms of itself:

$$\mathbf{b}'_c = \mathbf{a}'_c + \mathbf{Q}_{cc} \mathbf{b}'_c$$

This matrix equation can be solved for $\mathbf{b}'_c$ as follows, being careful not to reverse the order of a matrix multiplication:

$$\mathbf{b}'_c - \mathbf{Q}_{cc} \mathbf{b}'_c = \mathbf{a}'_c$$
$$(\mathbf{I} - \mathbf{Q}_{cc}) \mathbf{b}'_c = \mathbf{a}'_c$$
$$\mathbf{b}'_c = (\mathbf{I} - \mathbf{Q}_{cc})^{-1} \mathbf{a}'_c \qquad (4.28)$$

Putting Equations 4.27 and 4.28 together with the probability of the first four steps in the string gives the likelihood

$$P(ECCECC \cdots) = s_{1,e}Q_{ec}Q_{cc}Q_{ce}[a'_e + Q_{ec} (I - Q_{cc})^{-1}a'_c] \quad (4.29)$$

Analogous calculations determine the likelihood of any string.

The Fundamental Matrix

The matrix $(I - Q_{cc})^{-1}$ in the above calculation is important and deserves special comment. It, or matrices similar to it, appear frequently in matrix probability calculations. Consider any set of transient states and let Q be the portion of the transition matrix that contains the transition probabilities from the states in the set to themselves. The contribution to the likelihood of a stay of k trials in the set is Q^k, this term appearing between composite terms describing what happens before and after entry to the set as xQ^ky. Now suppose the process enters the set and stays for some unspecified number of trials, $k = 0, 1, 2, \ldots$. The likelihood of this is the sum of the likelihoods of stays of every duration:

$$xy + xQ^1y + xQ^2y + \cdots = x(I + Q + Q^2 + \cdots)y$$

The infinite sum in this,

$$N = I + Q + Q^2 + Q^3 + \cdots \qquad (4.30)$$

can be evaluated, using one of the methods employed to evaluate scalar sums (discussed following the treatment of the geometric distribution in Section A.3) to give

$$N = (I - Q)^{-1} \qquad (4.31)$$

Of course, if $I - Q$ is singular, the inverse does not exist, but this is never a problem when the states in the set are all transient. The matrix N is sometimes called the *fundamental matrix* of the set of states.

The matrix N takes the process from an entering state indicated by the row to the eventual exit state indicated by the column, but without specifying the number of trials needed for this to happen. In this respect, N acts like a transition submatrix in cases where the number of trials for the transition to take place is not given. In Equation 4.29, for example, it represents an indeterminate stay in the transient correct set.

In spite of this use, the elements of N are not probabilities. The identity matrix included in the sum in Equation 4.30 forces the diagonal elements to exceed 1; so they clearly cannot be probabilities. In fact, the entries are the expected number of trials in the set of states. A process entering a particular set of transient states eventually leaves, but only after staying some number of trials. An element n_{ij} of the matrix **N** gives the average number of trials that a process entering in S_i is in state S_j. A demonstration of this runs as follows. Consider a process entering in S_i. Let $X_{ij}^{(k)}$ be a Bernoulli random variable that equals 1 if the process is in $S_j k$ trials later, without having left the set of states. Then the total number of trials that this process is in S_j is

$$Y_{ij} = \sum_{k=0}^{\infty} X_{ij}^{(k)}$$

The expectation of $X_{ij}^{(k)}$ equals the probability that it is 1. Using the rule for the expectation of a sum (Equation A.18) gives

$$n_{ij} = E(Y_{ij})$$

$$= \sum_{k=0}^{\infty} E(X_{ij}^{(k)})$$

$$= \sum_{k=0}^{\infty} P(S_{j,t+k} \wedge [\text{no departure from set}] \,|\, S_{i,t})$$

The probabilities in this sum are elements of $\mathbf{Q}^k$, as can be seen by recalling (from Equation 4.11) that $\mathbf{T}^{(k)} = \mathbf{T}^k$ and noting that the use of **Q** rather than **T** excludes sequences leaving the set. Thus, Equation 4.30 is a single equation giving all the n_{ij} at once. A proof can also be based on a recursive argument similar to that which led to Equation 4.28. The notion of the expected number of trials in a state is an important one and is treated in a more general framework in Chapter 8.

4.3 *Distributions of Some Summary Statistics*

Matrix methods can be used to find the distribution of many other statistics. A representative selection is considered in this section (for others, see Millward, 1969; Polson, 1972). The basic strategy is the same as for the likelihood calculation: the statistics are expressed as residencies in sets of states; then the probability of these sets is written as a sequence of matrices. Although the discussion is phrased in terms of learning models, correct responses, and errors, the methods are general.

The Number of Errors

The distribution of the number of errors made in learning an item is developed quite directly, following an argument comparable to the one used in Section 3.3. As there, the case of zero errors is treated differently from the case of one or more errors. In order for no errors to be made, the process must start in a correct-response state, either absorbing or transient. In the former case no errors are ever made, while in the latter the process must be absorbed without ever entering an error state. However, it can remain in the correct state for an arbitrarily long time before being absorbed. This latter event is the one represented by the matrix $\mathbf{N}_{cc}$ in the likelihood calculation. Thus,

$$P(T = 0) = s_{1,a} + s_{1,c}\mathbf{N}_{cc}\mathbf{a}'_c \tag{4.32}$$

If $T > 0$, the process cannot start in the absorbing state, but may begin in either of the two transient-state sets. It must pass through the error set as many times as there are errors before its last entry into the correct states. In more detail, the occurrence of exactly k errors requires the following series of events (cf. Equation 3.20):

1. The process enters the error set, either directly or by starting in a correct state and then moving to an error state. Let the vector $\mathbf{f}$ contain the probabilities of entering each of the error states for the first time. It is given by an expression similar to Equation 4.32, but with the error states playing the role of the absorbing states:

$$\mathbf{f} = s_{1,e} + s_{1,c}\,\mathbf{N}_{cc}\mathbf{Q}_{ce}$$

This assures the first error.

2. For each error after the first, the process must either stay in the error-state set or leave it and return after a sojourn in the transient correct states. Let the matrix $\mathbf{D}$ give the probability of eventual passage from one error state to another. By the same reasoning as before,

$$\mathbf{D} = \mathbf{Q}_{ee} + \mathbf{Q}_{ec}\mathbf{N}_{cc}\mathbf{Q}_{ce}$$

For a process with k errors, $\mathbf{D}$ appears raised to the $k - 1$ power, giving $k - 1$ returns to error states.

3. Finally, the process is absorbed without further errors. The probability of this event following each of the error states has

already been found in Equation 4.27 to be

$$\mathbf{b}'_e = \mathbf{a}'_e + \mathbf{Q}_{ec}\mathbf{N}_{cc}\mathbf{a}'_c$$

Combining these steps, the complete distribution of the number of errors is

$$P(T = k) = \begin{cases} s_{1,a} + s_{1,c}\mathbf{N}_{cc}\mathbf{a}'_c & k = 0 \\ \mathbf{f}\mathbf{D}^{k-1}\mathbf{b}'_e & k > 0 \end{cases} \tag{4.33}$$

The expected value of T can be obtained directly from the definition of the expectation. The calculation is quite orthodox, except for the use of matrices.

$$\begin{aligned} E(T) &= \sum_{k=0}^{\infty} kP(T = k) \\ &= \sum_{k=1}^{\infty} k\mathbf{f}\mathbf{D}^{k-1}\mathbf{b}'_e \\ &= \mathbf{f}\left[\sum_{k=1}^{\infty} k\mathbf{D}^{k-1}\right]\mathbf{b}'_e \\ &= \mathbf{f}(\mathbf{I} - \mathbf{D})^{-2}\mathbf{b}'_e \end{aligned} \tag{4.34}$$

The evaluation of the infinite sum parallels the comparable sum for scalar quantities (Equation A.30). The variance of T is found in an analogous way (see Problem 4.4).

The value of $E(T)$ can also be found from the expected-trials interpretation of $\mathbf{N}$. Let

$$\mathbf{Q} = \begin{bmatrix} \mathbf{Q}_{cc} & \mathbf{Q}_{ce} \\ \mathbf{Q}_{ec} & \mathbf{Q}_{ee} \end{bmatrix}$$

be the transition submatrix for the transient states. Then the fundamental matrix for this set of states, $\mathbf{N} = (\mathbf{I} - \mathbf{Q})^{-1}$, contains the expected number of trials that the process resides in each state given a particular starting state. Thus, $[s_{1,c}, s_{1,e}]\mathbf{N}$ is a row vector containing the expected number of trials in each of the transient states. The expected number of errors is the sum of the entries of this vector that correspond to error states. This sum is expressed in matrix notation as postmultiplication by a vector with as many entries as there are transient states, those corresponding to correct states being 0 and those corresponding to errors being 1. Denoting this vector by $\mathbf{v}'$:

$$E(T) = [s_{1,c}, s_{1,e}]\mathbf{N}\mathbf{v}' \tag{4.35}$$

The results in Equations 4.34 and 4.35 appear different. In fact, they are not, as the following operations show (see Problem 4.5). By partitioning $\mathbf{N}$, $\mathbf{Q}$, and $\mathbf{v}$ into their correct and error portions, then using the formulas from Section C.4, Equation 4.35 becomes

$$E(T) = \mathbf{f}(\mathbf{I} - \mathbf{D})^{-1}\mathbf{1}'_e \tag{4.36}$$

The rows in a Markov matrix sum to 1, so

$$\mathbf{a}'_c + \mathbf{Q}_{cc}\mathbf{1}'_c + \mathbf{Q}_{ce}\mathbf{1}'_e = \mathbf{1}'_c$$

or

$$\mathbf{a}'_c = (\mathbf{I} - \mathbf{Q}_{cc})\mathbf{1}'_c - \mathbf{Q}_{ce}\mathbf{1}'_e$$

A similar equation holds for $\mathbf{a}'_e$. Substituting these in the formula for $\mathbf{b}_e$ gives

$$\mathbf{b}'_e = (\mathbf{I} - \mathbf{D})\mathbf{1}'_e$$

This changes Equation 4.34 into Equation 4.36. The apparent dissimilarity among Equations 4.34, 4.35, and 4.36 is a bit disconcerting. The same quantity appears very different in the different formulas. Unfortunately, it is quite common for superficial discrepancies of this sort to occur. Two methods of derivation cannot be judged inconsistent until one is quite sure that the results are really different.

The Trial of Last Error

Another useful statistic is the number of the trial on which the last error takes place. This statistic, denoted here by L, embodies quite different information from the number of errors. For example, one may be able to match the number of errors predicted by the all-or-none model and the two-stage model, but because the two-stage model allows the probability of an error to change before the final error (due to movement into state I), it predicts a larger trial of last error. This could provide a basis for comparing the models to data.

Finding the distribution of the trial of last error is straightforward (cf. Problem 3.9). By definition, the event of no errors is denoted as $L = 0$. So, copying Equation 4.32 gives

$$P(L = 0) = s_{1,a} + s_{1,c}\mathbf{N}_{cc}\mathbf{a}'_c$$

In all other cases, finding the last error is equivalent to finding the last passage of the chain through any member of the error-state set. For $L = t$, the process must be in an error state on trial t, then never reenter the set. If $s_{t,e}$ is the error-state portion of s_t, then

$$P(L = t) = s_{t,e}b_e' \tag{4.37}$$

In one sense, Equation 4.37 completes finding the distribution. Quite trivially, $s_{t,e}$ is that portion of $s_t = s_1 T^{t-1}$ associated with the error states. However, some computational work can be saved by reformulating $s_{t,e}$. If only items in transient states lead to errors, the probability of being in the absorbing state is not needed, and the smaller vector $[s_{1,c}, s_{1,e}]Q^{t-1}$ can be used in lieu of $s_1 T^{t-1}$. The extraction of the error-state vector from this is also a matrix operation. Consider the rectangular matrix

$$V_E = \begin{bmatrix} 0 & 0 & 0 & \cdots & 0 \\ 0 & 0 & 0 & \cdots & 0 \\ \vdots & \vdots & \vdots & & \vdots \\ 0 & 0 & 0 & \cdots & 0 \\ 1 & 0 & 0 & \cdots & 0 \\ 0 & 1 & 0 & \cdots & 0 \\ \vdots & \vdots & \vdots & & \vdots \\ 0 & 0 & 0 & \cdots & 1 \end{bmatrix} = \begin{bmatrix} 0_{ce} \\ I_{ee} \end{bmatrix} \tag{4.38}$$

composed of a $c \times e$ matrix of 0's above an $e \times e$ identity matrix. Multiplying by Matrix 4.38 reduces a large vector to a smaller one by keeping only entries for which there is a 1 in that row of V_E and putting them into new positions designated by the corresponding columns. The result is $s_{t,e}$. Thus, for $t > 0$, Equation 4.37 becomes

$$P(L = t) = [s_{1,c}, s_{1,e}]Q^{t-1}V_E b_e' \tag{4.39}$$

The expectation is found by a calculation similar to that which led to $E(T)$:

$$E(L) = [s_{1,c}, s_{1,e}](I - Q)^{-2}V_E b_e' \tag{4.40}$$

Note that $E(L)$ is not the same as the mean number of trials in the transient states. If absorption can occur from correct-response states, it is possible to make responses from the transient states after the last error.

Latency of Responses

Matrix multiplication can map the state probabilities onto quantities other than response probabilities. As long as a linear combination is involved, the procedure is the same. One example is the response latency. Ideally, the latency should be treated as a random variable and its complete distribution found. However, most models do not support sufficient detail to do this (for some exceptions, see Chapter 10). Fortunately, it is usually enough to work with the mean and variance. Suppose that plausible mean values, μ_i, can be assigned to the response latency from state S_i. Because of the linearity of the expectation (Equation A.18), the expected value over a linear combination of states is itself a linear combination. Let $\mathcal{L}$ denote the latency. Then

$$
\begin{aligned}
E(\mathcal{L}_t) &= \sum_{i=1}^{n} E(\mathcal{L}|S_i)P(S_{i,t}) \\
&= \sum_{i=1}^{n} \mu_i P(S_{i,t}) = s_t \boldsymbol{\mu}'
\end{aligned}
\tag{4.41}
$$

where $\boldsymbol{\mu} = [\mu_1, \mu_2, \ldots, \mu_n]$.

As a simple example of this, consider the all-or-none model in its three-state form and suppose that responses are slower by an average amount δ in the guessing states. If μ is the mean latency in the learned state, then

$$
\boldsymbol{\mu} = [\mu, \mu + \delta, \mu + \delta]
$$

Using the state probabilities developed in Chapter 3 (Equations 3.2 and 3.4, slightly modified) gives

$$
E(\mathcal{L}_t) = [1 - (1 - \alpha)^{t-1}, (1 - \alpha)^{t-1}g, (1 - \alpha)^{t-1}(1 - g)] \begin{bmatrix} \mu \\ \mu + \delta \\ \mu + \delta \end{bmatrix}
$$

$$
= \mu + (1 - \alpha)^{t-1}\delta
$$

This function starts at $\mu + \delta$ on trial 1 and falls exponentially toward μ.

Unfortunately, a formula such as Equation 4.41 does not apply to the variances of the latencies. As with the variance of other quantities, calculation must proceed via the moments about 0, for which Equation

4.41 works. Both $E(\mathcal{L})$ and $E(\mathcal{L}^2)$ are found as linear combinations; then var$(\mathcal{L})$ is calculated from them.

4.4   Selection of Items Taking Particular Paths

Most interesting questions about a Markov model can be phrased as questions about the joint probabilities of various events. To construct these joint probabilities, it is useful to have a way to select subsets of items that pass through a particular set of states on a particular trial. Such a selection was performed above in finding the distribution of the trial of last error: the matrix $\mathbf{V}_E$ selected items with an error on trial t for further consideration. This was done by keeping the probability of any process that was in an error state on that trial and dropping the probability of being in a correct-response state. In effect, processes that did not have an error on that trial were eliminated. Rows of $\mathbf{V}_E$ containing 1's passed the corresponding probabilities along, while rows containing 0's eliminated paths. The fact that $\mathbf{V}_E$ was not square served to reduce a larger vector to a smaller one, although this was not necessary to the selection process.

This method applies more generally. At any point in a sequence of matrix multiplications, a matrix can be inserted to eliminate all processes in certain states and allow others to continue. Such a matrix looks like an identity matrix in which some of the diagonal entries have been replaced by 0's. For example, suppose one desired to select only items that were in the intermediate state of the two-stage model on a particular trial. This means selecting states IC and IE, which are the second and fourth states of Matrix 4.16. Using a matrix in which the second and fourth rows (and columns) contain 1's and the remainder is 0's gives

$$[P(L), P(IC), P(GC), P(IE), P(GE)] \begin{bmatrix} 0 & 0 & 0 & 0 & 0 \\ 0 & 1 & 0 & 0 & 0 \\ 0 & 0 & 0 & 0 & 0 \\ 0 & 0 & 0 & 1 & 0 \\ 0 & 0 & 0 & 0 & 0 \end{bmatrix}$$

$$= [0, P(IC), 0, P(IE), 0] \quad (4.42)$$

Only $P(IC)$ and $P(IE)$ are preserved by this multiplication.

In terms of probabilities, the selection operation forms the joint probability of the original state distribution with residency in the selected set of states. On the left of Equation 4.42, for example, is a state-probability distribution; on the right are the joint probabilities of this distribution and residence in the intermediate state. More generally, if Z represents any event, then

$$[P(S_1 \wedge Z), \; P(S_2 \wedge Z), \; \ldots, \; P(S_n \wedge Z)]$$

$$= [P(Z|S_1)P(S_1), \; P(Z|S_2)P(S_2), \; \ldots, \; P(Z|S_n)P(S_n)]$$

$$= [P(S_1), \; P(S_2), \; \ldots, \; P(S_n)] \begin{bmatrix} P(Z|S_1) & 0 & \cdots & 0 \\ 0 & P(Z|S_2) & \cdots & 0 \\ \vdots & \vdots & & \vdots \\ 0 & 0 & \cdots & P(Z|S_n) \end{bmatrix} \quad (4.43)$$

When the conditional probabilities in Matrix 4.43 are either 0 or 1, construction of joint probabilities amounts to selection of states. Representation of joint probabilities in this way allows formulas to be written in a very unified manner.

In some respects, calculation using these selection matrices is inefficient. It is not necessary to multiply and sum all the 0's in Matrix 4.43, nor, for many purposes, to carry the 0's in the resultant vectors on to later calculations. To avoid doing so, simpler matrices can be used. For example, this is why V_E was not square: it selected the error states and dropped the correct-state probability. In writing a computer program, one would not multiply the full selection matrices out. Selection amounts to preserving certain elements of a vector and setting others to 0. There are much easier and faster ways to do this than matrix multiplication. Indeed, some computer languages (such as APL) contain selection operations of this sort as part of their basic vocabulary.

Likelihoods Again

One direct application of the selection process is to the likelihood of a string of responses. These were found in Section 4.2 using the matrices Q_{cc}, Q_{ce}, Q_{ec}, and Q_{ee} to match the sequence of responses. Selection matrices can also be used. The approach is similar, except that the full transition matrix is used and the result is more general.

Matrices to select the correct-response states and the error states are needed. The division of the states by responses makes these matrices simple. They contain 1's on the diagonal entries for the states selected and 0's elsewhere. If correct-response and error states are separated, as in Matrix 4.16, the 1's are blocked:

$$W_C = \begin{bmatrix} I_{cc} & 0_{ce} \\ 0_{ec} & 0_{ee} \end{bmatrix} \qquad W_E = \begin{bmatrix} 0_{cc} & 0_{ce} \\ 0_{ec} & I_{ee} \end{bmatrix} \qquad (4.44)$$

The subscripts indicate the size of the submatrices, a capital C being used to indicate that the correct-response set now includes the absorbing state as well as the transient-correct states. Inserted between successive applications of the transition matrix, $\mathbf{W}_C$ and $\mathbf{W}_E$ select the desired responses. Thus, $\mathbf{s}_1 \mathbf{W}_E$ selects those response sequences that begin with an error. Multiplying this by $\mathbf{T}$, to give $\mathbf{s}_1 \mathbf{W}_E \mathbf{T}$, produces a vector whose entries are $P(E_1 \wedge S_{i,2})$. Multiplying by $\mathbf{W}_C$ selects from these only those state sequences with the second response correct, matching response strings starting with $E_1 C_2$. In this way the probability of any string can be found.

If the likelihood of a string of responses up to a particular trial is to be found, the entries of the final state vector are summed by postmultiplication by $\mathbf{1}'$. For the sequence of responses, $X_1, X_2, \ldots, X_t$,

$$P(X_1 X_2 \cdots X_t) = \sum_{i=1}^{n} P(X_1 \wedge X_2 \wedge \cdots \wedge X_t \wedge S_{i,t})$$

$$= \mathbf{s}_1 \mathbf{W}_{X_1} \mathbf{T} \mathbf{W}_{X_2} \mathbf{T} \cdots \mathbf{T} \mathbf{W}_{X_t} \mathbf{1}' \qquad (4.45)$$

When the response string ends with an indefinitely long sequence of correct responses, the vector $\mathbf{1}'$ is replaced by a vector containing the probabilities of no further errors following a response in each state. The parts of this vector have already been found; in full, it is

$$\mathbf{b} = [1, \mathbf{b}_c, \mathbf{b}_e]$$

Thus, if X_t is followed by correct responses,

$$P(X_1 S_2 \cdots X_t C C C \cdots) = \mathbf{s}_1 \mathbf{W}_{X_1} \mathbf{T} \mathbf{W}_{X_2} \mathbf{T} \cdots \mathbf{T} \mathbf{W}_{X_t} \mathbf{b}' \qquad (4.46)$$

For practical computation, writing the likelihood in this way has no advantage over the procedures using the $\mathbf{Q}$ matrices developed in Section 4.2. In fact, because $\mathbf{T}$ has larger dimension than any of the $\mathbf{Q}$ matrices, that method is computationally more efficient. The advantage of the selection procedure lies in its generality, in the fact that its ideas can be extended to apply to more complicated statistics, and in the fact that the relative simplicity of such expressions as Equation 4.46 makes them easy to use as a basis for theoretical work. For example, the selection matrices form part of a proof that the $\mathbf{Q}$-matrix procedure is correct (see Problem 4.9).

Likelihood calculations can be made using probabilistic selection matrices, without expanding the state space to include the responses. Consider the all-or-none model. As Matrix 4.43 indicates, when a correct response is made, the joint state probability is determined by multiplying the state vector by

$$W_C = \begin{bmatrix} 1 & 0 \\ 0 & g \end{bmatrix}$$

Any sequence of states that passes through state L on that trial is selected, as is a proportion g of the sequences passing through G. On errors, the remaining paths through the guessing state are chosen, and so

$$W_E = \begin{bmatrix} 0 & 0 \\ 0 & 1-g \end{bmatrix}$$

Each of these matrices contains a column of the response mapping R (Equation 4.9) along the diagonal.

These matrices can be constructed from the basis change that takes one representation of the model into the other. In parallel with the reduction in Equation 4.24, the selection matrices obey

$$W_X = P\tilde{W}_X Q \qquad (4.47)$$

where again the tildes indicate the expanded model and P and Q are given in Equations 4.21 and 4.23. For example,

$$W_C = P\tilde{W}_C Q$$

$$= \begin{bmatrix} 1 & 0 & 0 \\ 0 & g & 1-g \end{bmatrix} \begin{bmatrix} 1 & 0 & 0 \\ 0 & 1 & 0 \\ 0 & 0 & 0 \end{bmatrix} \begin{bmatrix} 1 & 0 \\ 0 & 1 \\ 0 & 1 \end{bmatrix} = \begin{bmatrix} 1 & 0 \\ 0 & g \end{bmatrix}$$

The transformation in the opposite direction (comparable to Equation 4.22) does not work, for the larger matrix W_X potentially can represent a transformation too complicated to express in the smaller space of the reduced model. When the larger matrix has been produced from a smaller matrix by removing a probabilistic response mapping, this is no problem, however.

To demonstrate that identical results are obtained from calculations in either basis, start with the likelihood as written for the expanded model (Equation 4.45 identified with tildes), which has been shown in the first part of this section to be correct. Now write the initial vector $\tilde{s}_1$ and the transition matrix $\tilde{T}$ as quantities that are converted from the smaller basis, by substituting from Equations 4.20 and 4.22.

$$P(X_1 X_2 \cdots X_t) = \tilde{s}_1 \tilde{W}_{X_1} \tilde{T} \tilde{W}_{X_2} \tilde{T} \cdots \tilde{T} \tilde{W}_{X_t} \tilde{1}'$$

$$= (s_1 P) \tilde{W}_{X_1} (QTP) \tilde{W}_{X_2} (QTP) \cdots (QTP) \tilde{W}_{X_t} (Q1')$$

The final substitution here uses the fact that the rows of Q sum to 1, so that $Q1' = \tilde{1}'$. Associating the products differently and using the definition of W in Equation 4.47, the likelihood is written completely in the smaller space:

$$P(X_1 X_2 \cdots X_5) = s_1(P\tilde{W}_{X_1}Q)T(P\tilde{W}_{X_2}Q)T \cdots T(P\tilde{W}_{X_t}Q)1'$$

$$= s_1 W_{X_1} T W_{X_2} T \cdots T W_{X_t} 1'$$

If the response string ends in a long run of correct responses so that absorption can be assumed, the same analysis applies, but with $1'$ replaced by the probability of no further errors, as in Equation 4.46. The vectors b and $\tilde{b}$ in the smaller and the larger spaces are related by the basis transformation $\tilde{b}' = Qb'$, whence also $b' = P\tilde{b}'$.

The Backward Learning Curve

Response-selection matrices help to analyze situations in which two fixed events are separated by a given number of trials. One example of such a statistic is the backward learning curve, that is, the learning curve constructed so that the different response strings are lined up for averaging at the point of last error. Backward learning curves are useful in examining events in the vicinity of the learning event (if any), for they pool trials that anticipate the final step of learning by the same amount. In a conventional learning curve, where the strings are aligned on the first trial, the learning event is not localized in one part of the curve and cannot be examined directly. In the all-or-none model, for example, all responses prior to the last error are made from the guessing state; so although the learning curve falls off geometrically, the backward learning curve is flat at $1 - g$.

To see how the backward learning curve is constructed, consider the four strings of responses

$$ECCCCCCCC$$
$$EECCCCCCC$$
$$ECECEECCCC$$
$$CECECCCCC$$

Now stagger the strings so as to align them at the last error:

$$ECCCCCCCC$$
$$EECCCCCCC$$
$$ECECEECCCC$$
$$CECECCCCC$$

The backward learning curve is the proportion of errors on trials before the last error, using only those strings for which responses are actually made. Thus, the proportion of errors one trial before the last error is $\frac{2}{3}$, that two trials before is $\frac{1}{2}$, and so on. Of course, for realistic use a substantially larger number of items is needed.

More rigorously, the backward learning curve is the probability of an error t trials before the last error given that there is an opportunity for such an error. One part of this is the event of an error t trials back. If L is the trial of last error, this is the event E_{L-t}. However, the learning curve is not simply $P(E_{L-t})$, for this event is possible only for sequences in which $L > t$. When t is large, $P(E_{L-t})$ is small, not necessarily because errors are unlikely before learning, but simply because few items remain unlearned long enough to have a response t trials before the last error. It is for this reason that only sequences with $L > t$ are used to calculate the backward learning curve. Thus, the theoretical value of the curve is the conditional probability

$$P(E_{L-t}|L > t) = \frac{P(L > t \wedge E_{L-t})}{P(L > t)} \tag{4.48}$$

Both probabilities on the right-hand side of Equation 4.48 can be expressed as matrix products. The denominator is simplest. Let $\mathbf{Q}$ be the submatrix of transitions for the transient states, $\mathbf{N}$ the fundamental matrix of these states, and $\mathbf{V}_E$ the matrix that selects the error states from among the transient states and deletes the correct states (given above in Matrix 4.38). In order for L to be greater than t, the process must be in the transient states for at least $t + 1$ trials ending with an error. This is expressed by $\mathbf{Q}^t\mathbf{V}_E\mathbf{b}'_e$, as in the formula for the trial of last error (Equation 4.39). This sequence of trials may be preceded by an arbitrary number of other trials in the transient states, an event represented by $\mathbf{N}$. Putting these together gives

$$P(L > t) = [s_{1,c}, s_{1,e}]\mathbf{N}\mathbf{Q}^t\mathbf{V}_E\mathbf{b}'_e$$

The numerator of Equation 4.48, $P(L > t \wedge E_{L-t})$, is very similar to the denominator. It differs only in that the response on the tth trial preceding the last must be an error. Let $\mathbf{U}_E$ be a selection matrix similar to $\mathbf{W}_E$, but applying only to the transient states. By inserting $\mathbf{U}_E$ just prior to the run of t trials ending in the last error, the event E_{L-t} is assured. So

$$P(L > t \wedge E_{L-t}) = [s_{1,c}, s_{1,e}]\mathbf{N}\mathbf{U}_E\mathbf{Q}^t\mathbf{V}_E\mathbf{b}'_e \tag{4.49}$$

and the backward learning curve is

$$P(E_{L-t}|L > t) = \frac{[s_{1,c}, s_{1,e}]NU_EQ'V_Eb'_e}{[s_{1,c}, s_{1,e}]NQ'V_Eb'_e}$$ (4.50)

Because the operations in the numerator and denominator are matrix rather than scalar multiplication, common terms cannot be canceled.

The Backward Latency Curve

This selection procedure can be combined with the assignment of a numerical value to the states to give such statistics as the expected latency or confidence rating plotted around the last error. As above, let $\mathcal{L}_t$ be the latency on trial t and let μ_i be the mean latency in state S_i. Suppose also that S_1 is the absorbing state. To get the mean latency t trials before the last error, the items must be separated by state as they pass through trial $L - t$ and weighted by the expected latency for that state:

$$E(\mathcal{L}_{L-t}|L > t) = \sum_{i=2}^{n} \mu_i P(S_{i,L-t}|L > t)$$

Note that later error means that the absorbing state can be excluded from the sum. Selection is accomplished with matrices U_i that are 0 except for a 1 in the diagonal position corresponding to S_i. So, following Equations 4.49 and 4.50:

$$P(S_{i,L-t} \wedge L > t) = [s_{1,c}, s_{1,e}]NU_iQ'V_Eb'_e$$

and

$$E(\mathcal{L}_{L-t}|L > t) = \sum_{i=2}^{n} \mu_i \frac{[s_{1,c}, s_{1,e}]NU_iQ'V_Eb'_e}{[s_{1,c}, s_{1,e}]NQ'V_Eb'_e}$$

Since the μ_i are scalars, they commute with respect to the matrices, and the result can be written as

$$E(\mathcal{L}_{L-t}|L > t) = \frac{[s_{1,c}, s_{1,e}]N\left[\sum_{i=2}^{n} \mu_i U_i\right]Q'V_Eb'_e}{[s_{1,c}, s_{1,e}]NQ'V_Eb'_e}$$

The sum can be incorporated into a single matrix:

$$
\mathbf{U}_L = \begin{bmatrix} \mu_2 & 0 & \cdots & 0 \\ 0 & \mu_3 & \cdots & 0 \\ \vdots & \vdots & & \vdots \\ 0 & 0 & \cdots & \mu_n \end{bmatrix}
$$

to give

$$
E(\mathcal{L}_{L-t}|L > t) = \frac{[\mathbf{s}_{1,c}, \ \mathbf{s}_{1,e}]\mathbf{N}\mathbf{U}_L\mathbf{Q}'\mathbf{V}_E\mathbf{b}_e'}{[\mathbf{s}_{1,c}, \ \mathbf{s}_{1,e}]\mathbf{N}\mathbf{Q}'\mathbf{V}_E\mathbf{b}_e'} \tag{4.51}
$$

Expected values of other quantities are found in the same way.

Problems

4.1. Rewrite the model of Problem 2.7 in the proper form for matrix calculations (i.e., similar to Matrix 4.16). Identify the various submatrices of **T**.

4.2. Suppose the subject in a paired-associate task makes both a response and a confidence rating, high (H) or low (L). Thus, there are four observable events: low–correct, low–error, high–correct, and high–error. Consider a two-stage model. Further, suppose that responses from state G are always given a low confidence rating and responses from L are always rated high. Let $P(H|I) = \eta$, independent of the correctness of the response. Write a transition matrix for this model appropriate for matrix operations.

4.3. Use the method for the evaluation of geometric sums in Section A.3 to show that the sum in Equation 4.30 equals Equation 4.31.

4.4. a. Evaluate the sum $s = \mathbf{I} + 4\mathbf{X} + 9\mathbf{X}^2 + 16\mathbf{X}^3 + \ldots$.
   b. Find a general matrix expression for the variance of the total number of errors.

4.5. Complete the demonstration of the equivalence of Equations 4.34, 4.35, and 4.36.

4.6. Show that Equation 4.40 is the correct formula for the expected trial of last error.

4.7. Find a matrix formula for the distribution of the following statistics and for their mean and second central moment (see Problem 3.13).

    a. The number of errors before the first success, F.

    b. The length of the first run of errors, R.

4.8. For the model in Problem 4.2, write matrix expressions for

    a. The distribution of trials until the first high-confidence response, H.

    b. The probability that a high-confidence error is ever made.

4.9. The likelihood in Equation 4.45 can be associated

$$(s_1 W_{X_1})(T W_{X_2}) \cdots (T W_{X_t}) \mathbf{1}'$$

Partition the matrices $\mathbf{T}$ and $\mathbf{W}_X$ into absorbing, correct-transient, and error-transient states. Then show that if blocks of 0's are ignored, these products reduce to the $\mathbf{Q}$ matrices. With the more formal argument of Equation 4.43, this demonstrates that using the $\mathbf{Q}$ matrices correctly yields the likelihood.

4.10. The full transition matrix $\mathbf{T}$ and selection matrices $\mathbf{W}_X$ can be used to express statistics such as the trial of last error or the total number of errors. The only difficulty is correctly defining $\mathbf{b}'$ or, more generally, the analog of N_{cc}. Let $\mathbf{W}_c$ select the transient-correct states and $\mathbf{W}_a$ the absorbing states. Then

$$\mathbf{b}' = \mathbf{T}(\mathbf{W}_c \mathbf{b}' + \mathbf{W}_a \mathbf{1}')$$

    a. Explain why this equation works and solve it for $\mathbf{b}'$.

    b. Express the elements of the solution to part a as partitioned matrices and show that the solution reduces to $\mathbf{b}'_c$ and $\mathbf{b}'_e$, as given in Equations 4.27 and 4.28 in terms of the $\mathbf{Q}$ matrices.

    c. Write the distribution of the trial of last error in terms of the full matrices.

    d. Write the distribution of the total number of errors in terms of the full matrices.

4.11. In some theories of learning, responses before the first correct response are different from those following this response. Suppose that the response strings are aligned at the first correct response. Derive the formula for the subsequent learning curve.

4.12. Consider the last error in a paired-associate experiment.

    a. Find an expression for the expected latency t trials after this error. *Hint:* Remember that data will be conditional on at least one error having been made.

b. Suppose (as in Section 4.3) that the latency in the three states of the all-or-none model are μ, $\mu + \delta$, and $\mu + \delta$. Apply the results of part a to the simple all-or-none model (as in Matrix 4.14) and to the hypothesis-testing version of Equation 2.7. How do the results differ?

4.13. [C]† Using a computer language having matrix operations (such as APL), calculate the state-probability vector for the two-stage model on trials 1 through 6 using the parameter values $\alpha = 0.1$, $\beta = 0.3$, $\delta = 0.2$, $\sigma = 0.05$, and $\tau = 0.2$. Convert the state probabilities to response probabilities using $g = \frac{1}{5}$ and $\pi = \frac{1}{2}$. Check your answer by calculating the first three trials by hand.

4.14. [C] Write a program to calculate the response probabilities for the first T trials, taking as input an arbitrary matrix and response vector. Test it on the two-stage model from Problem 4.13.

4.15. [C] Write a program to calculate the distribution of the trial of last error and the number of errors for an arbitrary Markov chain. The program should take as input (or call a subprogram to calculate) the initial vector, the matrix of the chain (in numerical, rather than symbolic, form), and the mapping from states to responses. It should print (or return) the distributions and their expectations. Use subroutines to do the matrix calculations, or write in a language that directly allows matrix operations.

4.16. [C] Use the methods of Section 4.2 to compute the likelihood of the string

$$C_1 C_2 E_3 E_4 C_5 E_6 C_7 C_8 C_9 \cdots$$

using the two-stage model of Problem 4.13.

4.17. [C] Write a program that determines the likelihood of an arbitrary string of responses for an arbitrary model. Test it on a suitable example.

---

† Problems marked [C] require the use of a computer.

Chapter 5

Estimation of Parameters

The preceding two chapters show how to make predictions from Markov models. All of these models depend on the values of one or more numerical quantities. To tie the results to an actual experiment, these quantities must be assigned values. When the values can be assigned a priori by a logical analysis of the experimental procedure, things are simple. The random guessing rate g in the learning models is an example. However, in many cases, values cannot be assigned beforehand, but must be determined from the observed data. For example, in most cases, the learning rate α of the all-or-none model is not known. These unknown quantities, called *parameters*, are designated by Greek letters in this book. If a model correctly describes the process, there are true values of its parameters. Although it may be impossible to know these true values exactly, good guesses can be made by looking at observed data. These "guesses" are known as *parameter estimates*, and the formulas by which they are derived are called *estimators*. Several procedures for parameter estimation are discussed in this chapter.

The fit of any probability model to data can be good or poor, but there is no one set of data that represents perfect agreement. Statements about fit are always probabilistic. At best, one can ask whether the discrepancies between a model and data are small enough to be accidental or whether they are large enough to reject the model. Investigations of this sort are one form of the *statistical testing* of a model. A second type of statistical test concerns hypotheses about parameters, whether one parameter is equal to a particular value or whether the values of two parameters are equal to each other. These testing procedures are discussed in Chapter 6, largely as straightforward applications of conventional statistical methods to Markov models.

5.1 The Estimation Problem

To lay out the estimation problem clearly, a more formal notation is useful. Let $\mathcal{M}$ stand for a model that is to be fit to a body of data, that is, for s_1, $\mathbf{T}$, and $\mathbf{R}$. Suppose that $\mathcal{M}$ depends on the vector of parameters

$$\boldsymbol{\omega} = [\omega_1, \omega_2, \ldots, \omega_p]$$

For example, in the simplest all-or-none model, $\boldsymbol{\omega}$ is the single quantity α. If the initial probability $P(L_1)$ is also unknown, say it is σ, then $\boldsymbol{\omega}$ is the two-dimensional vector $[\alpha, \sigma]$. The two-stage model (Equations 2.15, 2.16, and 2.17) involves six parameters, and so

$$\boldsymbol{\omega} = [\alpha, \beta, \delta, \sigma, \tau, \pi]$$

The task of parameter estimation is to assign a value to $\boldsymbol{\omega}$.

Each of the parameters has a range of possible values. For example, with probabilities, usually $0 \leq \omega_i \leq 1$. Together these restrictions form a *parameter space* $\boldsymbol{\Omega}$ in which the values of $\boldsymbol{\omega}$ fall. Often this space is simply the Cartesian product of the individual parameter ranges. For the all-or-none model with unknown σ, both parameters are probabilities lying in the interval $[0, 1]$, so $\boldsymbol{\Omega}$ is the square:

$$\boldsymbol{\Omega} = [0, 1] \times [0, 1] = [0, 1]^2$$

as illustrated in Figure 5.1a.

Where other restrictions on the parameters exist, $\boldsymbol{\Omega}$ may not be square. For example, suppose that the probabilities of three mutually exclusive events are ϕ, ψ, and $1 - \phi - \psi$. In order for all three of these to be greater than 0, the sum of ϕ and ψ must be less than 1, leading to the triangular region in Figure 5.1b. Any point outside this triangle is not an acceptable parameter set.

Whatever the shape of $\boldsymbol{\Omega}$, the true value of the parameter vector is $\boldsymbol{\omega} \in \boldsymbol{\Omega}$, which the experimenter cannot know, but wishes to estimate. Data are collected, and, from these data and the model, a value $\hat{\boldsymbol{\omega}} \in \boldsymbol{\Omega}$ is calculated, using one of the methods to be described below. The

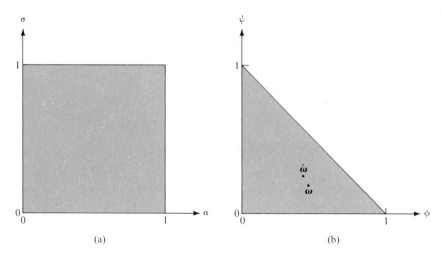

Figure 5.1 Parameter spaces for two models. For the model in part b, the true parameter **ω** and the estimated value **ω̂** are indicated.

vector **ω̂** is the estimate of **ω**. Typographically, the estimate is distinguished from the true parameter value either by placing the symbol ˆ (commonly read "hat") above it, or by using a Latin rather than a Greek letter (as M is used for the estimate of a mean μ).

Clearly, a good estimate is one for which **ω̂** is close to **ω**. However, the size of this distance cannot be used as a criterion to select **ω̂**, since **ω** is unknown. A more feasible procedure is to pick **ω̂** so as to minimize the difference between predictions of the model and the data. There are several ways to do this. One procedure is to take several numerical quantities predicted by the model, set them equal to the corresponding values in the data, then solve for the parameters. These *method-of-moments estimates* are relatively easy to find, but are not highly accurate. The method-of-moments procedure is considered in the next section. The second approach is more global in nature. First, some overall measure of agreement between theory and data is defined; then a search is made of Ω to find the value of **ω̂** that makes this measure as large as possible. Methods of this sort, such as the *maximum-likelihood estimators* and *minimum chi-square estimators,* also discussed below, usually give better results but require more work to find.

Although the underlying parameter **ω** is a fixed number, the estimate **ω̂** is a function of the observed data, and hence would vary from replication to replication of the experiment that obtained the data. Thus, **ω̂** is properly viewed as a random variable, with a distribution, known as its *sampling distribution,* that depends on the way in which the estimator is calculated. The sampling distribution plays an important role in evaluating the quality of an estimator. It is important to distinguish among the underlying value of ω (which is exact but unknown), the estimator $\hat{\omega}$ (which is a random variable defined as a function of the Markov model), and a numerical realization of $\hat{\omega}$ (which is the estimate obtained from a particular collection of data).

Each estimation procedure has different properties and different advantages and disadvantages. A number of criteria have been developed for evaluating estimators. Four of these properties are commonly used to describe estimators and are important enough to be worth examining here. Although in many situations there is no "best" estimator of a parameter, these criteria help to compare two estimators and to evaluate whether a particular estimator is good or poor.

1. *A consistent estimator* is one that converges (in probability) for large samples to the true parameter value. More rigorously, for any parameter ω and any positive number ϵ, the probability that the estimate $\hat{\omega}$ deviates from ω by more than ϵ goes to 0 as the number of observations, N, becomes large:

$$\lim_{N \to \infty} P(|\hat{\omega} - \omega| > \epsilon) = 0$$

   A vector of parameters, $\hat{\omega}$, is consistent if all its elements are. With a consistent estimator, collecting more observations is useful, for doing so makes the size of the error in the estimate shrink toward 0. All the estimators considered in this chapter are consistent.

2. *A sufficient estimator* is, roughly, one that makes use of all the information in the data that pertains to ω. A formal definition of "all the information" can be written, but is not very useful for the purposes here. Informally, if $\hat{\omega}$ is a sufficient estimator of ω, then there is no association between the data and ω other than that embodied in $\hat{\omega}$. Unfortunately, not all parameters have sufficient estimators.

3. *An unbiased estimator* is one for which the mean of the sampling distribution equals the true parameter value:

$$E(\hat{\omega}) = \omega$$

   Thus, there is no systematic tendency for an unbiased estimator to have values that are either too large or too small. In Figure 5.2, which shows the sampling distributions of three estimators of a single parameter ω, $\hat{\omega}_1$ is biased, while $\hat{\omega}_2$ and

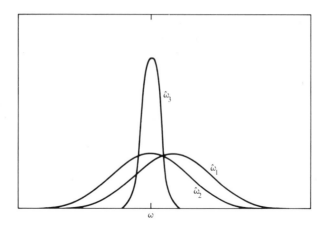

Figure 5.2   The sampling distribution of three esti-
mators—$\hat{\omega}_1$, $\hat{\omega}_2$, and $\hat{\omega}_3$—of a parameter ω. The estimator $\hat{\omega}_1$ is biased, and the estimator $\hat{\omega}_3$ is more efficient
than $\hat{\omega}_2$.

$\hat{\omega}_3$ are unbiased. It is frequently possible to correct a biased
estimator to remove the bias.

4. Regardless of the other properties, it is desirable that the variance of the sampling distribution of an estimator be as small as
possible, so that $\hat{\omega}$ is close to $E(\hat{\omega})$. For an estimator that
satisfies the other criteria, this variance cannot be made 0, as
there is a limit to the amount of information that can be extracted from any set of data. In fact, lower bounds for var($\hat{\omega}$)
can be found. The relative size of the actual variance as compared to the lower bound is referred to as the *efficiency* of the
estimator, and an estimator with minimum variance is said to be
efficient. Of the unbiased estimators $\hat{\omega}_2$ and $\hat{\omega}_3$ in Figure 5.2, $\hat{\omega}_3$
has the smaller variance, so is more efficient. Efficient es-
timators do not always exist, but, other factors being equal,
the most efficient of a set of estimators is the best.

Where two or more parameters are estimated from the same set of
data, the correlation between the estimates—a property of the multivariate sampling distribution of $\boldsymbol{\omega}$—is also important. If two parameters have a substantial correlation, the joint estimate of both is less
accurate than are the estimates of either one alone. Thus, the efficiency
of a joint estimator is overestimated by a univariate analysis. To illustrate this with a common situation, suppose that a learning model depends on two learning-rate parameters, ω_1 and ω_2. Further suppose that

overestimates of ω_1, which make learning too rapid in one part of the model, can be partially (although not completely) compensated for by lowering the value of the estimate $\hat{\omega}_2$ to slow learning elsewhere. Thus, over a series of experiments, the estimates scatter along a descending diagonal in Ω. This means that $\hat{\omega}_1$ and $\hat{\omega}_2$ are negatively correlated. If this correlation is appreciable, neither parameter can be estimated as accurately when the other parameter is unknown as it would have been had the other value been known. Where several parameters are involved, the intercorrelations can seriously limit the accuracy of the individual estimates.

There is a large literature on parameter estimation in both mathematical statistics and applied statistics. In this chapter it is not possible to consider more than a few of the methods that have found use with psychological models. Most texts on mathematical statistics have a substantial section on estimation to which one can refer for additional information; Kendall and Stewart (1979) have an extended (but difficult) treatment of estimation and the properties of estimators. Among texts for psychologists, the discussion by Hays (1981) is more extensive than most.

5.2   Method-of-Moments Estimators

One of the simplest estimation procedures is known as the *method of moments*. In it, an appropriate number of theoretical quantities are equated to their observed values and the resulting equations solved for the parameters. Usually, the moments of some distribution are used, hence the name of the procedure. When $p = 1$, these mechanics are straightforward. Suppose that X is a random variable that depends on the single unknown parameter ω. Now suppose that an experiment is conducted and a distribution of X with a mean of M_X is observed. The method-of-moments estimator of ω is formed by insisting that

$$E(X) = M_X \tag{5.1}$$

This equation has a formula that depends on ω on the left-hand side and a number (or its symbolic equivalent) on the right. The equation is solved for ω to get the estimate $\hat{\omega}$.

Consider the all-or-none model with the single unknown parameter α. The mean number of errors has a simple relationship to α, so is a good choice for use in a method-of-moments estimator. When all items start in the guessing state, its expected value (Equation 3.16) is

$$E(T) = \frac{1 - g}{\alpha}$$

This is equated with the mean number of errors made over the whole experiment, M_T. Thus, Equation 5.1 becomes

$$\frac{1 - g}{\hat{\alpha}} = M_T$$

Note that a hat has been placed over α to indicate that this equation holds for the estimate, not for the true population value. Solving for $\hat{\alpha}$ gives

$$\hat{\alpha} = \frac{1 - g}{M_T} \tag{5.2}$$

This is the desired estimate. As $E(T)$ equals the sum of $P(E_t)$ over all trials (as shown in Equation 3.15), this estimate has the effect of making the area under the theoretical learning curve agree with its observed value.

A numerical example may make the procedure clearer. Suppose that the all-or-none model, with $g = 0.25$, is to be fit to the eight items below. The strings are blocked in five-trial units as an aid to reading, and responses following the last error are indicated by lowercase letters.

> *Eccc ...*
> *EEccc ...*
> *ECECE EEccc ...*
> *EEccc ...*
> *EEEEE ccc ...*
> *EEECC CEEEE EEECE EEEEE Eccc ...*
> *Eccc ...*
> *EEEEE EECEE CCCEc cc ...*

The mean number of errors is

$$M_T = \frac{1 + 2 + 5 + 2 + 5 + 17 + 1 + 10}{8} = \frac{43}{8} = 5.375$$

The estimate of α is obtained by substituting this into Equation 5.2:

$$\hat{\alpha} = \frac{1 - g}{M_T} = \frac{0.75}{5.375} = 0.140$$

In a real situation there is no way to tell how accurate the estimate is, for the true α is unknown. However, in this example, the eight items are not real data, but were generated by simulation, using a random number table and $g = 0.25$, $\alpha = 0.15$. It is apparent that the estimated $\hat{\alpha}$ is quite close to the true α. Indeed, the values agree rather better than might be expected, in view of the small number of items.

Where more than one parameter must be estimated, the procedure is the same, but uses more statistics. With p parameters, p theoretical quantities, depending collectively on the unknown parameters, are equated to their data values. This gives a set of p simultaneous equations in p unknowns, which are solved for the estimates. It is possible to use the higher moments of a single distribution—the variance, the skew, the kurtosis, and so forth—to make the estimates. Where only one distribution is available, this is necessary; but for most practical problems, a better choice can be made by using the means of other statistics. The statistics that are used should be closely related to the parameters and should be different from each other, in order to extract as much information as possible from the data.

As an example, suppose that both the learning rate and the guessing probability in the all-or-none model are unknown. To emphasize its new status as a parameter, denote the guessing probability by γ rather than g. The estimate of α in Equation 5.2 no longer works, for it also involves the unknown γ. However, $E(T)$ can still be used to form one of the two equations that are needed:

$$\frac{1 - \hat{\gamma}}{\hat{\alpha}} = M_T \tag{5.3}$$

The variance of T (Equation 3.21) is not a good choice for the second statistic, as it is closely related to $E(T)$ and does not give much new information. The mean trial of last error, $E(L)$, is a better choice. The extent to which $E(L)$ exceeds the mean number of errors reflects the proportion of correct responses that are mixed in with the presolution errors. This, in turn, depends on γ. Equating $E(L)$ from Problem 3.9 with its observed value:

$$E(L) = \frac{1 - \hat{\gamma}}{\hat{\alpha}(1 - \hat{\gamma} + \hat{\alpha}\hat{\gamma})} = M_L \tag{5.4}$$

Equations 5.3 and 5.4 form a set that is to be solved. Using Equation 5.3 to eliminate $\hat{\alpha}$ from Equation 5.4 makes a quadratic equation in $\hat{\gamma}$:

$$M_L\hat{\gamma}^2 + (M_T - 1)M_L\hat{\gamma} + M_T(M_T - M_L) = 0$$

This is solved by the standard quadratic formula to give

$$\hat{\gamma} = \tfrac{1}{2}[-(M_T - 1) \pm \sqrt{(M_T - 1)^2 + 4M_T(M_L - M_T)/M_L}]$$

One of the two roots is the sum of two negative terms, so cannot be a probability; the other is $\hat{\gamma}$. Once $\hat{\gamma}$ has been found, substitution into Equation 5.3 gives $\hat{\alpha}$.

For the eight items above, the mean trial of last error is

$$M_L = \frac{1 + 2 + 7 + 2 + 5 + 21 + 1 + 14}{8} = 6.625$$

Combining this with $M_T = 5.375$ gives

$$\hat{\gamma} = 0.221 \qquad \hat{\alpha} = 0.145$$

The accuracy of these estimates is still quite good.

The principal advantage of the method of moments is its simplicity. It is faster than other methods and frequently gives simple functions for the estimators. These are substantial advantages, but the method also has several serious liabilities. The difficulties are of three sorts. First, it is often hard to find a set of equations that can be solved for the parameters without excessive labor. This practical problem can sometimes be overcome by finding a numerical solution on a computer, although that may entail a considerable programming effort (which may more profitably be spent on a better estimation procedure). A second, more serious liability is that the method of moments is without any very solid statistical basis. Even though estimates can be found, there is no assurance that they are good, in the sense of any of the four criteria above. Indeed, if the matching moments are poorly chosen, the result can be quite inaccurate and most of the information in the data can be lost. In practice, this leaves the quality of the estimate up to the skill and intuition of the investigator. The third problem is that the method of moments does not easily lead to a statistical-testing procedure. This makes it difficult to decide if a particular model fits adequately or whether one model is an improvement over another. Such questions are better treated with other estimation methods, as discussed in detail in Chapter 6.

5.3   Maximum-Likelihood Estimators

The second method of parameter estimation to be covered here, the *maximum-likelihood procedure*, eliminates many of the difficulties associated with the method of moments. Although somewhat more difficult to use than the method of moments, maximum-likelihood estimation is frequently the best of the relatively straightforward estimation procedures. As a method, it has been subject to extensive statistical analysis, so its properties are well understood. Thus, it should generally be the first choice in a serious attempt to fit a model, unless one is looking for quick, approximate estimates.

In the abstract, the maximum-likelihood procedure is quite simple. Given a set of data and a model, one picks the parameters that make the data most likely to have occurred. This is best illustrated with a miniature example. Suppose that the sequence of responses

$$EECECCEccc \ldots \tag{5.5}$$

has been recorded for a single paired-associate item with $g = \frac{1}{4}$ and that the parameter α in the all-or-none model is to be estimated. The probability of this string can be found by the methods of Chapter 3. The process must be in state G for the first seven trials, and, if no other errors are made, the probability of obtaining exactly that series of responses is

$$(1 - g)[(1 - \alpha)(1 - g)][(1 - \alpha)g][(1 - \alpha)(1 - g)][(1 - \alpha)g]$$
$$\times [(1 - \alpha)g][(1 - \alpha)(1 - g)]b = \frac{(1 - g)^4 g^3 (1 - \alpha)^6 \alpha}{1 - (1 - \alpha)g} \tag{5.6}$$

(Recall that $b = \alpha/[1 - (1 - \alpha)g]$ is the probability of no more errors following a response, found in Equation 3.18.) Ordinarily, this would be treated as the probability of a particular outcome, dependent on the model's parameters, in other words, as $P(\text{data}|\alpha)$, with the data free to vary. However, in the case of estimation, the data are known and the parameter unknown, so it makes sense to think of Equation 5.6 as a function of α with the data fixed. When thought of in this way, it is usually referred to as a *likelihood* and denoted by $L(\alpha)$. The new notation helps to emphasize the fact that $L(\alpha)$ is not the probability of a particular value of α (which, because α is not a random variable, it cannot be).

For some values of α, the data are quite unlikely and the likelihood in Equation 5.6 is small; while for others, the data are more probable and $L(\alpha)$ is larger. As the plot in Figure 5.3 indicates, $L(\alpha)$ has a single maximum lying between 0.1 and 0.15. The maximum-likelihood estimate is the value of α where this maximum occurs, that is, the value that makes the observed data most likely. A rough value for $\hat{\alpha}$ can be taken from Figure 5.3 or found more accurately using calculus (see the discussion of extrema in Section D.1). Differentiating Equation 5.6 gives

$$\frac{dL(\alpha)}{d\alpha} = \frac{(1 - g)^4 g^3 (1 - \alpha)^5}{[1 - (1 - \alpha)g]^2} [(1 - g) - 7(1 - g)\alpha - 6g\alpha^2]$$

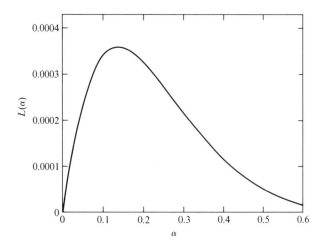

Figure 5.3   The likelihood function $L(\alpha)$ for the response string in Equation 5.5 with $g = 0.25$.

At the maximum of $L(\alpha)$, this derivative is 0. The only way for this to
happen is for $\alpha = 1$ or for the quadratic in brackets on the right to be 0.
A glance at Figure 5.3 or consideration of what $\alpha = 1$ means indicates
that this point is not a maximum and so the estimate must be one of the
roots of the quadratic. There is only one root of this quadratic between
0 and 1. This root is the estimate $\hat{\alpha} = 0.138$.

The maximum-likelihood procedure can be put in more formal terms
without much change. The parameter vector to be estimated is ω, and
the likelihood function is $L(\omega)$. This function takes a value over the
p-dimensional space Ω (as depicted, for example, in two dimensions by
Figure 5.4). The problem is to find the maximum point of $L(\omega)$ over all
$\omega \in \Omega$. As in the one-parameter example, the maximum is found by
differentiation, as the solution of the system of p equations:

$$\frac{\partial L(\omega)}{\partial \omega_1} = 0$$

$$\frac{\partial L(\omega)}{\partial \omega_2} = 0 \tag{5.7}$$

$$\vdots$$

$$\frac{\partial L(\omega)}{\partial \omega_p} = 0$$

Commonly, there are several vectors that satisfy Equations 5.7, some of
which are minima, some maxima, and some neither. Some of these

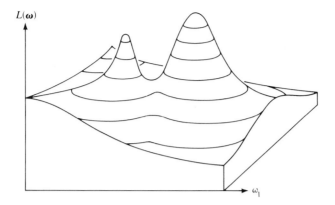

$L(\boldsymbol{\omega})$

ω_1

Figure 5.4   The likelihood $L(\boldsymbol{\omega})$ over a two-dimensional space Ω.

solutions may fall outside Ω. Of course, only maxima that are in Ω are of interest, for only these are meaningful estimates.

Where the data come from several items, the individual likelihoods must be combined. If the items can be treated as independent of each other, the probability of the results for several items is the product of the probabilities for each item. For N items, let the likelihood of the ith item be denoted by $l_i(\boldsymbol{\omega})$. Then the overall likelihood is

$$L(\boldsymbol{\omega}) = \prod_{i=1}^{N} l_i(\boldsymbol{\omega}) \qquad (5.8)$$

The assumption of independence is usually reasonable for items from different subjects, but is less so for different items from the same subject. It is a good first approximation, however, and seems not to cause major problems until statistical testing is attempted.

The combination Equation 5.8 allows maximum-likelihood estimates of α for the all-or-none model† to be found for more substantial collections of data than in the example above. Each individual item provides a sequence of correct and error responses, terminated (if the experiment continues long enough) by a string of correct responses. The method used in the example yields the probability of these strings of responses. A factor of $(1 - \alpha)g$ is included for each presolution correct response, $(1 - \alpha)(1 - g)$ for each error, and b for the final string of

---

† For a more extensive discussion of estimation in the all-or-none model, see Kraemer (1964).

correct responses. The resulting product is independent of the order of the responses before the last error, which means that the information about the string can be summarized in two quantities: the number of correct responses before the last error and the number of errors. For the ith item, let c_i and e_i denote the number of presolution correct responses and errors (for the string in Equation 5.5, $c_i = 3$ and $e_i = 4$). Then, after combining the probabilities of like responses:

$$l_i(\alpha) = \begin{cases} gb & e_i = 0 \\ (1 - g)^{e_i}g^{c_i}(1 - \alpha)^{e_i+c_i-1}b & e_i > 0 \end{cases} \qquad (5.9)$$

In practice, it is often slightly easier to maximize the natural logarithm† of the likelihood rather than the likelihood itself. Doing so does not change the estimates. Because the logarithm is a monotone function of its argument, the same value of ω that maximizes $\log L(\omega)$ also maximizes $L(\omega)$. Likelihoods often contain large numbers of products, which are converted to sums by the logarithm. It is a bit easier to differentiate a sum than a product, and the resulting algebra is somewhat simpler. Where a computer is used for numerical calculation, the use of logarithms has an additional advantage. Because any exact result of an experiment is quite unlikely, the actual value of $L(\omega)$ is always very small. Limits on the size of floating-point words in the computer may lead to underflow in calculating a direct likelihood, thereby losing all information about the data. Logarithms of likelihoods generally stay within acceptable size.

Taking logarithms, Equations 5.8 and 5.9 become

$$\log L(\alpha) = \sum_{i=1}^{N} \log l_i(\alpha)$$

and

$$\log l_i(\alpha) = \begin{cases} \log g + \log b & e_i = 0 \\ e_i \log(1 - g) + c_i \log g & \\ \quad + (e_i + c_i - 1)\log(1 - \alpha) + \log b & e_i > 0 \end{cases}$$

---

† The *natural logarithm* is the logarithm to the base e and must be distinguished from the common logarithm, which has the base 10. Instead of "log," the symbol "ln" is sometimes used for the natural logarithm (this is usually the case on calculators). The convention of using "log" for the natural logarithm is usual in mathematics (where the common logarithm finds little use) and therefore is adopted in this book.

Combining these equations gives

$$\log L(\alpha) = E \log(1 - g) + (C + Nz) \log g$$
$$+ (E + C - N + Nz)\log(1 - \alpha) + N \log b \quad (5.10)$$

where $E = \Sigma e_i$ and $C = \Sigma c_i$ are the total number of errors and pre-solution correct responses in the entire experiment, and z is the proportion of items on which no error is made. This function is to be maximized.

The advantage of the logarithmic form becomes clear when $\log L(\alpha)$ is differentiated. The terms involving $1 - g$ and g do not depend on α, and so vanish from the derivative with respect to α. Using the differentiation formulas in Section D.1 gives

$$\frac{d \log L(\alpha)}{d\alpha} = (E + C - N + Nz) \frac{d}{d\alpha} \log(1 - \alpha) + N \frac{d}{d\alpha} \log b$$

$$= -\frac{E + C - N + Nz}{1 - \alpha} + \frac{N(1 - g)}{\alpha[1 - (1 - \alpha)g]}$$

Combining these two terms, then writing $E + C = NM_L$ to express the result in terms of the mean trial of last error gives

$$\frac{d \log L(\alpha)}{d\alpha} = \frac{N(1 - g)(1 - \alpha) - (NM_L - N + Nz)\alpha[1 - (1 - \alpha)g]}{\alpha(1 - \alpha)[1 - (1 - \alpha)g]} \quad (5.11)$$

This derivative is 0 at the maximum. The value of the denominator plays no role in making a fraction 0, so Equation 5.11 is 0 only when its numerator is 0. Thus,

$$(1 - g)(1 - \hat{\alpha}) - (M_L - 1 + z)\hat{\alpha}[1 - (1 - \hat{\alpha})g] = 0$$

This is a quadratic equation in $\hat{\alpha}$. One of the two roots is a sum of two negative terms, so is not a permissible solution; the other is positive:

$$\hat{\alpha} = \frac{\sqrt{(1 - g)^2(M_L + z)^2 + 4g(1 - g)(M_L - 1 + z)} - (1 - g)(M_L + z)}{2g(M_L - 1 + z)}$$

$$(5.12)$$

This is the desired estimate.

For the eight items used as an example above, $g = 0.25$, $M_L = 6.625$, and $z = 0$. Thus, $\hat{\alpha} = 0.145$. Again, the result is quite accurate.

It is interesting to note that Equation 5.12 can be written in terms of the single quantity $M_L - 1 + z$, which equals the mean trial of last error when the first trial is dropped from the experiment. This reflects two properties of the all-or-none model. First, no information about α is provided by the first trial, which is a pure guess and so can be ignored without loss. Second, presolution responses are guesses unrelated to α, and neither the order of responses nor the relative proportion of correct responses and errors carries any information about α.

The maximum-likelihood estimate of Equation 5.12 is different from the estimate found by the method of moments in Equation 5.2, although the difference is not large. This is often the case. Where the model is fairly simple and the method-of-moments estimator is based on a good choice of statistic, the two estimates can be quite similar. However, if a poor choice of statistic is made for the method-of-moments estimator or if the model is so complex that no single summary statistic captures all the parameter information, the method-of-moments estimator is much inferior to the maximum-likelihood estimator.

Where both α and the guessing rate (denoted now by γ) in the all-or-none model are to be estimated, the derivatives of Equation 5.10 with respect to α (Equation 5.11) and with respect to γ are required. After removing terms that do not affect the maximum, the former gives

$$N(1 - \hat{\gamma})(1 - \hat{\alpha}) - (E + C - N + Nz)\hat{\alpha}[1 - (1 - \hat{\alpha})\hat{\gamma}] = 0$$

the latter,

$$[C + Nz - \hat{\gamma}(C + E + Nz)][1 - (1 - \hat{\alpha})\hat{\gamma}] + N(1 - \hat{\alpha})\hat{\gamma}(1 - \hat{\gamma}) = 0$$

These are solved simultaneously for $\hat{\alpha}$ and $\hat{\gamma}$. The solution to these equations is messy, but becomes much simpler when the initial probability σ is also estimated (see Problems 5.7 and 5.8).

Sometimes when equations such as these (more generally, the partial derivatives of Equation 5.7) are solved, the result is a point outside Ω. In such cases, the largest value of $L(\omega)$ within Ω usually lies on the boundary of Ω. Presumably, the impossible estimate is the result of sampling fluctuation about a point near the boundary. The most convenient way to deal with this situation is to fix the out-of-bounds parameters to lie on the boundary of Ω and to reestimate the remaining parameters. For example, when α and σ from the all-or-none model are simultaneously estimated, negative values of $\hat{\sigma}$ occasionally occur. So set $\hat{\sigma} = 0$. With this constraint, the appropriate estimate of α is obtained from Equation 5.12, rather than from the original joint-estimation equations.

Maximum-likelihood estimators have been extensively studied in the statistical literature, and much is known about their properties. In terms of the criteria for good estimators discussed above, it can be shown that maximum-likelihood estimators are always consistent. Although sufficient and efficient estimators for a particular parameter do not always exist, when they do, the maximum-likelihood procedure finds them (or functions of them). The four properties are better satisfied by maximum-likelihood estimation than by the other estimation procedures commonly used with Markov models. For this reason, the maximum-likelihood procedure is generally the best choice.

The major practical problem with maximum-likelihood estimators is the difficulty in calculation. In models with a larger number of states than the all-or-none model, the likelihoods are much more complicated and the derivative equations of Equation 5.7 are much harder to solve. For example, in the two-stage model, the response string $E_1C_2C_3E_4$ can arise from any of the 16 state sequences composed of state G or I, and the likelihood is the sum of 16 terms. Differentiation of this likelihood produces a very large expression. Problems of this sort make maximum-likelihood estimators less attractive. However, the general methods of Chapter 4 can be used to give numerical values for the likelihood (the four-response sequence above was the one analyzed in Equation 4.26); then the parameter set giving the maximum value is found by a numerical search of Ω using a computer. Some ideas about how to make such a search are considered in Section 5.5.

5.4   Minimum Chi-Square Estimators

In essence, a maximum-likelihood estimate provides the best fit between theory and data, using the likelihood function as the measure of fit. Other measures of goodness of fit could be used as well. The difficulty of obtaining exact expressions for the likelihood under general conditions has led to the use of the *Pearson chi-square* as another such measure.

In order to use the Pearson chi-square statistic, a set of mutually exclusive and exhaustive categories is defined, such that each item can be classified into exactly one of the categories. Sequential statistics— the responses on a short sequence of trials—are a common choice. For example, a partition based on the responses made on trials 2, 3, and 4 leads to the eight categories

$$C_2C_3C_4, \ C_2C_3E_4, \ C_2E_3C_4, \ C_2E_3E_4, \ E_2C_3C_4, \ E_2C_3E_4, \ E_2E_3C_4, \ E_2E_3E_4$$

Suppose that there are c categories in all and that the observed frequencies of these categories in a set of data are $f_1, f_2, \ldots, f_c$. For a particular parameter value ω, the model predicts theoretical probabilities for the categories, $\pi_1(\omega), \pi_2(\omega), \ldots, \pi_c(\omega)$. When the model is correct and ω is well chosen, the values of f_i mirror these probabilities. The Pearson chi-square statistic,

$$\chi^2(\omega) = \sum_{i=1}^{c} \frac{[f_i - N\pi_i(\omega)]^2}{N\pi_i(\omega)} \qquad (5.13)$$

compares these distributions, giving a measure of badness of fit. The numerator of this sum, $[f_i - N\pi_i]^2$, is the discrepancy between the data and the average frequencies predicted by the model. Thus, large values of chi-square indicate poor agreement of data and theory, while small values indicate good fit. By adjusting ω, the parameters that make $\chi^2(\omega)$ a minimum can be selected as estimates. These are the *minimum chi-square estimates*. Minimization of this statistic is appealing, as it automatically generates a statistical test of the model (discussed in Chapter 6).

Where the sequential statistics are used as the basis of the estimates, the theoretical probabilities, $\pi_i(\omega)$, are found by expanding each sequence to include the states as well as the responses, using the method of Chapter 3 (Equation 3.24 and Problems 3.16 and 3.17). Using the all-or-none model as an example, the event E_tC_{t+1} implies the state sequence G_tL_{t+1} or G_tG_{t+1}. The probabilities of these sequences, and of making the responses E_t and C_{t+1} from them, are easily calculated. In this way, the complete set of two-step sequential statistics on trial t are found to be

$$\pi_1(\alpha) = P(C_tC_{t+1}) = 1 - (1 - g)[1 + (1 - \alpha)g](1 - \alpha)^{t-1}$$
$$\pi_2(\alpha) = P(C_tE_{t+1}) = g(1 - g)(1 - \alpha)^t$$
$$\pi_3(\alpha) = P(E_tC_{t+1}) = (1 - g)[\alpha + (1 - \alpha)g](1 - \alpha)^{t-1}$$
$$\pi_4(\alpha) = P(E_tE_{t+1}) = (1 - g)^2(1 - \alpha)^t$$

$$(5.14)$$

These probabilities are inserted in the Pearson chi-square formula and the result minimized to find the best-fitting α. A numerical example, showing both data and estimates, appears in Chapter 6.

Unfortunately, the Pearson chi-square is usually even more difficult to minimize than the likelihood is to maximize. By expanding the square and simplifying, Equation 5.13 becomes

$$\chi^2(\omega) = \sum_{i=1}^{c} \frac{f_i^2}{N\pi_i(\omega)} - N \qquad (5.15)$$

which is often easier to compute. Nevertheless, it is almost always impossible to obtain a system of derivatives of $\chi^2(\omega)$ that can be solved.

Because the theoretical quantities $\pi_i(\omega)$ appear in the denominator of Equation 5.15, the derivatives are very complicated. Even in the simple case of the all-or-none model with two-step sequential statistics, differentiating Equation 5.15 results in an expression that cannot be readily solved for α. The alternative, as with the maximum-likelihood estimates, is direct numerical minimization by computer. In this minimization, the relative simplicity of probabilities such as Equation 5.14 makes calculation more rapid than when the likelihood is maximized.

The simplicity of the sequential-statistic probabilities comes largely from the fact that they extend over a short set of trials. However, this also limits their value. When only a three- or four-trial sequence is used, only part of the information in the data is incorporated in the estimate. Recall from the preceding section, for example, that the pattern of presolution responses in the all-or-none model is unrelated to α. Thus, the sequential statistics primarily serve to separate items that cannot be in state L from those that might be in L. This gives far less information than is available, say, to the maximum-likelihood estimate calculated in Equation 5.12. In models with more than two states, the pattern of correct responses and errors may help to identify the state, but the chance that many items show interesting transitions within a three- or four-trial sequence is small.

The natural solution to this problem would appear to be to increase the length of the string of responses. However, increasing the length of the string increases greatly the number of categories.[†] Unless N is very large, the frequencies in each cell become unacceptably small. These problems make most minimum chi-square estimates less accurate than maximum-likelihood estimates involving the full response string. Because fewer data are involved, the chi-square estimates are neither sufficient nor as efficient as those estimates. Unless the greater speed with which chi-square can be calculated is an issue, the likelihood solution is to be preferred.

The difference between the maximum-likelihood estimators and the minimum chi-square estimators, as discussed in the last paragraph, depends on the data that are incorporated in the estimate, rather than on the fitting procedure per se. In one respect, the two procedures are very similar. The data for the chi-square statistic (Equation 5.13 or 5.15) have a multinomial distribution with likelihood

$$L(\omega) = B \prod_{i=1}^{c} [\pi_i(\omega)]^{f_i} \qquad (5.16)$$

---

† For some attempts to circumvent this problem, see Holland (1967).

where B is a multinomial coefficient (generalizing Equation A.33),

$$B = \frac{f_1! f_2! \ldots f_c!}{(\Sigma f_i)!}$$

and a constant with respect to the argument ω of the likelihood function. It is shown in Problem 5.12 that as N gets large, the values of the parameters that maximize Equation 5.16 become the same as those that minimize Equation 5.13. In this sense, the two estimation methods are asymptotically equivalent and have the same properties.

5.5 Finding Numerical Extrema

Practical application of both the maximum-likelihood procedure and the minimum chi-square procedure requires a way to find the extrema of a function. Quite frequently, the values of a function $f(\omega)$ can be calculated, but derivatives such as Equation 5.7 cannot. This makes an analytical solution impossible. The alternative is to find the extrema by purely numerical means, using a computer to calculate successively better and better approximations to the extremum point. Procedures of this sort, known as *numerical optimization,* are important in many branches of engineering, and there is an extensive literature on optimization algorithms (see Daniels, 1978, for a fairly elementary introduction). A proper treatment of these algorithms is far beyond the scope of this book, but the issues are important enough to warrant a brief overview in this section.

In its simplest form, the optimization problem is almost trivial. To find the extrema of $f(\omega)$ over $\omega \in \Omega$, $f(\omega)$ is evaluated at a number of points in Ω, and the point that gives the best value is chosen as the answer. Of course, the points cannot be selected haphazardly if a solution is to be found in a reasonable amount of time. More systematic procedures are needed. One obvious way is to look at all the points in a regularly spaced grid covering Ω. If this grid is fine enough, a solution of any degree of accuracy can be obtained.

The problem with scanning a grid is the number of points that must be examined. On the one hand, if too few values of ω are examined, knowledge of the function is poor and the true extremum is easily overlooked. On the other, a very dense grid of parameter values contains too many points. For example, when a single probability is to be estimated to two decimal places, it may be practical to examine the function at the sequence of values 0.00, 0.01, 0.02, ... , 0.99, 1.00, for a total of 101 function evaluations. When two parameters are involved, a two-dimensional grid with this accuracy requires 101×101 or 10,201

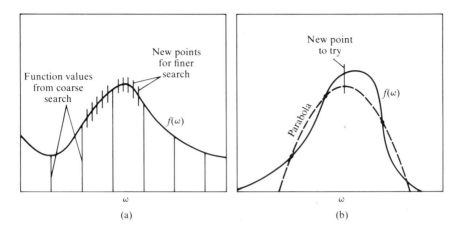

Figure 5.5   Searching for the maximum of a one-dimensional function. (a) A finer grid is used in the vicinity of the maximum. (b) A quadratic equation is fit to three points, and its maximum is taken as an approximate solution.

evaluations, which probably takes too long. More generally, with p parameters, 101^p evaluations are needed. This surely consumes too much computer time. Thus, in making the search, a balance must be struck between making errors due to lack of knowledge about the function and evaluating the function too often. The first error makes the answer useless; the second makes it too expensive. The solution is a more sophisticated search procedure.

When a single parameter is to be found, there are straightforward algorithms. The easiest way is to conduct a coarse search first, then make a finer search in the vicinity of the best point or points (see Figure 5.5a). If the function has no very narrow spikes or pits, this procedure is satisfactory and can be continued until any desired accuracy is attained. Better ways to search are based on the value of the function at several points. For instance, a quadratic equation can be fit to any three points and an approximation to the extremum taken as the turning point of this parabola (Figure 5.5b). Then new points are calculated, a new parabola fit, and so forth.

Where two or more parameters are to be estimated, this procedure is harder to use. On first thought, it might appear that one parameter could be estimated first, then a second, and so on. However, the best value for each parameter depends on the best value for all others, and these other values are not known. As a consequence of the intercorrelation of the estimates discussed at the end of Section 5.1, parameter surfaces are often characterized by long diagonal ridges. These ridges mean that the initial search on one parameter can locate a point that is quite a distance from the true extremum. It is necessary to go a step at a time, following a track through the space toward the highest point. This is known as *hill climbing*, after the two-parameter representation of the problem. Of course, to find a minimum rather than a maximum, the hill is descended rather than climbed, but the principles are the same. A great many hill-climbing algorithms exist, of varying degrees of sophistication. However, no one of these is uniformly the best. Whatever algorithm is used, a function can be found that leads it astray and on which another algorithm works better. Thus, the most sophisticated hill-climbing programs combine several strategies.

The simplest hill-climbing procedure is to use a series of one-dimensional searches. Consider the two-dimensional parameter space with the function indicated by the contours in Figure 5.6. The fine lines in this figure connect points where the value of the function is the same. The figure shows the steps taken by several hill-climbing algorithms. The steps in paths A and B are formed by incrementing or decrementing the value of one of the parameters at a time. First ω_1 is stepped to a maximum, then ω_2, then ω_1 again, and so forth, until neither parameter can be improved. By following this procedure, reducing the step size whenever the search gets stuck, the top is found.

As with the one-dimensional search, better procedures can be based on the value of the function at several points. Suppose that the function in Figure 5.6 has been evaluated at the three points c_1, c_2, and c_3. The point c_2 has the smallest value. For many functions, it is a good strategy to search in a direction away from the low point through the average of all the points, as indicated by the arrow. Algorithms combining information from several points in this way are appreciably faster than stepping along the axes.

Path D in Figure 5.6 is the most efficient, for it always takes steps pointing directly uphill. However, finding this path requires a knowledge of the slope of the surface, which may be difficult to obtain. The steepest uphill direction, or *gradient,* of the function is determined by the partial derivatives of the function with respect to each of the parameters. A step in which the distance moved along ω_j is proportional to $\partial f(\omega)/\partial \omega_j$ goes directly uphill (or downhill). Sometimes it is possible to find these partial derivatives analytically. For example, differentiating the Pearson chi-square in the form of Equation 5.15 gives

$$\frac{\partial \chi^2(\omega)}{\partial \omega_j} = -N \sum_{i=1}^{c} \left(\frac{f_i}{N \pi_i(\omega)}\right)^2 \frac{\partial \pi_i(\omega)}{\partial \omega_j} \qquad (5.17)$$

For simple problems, such as with the sequential statistics in Equation 5.14, it is possible to calculate the $\partial \pi_i/\partial \omega_j$ and evaluate Equation 5.17.

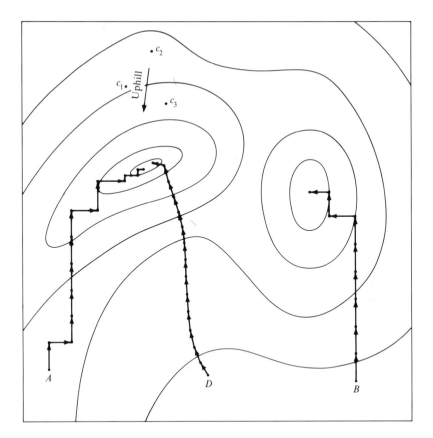

Figure 5.6 Maximization of a two-dimensional function (such as that shown in perspective in Figure 5.4) by hill-climbing algorithms. Paths A and B step along the axes; path D, along the gradient; and the three points c_1, c_2, and c_3 are used to determine an uphill direction.

Unfortunately, in most cases (such as the numerical likelihood calculations) the derivatives cannot be found. When this happens, the derivatives can still be estimated by the slope between two closely spaced values of ω_j. If $\Delta\omega_j$ is small with respect to ω_j, then

$$\frac{\partial f(\boldsymbol{\omega})}{\partial\omega_j} \approx \frac{f(\omega_1, \omega_2, \ldots, \omega_j, \ldots, \omega_p) - f(\omega_1, \omega_2, \ldots, \omega_j + \Delta\omega_j, \ldots, \omega_p)}{\Delta\omega_j}$$

This approximation (usually) determines the uphill direction.

For most functions, at least one of these hill-climbing procedures finds the maximum. However, several difficulties are commonly encountered that reduce the accuracy of the final estimate and can even make it completely incorrect. The most serious are the problems of local extrema, of ridges, and of flat spots.

The local-extremum problem arises because numerical hill-climbing procedures respond only to local properties of the space. They work their way uphill until a maximum is found, but there is no assurance that this maximum is the best maximum in the entire space. Path B in Figure 5.6 illustrates this. Because of its starting point, it became trapped on a subsidiary hill and found only a local maximum. The more contorted and bumpy the function, the more serious is the problem of local extrema.

If the parameters of the model are correlated, the maximum often lies at the top of a diagonal ridge. In such cases, there may be great difficulty in finding a path to the maximum once the edge of the ridge has been reached. Figure 5.7 shows two examples of this problem. Path E, generated by a program that moved parallel to the parameter axes, is trapped on a ridge. A step in any direction finds a lower point, even though the maximum has not been reached. Programs that change the direction of their steps can partly avoid this particular problem. For example, a gradient search could climb this particular ridge. Yet even a climb up the gradient can become trapped if the ridge bends sharply and the step size is too large to negotiate the turn. Path F shows this situation. A less serious effect of the ridges is that the final estimates are usually somewhat less accurate than they seem—often quite a bit further from the true maximum than the size of the final step that is attempted.

The third problem occurs when the parameter space contains regions of equally good fit. These form flat plateaus in the function, and once a search reaches one of them, there is no uphill direction, so the search stops without finding the maximum. Sometimes the maximum itself is a flat spot, so that there are many equally good parameter choices. This event is not uncommon; it results from the sort of indeterminacy in the model that is the topic of Chapter 7.

The best cure for all these problems is to start searches from many places in the space and pick the best of the resulting solutions. In that way different local extrema (if any) are found and the chance of being caught on a ridge is diminished. While flat spots cannot be avoided, they can be discovered if several different extremum points are found with exactly the same value of $f(\omega)$. The starting points for these paths may be chosen systematically to loosely cover Ω, may be selected randomly from it, or may be the best points found by scanning a coarse grid covering Ω. If these searches do not arrive, roughly, at the same point, both $f(\omega)$ and the model on which it is based should be examined to see what went wrong.

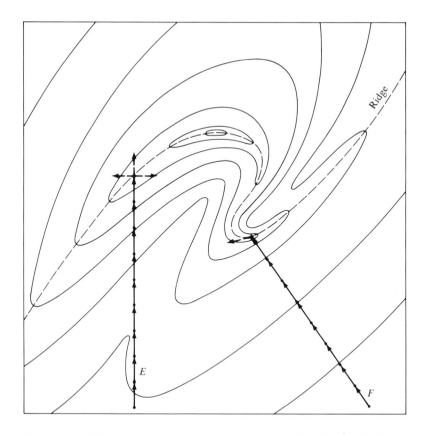

Figure 5.7 Hill-climbing procedures trapped on a ridge (dashed line). Path *E* is a search along the axes; path *F*, along the gradient.

Problems

5.1. Consider the following 20 items:

EEEEE CECCE CECEc cc ...   *EEccc ...*
CECCC CEEcc c ...   *EEccc ...*
CCEEE CCCEE ECEEE Eccc ...   *EEECC EEccc ...*
ccc ...   *CEccc ...*
EEEEC ECCEc cc ...   *ccc ...*
EEECE EEccc ...   *ECEEE EEccc ...*
Eccc ...   *EECEE EEECE ccc ...*
CEccc ...   *ECCCC Eccc ...*
CECEE ccc ...   *EECEc cc ...*
ccc ...   *ccc ...*

Suppose that they are fit by an all-or-none model with $\sigma = 0$ and $g = \frac{1}{3}$. Estimate α using the method-of-moments estimator developed in this chapter.

5.2. Find a method-of-moments estimator for the parameter α of the all-or-none model based on the mean trial of last error (found in Problem 3.9). Apply the result to the data of Problem 5.1.

5.3. Suppose that α and σ in the all-or-none model are unknown and that g is known. Find method-of-moments estimators for these parameters based on $E(T)$ and the proportion of errors on the first trial. Apply the results to the data of Problem 5.1.

5.4. Find method-of-moments estimators for γ and δ in the all-or-none model with variable item difficulties (see Section 3.5). Use the mean and variance of T (given by Equation 3.30 and Problem 3.20).

5.5. Calculate and plot the likelihood of the string

$$ECEEECCEEEEccc \; \ldots$$

for the all-or-none model with $g = 0.25$ as a function of α. Find the maximum.

5.6. Find the maximum-likelihood estimate of α for the data in Problem 5.1.

5.7. Suppose that both the parameters α and σ in the all-or-none model are unknown.
   a. Show that

$$
\begin{aligned}
&L(\alpha,\sigma) \\
&= \frac{(1 - \sigma)^{N(1-z)} g^C (1 - g)^E (1 - \alpha)^{C+E-N(1-z)} \alpha^{N(1-z)} [\sigma(1 - g) + \alpha g]^{Nz}}{[1 - (1 - \alpha)g]^N}
\end{aligned}
$$

$$(5.18)$$

   b. Differentiate $\log L(\alpha,\sigma)$ and show that maximum-likelihood estimators of α and σ are

$$
\hat{\alpha} = \frac{1 - z}{M_L} \quad \text{and} \quad \hat{\sigma} = z - \frac{(1 - z)^2 g}{M_L(1 - g)}
$$

A moderately large amount of algebra is involved.
   c. Apply these results to the data in Problem 5.1.

5.8. Use the likelihood in Problem 5.7 to find maximum-likelihood estimates for α, σ, and the guessing rate γ in the all-or-none model. Once again, apply the estimators to the data in Problem 5.1.

5.9. Consider the five-state choice model in Equation 2.22. Suppose that of N choices, A are observed to be of alternative A.

    a. Show that the probability of eventually choosing A is $\alpha^2/[1 - 2\alpha(1 - \alpha)]$. What is the likelihood, $L(\alpha)$? *Hint:* Let $\mathbf{Q}$ be the matrix of the transient states A_1, U, and B_1; let s be the initial vector for these states; and let a′ be the vector of transition probabilities into state A. Then the probability of eventual absorption is $\mathbf{s}(\mathbf{I} - \mathbf{Q})^{-1}\mathbf{a}'$. (Why?)

    b. Find a maximum likelihood estimator of α.

5.10. Consider the all-or-none model in which learning is possible only following an error (as given in Equation 2.7). Let the initial vector be $[\tau, (1 - \tau)g, (1 - \tau)(1 - g)]$.

    a. Set $\tau = 0$. Derive the method-of-moments estimator for β based on the total number of errors.

    b. Again with $\tau = 0$, find the maximum-likelihood estimator of β. Compare the result to that found in part a.

    c. Suppose the three parameters β, τ, and the guessing rate (now denoted by ϵ) are unknown. Find maximum-likelihood estimators.

5.11. Suppose that a homogeneous Markov chain has states $S_1, S_2, \ldots,$ S_n, which are directly observable in the data, and let $P(S_j|S_i) = \pi_{ij}$. Data on the process are collected, and the transition from S_i to S_j is observed with frequency $f_{ij}, i, j = 1, 2, \ldots, n$. Construct the likelihood function and show that the maximum-likelihood estimate of π_{ij} is

$$\hat{\pi}_{ij} = \frac{f_{ij}}{\displaystyle\sum_{k=1}^{n} f_{ik}}$$

Hint: Remember that the rows of a transition matrix sum to 1, so that $\Sigma_k \pi_{ik}$ is 1.

5.12. Consider a probability distribution $\pi_1(\omega), \pi_2(\omega), \ldots, \pi_c(\omega)$ that depends on the single parameter ω. Differentiate Equation 5.15 to get an equation that could be solved for the minimum chi-square estimate $\hat{\omega}_c$ of ω (but do not solve it). Do the same with Equation 5.16 to get an equation for the maximum-likelihood estimate $\hat{\omega}_l$. As N gets large, $f_i/\pi_i \to N$. Show that substituting N for this ratio makes the equation for $\hat{\omega}_c$ into a multiple of the equation for $\hat{\omega}_l$. Thus, $\hat{\omega}_c$ and $\hat{\omega}_l$ are asymptotically the same.

5.13. [C] Write a computer program that searches a one-dimensional space to find the maximum-likelihood estimate of α in the all-or-none model. The program should start with one size of step, then shift to a smaller step when it gets close to the maximum, as in Figure 5.5. Apply the program to the data in Problem 5.1 and compare the result to that obtained in Problem 5.6.

5.14. [C] Modify the program in Problem 5.13 to estimate α using chi-square and the three-trial sequential statistics from Problem 3.17 (given in Figure 6.2). Apply the program to the data of Problem 5.1.

5.15. [C] Write a computer program that searches a two-dimensional space to find maximum-likelihood estimates of α and σ for the all-or-none model. Maximize the function first for α, then for σ, then for α again, and so on, until the change in the parameters becomes small. Apply the program to the data in Problem 5.1 and compare the results to those of Problem 5.7.

Chapter 6

Statistical Testing

Once the parameters of a model have been estimated, the next step is to evaluate how well the model fits. Two general types of questions can be asked. The first concerns the overall fit: whether the data deviate from the model to a greater extent than can be attributed to chance fluctuation. The second concerns comparisons between two (or more) models and whether a more complicated model is an improvement over a simpler one. These questions are considered in this chapter.

Statistical tests with Markov models are similar to the tests in any statistical-testing situation (see any statistics text; Hays, 1981, and Kendall and Stewart, 1979, are appropriate). The next few paragraphs review these procedures. In essence, the point of statistical testing is to distinguish between a real effect in the data and the sort of chance fluctuation that is consistent with a probabilistic process. The test procedure starts by specifying a *null hypothesis,* denoted by H_0, that is to be tested. This hypothesis must be exact; it specifies that a model fits or that a parameter is equal to a particular value, or some such exact statement. A *test statistic,* say denoted by G, sensitive to deviations from this hypothesis is defined. Even if H_0 is true, G does not take on the same value for every set of observations. So G is treated as a random variable having a sampling distribution over the range of possible observations when H_0 is true. The top part of Figure 6.1 shows such

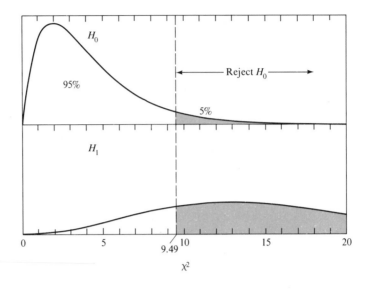

Figure 6.1   Sampling distributions of a test statistic under H_0 and H_1. The null-hypothesis distribution is a chi-square with four degrees of freedom and the decision criterion is set at the 5% level.

a distribution. The result of any single experiment is a realization of the statistic G.

The alternative to H_0 is the *alternative hypothesis, H_1*, which is usually the negation of H_0. Because H_0 is exact, H_1 is much less precise; it states, for example, that a model does not fit or that two parameters are unequal. The sampling distribution of the test statistic G under H_1 is different from that under H_0, generally displaced from it in one direction or another (Figure 6.1, bottom section). Because of the generality of H_1, any particular illustration of the alternative distribution is but one example from the infinity of possible alternatives.

The goal of the testing procedure is a decision between H_0 and H_1. To accomplish this, a *decision rule* for retaining or rejecting H_0 is based on G, with H_0 being rejected for values of G that are both rare under H_0 and in the direction indicated by H_1. Because the distributions of G under H_0 and H_1 usually overlap, no rule is correct all the time. So one picks a *significance level* for the test—frequently 5%—and rejects H_0 when the probability of a more deviate value of G is less than this number. When G is not so discrepant, H_0 is retained as still tenable. Because of the nonspecific nature of H_1, however, it is rarely possible to assert that H_1 is not true. Deviations from H_0 so small as to be undetectable are part of H_1, and so one speaks of retaining H_0, rather than accepting it.

6.1   Goodness-of-Fit Tests

At first thought, it may appear that tests of the overall goodness of fit of a model are most important. Surely, the first issue should be whether a model is right or wrong. Yet in many respects this question is less interesting than the comparison of models. As was argued in Chapter 1, models are approximations to psychological processes, and so are always wrong in detail. Any model can be rejected with a sufficiently large sample of data. Hence, the simple failure of a model to fit gives little useful information about the process. Similarly, the fact that a model is retained may only be an indication of the low power of the test or of the poor quality of the data. These considerations limit the value of pure goodness-of-fit tests. Nevertheless, such tests are sufficiently useful, if applied with understanding, to warrant some discussion.

One goodness-of-fit test arises quite naturally from the minimum chi-square estimation procedure. With N observations distributed into c categories, the Pearson chi-square, used as an estimation criterion in Chapter 5 (see Equation 5.13), is

$$\chi^2 = \sum_{i=1}^{c} \frac{(f_i - N\pi_i)^2}{N\pi_i} \tag{6.1}$$

When the model holds and N is reasonably large, this statistic has a distribution that is well approximated by the chi-square distribution (discussed in Section A.4 and tabled in Appendix F). The null-hypothesis distribution in the upper part of Figure 6.1 is of this type. When the model is wrong—when some variant of H_1 holds—the discrepancies between model and data are larger than chance factors would indicate. The result is the shifted distribution at the bottom of Figure 6.1. If χ^2 falls in the rightmost tail of the null-hypothesis distribution, H_0 is rejected, and the model is deemed not to fit.

The particular chi-square distribution to use depends on the number of *degrees of freedom* for the problem, which is determined by the number of categories into which the observations are partitioned and the number of parameters estimated. If no parameters are estimated, then χ^2 is distributed on $c - 1$ degrees of freedom. These correspond to the c categories, less 1 because the π_i are a probability distribution and constrained to sum to 1. When the parameter values can be found from an analysis of the task or are determined in another experiment, this is the correct degrees-of-freedom value. When parameters are estimated from the same data used to make the test, the number of degrees of freedom must be reduced. Each additional parameter that is estimated allows the model to fit the data somewhat better. Accidental characteristics of the data are accommodated by the estimation procedure; so even when the model is correct, χ^2 is smaller when parameters are estimated than when they are not. This better fit is reflected in the sampling distribution of χ^2 by a reduction in its degrees of freedom. Every parameter estimated creates one additional constraint. Thus, when p parameters are estimated, the minimum value of chi-square is distributed on $c - p - 1$ degrees of freedom.

For example, if three parameters are estimated using eight categories, the chi-square has $8 - 3 - 1 = 4$ degrees of freedom. This gives the distribution shown in Figure 6.1. From Appendix F, 5% of the scores in the chi-square distribution fall above 9.49; so if the observed chi-square exceeds 9.49, the model is rejected at the 5% level. For $\chi^2 < 9.49$, the model is retained.

For Equation 6.1 to closely approximate a chi-square distribution, several assumptions must be satisfied. Discussions of these can be found in most statistics texts. Two pose fairly serious problems in model testing. The first involves the size of the sample of data. The chi-square test is an asymptotic one, strictly correct only as $N \to \infty$. For it to be applicable, the predicted frequencies for each category (although not necessarily the obtained frequencies) must be reasonably large. Usually values of $N\pi_i$ greater than about 5 are sufficient, although several smaller cells can be tolerated when the number of degrees of freedom in the test is more than 3 or 4. Unfortunately, this criterion frequently fails to be satisfied because certain events are very unlikely. For example, most learning models predict, appropriately, a low probability for errors following runs of correct responses. This makes certain of the sequential statistics unlikely. Where the problem can be anticipated in advance, it may be advisable to pool some rare but related categories together. When fitting an all-or-none model with small g using the sequential statistics of length 4, for example, the cells *CCCE, CCEC,* and *CCEE* are unlikely and can be pooled together. Pooling of this sort should not be based solely on small frequencies, but also on the fact that the pooling makes sense in terms of the model.

A more serious problem involves the independence of the observations. For the chi-square distribution to apply, every observation must be statistically independent of every other observation. Where several observations are taken from each subject, this does not hold. Learning experiments, for example, typically use lists of many items. As a list is learned, good or bad performance on one item affects other items. Clearly, such items are not independent. The exact nature of the bias produced in the test depends on the way in which the items interact and on the particular character of the model. To the extent that items tend to behave more alike than they otherwise might, a bias in favor of rejection results. Other types of dependency create the opposite bias. The statistically ideal solution to the problem would be to take only a single item from each subject. Of course, this is an inefficient use of subject resources. Most often one lives with whatever bias in the test exists, interprets the results with caution, and does not take the significance levels too seriously.

The Pearson chi-square is not the only test statistic that compares observed and predicted frequency distributions. When N is reasonably large,

$$\chi^2 = 2 \sum_{i=1}^{c} f_i \log \frac{f_i}{N \pi_i} \tag{6.2}$$

$$= 2 \left(\sum_{i=1}^{c} f_i \log f_i - \sum_{i=1}^{c} f_i \log \pi_i - N \log N \right)$$

is also distributed as a chi-square variable with $c - p - 1$ degrees of freedom. For reasons to be discussed at the end of the next section, this is called the *likelihood-ratio chi-square*. The likelihood-ratio chi-square is not greatly different from the Pearson chi-square. The way in which the tests are run with the two statistics is the same, they have the same null-hypothesis distribution, and, when based on the same data, their values rarely differ by much. Asymptotically, as $N \to \infty$, they are identical.

The likelihood-ratio chi-square statistic is closely related to the maximum-likelihood estimation procedure. The likelihood for a set of frequencies, Equation 5.16, is

$$L(\omega) = B \prod_{i=1}^{c} \pi_i^{f_i} \tag{6.3}$$

Taking the logarithm gives

$$\log L(\omega) = \log B + \sum_{i=1}^{c} f_i \log \pi_i \tag{6.4}$$

The second term in Equation 6.4 is identical to the second sum in the line below Equation 6.2. Both likelihoods depend on the model's predictions only through this sum. Thus, the parameters that maximize the likelihood (Equation 6.3) also minimize the likelihood-ratio chi-square (Equation 6.2). Maximum-likelihood estimates are the same as minimum-likelihood-ratio chi-square estimates. Hence, the likelihood-ratio chi-square is the appropriate choice for a test statistic where maximum-likelihood estimates are used. Where parameters are estimated by the minimum Pearson chi-square procedure, Equation 6.1 is the better choice.

The gist of the last remark is that the same form of chi-square statistic should be used both to estimate parameters and to test fit. Only then is the sampling distribution correct. When the parameters are not estimated by finding the extremum of the Pearson chi-square or of the likelihood, neither chi-square statistic gives an exact test. For example, when method-of-moments estimators are used or likelihood is maximized on a string other than that used in the chi-square test, both Equation 6.1 and Equation 6.2 are only approximate. The minimum chi-square procedure, by its nature, makes the statistic as small as possible, and any other estimation procedure, even when the model is correct, gives a somewhat worse fit. Mismatching of estimation and testing procedures most frequently occurs when one wants to use a chi-square test without the numerical minimization needed to get the proper parameter estimates.

For many practical applications, the problem of mismatched estimates and tests can be circumvented by setting bounds on the value of χ^2. Suppose that the null hypothesis is true, i.e., that the model fits. If the parameters are known a priori, then the test statistic has a chi-square distribution on $c - 1$ degrees of freedom. As any estimation procedure is somewhat sensitive to the data, the goodness of fit cannot be worse than this, so the test statistic is bounded above by this distribution. At the other extreme, no estimation procedure can do better than minimize χ^2, which gives a distribution with $c - p - 1$ degrees of freedom. The unknown true distribution lies somewhere between these two distributions. In terms of testing procedure, the conclusions are accurate (up to the uncertainty of any statistical decision) if the model is rejected with $c - 1$ degrees of freedom or retained with $c - p - 1$ degrees of freedom. Values of χ^2 rejected at $c - p - 1$ degrees of freedom and retained at $c - 1$ cannot be interpreted unambiguously. Fortunately, to the precision to which the statistical testing of models is done, this is rarely a critical difference.

The data from the numerical examples of the last chapter are not appropriate for chi-square tests. Because of the small number of items involved, the expected frequencies are far too small for the chi-square approximation to be accurate. Instead, suppose that 208 items are observed in an experiment with $g = 0.2$, and the data in the "Data" column of Figure 6.2 are obtained for the three-item sequential statistics over trials 2, 3, and 4. Under the all-or-none model, the probability of these sequences is given by the probability in the "Theory" column (see Problem 3.17). Numerical minimization of the Pearson chi-square gives the parameter estimates $\hat{\alpha} = 0.0604$ and $\hat{\sigma} = 0.2201$, producing the expected frequencies and minimum χ^2 shown in Figure 6.2. A similar analysis, based on minimizing the likelihood-ratio chi-square (Equation 6.2) gives $\hat{\alpha} = 0.0762$ and $\hat{\sigma} = 0.2314$. In either case, the reference distribution has $8 - 2 - 1 = 5$ degrees of freedom. By either statistic,

String	Data	Theory	Pearson chi-square		Likelihood chi-square	
	f_i	π_i	π_i	$N\pi_i$	π_i	$N\pi_i$
$C_2C_3C_4$	64	$1 - \text{others}$	0.2829	58.8	0.3076	64.0
$C_2C_3E_4$	15	$(1-\sigma)(1-\alpha)^3 g^2(1-g)$	0.0207	4.3	0.0194	4.0
$C_2E_3C_4$	10	$(1-\sigma)(1-\alpha)^2 g(1-g)A$	0.0274	5.7	0.0274	5.7
$C_2E_3E_4$	12	$(1-\sigma)(1-\alpha)^3 g(1-g)^2$	0.0828	17.2	0.0776	16.1
$E_2C_3C_4$	13	$(1-\sigma)(1-\alpha)(1-g)[\alpha + (1-\alpha)gA]$	0.0628	13.1	0.0707	14.7
$E_2C_3E_4$	21	$(1-\sigma)(1-\alpha)^3 g(1-g)^2$	0.0828	17.2	0.0776	16.1
$E_2E_3C_4$	23	$(1-\sigma)(1-\alpha)^2(1-g)^2 A$	0.1094	22.8	0.1095	22.8
$E_2E_3E_4$	50	$(1-\sigma)(1-\alpha)^3(1-g)^3$	0.3312	68.9	0.3102	64.5
Total	208	1	1.0000	208.0	1.0000	207.9
χ^2				37.81		26.31

Figure 6.2 Chi-square tests of the all-or-none model using the sequential statistics. Both formulas for chi-square are used. In the theory column, $A = \alpha + (1-\alpha)g$.

the observed value exceeds the critical 11.07; so the all-or-none model can be rejected.

It is rarely enough to stop with the rejection of a model. Some information about the way in which the model fails can be obtained by looking at the particular statistic values. The difference between the observed and the expected value is useful, and the components of χ^2, such as $(f_i - N\pi_i)^2/N\pi_i$, which give a picture of the relative size of the error, can be even more useful. For this example, the largest relative discrepancy involves the CCE statistic, which is substantially overrepresented in the data. Such an occurrence suggests that errors are somewhat more likely to follow runs of correct responses than the all-or-none model predicts, perhaps indicating the presence of some form of partial learning state.

6.2   *Tests of Parameters and Comparison of Models*

More useful than tests of the overall fit of a model are tests that compare different models. Tests of this type answer two sorts of questions: first, whether a parameter takes a particular hypothesized value, and, second, whether a complex model is an improvement over a simpler one. Both of these questions can be restated as questions about the extent to which a model's fit worsens when one or more of its parameters are held fixed.

A test of the first type of question is easier to state. Suppose that one has data that fit the all-or-none model with the guessing rate γ free. Suppose also that there is some reason to think that γ truly equals a particular value, say $\frac{1}{4}$. Then one would want to test the hypothesis H_0: $\gamma = 0.25$ against the alternative hypothesis H_1: $\gamma \neq 0.25$. The statistical question to be answered is whether making the restriction H_0 leads to an appreciably worse fit than when γ is free under H_1.

Questions of the second type can also be expressed in terms of parameter values. Suppose that one wished to see if the two-stage model,

$$\mathbf{s}_1 = [\sigma, (1 - \sigma)\tau, (1 - \sigma)(1 - \tau)]$$

$$\mathbf{T} = \begin{matrix} L \\ I \\ G \end{matrix} \begin{bmatrix} 1 & 0 & 0 \\ \delta & 1 - \delta & 0 \\ \alpha\beta & \alpha(1 - \beta) & 1 - \alpha \end{bmatrix} \qquad \mathbf{r} = \begin{bmatrix} 1 \\ \pi \\ g \end{bmatrix}$$

fits a set of data better than the all-or-none model,

$$\mathbf{s}_1 = [\sigma, 1 - \sigma] \qquad \mathbf{T} = \begin{matrix} L \\ G \end{matrix} \begin{bmatrix} 1 & 0 \\ \alpha & 1 - \alpha \end{bmatrix} \qquad \mathbf{r} = \begin{bmatrix} 1 \\ g \end{bmatrix}$$

The two-stage model contains the all-or-none model as a special case, giving the pair of models a hierarchical structure. The probability α in either model governs the rate at which items leave state G, σ gives the probability that an item starts in L, and g is the guessing rate. The other parameters are unique to the two-stage model. If β is set to 1, then items in state G do not go through state I, and for these items the transition matrix reduces to that of the all-or-none model. Setting $\tau = 0$ eliminates state I from the initial vector. Hence, a comparison of the two-stage model with the all-or-none model amounts to a test of the hypothesis that $\beta = 1$ and $\tau = 0$. When β and τ take these values, the learning rate, δ, and the response probability, π, both associated with the intermediate state, become irrelevant and vanish from the model. Thus, there are four fewer parameters to be estimated for the all-or-none model than for the two-stage model. The statistical question to be answered is whether eliminating these four parameters leads to an appreciably worse fit.

The idea of creating a hierarchy of models by fixing parameter values is an important one. In terms of the notation introduced in the last chapter, the starting point is the most general or *unrestricted model*, $\mathcal{M}$, with parameter vector $\omega \in \Omega$. A *restricted model*, $\mathcal{M}^*$, is formed by limiting the parameters to a subset of the original parameter space, $\Omega^* \subset \Omega$. For the test of γ in the all-or-none model, these spaces are depicted in Figure 6.3. The space Ω of $\mathcal{M}$ consists of points $\omega =$

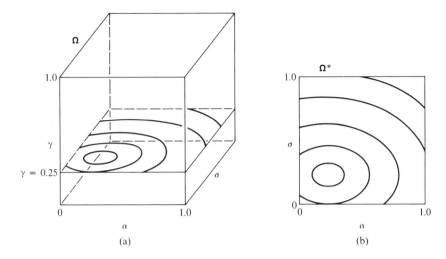

Figure 6.3   Parameter spaces (a) for the all-or-none model with free guessing probability γ and (b) for the same model with γ restricted to 0.25.

$[\alpha, \sigma, \gamma]$ and is three-dimensional, defined by inequalities $0 \le \alpha \le 1$, $0 \le \sigma \le 1$, and $0 \le \gamma \le 1$. The restricted parameter space, Ω^*, is a plane through this space, fixed at $\gamma = 0.25$ and defined by the first two of the three inequalities. It consists of points $\boldsymbol{\omega} = [\alpha, \sigma, 0.25]$. Similarly for the two-stage model, $\boldsymbol{\omega} = [\alpha, \beta, \delta, \sigma, \tau, \pi]$, so Ω is the six-dimensional "cube," $\Omega = [0, 1]^6$. The all-or-none model is obtained from this by restricting $\beta = 1, \tau = 0$, and holding δ and π to any convenient values, say, 0:

$$\Omega^* = \{[\alpha, 1, 0, \sigma, 0, 0], 0 \le \alpha, \sigma \le 1\} \qquad (6.5)$$

Because every $\boldsymbol{\omega}^* \in \Omega^*$ is also in Ω, $\mathcal{M}$ must fit the data at least as well as $\mathcal{M}^*$. In fact, Ω is so much larger than Ω^* that it is essentially certain that the unrestricted model fits better. The statistical question is whether the fit to $\mathcal{M}$ is sufficiently superior to the fit to $\mathcal{M}^*$ that it cannot be due to chance. If so, then $\mathcal{M}^*$ can be rejected in favor of $\mathcal{M}$; otherwise, the restricted model $\mathcal{M}^*$ is retained. The logic of this testing procedure is very standard and is used in many areas of statistics. For example, in a two-way analysis of variance, one asks whether a model that includes an interaction ($\mathcal{M}$) is an improvement on a model with only main effects ($\mathcal{M}^*$). If the more general model is sufficiently better, an interaction is deemed present. The tests used with multiple-regression models (of which the analysis of variance is a special case) exploit this logic even more explicitly.

To complete the test, a way is needed to evaluate the difference between the fits to $\mathcal{M}$ and $\mathcal{M}^*$. The procedure presented here, known as *likelihood-ratio testing*, starts with maximum-likelihood estimation of the parameters. Both models are fit to the data by finding maximum-likelihood estimates in the appropriate spaces. For $\mathcal{M}$, one obtains $\hat{\omega} \in \Omega$ such that $L(\hat{\omega})$ is the largest value that $L(\omega)$ takes over all $\omega \in \Omega$. Similarly, $\hat{\omega}^* \in \Omega^*$ is chosen to maximize $L(\omega)$ over Ω^*. The maximum cannot be smaller in the bigger space, so $L(\hat{\omega}) \geq L(\hat{\omega}^*)$. Under the null hypothesis that $\mathcal{M}^*$ fits, the size of the chance difference between these two likelihoods has a known statistical distribution. If the true value of ω is in the restricted space, Ω^*, then as the number of observations becomes large, the quantity

$$\chi^2 = -2 \log \left(\frac{L(\hat{\omega}^*)}{L(\hat{\omega})} \right) \qquad (6.6)$$

$$= 2 \left[\log L(\hat{\omega}) - \log L(\hat{\omega}^*) \right]$$

develops a chi-square distribution, with degrees of freedom equal to the number of parameters that are restricted in reducing Ω to Ω^* (or more exactly, the amount by which the dimensionality of Ω^* is less than that of Ω). The observed value of this statistic can be compared to the critical value of chi-square from Appendix F. If the data are not consistent with $\mathcal{M}^*$, but fit $\mathcal{M}$, then $L(\hat{\omega})$ much exceeds $L(\hat{\omega}^*)$ and the value of Equation 6.6 is large. Thus, when χ^2 exceeds the tabled value at the desired level of significance, the hypothesis that the true value of ω is in Ω^* is rejected in favor of a location somewhere in the remainder of Ω. The restricted model is wrong, and a model of at least the complexity of $\mathcal{M}$ must be used. If χ^2 is less than the tabled value, $\mathcal{M}^*$ can be retained.

When $\mathcal{M}^*$ is retained, this indicates that $\mathcal{M}$ is no improvement, but it is important to realize that this result does not reflect the absolute quality of the model. The value of χ^2 measures only the difference between $\mathcal{M}$ and $\mathcal{M}^*$, not how well $\mathcal{M}^*$ fits. Likewise, the fact that $\mathcal{M}^*$ is rejected does not mean that $\mathcal{M}$ is a satisfactory model, only that it is better than $\mathcal{M}^*$. Furthermore, the value of $\log L(\hat{\omega})$ itself cannot be used for a test. To investigate overall fit, some other test must be used. A test such as those in the preceding section is one possibility, and a likelihood-ratio test against a still more general alternative is another.

As its name suggests, the likelihood-ratio chi-square used to test the overall fit of a model (Equation 6.2) is an example of a likelihood-ratio test. The model to be tested, representing $\mathcal{M}^*$, is compared to an unrestricted model $\mathcal{M}$ that fits perfectly. The data are frequencies of observations in each of c categories. The logarithm of the likelihood of a frequency distribution (given in Equation 6.4) is

$$\log L(\omega) = \log B + \sum_{i=1}^{c} f_i \log \pi_i$$

The model $\mathcal{M}^*$ can always be generalized to a $c - 1$ parameter model that fits the distribution perfectly, for $c - 1$ parameters always suffice to determine the probabilities in a c-category distribution. How the $c - 1$ parameters are used to form the unrestricted model is unimportant; it suffices to know that $N\pi_i = f_i$. Then, using f_i/N for the full model's probabilities and π_i for the probabilities in the reduced model, Equation 6.6 becomes

$$\chi^2 = 2 \left(\sum_{i=1}^{c} f_i \log \frac{f_i}{N} - \sum_{i=1}^{c} f_i \log \pi_i \right)$$

$$= 2 \sum_{i=1}^{c} f_i \log \frac{f_i}{N\pi_i}$$

This is the likelihood-ratio chi-square of Equation 6.2.

6.3   *Examples of Likelihood-Ratio Testing*

Two examples of parameter restriction were given in the preceding section: the first to test the value of the parameter g in the all-or-none model, and the second to compare the all-or-none to the two-stage model. This section completes these examples. The test of g is based purely on the all-or-none model. Parameter spaces for this test were shown in Figure 6.3, with the more general model, $\mathcal{M}$, depending on the parameter vector $[\alpha, \sigma, \gamma]$ and the restricted model, $\mathcal{M}^*$, on the vector $[\alpha, \sigma, 0.25]$. A comparison of the two models tests the hypothesis that $\gamma = 0.25$ against an alternative of some other value.

Estimates of the parameters are found by differentiating the likelihood function and solving the resulting set of simultaneous differential equations for the unknown parameters. These estimates were obtained in Problems 5.7 and 5.8. The parameters of $\mathcal{M}^*$ are estimated by

$$\hat{\alpha}^* = \frac{1 - z}{M_L} \qquad \hat{\sigma}^* = z - \frac{(1 - z)^2 g}{M_L(1 - g)} \tag{6.7}$$

while those of $\mathcal{M}$ are

$$\hat{\alpha} = \frac{1 - z}{M_L} \qquad \hat{\sigma} = z - \frac{(1 - z)^2(M_L - M_T)}{M_L(M_T - 1 + z)} \qquad \hat{\gamma} = \frac{M_L - M_T}{M_L - 1 + z} \tag{6.8}$$

where M_L is the mean trial of last error and M_T is the mean number of errors. For both models,

$$\log L(\omega) = N(1 - z)[\log(1 - \sigma) + \log \alpha]$$
$$+ C \log g + E \log(1 - g) + [C + E - N(1 - z)] \log(1 - \alpha)$$
$$+ Nz \log[\sigma(1 - g) + \alpha g] - N \log[1 - (1 - \alpha)g]$$

As Figure 6.3 makes obvious, the dimensions of the two parameter spaces differ by 1, so if the null hypothesis is true, the likelihood ratio (Equation 6.6) is distributed as χ^2 with one degree of freedom. From Appendix F, χ^2 has a 5% chance of exceeding 3.84. If the likelihood-ratio statistic is larger than 3.84, than there are grounds to reject $\gamma = 0.25$.

In particular, consider the following items:

ECEEE EEEcc c ...   *EEECE ECEEE CECEE EEEEE EEccc ...*
EEEEc cc ...   *ECEEC EEECE EEEEE ccc ...*
EEECE EEEEc cc ...   *EEEEC EECEE EEccc ...*
ccc ...   *Eccc ...*
ECEcc c ...   *EEccc ...*
ccc ...   *EEEcc c ...*
ccc ...   *Eccc ...*
EEccc ...   *Eccc ...*
CCCEE ccc ...   *Eccc ...*
ccc ...   *ccc ...*

This is too small a set of data for an accurate statistical test, but makes a satisfactory example. For model $\mathcal{M}^*$, with $\gamma = 0.25$, the maximum-likelihood estimates (Equation 6.7) are $\hat{\sigma}^* = 0.208$ and $\hat{\alpha}^* = 0.168$, with $\log L(\hat{\alpha}^*, \hat{\sigma}^*) = -89.38$. For the more general model, Equation 6.8 gives somewhat different estimates, $\hat{\sigma} = 0.218$, $\hat{\alpha} = 0.169$, and $\hat{\gamma} = 0.203$, and the fit is better, $\log L(\hat{\alpha}, \hat{\sigma}, \hat{\gamma}) = -88.92$. The likelihood-ratio test statistic is

$$\chi^2 = 2[\log L(\hat{\alpha}, \hat{\sigma}, \hat{\gamma}) - \log L(\hat{\alpha}^*, \hat{\sigma}^*, 0.25)]$$
$$= 2[-88.92 - (-89.38)] = 0.92$$

This does not exceed the critical value of 3.84, so the hypothesis cannot be rejected. As in any statistical test, an exact null hypothesis cannot be proved true—for example, γ could equal 0.2 without problem—but there is, at least, insufficient evidence to reject $\gamma = 0.25$. Adding the parameter γ to the all-or-none model does not make a significant improvement in fit over $\gamma = 0.25$.

Again, it must be emphasized that this test does not establish either $\mathcal{M}$ or $\mathcal{M}^*$ as a satisfactory model. The chi-square test permits $\gamma = 0.25$ to be retained when the all-or-none model is fit, but does not show whether the all-or-none model is really appropriate. That can be established only by one of the goodness-of-fit tests in the preceding section or by showing that the all-or-none model cannot be rejected in favor of a more general model. One of the best ways to test the overall satisfactoriness of the all-or-none model is by comparing it to the two-stage model. Almost any failure of the all-or-none property makes the best-fitting two-stage model a significant improvement, even when the two-stage model itself is not correct.

The logic of a comparison of all-or-none and two-stage models is similar to the test just run. Again, let $\mathcal{M}^*$ be the two-parameter version of the all-or-none model, but now use the six-parameter two-stage model for $\mathcal{M}$. The parameter spaces for these models were defined above (see Equation 6.5). There are four fewer free parameters in $\mathcal{M}^*$. For example, take the following 16 items:

EECEE ccc ...
EEEEE CEEEE EEccc ...
EECCE CEECE ccc ...
ECEEE EEccc ...
EEccc ...
EECEC CEEEE ccc ...
EECEE CECCC EEccc ...
CECEE CEEEE ccc ...
CEEEC ECEEE CEEEC CEEEC EEEEC EECCC CCEEE ccc ...
CEEEE EECEC CECEc cc ...
ECCEC EEEEC ECEEE ECECE CECCE EECEc cc ...
EEEEE EEEEE EEEEE CECEC Eccc ...
EEEEE EECEE EECEE EEccc ...
CEEEE EEECC CCECC Eccc ...
CEEEE ECEEE CECCE ccc ...
EEEEE CECEC EEEEc cc ...

Applying the estimators for $\mathcal{M}^*$ (Equation 6.7) with $g = 0.25$ gives $\hat{\sigma}^* = -0.233$, which is outside of Ω^*. Hence $\hat{\sigma}^* = 0$. Maximizing the likelihood for the remaining parameter α (by Equation 5.12) gives $\hat{\alpha}^* = 0.068$ and a log-likelihood of -199.44. The complexity of the likelihood function for the two-stage model makes analytic formulas for maximum-likelihood estimators very difficult. Estimation is better done by numerical minimization. Using a computer search procedure and holding $g = 0.25$, the estimates $\hat{\alpha} = 0.109$, $\hat{\beta} = 0$, $\hat{\delta} = 0.159$, $\hat{\sigma} = 0$,

$\hat{\tau} = 0$, $\hat{\pi} = 0.488$ are obtained. The log-likelihood for this point $\hat{\omega}$ is -189.57. Thus, the test statistic comparing the models is

$$\chi^2 = 2[-189.57 - (-199.44)] = 19.74$$

on four degrees of freedom. The critical value of chi-square is 9.49 at the 5% level, which indicates that the all-or-none model is not satisfactory. A model of at least the complexity of the two-stage model is required.

Problems

6.1. For a particular set of data, the sequential statistics on trials 3, 4, and 5 have frequencies

$$42, 5, 3, 13, 12, 15, 20, 38$$

(in the same order as Figure 6.2). Fitting an all-or-none model with $g = 0.25$ to these frequencies by minimizing the Pearson chi-square gives the estimates $\hat{\alpha} = 0.746$ and $\hat{\sigma} = 0.130$. Can the all-or-none model be rejected?

6.2. Use the parameter estimates obtained in Problems 5.7c and 5.8 to test whether $g = \frac{1}{3}$ is appropriate for the data in Problem 5.1.

6.3. For the data in the first example of Section 6.3, parameter estimates for the two-stage model are $\hat{\alpha} = 0.148$, $\hat{\beta} = 0.945$, $\hat{\delta} = 1$, $\hat{\pi} = 0.526$, $\hat{\sigma} = 0.102$, and $\hat{\tau} = 0.250$, with a log-likelihood of -88.82. Is the all-or-none model satisfactory?

6.4. For a certain body of data, five estimates of the parameters of the two-stage model are made, constraining some parameters and estimating others. Values of the log-likelihood are

α	β	δ	π	γ	σ	τ	$\log L(\omega)$
free	1	0	0	0.2	0	0	-158.63
free	1	0	0	0.2	free	0	-156.99
free	free	free	free	0.2	0	0	-141.08
free	0	free	free	0.2	free	free	-128.15
free	free	free	free	0.2	free	free	-127.63

a. Can the all-or-none model be rejected?
b. For the model that was retained in part a, do any items start in other than state G?

c. If the two-stage model is used, is there a path from state G directly to L, without passing through I?

6.5. Tests of the hypothesis-testing version of the all-or-none model (see Problem 5.10) are particularly simple. Show, by calculating the likelihood ratios, that a test for a particular value of the model's parameters, $[\beta_0, \tau_0, \epsilon_0]$ can be divided into three separate tests, one for each parameter. Write formulas for these tests.

6.6 Apply the test from Problem 6.5 above to the hypothesis $\omega = [0.2, 0.2, 0.5]$ for the following items:

ccc ...
CCEcc c ...
ccc ...
CEEcc c ...
ccc ...
CEECE EEEcc c ...
EEECC CCCEE ccc ...
CCECC CCEEc cc ...
ECCEE CCCEE EEccc ...
ccc ...
CECEE CECCE CECEC CEECE CECCE Eccc ...
EECEE EECEE CEECE CCEEC CCCCE ECCEE CEECC
  CCCCE ECEEE ccc ...
CCECE CECEE CCCEC EECEc ccc ...
CCEEE ECCEC ECECC CCEEE CEECC EECCE EEccc ...
CECCC ECEEC CCEEC ECECC CEEcc c ...
CCCEE ECCEC ECEEE ECECE ccc ...
ECCEC CEccc ...
ECCCC CEEEC ECEEE CCCCE ECECC EECEE EEccc ...
CEEEc cc ...
EECEE ECEEc cc ...

6.7. Suppose that an experiment is run to see which of two types of items (type A or type B) is learned more rapidly. Data are collected from 200 items of each type. A summary of the results is

Type	M_T	M_L	z
A	17.140	21.085	0.005
B	11.050	13.460	0.035

From the experimental procedure, suppose that it can reasonably be assumed that $\sigma = 0$ and $g = 0.2$ for both sets of items. Use the following procedure to test whether the learning rate is different for the two item types.

a. Estimate parameters α_A and α_B for the two types of items.
b. Pool the items and estimate a common value of α.
c. Find the likelihoods for the estimates in parts a and b; then test the null hypothesis $\alpha_A = \alpha_B$. Draw a conclusion about the learning rates.

Chapter 7

Identification of Models
and Parameters

The methods presented in the preceding two chapters allow the parameters of a Markov model to be estimated and two different models to be compared. It would appear that most psychologically interesting questions could be investigated in this way. For any theory, a model can be set up and its parameters estimated. The fit of the model tells how well the theory works, and the value of the parameters indicates the relative importance of its processes. Unfortunately, there are limitations to this way of proceeding. Not every question about a model can be answered by fitting it to data, nor can every pair of models be discriminated from each other. The ways in which these limitations affect the testing of models are discussed in this chapter.

One way to understand the difficulty is to view it as the result of equivalent models. Sometimes two models, although appearing different, make precisely identical predictions. There is no way to choose between such models, for each fits a given set of data equally well. Models that are not confounded in this way are said to be *identifiable*, while models that cannot be distinguished are said to be *not identifiably different*. The equivalence of models can be expressed in terms of their parameters. As Section 6.2 suggests, two different models are distinguished by the value of one or more parameters. If the two models are not identifiably different, the distinguishing parameters cannot be estimated, nor can questions that depend on them be answered. When parameters can be estimated, they are called *estimable* or *identifiable*.

If it were easy to spot which parameters are estimable, and thereby which models are identifiable, the problem would not be a serious one. Unfortunately, the difficulty is rarely obvious. Parameters that are quite reasonable in terms of the psychological assumptions of a model may be unestimable, and models based on very different theories may be unidentifiable. A deeper analysis of the mathematical structure of the model is needed. Although this analysis is frequently arduous, it is crucial for the user of Markov models to be sensitive to the potential problem.

With respect to the problem of model identification, it is sometimes helpful to reinterpret the difficulty as one involving the data that are used. In this view, when two models are equivalent or when parameters are not estimable, the problem is that the data are not sufficiently rich to make the necessary tests. The issue is not that an insufficient quantity of data is available; rather it is that, in terms of the model, the data contain no information about the question of interest. In this sense, data of a qualitatively different type must be found before the problem can be solved.

Problems with the identification of models are not confined to psychology, but occur whenever models are constructed that cannot be entirely observed. In statistics, for example, the conventional constraint that the effects in the analysis of variance sum to 0 serves to identify the parameters. Identifiability problems were noticed in econometrics before they became apparent in psychology (e.g., Koopmans, 1950). Much of the work with Markov models in a psychological context has been done by Greeno and his coworkers (Greeno, Millward, and Merryman, 1971; Greeno and Steiner, 1964; Steiner and Greeno, 1969; Wandell, Greeno, and Egan, 1974; see also Larkin and Wickens, 1980; Polson and Huizinga, 1974).

7.1   Unidentifiable Parameters and Equivalent Models

Two examples serve to illustrate the identifiability problem more clearly. Both are based on the all-or-none model of paired-associate learning, although in different ways. The first example is quite simple and the problems are very obvious. Suppose that one believed that learning an item required two operations. First, a code for the item is developed; then that code is stored. If not stored, the code must be developed again on the next presentation of the item. This simple theory is readily formulated as a two-state Markov model. In one state the code is known; in the other it must be developed. Let the probability of constructing a usable code be κ and the probability of storing it once constructed be σ. If these events are independent of each other, the probability of learning is $\kappa\sigma$, and the matrix of the chain is

$$\mathbf{T} = \begin{bmatrix} 1 & 0 \\ \kappa\sigma & 1 - \kappa\sigma \end{bmatrix} \tag{7.1}$$

Except for the parameters, this model is identical to the familiar all-or-none model, and all of the analysis of Chapters 3–6 applies, using $\kappa\sigma$ instead of α.

The difficulty with this model is that it depends on κ and σ only through their product; so any parameters that produce the same product make the same predictions. For example, the model with parameter vector [0.1, 0.4] cannot be distinguished from the model with parameters [0.2, 0.2], or from any other model in which $\kappa\sigma = 0.04$. Clearly, there is no way to answer questions about the individual parameter values, which are completely confounded with each other.

If this confounding is not noticed before, the difficulty appears when the parameters are estimated. When the likelihood (Equation 5.10), appropriately modified) is differentiated with respect to κ and σ, then set to 0, two independent equations are not obtained, only the same equation twice. This single equation cannot be solved for both parameters. This indicates that something is wrong. The problem is not with the maximum-likelihood procedure, for one encounters similar difficulties with any other method of estimation.

With a computer doing numerical maximization, the difficulty is not so obvious. The effect of the confounded parameters is to make the goodness-of-fit function flat in one direction or another. In this example, the likelihood is constant along the lines of constant $\kappa\sigma$. How a hill-climbing algorithm reacts to this situation depends on the way that it treats tied values. Usually an answer is produced, but the estimate is not unique. As the program does not inform the user of the difficulty, one might proceed as if the estimate had been good, even though it is not. There are usually danger signs that can be spotted, the exact nature of which depends on the particular hill-climbing algorithm. In some programs, one of the confounded parameters never changes from its initial value during the search. Other programs tend to move one of the confounded parameters to the edge of Ω and estimate the others (e.g., setting $\kappa = 1$ and estimating σ). For other algorithms, different starting points give different solutions. In every case, the result is to find a maximum, but this maximum is but one of the equivalent solutions. This multiplicity of solutions is often the best indication that there is a problem. When different starting configurations produce different parameter estimates with exactly the same function value, there is almost surely some sort of parameter confounding in the model.

The example just discussed is simple, and the problems in estimating κ and σ are obvious from an inspection of the transition matrix. More subtle problems occur when the unidentified parameters are not algebraically confounded in a simple way. Such a failure of identification occurs in the analysis of the role of errors in the all-or-none model.

Two versions of the all-or-none model are presented in Chapter 2. In the first version, the probability of passing from the guessing state to the learned state is independent of the response. As modified to three-state form in Matrix 4.14 and with the guessing rate treated as a parameter, the model is

$$s_1^{(1)} = [\sigma, (1 - \sigma)\gamma, (1 - \sigma)(1 - \gamma)]$$

$$\mathbf{T}_1 = \begin{matrix} L \\ GC \\ GE \end{matrix} \begin{bmatrix} 1 & 0 & 0 \\ \alpha & (1 - \alpha)\gamma & (1 - \alpha)(1 - \gamma) \\ \alpha & (1 - \alpha)\gamma & (1 - \alpha)(1 - \gamma) \end{bmatrix} \qquad (7.2)$$

Denote this model by $\mathcal{M}_1^*$. A second all-or-none model is developed for hypothesis-testing theories in Section 2.2 (Equation 2.7). In this model, call it $\mathcal{M}_2^*$, learning takes place only after errors:

$$s_1^{(2)} = [\tau, (1 - \tau)\epsilon, (1 - \tau)(1 - \epsilon)]$$

$$\mathbf{T}_2 = \begin{matrix} L \\ GC \\ GE \end{matrix} \begin{bmatrix} 1 & 0 & 0 \\ 0 & \epsilon & 1 - \epsilon \\ \beta & (1 - \beta)\epsilon & (1 - \beta)(1 - \epsilon) \end{bmatrix} \qquad (7.3)$$

These two models suggest a third, in which learning is possible from either the correct or the error guessing state, but at differing rates:

$$s_1 = [\rho, (1 - \rho)\pi, (1 - \rho)(1 - \pi)]$$

$$\mathbf{T} = \begin{matrix} L \\ GC \\ GE \end{matrix} \begin{bmatrix} 1 & 0 & 0 \\ \zeta & (1 - \zeta)\pi & (1 - \zeta)(1 - \pi) \\ \eta & (1 - \eta)\pi & (1 - \eta)(1 - \pi) \end{bmatrix} \qquad (7.4)$$

This model includes the others as special cases: $\mathcal{M}_1^*$ when $\zeta = \eta$ and $\mathcal{M}_2^*$ when $\zeta = 0$. Adopting the notation of likelihood-ratio testing, this is model $\mathcal{M}$.

The most general of the three models, $\mathcal{M}$, has a four-dimensional parameter space:

$$\boldsymbol{\omega} = [\zeta, \eta, \pi, \rho] \in \boldsymbol{\Omega} = [0, 1]^4$$

The other models have three-dimensional parameter spaces formed by restrictions of this space. Model $\mathcal{M}_1^*$ has parameter vector $[\alpha, \alpha, \gamma, \sigma]$ in the space $\Omega_1^* \subset \Omega$, in which the first components of $\boldsymbol{\omega}$ are identical. The parameter space of $\mathcal{M}_2^*$, Ω_2^*, is created by restricting $\boldsymbol{\omega}$ to $0 \times [0, 1]^3$. The hierarchical structure of the three models makes it appear that the assumptions leading to $\mathcal{M}_1^*$ and $\mathcal{M}_2^*$ can be tested with likelihood-ratio tests. A comparison of maximum-likelihood estimates over Ω and Ω_1^* tests the null hypothesis $\zeta = \eta$, leading to $\mathcal{M}_1^*$. Similarly, the assumptions leading to $\mathcal{M}_2^*$ are tested by the hypothesis $\zeta = 0$. As is shown below, these tests cannot be made, for the predictions of the three models are identical.

The identical nature of the three models is expressed most generally by the fact that the probability of any set of data is the same under all three models. Formally the likelihood functions are the same. Following the procedures discussed in Section 5.3, the likelihood function for $\mathcal{M}$ is

$$L(\zeta, \eta, \pi, \rho) = (1 - \rho)^{N(1-z)}\pi^C(1 - \pi)^E(1 - \zeta)^C$$
$$\times (1 - \eta)^{E-N(1-z)}b_e^{N(1-z)}[\rho + (1 - \rho)\pi b_c]^{Nz} \quad (7.5)$$

where N is the number of items, z the proportion of items for which no errors are made, E the total number of errors made over all items, C the total number of presolution correct responses, and the quantities

$$b_c = \frac{\zeta}{1 - (1 - \zeta)\pi} \quad (7.6)$$

$$b_e = \eta + (1 - \eta)\pi b_c \quad (7.7)$$

are the probabilities of no more errors following a correct response and an error, respectively. In order to find the likelihood under the reduced models, the parameter space Ω is restricted, and the parameters are renamed as those of the reduced model. For $\mathcal{M}_2^*$, setting $\zeta = 0$ in Equations 7.5–7.7 gives

$$L(0, \eta, \pi, \rho) = (1 - \rho)^{N(1-z)}\pi^C(1 - \pi)^E(1 - \eta)^{E-N(1-z)}\eta^{N(1-z)}\rho^{Nz}$$

which becomes

$$L_2^*(\beta, \epsilon, \tau) = (1 - \tau)^{N(1-z)}\epsilon^C(1 - \epsilon)^E(1 - \beta)^{E-N(1-z)}\beta^{N(1-z)}\tau^{Nz} \quad (7.8)$$

Analogous restriction obtains Equation 5.18 for L_1^*.

If $\mathcal{M}_2^*$ is really a restriction of $\mathcal{M}$, the maximum value of $L(\zeta, \eta, \pi, \rho)$

over Ω is almost always larger than the maximum value of $L_2^*(\beta, \epsilon, \tau)$ over Ω_2^*. If $\mathcal{M}_1^*$ is not a restriction, then by assigning appropriate values to the parameters of Equation 7.8, $L_2^*(\beta, \epsilon, \tau)$ can take on any value that is attained by Equation 7.5. In fact, this is the case. When the substitutions

$$\beta = b_e = \frac{\zeta\pi + \eta(1 - \pi)}{1 - (1 - \zeta)\pi}$$

$$\epsilon = (1 - \zeta)\pi \tag{7.9}$$

$$\tau = \rho + (1 - \rho)\pi b_c = \rho + \frac{(1 - \rho)\pi\zeta}{1 - (1 - \zeta)\pi}$$

are made in Equation 7.8, then Equation 7.5 is obtained (see Problem 7.1). So the two likelihoods are identical. Just as the predictions of the coding-and-storage all-or-none model (Equation 7.1) depend only on the single product $\kappa\sigma$, the predictions of $\mathcal{M}$ depend only on the three parameters of Equations 7.9. Similar assignments make model $\mathcal{M}$ equivalent to $\mathcal{M}_1^*$ (see Problem 7.3).

The three substitutions (Equations 7.9) are not so arbitrary as they may at first seem. They are the quantities in model $\mathcal{M}$ that correspond to the parameters of $\mathcal{M}_2^*$. Thus, β is the probability that no more errors follow an error, ϵ is the probability that one presolution correct response follows another, and τ is the probability that no errors are made during learning. Of course, setting corresponding quantities equal does not make the likelihood for any two models identical, but in the case of these models it does.

The equivalence of the likelihoods means that $\mathcal{M}_2^*$ is not a restriction of $\mathcal{M}$ and that there is no hope of testing the hypothesis that reduces $\mathcal{M}$ to $\mathcal{M}_2^*$. For any maximum-likelihood estimate $\hat{\omega} = [\hat{\zeta}, \hat{\eta}, \hat{\pi}, \hat{\rho}]$ from $\mathcal{M}$, Equations 7.9 give values of $\hat{\omega}_2$ with the same likelihood. Thus, the ratio of likelihoods is 1, and the chi-square testing their difference is 0.

Not only is it impossible to test the parameter restriction of $\mathcal{M}$, but the parameters of $\mathcal{M}$ cannot even be estimated. Because a four-parameter model is equivalent to a three-parameter model, there are many combinations of ζ, η, π, and ρ that produce the same three parameters of $\mathcal{M}_2^*$. These have the same likelihood, so a maximum-likelihood solution cannot distinguish among them. Hence, $\mathcal{M}$ contains an excess parameter and ω is underdetermined. The practical problem is exactly the same as in the more obvious case of estimating κ and σ in Equation 7.1. When the likelihood in $\mathcal{M}$ (Equation 7.5) is differentiated with respect to each of the four parameters and the four results set equal to 0, only three independent equations are obtained. From this, only three parameters can be uniquely estimated, so the parameters of $\mathcal{M}$ cannot be identified.

This analysis shows the importance of investigating questions of identifiability before testing models. If one were unaware of the problem, one might formulate a psychological question as a comparison of $\mathcal{M}$ and $\mathcal{M}_2^*$, without recognizing that failure to reject the hypothesis $\zeta = 0$ has nothing to do with the data.

Even when testing models that are truly different, problems of parameter identifiability are important. In a hierarchy of models, the number of degrees of freedom in a likelihood-ratio test depends on the difference between the number of parameters in the two models. However, parameters that are not estimable cannot be counted here. For example, consider a very general version of the two-stage model:

$$s_1 = [\rho, (1 - \rho)\theta\epsilon, (1 - \rho)\theta(1 - \epsilon), (1 - \rho)(1 - \theta)\pi,$$
$$(1 - \rho)(1 - \theta)(1 - \pi)]$$

$$T = \begin{bmatrix} 1 & 0 & 0 & 0 & 0 \\ \phi & (1 - \phi)\epsilon & (1 - \phi)(1 - \epsilon) & 0 & 0 \\ \psi & (1 - \psi)\epsilon & (1 - \psi)(1 - \epsilon) & 0 & 0 \\ \zeta\phi & \zeta(1 - \phi)\epsilon & \zeta(1 - \phi)(1 - \epsilon) & (1 - \zeta)\pi & (1 - \zeta)(1 - \pi) \\ \eta\psi & \eta(1 - \psi)\epsilon & \eta(1 - \psi)(1 - \epsilon) & (1 - \eta)\pi & (1 - \eta)(1 - \pi) \end{bmatrix}$$
$$(7.10)$$

correct responses being made from the first, second, and fourth states and errors from the third and fifth. The all-or-none model is a special case of Equations 7.10; the restrictions $\phi = \psi = 1$ and $\theta = 0$ reduce this model to Equations 7.4. Eight parameters (ϕ, ψ, ζ, η, ϵ, π, ρ, and θ) must be estimated for Equations 7.10, and only four (ζ, η, π, and ρ) for Equations 7.4. Thus, a likelihood-ratio test on four degrees of freedom apparently results. Knowing π or ρ from the experimental situation does not alter this difference. But things are not so simple. It has already been demonstrated that Equations 7.4 represent the same model as the simpler matrices in Equations 7.2 or Equations 7.3. These have one fewer parameter than Equations 7.4, which suggests that the test should be based on $8 - 3 = 5$ degrees of freedom. However, to complicate things still more, Equations 7.10 also contain unidentifiable parameters—for example, as in Equations 7.4, ζ and η are not identifiable. In fact, it can be shown that the model of Equations 7.10 is equivalent to a special case of the two-stage model:

$$\mathbf{s_1} = [\sigma, (1 - \sigma)\tau, (1 - \sigma)(1 - \tau)]$$

$$\mathbf{T} = \begin{bmatrix} 1 & 0 & 0 \\ \beta & 1 - \beta & 0 \\ \alpha\beta & \alpha(1 - \beta) & 1 - \alpha \end{bmatrix}$$

$$\mathbf{R} = \begin{bmatrix} 1 & 0 \\ \pi & 1 - \pi \\ \gamma & 1 - \gamma \end{bmatrix}$$

This model has six parameters. The appropriate reduced model—either Equations 7.2 or Equations 7.3—has three parameters, and so the correct test is on $6 - 3 = 3$ degrees of freedom.

Problems of identifiability are not unique to Markov models. They arise in any situation where models are compared or theories are tested against each other. Models or theories expressed only as verbal statements suffer from identification problems, although the theories are rarely specified precisely enough to make the problems obvious. Differences between many verbal theories are illusory, and no amount of discussion renders the differences testable. The formal structure of the stochastic models makes it possible to discover and analyze the problem. Quite simply, models that are not identifiably different have identical likelihood functions for any experimental outcome. Only when the models are sufficiently exact for the likelihood function to be calculated is this similarity evident.

7.2 Vector-Space Representation†

Viewing Markov models as transformations between vector spaces, as discussed at the end of Section 3.1, makes identifiability problems somewhat clearer. In essence, models that are equivalent to each other are representations of the same vector-space operations, but appear different because they are expressed in terms of different bases (see Section C.5). Conversely, two models that are the same when viewed as vector-space transformations must be equivalent, even when their matrices are different. Recall the illustration of the transition process (Figure 3.1), which showed successive state vectors as points in a vector space. If the basis that is used to describe this space is changed,

---

† Material in this section is largely drawn from Larkin and Wickens (1980); see also Wandell, Greeno, and Egan (1974).

the mathematical form of the matrix that represents the transformation changes, but the geometric picture stays the same. This is what happens with equivalent models.

An example that prefigures the material in this section, appeared in Chapter 4. In Section 4.2, it was demonstrated that the three-state version of the all-or-none model derives from that of the two-stage version by a basis change (see Equation 4.21). The movement between the points of the state vectors, shown in Figure 4.1, does not change. Thus, the response predictions are the same, and the two- and three-state models are not identifiably different.

The equivalence of the likelihood under a basic change is readily demonstrated. Suppose that the responses on the first t trials are X_1, X_2, ..., X_t. The likelihood of this sequence, using selection matrices $\mathbf{W}_X$ (which can be either probabilistic or deterministic) and the full transition matrix, is

$$L(\omega) = \mathbf{s}_1 \mathbf{W}_{X_1} \mathbf{T} \mathbf{W}_{X_2} \mathbf{T} \ldots \mathbf{T} \mathbf{W}_{X_t} \mathbf{1}' \qquad (7.11)$$

(see the discussion of likelihoods in Section 4.4, particularly Equation 4.45). Now consider what happens to Equation 7.11 when the basis of the space is changed. Let $\mathbf{B}$ be a matrix with rows containing the new basis elements expressed in terms of the old. If the new basis expresses exactly the same space as the original basis, then $\mathbf{B}$ is nonsingular and $\mathbf{B}^{-1}$ exists. Then, a vector such as $\mathbf{s}_1$ is changed to the new basis by multiplication:

$$\tilde{\mathbf{s}}_1 = \mathbf{s}_1 \mathbf{B}^{-1} \qquad (7.12)$$

The tilde denotes the model in the new basis. In order to assure that the elements of $\tilde{\mathbf{s}}$ sum to 1 for any vector $\mathbf{s}$ in the original basis, it is necessary that the new basis vectors (or rows of $\mathbf{B}$) sum to 1, that is,

$$\mathbf{B1}' = \mathbf{1}' \qquad (7.13)$$

A transformation $\mathbf{T}$, in this case the transition matrix, is converted to

$$\tilde{\mathbf{T}} = \mathbf{B} \mathbf{T} \mathbf{B}^{-1} \qquad (7.14)$$

(see Equation C.30). The selection matrices $\mathbf{W}_X$ are also transformations of a space into itself, so Equation C.30 applies again:

$$\tilde{\mathbf{W}}_X = \mathbf{B} \mathbf{W}_X \mathbf{B}^{-1} \qquad (7.15)$$

Writing the likelihood in the new basis using Equation 7.11 with tildes, then applying the basis transformation as expressed in Equations 7.12–7.15 gives

$$L(\tilde{\omega}) = \tilde{s}_1 \tilde{W}_{X_1} \hat{T} \tilde{W}_{X_2} \hat{T} \cdots \hat{T} \tilde{W}_{X_t} 1'$$
$$= (s_1 B^{-1})(BW_{X_1} B^{-1})(BTB^{-1})(BW_{X_2} B^{-1})(BTB^{-1}) \cdots$$
$$\times (BTB^{-1})(BW_{X_t} B^{-1})(B1')$$
$$= s_1 I W_{X_1} ITIW_{X_2} IT \cdots TIW_{X_t} I1'$$
$$= s_1 W_{X_1} TW_{X_2} T \cdots TW_{X_t} 1' = L(\omega)$$

The last line is Equation 7.11 in the original basis, proving that the two likelihoods are the same.[†] Thus, models differing by a basis change are not identifiable, at least for the correct and error responses used here.

For example, version $\mathcal{M}$ of the all-or-none model is transformed into the $\mathcal{M}_2^*$ version by the basis-change matrices

$$B = \begin{bmatrix} 1 & 0 & 0 \\ \dfrac{-b_c}{1-b_c} & \dfrac{1}{1-b_c} & 0 \\ 0 & 0 & 1 \end{bmatrix} \quad \text{and} \quad B^{-1} = \begin{bmatrix} 1 & 0 & 0 \\ b_c & 1-b_c & 0 \\ 0 & 0 & 1 \end{bmatrix}$$

where b_c is given by Equation 7.6. Applying these to the transformation matrix from Equations 7.4 gives

$$\tilde{T} = BTB^{-1}$$

$$= \begin{bmatrix} 1 & 0 & 0 \\ \dfrac{-b_c}{1-b_c} & \dfrac{1}{1-b_c} & 0 \\ 0 & 0 & 1 \end{bmatrix} \begin{bmatrix} 1 & 0 & 0 \\ \zeta & (1-\zeta)\pi & (1-\zeta)(1-\pi) \\ \eta & (1-\eta)\pi & (1-\eta)(1-\pi) \end{bmatrix}$$

$$\begin{bmatrix} 1 & 0 & 0 \\ b_c & 1-b_c & 0 \\ 0 & 0 & 1 \end{bmatrix}$$

$$= \begin{bmatrix} 1 & 0 & 0 \\ 0 & (1-\zeta)\pi & 1-(1-\zeta)\pi \\ b_e & (1-b_e)(1-\zeta)\pi & (1-b_e)[1-(1-\zeta)\pi] \end{bmatrix}$$

[†] This demonstration is more delicate when the size of the models' state spaces are not the same, as with Equation 7.4 and the two-state version of the all-or-none model (Equation 2.5). However, the same result can be obtained if some fairly natural restrictions are placed on the larger model. The resulting analysis is quite similar to that at the end of the discussion of likelihoods in Section 4.4.

employing the notational simplification $b_e = \eta + (1 - \eta)\pi b_c$ from Equation 7.7. The initial vector of $\mathcal{M}$ is transformed by Equation 7.12 to

$$\tilde{s}_1 = s_1 B^{-1} = [C, (1 - C)(1 - \zeta)\pi, (1 - C)(1 - (1 - \zeta)\pi)]$$

where $C = \rho + (1 - \rho)\pi b_c$. With the exception of notation, these results are identical to the transition matrix and initial vector of model $\mathcal{M}_2^*$ in Equations 7.3. The parameter definitions needed to make the notation identical are exactly those in Equations 7.9.

The above discussion shows that models differing only by a basis change in their representations are not identifiably different from each other, but it does not give an easy way to spot when this is true, nor to select the matrix B of the basis change that turns one model into another. A complete analysis requires a closer look at what characteristics of the matrix transformations T and W_X are the same under any basis, that is, at the geometry of the model. One invariant property of a linear transformation is the set of eigenvectors and eigenvalues of the transformation (see Section C.6). The eigenvectors and eigenvalues of the transition matrix, which characterize the way that the model evolves toward its final state, are the same for any two equivalent models. For example, the eigenvalues of T for the all-or-none model $\mathcal{M}$ are

$$\lambda_1 = 1 \qquad \lambda_2 = 1 - \zeta\pi - \eta(1 - \pi) \qquad \lambda_3 = 0 \qquad (7.16)$$

while those for $\mathcal{M}_2^*$ are

$$\lambda_1 = 1 \qquad \lambda_2 = 1 - \beta(1 - \epsilon) \qquad \lambda_3 = 0 \qquad (7.17)$$

For the models to be equivalent, Equations 7.16 and 7.17 must be identical. The first and last eigenvalues are no problem; while for λ_2 to be the same, $\beta(1 - \epsilon)$ must equal $\zeta\pi + \eta(1 - \pi)$. This property is embodied in the substitutions of Equations 7.9.

Making the eigenvalues, such as Equations 7.16 and 7.17, identical is one step in finding the change of basis that turns one model into another. Constructing the remainder of the basis change is more complicated. In essence, it involves selecting B so that the relationships among the eigenvectors of T are preserved and so that the new response-selection operators, W_X, are diagonal matrices containing the correct mappings (see Larkin and Wickens, 1980). Although these conditions are relatively straightforward, the mechanics of the calculation are rather tedious for all but the simplest models, and so are not treated here.

Fortunately, much useful analysis can be done by examining the eigenvalues alone. Where the eigenvalues of two models can be brought into correspondence by a parameter substitution, as was the case with Equations 7.16 and 7.17, it is wise to suspect equivalence. On the other hand, the transition matrix of the general two-stage model,

$$\mathbf{T} = \begin{bmatrix} 1 & 0 & 0 \\ \delta & 1 - \delta & 0 \\ \alpha\beta & \alpha(1 - \beta) & 1 - \alpha \end{bmatrix}$$

has eigenvalues

$$\lambda_1 = 1 \qquad \lambda_2 = 1 - \delta \qquad \lambda_3 = 1 - \alpha \qquad (7.18)$$

No relationship between the parameters of this model and those of the all-or-none model can make Equations 7.18 the same as Equations 7.17. Only two eigenvalues in Equations 7.17 are nonzero, while all three in Equations 7.18 can be nonzero. So the models are identifiably different.

The nonzero eigenvalues of $\mathbf{T}$ are important in matching models, for these values, with their associated eigenvectors, convey all information about repeated applications of $\mathbf{T}$. Models may contain additional zero eigenvalues without compromising equivalence. For example, the eigenvalues of the long-and-short model (Equations 2.18) are

$$\lambda_1 = 1 \qquad \lambda_2 = 1 - \gamma(1 - \phi) - \delta\phi \qquad \lambda_3 = 1 - \alpha \qquad \lambda_4 = 0$$

Although this model has four eigenvalues, only three are nonzero, and these can be matched to those in Equations 7.18. This correspondence suggests (correctly) that the long-and-short model cannot be differentiated from the general two-stage model. Furthermore, the fact that the long-and-short model (with its initial vector) contains more parameters than does the fully parameterized two-stage model suggests that some of its parameters are not identifiable. More extensive analysis is needed to reveal the details, but the danger has been indicated.

7.3 Treatment of Identifiability Problems

The problems of identifiability are real and serious, and a researcher must be prepared to face them in one way or another. This section discusses some of the options that are available. In essence, there are three choices. The first is simply to recognize and accept the fact that one is working with a class of equivalent models. If this is not possible, one must either make additional assumptions to render the model identifiable or else change the experiment that is used to investigate it.

Equivalence Classes of Models

It is neither necessary nor possible to resolve all the problems of identifiability before many important questions can be answered. The set of equivalent models form a class whose members are not distinguishable from each other, but that has properties that can be tested against the properties of other classes of models. Even models with surplus parameters have likelihoods, although there are no unique parameter estimates. In essence, the whole class of models with identical likelihoods is considered at once. Likelihood-ratio tests compare this class with different classes of models that subsume the class in question or are subsumed by it. For example, although the three forms of the all-or-none model cannot be distinguished from each other, they all restrict the data more than do any of the many equivalent two-stage models. The need for an intermediate state can be tested without making a choice among the members of the classes.

Something like this always happens when models are tested, for every model has a host of other models that are equivalent to it. One always works, at least implicitly, with equivalence classes. The important thing is to recognize whether one's questions refer to other classes or to different members of the same class. In the former case, identifiability problems are irrelevant. Often only one member of the equivalence class is of interest, and the rest can be ignored. In a hypothesis-testing situation, for example, the experimental paradigm and the theory dictate that one look at the all-or-none model in the form $\mathcal{M}_2^*$, not in the form of $\mathcal{M}$ or $\mathcal{M}_1^*$.

When several equivalent models are potentially of interest, it is helpful to pick a simple version as representative of the class. Among the all-or-none models, for example, there is little point in working with model $\mathcal{M}$ (Equations 7.4), which contains unidentifiable parameters. Both model $\mathcal{M}_1^*$ and model $\mathcal{M}_2^*$ (Equations 7.2 and 7.3) are easier to use. Either one can be selected as the representative all-or-none model. One advantage of working with models for which all parameters are estimable is that the number of degrees of freedom for a likelihood-ratio (or other) test is easier to determine. Parameters that cannot be identified cannot be counted as part of either the full or the reduced model. With simple representatives of the equivalence classes, these numbers are clear.

Which member of a class of models is the simplest depends on what one is going to do with it. Where there is much numerical calculation to be done, the version with the smallest number of states may be best. This suggests using the two-state version of $\mathcal{M}_1^*$. But this is not the only criterion. Among the three-parameter versions of the all-or-none model, there is sometimes an advantage in selecting $\mathcal{M}_2^*$ because it does not allow transitions from the transient correct-response state into the absorbing state and has what are known as *observable states*. This means that the state of the process on any trial can be determined exactly (rather than probabilistically) from the string of responses. For example, the response string $C, E, E, C, E, c, c, c, \ldots$, implies the sequence of states $GE, GE, GE, GC, GE, L, L, L, \ldots$, and no other. Neither model $\mathcal{M}$ nor model $\mathcal{M}_1^*$ has the property. In both of these models, correct responses following the last error can be made from either GC or L. Models with observable states generally have fewer internal transitions than do other equivalent models. Maximum-likelihood estimates of the transition probabilities between states are also simple: they are just the relative frequency of passage from the originating to the final state (see Problems 5.10, 5.11, and 6.5). Not all classes of models contain simple versions with observable states, but the concept provides one reasonable guideline in picking a representative version.

Parametric Restrictions

At times one is interested in questions that concern two members of the same equivalence class. Ultimately one wants to construct psychologically plausible models, and such models cannot be chosen only on the basis of mathematical convenience. As the representation of a psychological theory, there is nothing wrong with an overparameterized model, and important questions may concern models that are not identifiable. Obviously, tests of these models cannot be made directly. One way to make the test is to place *identifying restrictions* on some of the parameters so as to make the models different. In this way, the least interesting parameters can be eliminated from the model in order to test the more interesting ones.

The all-or-none example again provides an illustration (for other examples, see Greeno, 1967, 1968). The hypothesis $\zeta = \eta$ in model $\mathcal{M}$, which reduces the model to $\mathcal{M}_1^*$, implies that the effectiveness of a response for learning is independent of its correctness. Clearly this question has psychological interest. However, a model for which this hypothesis holds has the same likelihood as one for which it does not, which means that the hypothesis cannot be directly tested. Model $\mathcal{M}$ depends on the four parameters ζ, η, π, and ρ, only three of which can be estimated, and so the hypothesis provides no true restriction. Suppose now that $\rho = 0$. With this restriction, the model's other parameters become identifiable and a reduced model similar to $\mathcal{M}_1^*$ can be compared with the full model. To assure that the assumption $\rho = 0$ is appropriate, an experiment must be designed in which it is not possible for an item to start in the learned state. This can be done by using sufficiently new and difficult material.

Equations 7.9, which relate the parameters of $\mathcal{M}$ to those of $\mathcal{M}_2^*$, provide another view of this restriction. The parameters of $\mathcal{M}_2^*$ (β, ϵ, and τ) are estimable, while the parameters of $\mathcal{M}$ would be estimable only if the three equations could be solved to get ζ, η, π, and ρ. As three equations cannot be solved for four parameters, a fourth equation is needed. The restriction $\rho = 0$ provides the missing equation. Solving the complete set gives

$$\zeta = \frac{\tau(1 - \epsilon)}{\epsilon + \tau(1 - \epsilon)} \qquad \eta = \frac{\beta - \tau}{1 - \tau} \qquad \pi = \epsilon + \tau(1 - \epsilon) \qquad (7.19)$$

These equations translate estimates of the parameters of $\mathcal{M}_2^*$ to parameters of the restricted $\mathcal{M}$. The hypothesis $\zeta = \eta$ can now be expressed as a hypothesis about the parameters of $\mathcal{M}_2^*$. Equating the first two members of Equations 7.19, then simplifying gives

$$\tau = \frac{\beta\epsilon}{1 - \beta(1 - \epsilon)} \qquad (7.20)$$

As Equation 7.20 is expressed in terms of the estimable parameters of $\mathcal{M}_2^*$, it is a true restriction and a testable hypothesis. Thus, it can be used to address the original question.

The analysis in the preceding paragraph also brings to light a limitation with the test. The parameter relationships (Equations 7.19) depend critically on the parameter τ of $\mathcal{M}_2^*$, and the hypothesis about learning rates is turned into a hypothesis about τ in Equation 7.20. In the data, τ is estimated by the probability of learning without errors. However, unless the learning rate is very high, only a small proportion of the items show zero errors, making τ very hard to determine accurately. Unless the number of items is very large, Equations 7.19 are not very accurate, and there is little power to detect violations of the hypothesis. Still worse, the critical data come from the early trials of the experiment, during which the subject is likely to behave in a relatively less stable manner so that minor violations of the model are likely. Thus, even though the restrictions enable a test to be run, the test is a weak one.

Analysis in a Broader Domain

When faced with a question concerning two models that cannot be identified, the best and most powerful solution is to expand the experiment. The fact that two models are equivalent means that the data at hand do not bear on their difference. By expanding the model to permit a wider range of data to be interpreted, one can address the difference between models directly.

For example, so far in this chapter, responses are treated as correct or in error, and only that information is modeled in the response process and incorporated into the likelihood function. The response mapping considerably simplifies the information in the state space. If more detailed information about the state is available, many of the identification problems go away. The trick is to locate additional data that relate to the state.

In many experiments, such additional sources of information are not hard to find. Sometimes the exact response that is made, rather than just its correctness, provides the needed information; sometimes the relationship between the particular stimulus that is presented and the particular response that it elicits provides the information. The response latency, $\mathscr{L}$, can often be used. For example, consider the expected latency on trials following the last error (see Problem 4.12). Although the sequence of errors predicted by models $\mathcal{M}_1^*$ and $\mathcal{M}_2^*$ is the same, whenever the latencies in the two correct-response states are different, the two models predict different latency functions (see Figure 7.1). In model $\mathcal{M}_2^*$, the trial of last error (L) occurs when the process passes the absorbing state, and $E(\mathscr{L}_{L+t})$ is constant. For $\mathcal{M}_1^*$, however, some responses from state GC may follow the last error; so $E(\mathscr{L}_{L+t})$ starts nearer to the expected latency for guesses, $E(\mathscr{L}|G)$, and asymptotes to $E(\mathscr{L}|L)$ as t increases. This discriminates the models.

When no additional response information is available, the experiment can be broadened. Although two theories give rise to models that make identical predictions for a particular experiment, there are larger contexts in which the predictions differ. The models are expanded so that they make predictions about a wider domain of behavior and so that previously unidentified parameters generate differential predictions.

As an example of this procedure, consider the all-or-none model presented in Equation 7.1, in which the two parameters κ and σ are completely confounded. These parameters appear only as the product $\kappa\sigma$, and so cannot be identified; nor can the model be discriminated from version $\mathcal{M}_1^*$ of the all-or-none model, with a single learning parameter α. Clearly, no mathematical treatment is going to correct this problem. However, suppose that two manipulations of the items could be devised, one of which primarily affected κ, the other σ. To select these, one must go back to the theory underlying the model. For example, the theory may suggest that when items are very similar to each other, it is difficult to develop a good code, but that very discriminable items are easy to code. Thus, manipulating item discriminability should

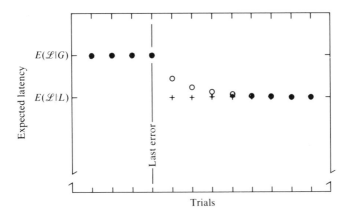

Figure 7.1   Predicted mean latencies under models $\mathcal{M}_1^*$ (circles) and $\mathcal{M}_2^*$ (crosses) for responses following the last error.

change κ. Storage of the resulting codes (σ) may be relatively unaffected by this manipulation, but depend, say, on the amount of time allotted to study the items. Thus, the model is expanded to predict learning rates over several conditions.

Now consider an experiment in which items are chosen so as to vary these two characteristics independently, say, by combining three levels of similarity with three different study times to create nine types of items organized in two crossed factors. The nine cells and the learning rates under the $\kappa\sigma$ model are

		Study time		
		Short	Medium	Long
	Low	$\kappa_1\sigma_1$	$\kappa_1\sigma_2$	$\kappa_1\sigma_3$
Similarity	Intermediate	$\kappa_2\sigma_1$	$\kappa_2\sigma_2$	$\kappa_2\sigma_3$
	High	$\kappa_3\sigma_1$	$\kappa_3\sigma_2$	$\kappa_3\sigma_3$

A test of this model is analogous to the test for an interaction in an analysis of variance. Let i index the similarity manipulation and j the study-time manipulation. The specific model in each cell is the two-state all-or-none model, and the parameter values across cells form a hierarchical pair of models with parameters as follows:

Full model: The learning rate for items of type ij is α_{ij}, estimated separately for each item type. Ignoring the initial parameters, the full parameter vector is

$$\boldsymbol{\omega} = [\alpha_{11}, \alpha_{12}, \alpha_{13}, \alpha_{21}, \alpha_{22}, \alpha_{23}, \alpha_{31}, \alpha_{32}, \alpha_{33}]$$

Reduced model: The learning rate for items of type ij is $\alpha_{ij} = \kappa_i \sigma_j$. The restricted parameter vector is

$$\boldsymbol{\omega}^* = [\kappa_1, \kappa_2, \kappa_3, \sigma_1, \sigma_2, \sigma_3]$$

The second model is a reduced version of the first, so it can be tested against the first with a likelihood-ratio test. If the reduced model can be rejected, there are grounds to reject the simple $\kappa\sigma$ model.

In making this test, it is important to be sure that the parameters of both models are identifiable, so that the correct number of degrees of freedom is used. All the parameters of the general model are estimable, but, as written above, there is a problem with the reduced model. One could multiply every κ_i by a constant and divide every σ_j by the same constant without changing the learning rates. To make the parameters identifiable, one further restriction is needed. There are many ways to do this; the value of any one of the κ_i or σ_j could be fixed, as could some combination, such as the sum or the product of either the three κ values or the three σ values. An analogy can be made to the analysis of variance, where side conditions are put on the parameters of the main effects to make them estimable. Whatever restriction is chosen, $\boldsymbol{\omega}^*$ has five, not six, free parameters. The vector $\boldsymbol{\omega}$ still has nine parameters; so a likelihood-ratio test of the $\kappa\sigma$ model is on four degrees of freedom.

The construction of this revised experiment has done more than solve the identifiability problem; it has also put the experimenter in a much better position with regard to statistical testing. The situation has been changed from one in which the $\kappa\sigma$ model could be tested only by fitting it to the data and looking at the overall fit to one in which it is tested as an explicit null hypothesis against a more general alternative. As discussed in Chapter 6, this gives more useful evidence for or against the model. Of course, the additional assumptions about the dependency of κ and σ on the items' properties go beyond the original statement of the model and may themselves be incorrect. In fact, these assumptions are what are tested, rather than simple goodness of fit of the all-or-none model. But questions of this sort get more deeply at the relationship between coding and storage at the foundation of the $\kappa\sigma$ model, and so these questions are the ones that best test the underlying theory. Dealing with the identifiability problem of the model leads to a sharper analysis of the underlying theory.

Problems

7.1. Show that the substitutions of Equations 7.9 make Equation 7.8 identical to Equation 7.5.

7.2. Use model $\mathcal{M}_1^*$ to express the quantities represented by the parameters of model $\mathcal{M}_2^*$, thus finding the parameter equivalences that make the two models identical. Solve the equations to express the parameters of $\mathcal{M}_2^*$ in terms of those of $\mathcal{M}_1^*$.

7.3. The parameters β, τ, and ϵ of $\mathcal{M}_2^*$ are easy to estimate and to test (see Problems 5.10 and 6.5), while those of $\mathcal{M}_1^*$ are much more difficult to work with. Because the two models are equivalent, the simpler can be used. Take the estimators $\hat{\beta}$, $\hat{\tau}$, and $\hat{\epsilon}$ from Problem 5.10 and substitute them in the relationships derived in Problem 7.2 to obtain estimators of α, σ, and γ for $\mathcal{M}_1^*$. The results should be identical to the estimators originally derived in Problem 5.8 and given in Equation 6.8.

7.4. For the expanded $\kappa\sigma$ model, construct appropriate parameter vectors $\boldsymbol{\omega}$ and $\boldsymbol{\omega}^*$ to examine the following questions. Assume τ (unknown) and g (known) are the same for all items. Indicate the correct degrees of freedom for the tests.
   a. Is the $\kappa\sigma$ model better than the simple model $\mathcal{M}_1^*$?
   b. Does κ vary with discriminability?
   c. Does σ vary with study time?
   d. Why is it not possible to test whether κ varies with study time in this way?

7.5. Consider the following paired-associate model. The subject starts in one of a pair of guessing states GE and GC related by the guessing rate g. There is a probability of α of departing from these states by permanent learning, going to an absorbing state L; alternatively, with probability $(1 - \alpha)\delta$, the process passes to a short-term memory state, S. From S, there is a probability β that the item is learned on each trial (passing to L) and a probability $(1 - \beta)(1 - \delta)$ that it is forgotten. Thus, the matrix of the chain is

$$
\begin{array}{c}
L \\ S \\ GC \\ GE
\end{array}
\begin{bmatrix}
1 & 0 & 0 & 0 \\
\beta & (1 - \beta)\delta & (1 - \beta)(1 - \delta)g & (1 - \beta)(1 - \delta)(1 - g) \\
\alpha & (1 - \alpha)\delta & (1 - \alpha)(1 - \delta)g & (1 - \alpha)(1 - \delta)(1 - g) \\
\alpha & (1 - \alpha)\delta & (1 - \alpha)(1 - \delta)g & (1 - \alpha)(1 - \delta)(1 - g)
\end{bmatrix}
$$

Correct responses are made from states GC, S, and L; and errors, from state GE. Find the eigenvalues and show that they can be put in correspondence with those of the all-or-none model (say, version $\mathcal{M}_1^*$). In fact, this model is equivalent to the all-or-none model (see Greeno, 1967; Greeno, Millward, and Merryman, 1971; Larkin and Wickens, 1980). *Note:* Finding eigenvalues using the characteristic equation (Equation C.38) is much simplified by the following identity for the determinant of a partitioned matrix containing a block of zeros:

$$\begin{vmatrix} \mathbf{A} & \mathbf{0} \\ \mathbf{B} & \mathbf{C} \end{vmatrix} = |\mathbf{A}||\mathbf{C}|$$

7.6. Show that the model with transition matrix and response mapping

$$\mathbf{T} = \begin{bmatrix} 1 & 0 & 0 & 0 \\ \alpha & (1-\alpha)\delta & (1-\alpha)(1-\delta) & 0 \\ \beta & (1-\beta)\delta & (1-\beta)(1-\delta) & 0 \\ 0 & \epsilon\delta & \epsilon(1-\delta) & 1-\epsilon \end{bmatrix} \qquad \mathbf{r} = \begin{bmatrix} 1 \\ \gamma \\ \pi \\ g \end{bmatrix}$$

cannot be an all-or-none model, but may be equivalent to a two-stage model. See the note to Problem 7.5.

7.7. Show that the eigenvalues of the five-state version of the two-stage model of Equations 7.10 can be put in correspondence with those of the three-state version, Equations 7.18. What values must α and δ take in the reduced model for it to be equivalent to Equations 7.10?

7.8. Show that model $\mathcal{M}$ is changed into model $\mathcal{M}_1^*$ by the basis transformation

$$\mathbf{B} = \begin{bmatrix} 1 & 0 & 0 \\ \dfrac{\eta-\zeta}{1-\zeta} & \dfrac{1-\eta}{1-\zeta} & 0 \\ 0 & 0 & 1 \end{bmatrix}$$

Chapter 8

Markov Chains
Without Absorbing States

The Markov chains in Chapters 3–7 are finite and have at least one state in which the process is absorbed. Both of these restrictions—the need for an absorbing state and the requirement that the number of states be finite—can be relaxed. The next two chapters treat chains of these classes: chains without absorbing states in this chapter and chains with an infinite number of states in the next.

Several finite-state models without absorbing states are discussed in Chapter 2. The prime examples are the sequence-of-choice models (Matrices 2.23, 2.24, and 2.25) and the probability-learning models, say, in the form of Matrix 2.28. As a simple prototype of a choice model, suppose that when the first of two alternatives, A and B, is chosen, the subject selects A again on the next trial with probability $1 - \alpha$ and changes to B with probability α; while if B is chosen, the corresponding probabilities of staying with B or shifting to A are $1 - \beta$ and β. Thus, generalizing Matrix 2.23 gives

$$\mathbf{T} = \begin{bmatrix} 1 - \alpha & \alpha \\ \beta & 1 - \beta \end{bmatrix} \qquad (8.1)$$

The random-walk process discussed in Section 2.4 provides a second example. In the transition among states $S_0, S_1, \ldots, S_{n-1}$, suppose that S_0

and S_{n-1} reflect the process in the opposite direction (Equation 2.32). For example, when $n = 4$, the model has the form

$$
\mathbf{T} = \begin{bmatrix}
1 - \gamma\eta & \gamma\eta & 0 & 0 \\
\gamma(1 - \eta) & 1 - \gamma & \gamma\eta & 0 \\
0 & \gamma(1 - \eta) & 1 - \gamma & \gamma\eta \\
0 & 0 & \gamma(1 - \eta) & 1 - \gamma(1 - \eta)
\end{bmatrix} \quad (8.2)
$$

Clearly, models with transition matrices such as Matrix 8.1 or Matrix 8.2 have very different properties from absorbing chains. Except in a few special cases (such as γ or η being 0), by allowing a sufficiently large number of transitions, it is possible to get from any state to any other state and back again. Two states with this property are said to *communicate* with each other. In a chain with an absorbing state, not all states communicate, for there is no way to get from the absorbing state to any other state. In Matrices 8.1 and 8.2, every pair of states communicates with each other, so the process certainly returns to any given state again and again, although the number of trials required for each return is not always the same.

The chains just described generate an indefinitely long sequence of states (choices in the example of Matrix 8.1) that fluctuate among the alternatives, but never remain with any one of them. Thus, any statement about the ultimate fate of the process must be probabilistic in nature. The likelihood of ultimately being in each of the states can be specified, but no final state can be given. With this in mind, three types of questions about this sort of Markov process can be raised:

1. What is the time course of the process? From a given starting configuration, what happens to the chain? How do the state probabilities change with time?

2. What is the ultimate fate of the process? Are there probabilistically stable state distributions, that is, vectors of state probabilities that remain unchanged from trial t to trial $t + 1$? If these exist, what are they?

3. How often does the process pass through a particular state? When it leaves a state, does it ever return? If so, how often?

These questions are closely related and have very similar answers. They are, largely, the topic of this chapter.

8.1   Classification of Markov States and Chains

The states of a general Markov chain can be divided into several qualitatively different classes. These classes have different properties, and the answers to the three questions above depend on the class of the state that is being investigated. The first step toward answering the questions is to define the different behaviors of a Markov state.

The most important division of states has already been presented. Those states to which the process returns an infinite number of times can be distinguished from those states that are eventually left and to which return is impossible. This creates two large classes:

Transient states are visited a finite number of times (if at all) in the life of the process. Whenever the process leaves a transient state, there is a nonzero probability that the state is never revisited.

Persistent states are revisited from time to time throughout the life of the process. Whenever the process leaves a persistent state, it surely returns to it; that is, it returns with a probability of 1.†

In Chapters 3 and 4, the focus of attention was on the way in which the process moved from the initial state to the absorbing state, and particularly on the transient—that is, presolution—behavior. The single persistent state was more or less ignored. In a more general chain, the persistent states are much more important, and distinctions among a number of types need to be made. The first of these classes is familiar:

Absorbing states are states from which transitions to other states are impossible. Once an absorbing state is entered, the process stays there indefinitely.

This means that the row of the transition matrix corresponding to an absorbing state contains only one nonzero entry: a 1 in the diagonal position.

In some chains, opportunities to enter a state do not occur on every trial, but take place at regular intervals. For example, it might be possible to be in a particular state on trials 1, 4, 7, ... , $3t + 1$, but not on trials 2, 3, 5, 6, 8, ... On leaving this state, the process passes through a sequence of other states and returns to the original state only after a multiple of some fixed number of trials (here 3). This is characteristic of the next type of state:

Periodic states are states to which return is possible at some regular interval, but not on every trial.

---

† Unfortunately, there is some variation in terminology; sometimes persistent states are called *recurrent states*.

The number of trials between possible returns is called the *period* of the state. A more formal definition of the period is given with the discussion of recurrence probabilities in Section 8.3.

The simplest example of a periodic state is the trivial two-state chain with the transition matrix

$$\mathbf{T} = \begin{bmatrix} 0 & 1 \\ 1 & 0 \end{bmatrix} \tag{8.3}$$

If started in either state, the process passes to the other state on the next trial and returns to the original state on the third trial. Returns to the starting state take place after the second transition, the fourth, the sixth, and so on, but never after an odd number of transitions. The other state is entered after the first transition, the third, the fifth, and so on. Thus, the period of this chain is 2.

For a state to be periodic, the process need not enter it on every opportunity. Consider the transition matrix

$$\mathbf{T} = \begin{bmatrix} 0 & 0 & 0.7 & 0.3 \\ 0 & 0 & 0.6 & 0.4 \\ 0.1 & 0.9 & 0 & 0 \\ 0.2 & 0.8 & 0 & 0 \end{bmatrix} \tag{8.4}$$

The states of this chain are periodic with period 2, although they are not necessarily occupied on any particular trial. For example, if started in state 1, the process may or may not be in state 3 after the first, third, fifth, ... , transition, but can never be in that state after an even number of steps. To make the state periodic, it suffices for the chance of returning to be positive only at regular intervals. Note the similarity between the blocks of zero and nonzero elements in this chain and the zeros and ones in the two-state chain of Matrix 8.3. The process passes between the blocks of states in Matrix 8.4 just as it did between the individual states of Matrix 8.3. Something of this sort always happens with chains containing periodic states, although the fact may be somewhat disguised if the states are not written in the most convenient order.

The remaining persistent states are the most interesting. These states are not absorbing, so are entered and left forever, and they are not periodic. The process passes back and forth among them without remaining permanently in any one. Chains containing these types of states provide the simplest example of a process that continues to change state indefinitely. One class of these states is the principal subject of this chapter:

Ergodic states are nonperiodic, persistent states for which the mean time to return to the state after leaving it is finite.

The portion of this definition regarding return time is unnecessary now, for the time to return to any persistent state is finite in a finite chain. In Chapter 9, a new class of states, called *null states*, is introduced, and the return time is important.

A chain can contain states of several different types. For example, the chain with the transition matrix

$$\mathbf{T} = \begin{array}{c} S_1 \\ S_2 \\ S_3 \\ S_4 \\ S_5 \end{array} \begin{bmatrix} 0.4 & 0.3 & 0.3 & 0 & 0 \\ 0.5 & 0.1 & 0.4 & 0 & 0 \\ 0.2 & 0.2 & 0.6 & 0 & 0 \\ 0 & 0 & 0.2 & 0.3 & 0.5 \\ 0 & 0 & 0 & 0.4 & 0.6 \end{bmatrix} \tag{8.5}$$

contains both transient and ergodic states. States S_1, S_2, and S_3 form a cluster that the process cannot leave. They are neither absorbing nor periodic, and thus all three are ergodic. The other two states are different. Processes started in S_4 or S_5 eventually pass into the first cluster via the link from S_4 to S_3, and once there do not return. Processes started in S_1, S_2, or S_3 never reach S_4 or S_5 at all. Hence S_4 and S_5 are transient states. Note that the classification of a particular state is not determined by its own transition probabilities alone, but by those of the complete chain. The transition probabilities for S_5, for example, do not show that it is transient; that can be determined only by looking at the other four states. If transitions from S_1 to S_4 were possible—say, the first row of Matrix 8.5 read 0.4, 0.3, 0.2, 0.1, 0—then S_5 would be ergodic, even though the transitions both into and out of S_5 are unchanged.

In spite of the fact that a chain can contain several types of states, there are certain cases where the entire Markov chain is named according to the states it contains. A chain consisting of periodic states is called a *periodic chain;* one consisting only of ergodic states, an *ergodic chain.*† A chain containing an absorbing state is called an *absorbing chain* to distinguish it from chains such as ergodic chains in which several states are visited infinitely often.

The simplest case of an ergodic or a periodic chain is one in which every state communicates with every other state. Such chains are called *irreducible chains.* Irreducible chains are important because the properties of their states are all the same. For example, if an irreducible chain contains any periodic states, it can be shown that all the states of the chain are periodic and that they have the same period (see Problem 8.3). Chains that are not irreducible are called *reducible chains.* The set

---

† Sometimes the terms *cyclic chains* and *regular chains* are used for what are here called periodic chains and ergodic chains, respectively.

of states of a reducible chain can be divided into subsets, at least one of which forms an irreducible chain.

Some examples illustrate this. The first is almost trivial. Sometimes the states of a Markov chain can be divided into two or more sets that are completely disjoint from each other, so that neither set communicates with the other. The chain with the matrix

$$\mathbf{T} = \begin{bmatrix} 0.5 & 0.5 & 0 & 0 \\ 0.4 & 0.6 & 0 & 0 \\ 0 & 0 & 0.3 & 0.7 \\ 0 & 0 & 0.2 & 0.8 \end{bmatrix}$$

is an example. A process started in one set never reaches the other set. When this happens, there is no need to keep the whole chain together. Each part is a Markov chain in its own right. Here, two ergodic chains result, with the matrices

$$\mathbf{T}_1 = \begin{bmatrix} 0.5 & 0.5 \\ 0.4 & 0.6 \end{bmatrix} \quad \text{and} \quad \mathbf{T}_2 = \begin{bmatrix} 0.3 & 0.7 \\ 0.2 & 0.8 \end{bmatrix}$$

Thus, chains with disjoint sections are no more complicated than simple chains and do not need special analysis. Another simple example is an absorbing chain. The absorbing state does not communicate with the transient states, so the chain is reducible. The single absorbing state forms an irreducible class, consisting of the rather uninteresting chain that sits in a single state.

Other examples are more complicated. The chain with Matrix 8.5 is reducible, because there is no route from the set $\{S_1, S_2, S_3\}$ to the set $\{S_4, S_5\}$. The chain contains the irreducible ergodic chain consisting of S_1, S_2, and S_3 as a subunit. The other two states neither are part of an irreducible set nor form an irreducible set in themselves. Further examples of irreducible units appear in the course of the discussion below.

8.2   State Probabilities

With these definitions, it is possible to return to the three questions posed at the start of this chapter. The first two of these questions concerned the state probabilities. In one sense, the problem of finding these probabilities has already been solved. For a chain with transition matrix $\mathbf{T}$, the basic state probability equation (Equation 4.4) holds, regardless of the type of state; so

$$s_t = s_{t-1}\mathbf{T} \tag{8.6}$$

or, in terms of the initial state,

$$s_t = s_1 T^{t-1} \tag{8.7}$$

From any particular initial distribution, state-probability distributions on subsequent trials can be worked out.

For example, if the initial vector for the five-state chain with Matrix 8.5 is

$$s_1 = [0.1, 0.2, 0.1, 0.2, 0.4]$$

then

$$s_2 = [0.1, 0.2, 0.1, 0.2, 0.4] \begin{bmatrix} 0.4 & 0.3 & 0.3 & 0 & 0 \\ 0.5 & 0.1 & 0.4 & 0 & 0 \\ 0.2 & 0.2 & 0.6 & 0 & 0 \\ 0 & 0 & 0.2 & 0.3 & 0.5 \\ 0 & 0 & 0 & 0.4 & 0.6 \end{bmatrix}$$

$$= [0.16, 0.07, 0.21, 0.22, 0.34]$$

Successive applications of T give the probabilities plotted in Figure 8.1. If exact formulas for the state probabilities are desired, Equation 8.6 can be written as a set of difference equations and solved by the methods of Appendix B, using s_1 as the initial conditions. The methods are not difficult in principle, although they are algebraically quite tedious when there are very many states in the chain. For large chains, the eigenvector methods of Section C.6 applied to Equation 8.7 are more systematic.

It is clear from Figure 8.1 that the properties of the ergodic states ($S_1, S_2,$ and S_3) and the transient states (S_4 and S_5) are quite different. As the trial number increases, the probability of being in either S_4 or S_5 falls to 0, while the probability of being in each of the ergodic states converges to a fixed value. More generally, the states of each different class have different properties. These properties are best examined for each state type separately.

Transient States

Transient states are discussed in considerable detail in Chapters 3 and 4, and the methods given there can be applied to any set of transient states. For example, to find the distribution of the last passage through state S_4 in the five-state chain of Matrix 8.5 or the distribution of the

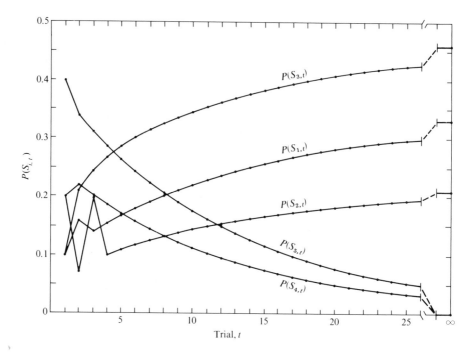

Figure 8.1   State probabilities for a Markov chain with Matrix 8.5.

number of passages through S_5, one uses calculations exactly analogous to the calculations of the distribution of the trial of last error and the number of errors in Section 4.3.

Consider the first of these distributions (the second is left to Problem 8.4). The ergodic states are not of interest here, as they do not communicate with S_4, so they can be lumped into a single absorbing state. As far as the transient states S_4 and S_5 are concerned, the chain with Matrix 8.5 has the same properties as one with the matrix

$$\mathbf{T} = \begin{matrix} A \\ S_4 \\ S_5 \end{matrix} \begin{bmatrix} 1 & 0 & 0 \\ 0.2 & 0.3 & 0.5 \\ 0 & 0.4 & 0.6 \end{bmatrix}$$

and initial vector $\mathbf{s}_1 = [0.4, 0.2, 0.4]$. Let L_5 be the number of the last trial in S_5. Then, letting S_5 correspond to the block of error states and S_4 to the transient correct states, in parallel to Equation 4.39, gives

$$P(L_5 = t) = [s_{1,4}, s_{1,5}]\mathbf{Q}^{t-1}\mathbf{V}_5\mathbf{b}'_5 \qquad t > 0$$

with (see Equations 4.27 and 4.28)

$$\mathbf{b}_5' = \mathbf{a}_5' + \mathbf{Q}_{54}(\mathbf{I} - \mathbf{Q}_{44})^{-1}\mathbf{a}_4'$$

Exact probabilities are easily calculated, particularly in this example where many of the vectors and matrices are of size 1:

$$\mathbf{b}_5' = [0] + [0.4]([1] - [0.3])^{-1}[0.2] = [0.1143]$$

$$P(L_5 = t) = [0.2, 0.4]\begin{bmatrix} 0.3 & 0.5 \\ 0.4 & 0.6 \end{bmatrix}^{t-1}\begin{bmatrix} 0 \\ 1 \end{bmatrix}[0.1143]$$

(where numbers in brackets indicate vectors or matrices of unit size). The value of $P(L_5 = 0)$ must be calculated separately, using an analog of Equation 4.32. The distribution of L_5 starting from $t = 0$ is

   0.4571, 0.0457, 0.0387, 0.0359, 0.0331, 0.0305, 0.0281, 0.0259, ...

Most questions about transient states can be answered in this way; because these methods are extensively covered above, no further discussion of transient states is needed.

Ergodic States and Chains

The most important class of states considered in this chapter is the ergodic class. These states form ergodic chains such as Matrices 8.1 and 8.2, as well as being an important constituent of chains with matrices like Matrix 8.5. As always the basic state probabilities for ergodic chains can be calculated by matrix multiplication (as in Equation 8.6) or by setting up and solving the equivalent set of simultaneous difference equations. However, often the most important results concern the long-term behavior of the chain, that is, the limiting value of s_t as t gets very large. A glance at Figure 8.1 suggests that the state probabilities for the ergodic states (S_1, S_2, and S_3) are converging to stable nonzero values that do not change from trial to trial. Apparently, in answer to the second of the three questions above, there are stable ultimate distributions.

Consider first an irreducible ergodic chain. It is possible to prove that, for such a chain, the state probabilities eventually converge to a unique, stable distribution that does not depend on the initial vector. Once this distribution is reached, the state-probability vector does not change from trial to trial. This stable distribution is known as the *stationary distribution* of the chain and is denoted here by s_∞. It should be remembered that the fact that the process eventually reaches this distribution does not mean that the process becomes locked into any one state (which would make it an absorbing chain), but rather that the probability of finding the process in any particular state remains unchanged from trial to trial. The stability is probabilistic, not absolute.

Calculation of s_∞ is straightforward. For a state distribution to be stationary, it must be left unchanged by the transition from one trial to the next; so for very large t, both s_t and s_{t+1} are the same. Thus, applying $\mathbf{T}$ does not change the state vector:

$$s_\infty = s_\infty \mathbf{T} \tag{8.8}$$

(cf. Equation 8.6). This equation cannot be solved directly for s_∞ in matrix form, except trivially by $s_\infty = \mathbf{0}$. To find a solution, express the equation in terms of its components. Let

$$s_\infty = [p_1, p_2, \ldots, p_n]$$

and let p_{ij} be an entry of $\mathbf{T}$. Then Equation 8.8 is equivalent to the set of equations

$$p_{11}p_1 + p_{21}p_2 + \cdots + p_{n1}p_n = p_1$$
$$p_{12}p_1 + p_{22}p_2 + \cdots + p_{n2}p_n = p_2$$
$$\vdots \tag{8.9}$$
$$p_{1n}p_1 + p_{2n}p_2 + \cdots + p_{nn}p_n = p_n$$

Although there are n equations in n unknowns here, they are not independent (remember that the rows of $\mathbf{T}$ sum to 1), and so only determine s_∞ up to a multiplicative constant. The fact that s_∞ is a probability distribution provides a final relationship:

$$\sum_{i=1}^{n} p_i = 1 \tag{8.10}$$

With this equation, a solution to Equation 8.8 is possible.

For one example of a stationary distribution, consider the two-state chain with the matrix in Matrix 8.1. Then Equation 8.8 is

$$[p_1, p_2] \begin{bmatrix} 1 - \alpha & \alpha \\ \beta & 1 - \beta \end{bmatrix} = [p_1, p_2] \tag{8.11}$$

or, in the form of Equations 8.9,

$$(1 - \alpha)p_1 + \beta p_2 = p_1$$
$$\alpha p_1 + (1 - \beta)p_2 = p_2$$

Both of these equations are equivalent to

$$\alpha p_1 = \beta p_2$$

Equation 8.10 is

$$p_1 + p_2 = 1$$

and solving these two equations:

$$p_1 = \frac{\beta}{\alpha + \beta} \qquad p_2 = \frac{\alpha}{\alpha + \beta} \qquad (8.12)$$

It is easy to verify that, with this value of s_∞, Equation 8.11 holds.
For a numerical example, consider the transition matrix

$$\mathbf{T} = \begin{bmatrix} 0.4 & 0.3 & 0.3 \\ 0.5 & 0.1 & 0.4 \\ 0.2 & 0.2 & 0.6 \end{bmatrix} \qquad (8.13)$$

From Equations 8.9 and 8.10,

$$0.4p_1 + 0.5p_2 + 0.2p_3 = p_1$$
$$0.3p_1 + 0.1p_2 + 0.2p_3 = p_2$$
$$0.3p_1 + 0.4p_2 + 0.6p_3 = p_3$$
$$p_1 + p_2 + p_3 = 1$$

These have solution

$$s_\infty = [0.3294, 0.2118, 0.4588] \qquad (8.14)$$

When the matrix is in numerical form, as in the last example, another method can be used to find the stationary distribution. This method is based on the fact that, if a stable distribution exists, then any initial vector is transformed into it by a sufficiently high power of $\mathbf{T}$; that is,

sT^K approaches s_∞ for any s and large K. This can only happen if T^K is a matrix with identical rows, each containing s_∞ (consider what the ith row of T^K must look like in order to turn a population entirely in S_i into s_∞). Thus, it is only necessary to look at a large power of T to find s_∞. To minimize calculation (and the propagation of rounding errors), it is easiest to do this by successive squaring, forming T^2, T^4, T^8, and so on. These usually converge fairly rapidly. For example, using Matrix 8.13, gives

$$T^2 = TT = \begin{bmatrix} 0.37 & 0.21 & 0.42 \\ 0.33 & 0.24 & 0.43 \\ 0.30 & 0.20 & 0.50 \end{bmatrix} \tag{8.15}$$

$$T^4 = (T^2)(T^2) = \begin{bmatrix} 0.3322 & 0.2121 & 0.4557 \\ 0.3303 & 0.2129 & 0.4568 \\ 0.3270 & 0.2110 & 0.4620 \end{bmatrix}$$

$$T^8 = (T^4)(T^4) = \begin{bmatrix} 0.32943 & 0.21177 & 0.45880 \\ 0.32942 & 0.21177 & 0.45881 \\ 0.32940 & 0.21176 & 0.45884 \end{bmatrix}$$

and the result if already quite close to the value of s_∞ found algebraically to be Equation 8.14.

The same procedure, either analytically or numerically, could be used to work with reducible matrices such as Matrix 8.5. However, the larger number of states makes the numerical convergence slower (one must double Matrix 8.5 out to T^{128} before correct four-digit answers are obtained). It is better to first classify the states. For transient states, such as S_4 and S_5, the components of s_∞ are 0. Irreducible sets of ergodic states within a larger matrix can be analyzed in the same way as ergodic chains. Thus, once the process with Matrix 8.5 reaches the ergodic states, or if it is started there, the transient states are irrelevant, and the dynamics of the process are just those of a simple ergodic chain with a matrix composed of the rows and columns of Matrix 8.5 that correspond to S_1, S_2, and S_3. This matrix was just analyzed as Matrix 8.13. Putting all this together, for Matrix 8.5, gives

$$s_\infty = [0.3294, 0.2118, 0.4588, 0, 0] \tag{8.16}$$

These are the asymptotes depicted in Figure 8.1.

Finding the stationary distribution is a special case of the eigenvector problem discussed in Section C.6. The left eigenvectors e of a matrix A are those vectors that are changed only in scale when multiplied by A:

$$eA = \lambda e \qquad (8.17)$$

for some number λ (see Equation C.31). The scalar λ in Equation 8.17 is the eigenvalue associated with e. Equation 8.8 is Equation 8.17 with $\lambda = 1$; thus, s_∞ is a left eigenvector of T with an eigenvalue of 1. Of course, not all matrices have a unit eigenvalue, but it is easy to prove that one always exists for a Markov transition matrix. The rows of T sum to 1, so $T1' = 1'$, which is the definitional equation for the right eigenvalue, Equation C.32, and shows that $1'$ is a right eigenvector with unit eigenvalue. As left and right eigenvectors always come in pairs with the same eigenvalue, this assures the existence of a left eigenvector with $\lambda = 1$. Unfortunately, this proof is not constructive. Finding s_∞ still involves either solving equations like Equation 8.9 or using numerical methods such as raising T to a high power.

It is sometimes useful to conceive of the states of a Markov chain in a different way. Thus far, the term *state* has been used to characterize the condition of a particular subject or item at a particular time. In this sense, s is the probability distribution for a subject or an item over the state space. One can also think of s as giving the state of a population of subjects or items. In this view, it is the populations that are important, not the individuals. One works directly with *population states* or *system states,* which are the vectors s and represent the distribution of individual states.

Viewing a Markov process in terms of population states is not a large change. As probabilistic processes, Markov chains deal with probability distributions, not with individuals. For example, one never fits data from a single item to a Markov chain, but works with data from a good-sized sample of observations. The individuals never enter the calculations at all. Considering the model as describing changes among the population states, the transition matrix acts to transform one state, s_t, into a new state, s_{t+1}. This picture is particularly natural when one analyzes the process in terms of its vectors, rather than in terms of individual subjects or items, as discussed in Section 4.2. The vectors in Figure 4.1 are the population states.

One advantage of the population-state view is that it unifies some results across the different types of states and chains. For all nonperiodic chains, the population passes from an initial population state given by s_1, through a series of intermediate states, to a final population state, s_∞. The only difference between an ergodic chain and an absorbing chain is that, for the latter, s_∞ is a degenerate distribution in which all the probability falls in one component. Like an absorbing chain, an ergodic chain is absorbed into a stable state, but in the sense that the population state is stable, not in the sense that individuals do not change their individual state.

Periodic States

A chain containing periodic states presents no major new problems, for it is easily converted into simpler ergodic or absorbing chains. Consider the periodic chain with the matrix

$$\mathbf{T} = \begin{bmatrix} 0 & 0 & 0.7 & 0.3 \\ 0 & 0 & 0.6 & 0.4 \\ 0.1 & 0.9 & 0 & 0 \\ 0.2 & 0.8 & 0 & 0 \end{bmatrix}$$

which was presented above as Matrix 8.4. This chain has a period of 2, indicating that return to the starting state is possible only every second trial. The fact that returns can take place every other trial suggests that looking at the two-step transitions may simplify things. The matrix of these probabilities is the second power of $\mathbf{T}$ (recall Equation 4.11):

$$\mathbf{T}^{(2)} = \mathbf{T}^2 = \begin{bmatrix} 0.13 & 0.87 & 0 & 0 \\ 0.14 & 0.86 & 0 & 0 \\ 0 & 0 & 0.61 & 0.39 \\ 0 & 0 & 0.62 & 0.38 \end{bmatrix}$$

This chain is no longer periodic; in fact, it is ergodic. Furthermore, its matrix is reducible, for it can be broken into two nonconnecting parts, each involving two states:

$$\mathbf{T}_{odd} = \begin{bmatrix} 0.13 & 0.87 \\ 0.14 & 0.86 \end{bmatrix} \quad \text{and} \quad \mathbf{T}_{even} = \begin{bmatrix} 0.61 & 0.39 \\ 0.62 & 0.38 \end{bmatrix}$$

The matrix $\mathbf{T}_{odd}$ acts on the set $\{S_1, S_2\}$, while $\mathbf{T}_{even}$ acts on $\{S_3, S_4\}$. Each of these describes the process on alternate trials. If started in either S_1 or S_2 on trial 1, then the process is in the set $\{S_1, S_2\}$ on odd-numbered trials, and $\mathbf{T}_{odd}$ is the relevant two-step transition matrix. On even-numbered trials, the process is in $\{S_3, S_4\}$, acting according to $\mathbf{T}_{even}$. Both $\mathbf{T}_{odd}$ and $\mathbf{T}_{even}$ are simple, irreducible, ergodic Markov chains, and can be analyzed as such. From the limiting distribution for $\mathbf{T}_{odd}$, the process started in S_1 or S_2 eventually has the state distribution [0.1386, 0.8614, 0, 0] on odd-numbered trials; and from $\mathbf{T}_{even}$, the limiting distribution [0, 0, 0.6139, 0.3861] on even-numbered trials.

More generally, for an irreducible, periodic chain with period p, the process with matrix $\mathbf{T}^{(p)}$ is reducible and breaks the state space into p disjoint sets. The process returns to each set at intervals of p trials. The transition matrix for each of these p-step transitions is that of a simple, aperiodic chain, easily analyzed.

Where the original chain is not irreducible, it is possible for one section to have one period and another section to have a different period. For example, the process may start in a set of transient states with period p_1, then move into an ergodic set with period p_2. Because there is no way to get from the second set back to the first, the second periodicity cannot interfere with the first. In cases like this, breaking the chain into irreducible parts solves any problem. The various parts are analyzed for their periodic properties separately.

8.3 Renewal Properties of a Finite Markov Chain

The third of the three questions posed at the start of this chapter concerns the frequency with which a process returns to a state. For example, looking at the random walk in Matrix 8.2, one may ask how frequently returns to state S_1 occur. Started in S_1, does the process return on the next trial, the trial after, or when? The remainder of this chapter concerns return properties of this sort.

It is easy to state abstractly what is required. Suppose that a process is in state S_i on trial t_0. On the next trial, the process may still be found in S_i, or it may have left and gone to some other state. In the first case, return to S_i is immediate, on trial $t_0 + 1$ (it is called a "return" even though the process never leaves S_i). If the process does leave S_i, some trials are spent out of S_i; and the next return, if there is one, takes place on trial $t_0 + t$, $t > 1$. The problem is to determine the probabilities of these events, known as *recurrence probabilities,* as well as the moments of their distributions.

An analysis of this sort is part of the theory of *renewal processes.*† A renewal process concerns a series of events with the property that the process, in effect, starts over again whenever an event takes place. Such restarting events are referred to as *recurrent events.* Because of their memory-less property, the states of a Markov chain are examples of recurrent events. The idea of a recurrent event (and of renewal processes) originated as a model of the replacement of parts, and this description provides a good way to think of them. For example, think of a light fixture in which a bulb is installed and allowed to burn. It burns, then blows out after some period of time for which the distribution is known (it is a property of the brand of bulb). When a bulb burns out, it is replaced by a new bulb, which is similar to the old one in that it has, probabilistically, exactly the same properties. Thus, the process

---

† Most texts on stochastic processes include a discussion of renewal processes; see also Cox (1962).

begins again. One can now raise questions about such things as the average life span of a bulb, how likely it is to burn out at time T, and so forth. The theory of renewal processes is actually much more complicated than this example suggests (or than will be presented here). As is common, the mathematics have been generalized beyond the initial physical model. Restricting consideration to finite, homogeneous Markov chains in discrete time, as in this chapter, also simplifies the picture considerably.

Many questions relating to the properties of a psychological model can be expressed in terms of renewal theory. The temporal properties of a process modeled by a Markov chain—for example, how long one must wait for an event or how frequently an event takes place—usually can be expressed as questions about passage between states or sets of states, in the manner of Chapter 4. These questions are the domain of renewal theory. For example, in the models of successive choices (Equations 2.23, 2.24, and 2.25, as well as Equation 8.1, passage into a state represents the choice of the corresponding alternative. The return probabilities express how long until the same alternative is chosen again.

It is fairly obvious that the theory of renewal process is easily applied to homogeneous Markov chains. The Markov property assures that state occupancy is a recurrent event. If the process is in state S_i, the future behavior of the process, and thus the probability of its return to S_i on a later trial, are probabilistically the same regardless of the history of the process. Whenever the process enters S_i, be it for the first, tenth, or thousandth time, its future is the same. Assuming homogeneity makes things a bit easier, as the results need not be indexed by the absolute time.

The fact that the states of a Markov chain are recurrent events does not mean that all events associated with a Markov model are recurrent. Functions of the Markov states other than the states themselves are not necessarily recurrent events, just as they are not necessarily Markovian. This gives a Markov model the power to describe nonrecurrent processes. For example, the responses in the learning models of Chapter 2 are usually not recurrent. In fact, the notion that an event is recurrent is a fairly strong one and, where it applies to an observable event, has substantial psychological implications. It indicates that there is no change in the subject with successive occurrences of the event and frequently means that the event can be associated with a single state in the model.

Recurrent events play an important role in the all-or-none model. In any version of the model (Equations 2.5 and 2.7 or Equations 7.2, 7.3, and 7.4), there is only one error state, so each error leaves the process in the same place and learning starts over from the beginning. This is not true for a model like the two-stage model (Equation 2.15), in which errors are generated from two different states. If the all-or-none model fits, and errors are recurrent, some very definite limits are implied as to what the subject must be doing. Because each error leaves the subject in the same state, no information can be retained from previous errors. For example, under the hypothesis-testing view of the all-or-none model, the recurrence property means that the subject is unable to distinguish between hypotheses that have been tested on prior trials and those that have not. Each error initiates a new search among all the possible hypotheses. Some of the early analyses of the all-or-none model (e.g., Bower and Trabasso, 1964; Restle, 1962) rely heavily on this property.

Recurrence Probabilities

Central to any analysis of a renewal process are the recurrence probabilities, that is, the probabilities that a recurrent event occurring on trial t_0 next occurs on trial $t_0 + t$, $t = 1, 2, \ldots$. Such recurrence probabilities can be found for each state of a Markov chain. Because homogeneous processes are being considered, these probabilities do not depend on the original trial number (t_0), only on the offset relative to this initial trial. For the state S_i, they are denoted here by $f_i^{(t)}$.

It is important to distinguish between the recurrence probabilities $f_i^{(t)}$ and the t-step transition probabilities of going from S_i itself, which are elements of $\mathbf{T}^{(t)} = \mathbf{T}^t$. Let $p_{ii}^{(t)}$ denote an element from the matrix $\mathbf{T}^t$ (which is not the same thing as an element of $\mathbf{T}$ that has been raised to the tth power, or p_{ii}^t). The value of $p_{ii}^{(t)}$ includes the probability of any path that goes from S_i to S_i in t trials, including paths that pass through S_i on the way. In contrast, $f_i^{(t)}$ is the probability of a first return only, so it excludes any paths that touch S_i. This makes $f_i^{(t)}$ something like a distribution function; because there can be at most one first return to S_i, the sum of $f_i^{(t)}$ over t cannot be larger than 1. The same is not true of $p_{ii}^{(t)}$.

The value of $f_i^{(t)}$ can be related to $p_{ii}^{(t)}$ by subtracting the extra paths. When $t = 1$, $f_i^{(t)}$ and $p_{ii}^{(t)}$ are the same. The recurrence probability, $f_i^{(1)}$, is the probability of staying in S_i for a trial, so

$$f_i^{(1)} = p_{ii} = p_{ii}^{(1)} \tag{8.18}$$

The probability of first return on the second trial is not quite so simple. To be in S_i on trial $t_0 + 2$, the process must either make a first return on the second trial or make a first return immediately, then stay there for one trial. Expressing this statement in terms of probabilities gives

$$p_{ii}^{(2)} = f_i^{(2)} + f_i^{(1)}p_{ii}^{(1)}$$

and solving for $f_i^{(2)}$ gives

$$f_i^{(2)} = p_{ii}^{(2)} - f_i^{(1)}p_{ii}^{(1)} \tag{8.19}$$

In effect, the probability of the path returning to S_i too quickly is subtracted from $p_{ii}^{(2)}$. Likewise, $p_{ii}^{(3)}$ includes the probabilities of returns on the first, second, or third trial, and so the first two of these can be subtracted to get

$$f_i^{(3)} = p_{ii}^{(3)} - f_i^{(2)}p_{ii}^{(1)} - f_i^{(1)}p_{ii}^{(2)}$$

Generalizing this logic gives

$$f_i^{(t)} = p_{ii}^{(t)} - \sum_{u=1}^{t-1} f_i^{(u)}p_{ii}^{(t-u)} \tag{8.20}$$

In words, the probability of first return to S_i after t trials equals the probability of being there after t trials, less the probability of making a first return before trial t and still getting to S_i on the tth trial. The values of $f_i^{(u)}$, $u < t$, can be substituted into Equation 8.20 to obtain a solution in terms of the $p_{ii}^{(u)}$ only; however, the complexity of the sums that result makes a general formula fairly useless. For calculation, it is simpler to start with $f_i^{(1)}$ and work up or to use the more advanced methods to be presented in Section 9.4 below (see Equation 9.34).

For example, consider S_1 in the five-state chain with Matrix 8.5. Values of $p_{11}^{(t)}$ can be obtained from powers of Matrix 8.5, but using the classification of the states saves some algebra. Because transitions out of the irreducible set $\{S_1, S_2, S_3\}$ are impossible, only this set need be considered. The transition probabilities among these states (as in Matrix 8.13) are

$$\mathbf{T} = \begin{bmatrix} 0.4 & 0.3 & 0.3 \\ 0.5 & 0.1 & 0.4 \\ 0.2 & 0.2 & 0.6 \end{bmatrix}$$

By Equation 8.18, the one-trial first-return probability is p_{11},

$$f_1^{(1)} = 0.4$$

Using the square of **T** (given in Matrix 8.15), $p_{11}^{(2)} = 0.37$; and by Equation 8.19,

$$f_1^{(2)} = p_{11}^{(2)} - f_1^{(1)} p_{11}^{(1)}$$
$$= 0.37 - (0.4)(0.4) = 0.21$$

Cubing **T** gives $p_{11}^{(3)} = 0.337$, so

$$f_1^{(3)} = 0.337 - (0.4)(0.37) - (0.21)(0.4) = 0.105$$

The next steps are

$$p_{11}^{(4)} = 0.3322 \qquad f_1^{(4)} = 0.0777$$
$$p_{11}^{(5)} = 0.3300 \qquad f_1^{(5)} = 0.0564$$

and the series of $f_1^{(t)}$ continues with 0.0411, 0.0299, and 0.0217. First-return probabilities for other states in the chain are found in the same way. For the transient states S_4 and S_5, only the matrix of transitions among them,

$$\mathbf{Q} = \begin{bmatrix} 0.3 & 0.5 \\ 0.4 & 0.6 \end{bmatrix}$$

need be used to get the $p_{ii}^{(t)}$.

When the transition matrix is expressed in symbolic form, application of Equation 8.20 is more work, but a general formula can sometimes be obtained. Consider as an example, the all-or-none model in the version with the transition matrix

$$\mathbf{T} = \begin{bmatrix} 1 & 0 & 0 \\ \alpha & (1-\alpha)\gamma & (1-\alpha)(1-\gamma) \\ \alpha & (1-\alpha)\gamma & (1-\alpha)(1-\gamma) \end{bmatrix} \qquad (8.21)$$

Powers of Matrix 8.21 are readily found to be

$$\mathbf{T}^t = \begin{bmatrix} 1 & 0 & 0 \\ 1-(1-\alpha)^t & \gamma(1-\alpha)^t & (1-\gamma)(1-\alpha)^t \\ 1-(1-\alpha)^t & \gamma(1-\alpha)^t & (1-\gamma)(1-\alpha)^t \end{bmatrix}$$

The error state, being associated with a unique response, is the most interesting. For this,

$$p_{EE}^{(t)} = (1-\gamma)(1-\alpha)^t \qquad (8.22)$$

Then, applying Equation 8.20 gives

$$f_E^{(1)} = p_{EE}^{(1)} = (1 - \gamma)(1 - \alpha)$$
$$f_E^{(2)} = p_{EE}^{(2)} - f_E^{(1)}p_{EE}^{(1)} = (1 - \gamma)\gamma(1 - \alpha)^2$$
$$f_E^{(3)} = p_{EE}^{(3)} - [f_E^{(2)}p_{EE}^{(1)} + f_E^{(1)}p_{EE}^{(2)}] = (1 - \gamma)\gamma^2(1 - \alpha)^3$$

This sequence suggests

$$f_E^{(t)} = (1 - \gamma)(1 - \alpha)[\gamma(1 - \alpha)]^{t-1} \tag{8.23}$$

a result that can be proved by induction as follows. Clearly, Equation 8.23 holds when $t = 1$. Now suppose that it holds for any $u < t$. Substituting into Equation 8.20 gives

$$f_E^{(t)} = p_{EE}^{(t)} - \sum_{u=1}^{t-1} f_E^{(u)}p_{EE}^{(t-u)}$$

$$= (1 - \gamma)(1 - \alpha)^t - \sum_{u=1}^{t-1} [(1 - \gamma)\gamma^{u-1}(1 - \alpha)^u][(1 - \gamma)(1 - \alpha)^{t-u}]$$

$$= (1 - \gamma)(1 - \alpha)^t \left(1 - (1 - \gamma) \sum_{u=1}^{t-1} \gamma^{u-1} \right)$$

$$= (1 - \gamma)(1 - \alpha)^t\gamma^{t-1}$$

This establishes Equation 8.23 and completes the proof.

Sometimes the recurrence probabilities can be found by a careful inspection of the model, without formally applying Equation 8.20. For example, in the two-state chain with Matrix 8.1, return to a state can be avoided only by staying in the other state. By directly looking at the possible paths:

$$f_A^{(t)} = \begin{cases} 1 - \alpha & t = 1 \\ \alpha\beta(1 - \beta)^{t-2} & t > 1 \end{cases} \tag{8.24}$$

A similar equation applies for the second state (see Problem 8.14). Of course, this result agrees with the results of more formal calculation using Equation 8.20.

Clearly, the calculations in the last two examples are getting complicated, and they capitalize on special properties of the problem or on the recognition of a general form from special cases. The difficulty is that the value of $f_i^{(t)}$ in Equation 8.20 depends on $f_i^{(u)}$ for $u < t$, so it is hard to find a general formula. Problems of this sort are often easier to solve using mathematical entities known as generating functions. These are discussed in Section 9.4.

The recurrence probabilities can be used to provide a more formal definition of a periodic state than that given above. Return to a periodic state is possible only at fixed intervals, so $f_i^{(t)}$ is zero except when t is a multiple of the period. Conversely, any state for which $f_i^{(t)}$ is zero except at some regular interval is a periodic state, and the period is that interval for which $f_i^{(t)}$ is nonzero. A rigorous definition of the period can easily be based on this property of the recurrence probabilities.

Recurrence of Transient States

The probability of eventual return to S_i is

$$f_i = \sum_{i=1}^{\infty} f_i^{(t)} \tag{8.25}$$

For transient states this is less than 1, while for persistent states it equals exactly 1. When $f_i < 1$, there is a positive probability that the process never returns to S_i, no matter how long one waits, and so the distribution function given by the $f_i^{(t)}$ values is defective. For this reason, return to a transient state is sometimes referred to as an *uncertain recurrent event*—recurrent because it starts the process over, but uncertain because it may never happen. The sum from Equation 8.25 can be used to rigorously define the concept of transient and persistent states, replacing the less formal definitions given above. If $f_i < 1$, then S_i is transient; if $f_i = 1$, it is persistent.

For example, the states of the two-state choice model are persistent. Summing Equation 8.24 gives

$$f_A = (1 - \alpha) + \sum_{t=2}^{\infty} \alpha\beta(1 - \beta)^{t-2}$$

$$= (1 - \alpha) + \alpha = 1$$

On the other hand, an error in the all-or-none model is transient. From Equation 8.23,

$$f_E = (1 - \alpha)(1 - \gamma) \sum_{t=1}^{\infty} [(1 - \alpha)\gamma]^{t-1}$$

$$= \frac{(1 - \alpha)(1 - \gamma)}{1 - (1 - \alpha)\gamma} \tag{8.26}$$

Unless $\alpha = 0$ (which means that no learning takes place), the numerator of Equation 8.26 is always less than the denominator, which makes the quotient less than 1. Eventually, errors must cease. Note that $1 - f_E$ is the quantity b that figured heavily in the algebraic analysis of the all-or-none model (e.g., the distribution of T in Equation 3.20).

At times, one may be interested in recurrence-time distributions for transient states, considering returns only when they actually happen. If $f_i^{(t)}$ is conditioned on the fact that a return takes place, by dividing each $f_i^{(t)}$ by f_i, a proper probability distribution will result:

$$f_i^{(t)*} = f_i^{(t)}/f_i \tag{8.27}$$

Now $f_i^{(t)*}$ gives the probability of return to S_i after t trials given that return ever takes place. For example, considering the all-or-none model errors, then combining Equations 8.23 and 8.26 in Equation 8.27 gives

$$f_E^{(t)*} = [1 - \gamma(1 - \alpha)][\gamma(1 - \alpha)]^{t-1} \tag{8.28}$$

which is a proper probability distribution, in this case one that follows naturally from inspection of the probabilities in the transition matrix (Matrix 8.21).

The calculations leading to Equation 8.28 are important. In practice, many psychological events are transient and lead to defective recurrence distributions. But data can be collected only for recurrences that actually take place, so the observed distributions are conditional on the event occurring. Then the conditional recurrence probabilities (Equation 8.27) are the appropriate predictions and match the data better than the unconditional values of $f_i^{(t)}$.

Expected Return Times

For many purposes, there is no need to look at the full distribution of $f_i^{(t)}$, only at its expected value. If a state is persistent and the full distribution of $f_i^{(t)}$ is known, the mean time to the first return can be calculated from the definition of the mean:

$$\mu_i = \sum_{t=1}^{\infty} t f_i^{(t)} \tag{8.29}$$

For persistent states this equation is correct, but it does not apply to transient states because $f_i^{(t)}$ is not a proper probability distribution. With positive probability, the process never returns to a transient state. If a failure to return is treated as $t = \infty$, then Equation 8.29 can be interpreted as evaluating to $\mu_i = \infty$.

In many cases, it is neither easy nor practical to calculate $f_i^{(t)}$ in general when μ_i is wanted. Fortunately, it is not necessary to do so. For ergodic chains, a very important theorem relates μ_i to the stationary distribution, s_∞. Recall that the stable state probability for S_i is p_i; then

$$\mu_i = \frac{1}{p_i} \tag{8.30}$$

When S_i is transient, p_i is 0 and the division in Equation 8.30 is undefined. This fits with the fact that Equation 8.29 is also not properly defined. A proof of this theorem is fairly complicated and is not given here. It can be found in most books on Markov chains or stochastic processes.

The formula in Equation 8.30 nearly holds for periodic states. As in the calculations in Section 8.2, let s_∞ be the stable distribution on trials where occupancy of a state is possible (and 0 on other trials). Suppose that the matrix $\mathbf{T}^{(p)}$ indicates a mean return time of $1/p_i$, which is based on a p-step time interval. Thus, to express the returns in terms of basic trials, multiply by the period to give

$$\mu_i = \frac{p}{p_i} \tag{8.31}$$

Equation 8.30 is a special case of Equation 8.31 when $p = 1$.

A little thought should indicate that Equations 8.30 and 8.31 are not surprising. As the process moves into a stationary distribution, s_∞, this distribution determines the return frequency. In order for the process to occupy S_i, say, $\frac{1}{5}$ of the time, it must average one trial out of five in the state; hence returns to S_i take place, on the average, at five trial intervals. Equation 8.30 is just an assertion of the fact that the rate of an event and its mean time to occur are reciprocals. However, the simple relationship between μ_i and the asymptotic s_∞ does not mean that the value of μ_i is an asymptotic property only. Although s_∞ is the state-probability vector only in the limit of a long-run process, Equation 8.30 is true whether S_i occurs on the first trial or the thousandth.

As an example, consider the five-state chain in Matrix 8.5 again. The stable distribution for this chain (calculated as Equation 8.16) is

$$s_\infty = [0.3294, 0.2118, 0.4588, 0, 0]$$

For state S_1, the mean time to recurrence is

$$\mu_1 = 1/p_1 = 1/0.3294 = 3.036$$

A similar calculation gives $\mu_2 = 4.721$ and $\mu_3 = 2.180$. The same quantities could be obtained by finding the distribution of $f_i^{(t)}$ and calculating the expectation from Equation 8.29, but a great many more than the eight terms that were determined above are needed. Brute force is not very rewarding here. The values of μ_4 and μ_5 are undefined, as appropriate for transient states. It is possible to wait forever without a return to these states.

The relationship between $f_i^{(t)}$ and μ_i can be verified for the two-state choice model in Matrix 8.1. From Equation 8.12,

$$\mathbf{s}_\infty = \left[\frac{\beta}{\alpha + \beta}, \frac{\alpha}{\alpha + \beta} \right]$$

Taking reciprocols gives

$$\mu_1 = \frac{\alpha + \beta}{\beta} \qquad \mu_2 = \frac{\alpha + \beta}{\alpha}$$

The complete distribution of $f_1^{(t)}$, given in Equation 8.24, also lets Equation 8.29 be used to find these means:

$$\mu_1 = \sum_{t=1}^{\infty} t f_1^{(t)}$$

$$= 1 - \alpha + \alpha\beta \sum_{t=2}^{\infty} t(1 - \beta)^{t-2}$$

$$= 1 - \alpha + \alpha\beta \left(\frac{1 + \beta}{\beta^2} \right) = \frac{\alpha + \beta}{\beta}$$

The results agree.

Matrix Formulation

The mean first-passage times to go from any S_i to any S_j can also be found. Consider an ergodic chain and let μ_{ij} be the mean trial of first passage from S_i to S_j (so μ_i in Equation 8.29 or Equation 8.30 is now denoted μ_{ii}). Consider an item starting in S_i on trial t. The value of μ_{ij} can be decomposed into a sum based on where the item is on trial $t + 1$:

$$\mu_{ij} = \sum_{k=1}^{n} p_{ik} E \text{ (first-passage time from } S_{i,t} \text{ to } S_j \ S_{k,t+1})$$

Two situations can be distinguished in this sum. If $k = j$, the first passage occurs and the conditional mean first-passage time is exactly 1. If $k \neq j$, the mean first-passage time is the sum of the one trial taken to get to S_k and the μ_{kj} trials to get from S_k to S_j. So

$$\mu_{ij} = (p_{ij})(1) + \sum_{k \neq j} (p_{ik})(1 + \mu_{kj})$$

$$= \sum_{k=1}^{n} p_{ik} + \sum_{k \neq j} p_{ik}\mu_{kj}$$

The first sum equals 1; the second can be completed by adding and subtracting the excluded term $p_{ij}\mu_{jj}$. This gives

$$\mu_{ij} = 1 + \sum_{k=1}^{n} p_{ik}\mu_{kj} - p_{ij}\mu_{jj} \tag{8.32}$$

Solving this system of simultaneous equations gives the μ_{ij}.

The middle sum in Equation 8.32 looks like a matrix multiplication. In fact, Equation 8.32 can be restated in matrix form. Let **M** be the matrix of the μ_{ij} and define

$$\mathbf{D} = \begin{bmatrix} \mu_{11} & 0 & \cdots & 0 \\ 0 & \mu_{22} & \cdots & 0 \\ \vdots & \vdots & & \vdots \\ 0 & 0 & \cdots & \mu_{nn} \end{bmatrix} \quad \mathbf{E} = \begin{bmatrix} 1 & 1 & \cdots & 1 \\ 1 & 1 & \cdots & 1 \\ \vdots & \vdots & & \vdots \\ 1 & 1 & \cdots & 1 \end{bmatrix}$$

Then Equation 8.32 is

$$\mathbf{M} = \mathbf{E} + \mathbf{TM} - \mathbf{TD} \tag{8.33}$$

The elements in **D** are known from Equation 8.30 to be $1/p_i$, so only **M** in Equation 8.33 is unknown.

The solution to Equation 8.33 is less simple than it seems, however. Manipulation of Equation 8.33 gives $(\mathbf{I} - \mathbf{T})\mathbf{M} = \mathbf{E} - \mathbf{TD}$, but $\mathbf{I} - \mathbf{T}$ is singular and cannot be inverted. An analysis in detail goes beyond this book. It can be shown (see Kemeny and Snell, 1960) that

$$\mathbf{M} = (\mathbf{I} - \mathbf{Z} + \mathbf{Z}_c)\mathbf{D} \tag{8.34}$$

where

$$\mathbf{Z} = [\mathbf{I} - (\mathbf{T} - \mathbf{T}^{(\infty)})]^{-1} \qquad (8.35)$$

$$\mathbf{T}^{(\infty)} = \lim_{K \to \infty} \mathbf{T}^{(K)} = \mathbf{1}'\mathbf{s}_\infty$$

$$= \begin{bmatrix} p_1 & p_2 & \cdots & p_n \\ p_1 & p_2 & \cdots & p_n \\ \vdots & \vdots & & \vdots \\ p_1 & p_2 & \cdots & p_n \end{bmatrix}$$

and $\mathbf{Z}_c$ is a matrix whose columns contain the diagonal elements of $\mathbf{Z}$,

$$\mathbf{Z}_c = \begin{bmatrix} z_{11} & z_{22} & \cdots & z_{nn} \\ z_{11} & z_{22} & \cdots & z_{nn} \\ \vdots & \vdots & & \vdots \\ z_{11} & z_{22} & \cdots & z_{nn} \end{bmatrix}$$

The matrix $\mathbf{Z}$ is known as the *fundamental matrix* for the ergodic chain and is in some respects analogous to the fundamental matrix for a set of transient states discussed at the end of Section 4.2 (see Equation 4.31). The role of the transient-state probabilities, $\mathbf{Q}$, in Chapter 4 is now played by $\mathbf{T} - \mathbf{T}^{(\infty)}$. This is the difference between the single-trial and the long-term transition probabilities, so it also reflects transient aspects of the chain. Unfortunately, many of the properties that made the fundamental matrix for a set of transient states so useful do not hold for Equation 8.35. It cannot, for example, be used to help find the probabilities of a sequence of states of unspecified length. The principal importance of Equation 8.34 is to simplify and unify calculation. Given $\mathbf{T}$, Equation 8.34 makes $\mathbf{M}$ easy to find. Other quantities, such as variances and covariances, can be found in similar ways (again, see Kemeny and Snell, 1960).

Problems

8.1. Classify the states of Markov chains having the following transition matrices. Identify irreducible sets and, for periodic states, find the period. It may be helpful to rewrite some of the matrices with the states in a different order, so as to bring together blocks of zeros, states of a similar type, and so on. As the asymptotic state probabilities are determined only by the location of zeros and ones in the transition matrix, it may simplify the problem to replace any nonzero, nonunit entries by a common symbol such as x.

a. $\begin{bmatrix} 1.0 & 0 \\ 0.6 & 0.4 \end{bmatrix}$

b. $\begin{bmatrix} 0.8 & 0.2 \\ 0.7 & 0.3 \end{bmatrix}$

c. $\begin{bmatrix} 0 & 0.5 & 0.5 \\ 0.6 & 0 & 0.4 \\ 0 & 0.2 & 0.8 \end{bmatrix}$

d. $\begin{bmatrix} 0.4 & 0 & 0.6 \\ 0.2 & 0.7 & 0.1 \\ 0.8 & 0 & 0.2 \end{bmatrix}$

e. $\begin{bmatrix} 0.2 & 0.3 & 0.5 \\ 0 & 1.0 & 0 \\ 0.8 & 0.1 & 0.1 \end{bmatrix}$

f. $\begin{bmatrix} 0 & 0.4 & 0.6 & 0 \\ 0.7 & 0 & 0 & 0.3 \\ 0.1 & 0 & 0 & 0.9 \\ 0 & 0 & 1.0 & 0 \end{bmatrix}$

g. $\begin{bmatrix} 0 & 0 & 1 & 0 \\ 0 & 1-\beta & \beta & 0 \\ \alpha & 0 & 0 & 1-\alpha \\ 0 & 0 & 1 & 0 \end{bmatrix}$

h. $\begin{bmatrix} 0 & 0.2 & 0.3 & 0.3 & 0.2 \\ 0 & 0.5 & 0 & 0.5 & 0 \\ 0.6 & 0.3 & 0 & 0.1 & 0 \\ 0 & 0.7 & 0 & 0.3 & 0 \\ 0.4 & 0.3 & 0 & 0.3 & 0 \end{bmatrix}$

8.2. Give an example of a Markov chain containing
   a. All ergodic states.
   b. Transient and ergodic states.
   c. Periodic states and an absorbing state.
   d. Periodic transient states and aperiodic ergodic states.

8.3. An irreducible Markov chain cannot contain sections that are periodic with different periods; all states must have the same period. Use examples to try to explain why.

8.4. Find the distribution of the number of passages through S_5 in the chain with Matrix 8.5.

8.5. Consider the random walk in Matrix 8.2. Suppose the process is started in S_0. How many trials, on the average, are needed to reach S_3? *Hint:* Treat S_3 as absorbing.

8.6. Raise the matrices in Problem 8.1, parts a and b, to successively higher powers to find their asymptotic state probabilities.

8.7. Find the asymptotic state distribution and the mean recurrence time for the chains in Problem 8.1.

8.8. Find the stable distribution for the random-walk model with Matrix 8.2. What happens to γ in the solution? Why?

8.9. What is the asymptotic error probability for the model in Problem 2.2?

8.10. Consider the probability-learning model in Equation 2.28.
   a. Show that the asymptotic state distribution is $[\pi^2, \pi(1-\pi), \pi(1-\pi), (1-\pi)^2]$. Find the asymptotic values of the re-

sponse probabilities, $P(R_1)$ and $P(R_2)$, and of the probability of a correct response and of an error.

   b. A subject is run at $\pi = 0.7$. After stable behavior is obtained, π is changed to 0.4. If $\sigma = 0.2$, how does $P(R_1)$ change?

8.11. Consider the simpler (four-state) form of the probability-learning model with response-dependent events defined in Problem 2.11.

   a. What are the asymptotic values of $P(R_1)$, $P(E_1)$, and P(correct)? Does the model predict matching of $P(E_1)$ and $P(R_1)$?

   b. Suppose that $\delta_1 = \delta_2 = 0.7$, and let σ be as in Problem 8.10b. After the subject has been responding under these conditions for enough time to perform stably, δ_1 and δ_2 are switched to 0.9 and 0.4. What happens to $P(E_1)$, $P(R_1)$, and the probability of a correct response?

8.12. [C] Write a computer program that will take the transition matrix of an ergodic chain and successively square it to calculate the stable distribution, s_∞, for the chain. Apply it to the matrices of Problem 8.1.

8.13. Calculate the first few values of $f_4^{(t)}$ for the chain in Matrix 8.5.

8.14. Write an equation similar to Equation 8.24 for the renewal-time distribution of state S_2 of Equation 8.1.

8.15. What is the mean number of trials to return to each of the states of the random walk with Matrix 8.2?

8.16. Consider the probability-learning model of Problem 8.10.

   a. An R_2 response is made and is followed by an E_1 event. How many R_1 responses, on the average, precede the next R_2 response?

   b. On the average, how many R_1 responses immediately follow an R_2 response without considering the event that follows it?

8.17. Consider S_4 of Matrix 8.5. After two of the three transitions from this state, return is inevitable; after the other, return is impossible. So find f_4, then use this to normalize the values of $f_4^{(t)}$ found in Problem 8.13, giving the recurrence distribution conditional on return taking place.

8.18. Find the mean recurrence time for errors in the all-or-none model of Matrix 8.21, given that an error takes place.

8.19. [C] Write a computer program that takes a transition matrix and calculates the probabilities $f_i^{(t)}$ for a range of t. Apply it to answer Problems 8.13 and 8.16.

8.20. [C] Write a computer program that takes the matrix of an ergodic chain in numerical form and determines the mean first-passage times for all pairs of states.

Chapter 9

Markov Chains with Unbounded State Spaces

The finite state spaces used in Chapters 3–8 make the models relatively easy to work with. The models can be constructed by considering the transitions between each pair of states separately and can be analyzed using either simple or matrix algebra. While this is convenient, there are a number of situations in which it is difficult to write the model with a small set of states, and it is more natural to think of a state space with a very large, or even infinite, number of states. Several examples of such models appeared in Chapter 2—the linear model and the random-trials-increment (RTI) model of learning (Equations 2.9 and 2.14) and, more generally, the unbounded random walks (Equation 2.34). These models require somewhat different methods of analysis, which are treated in this chapter.

Of course, for a Markov process in discrete time, an "infinite" number of states is not needed to describe any finite collection of data. A large, but finite state space always suffices for any particular case. However, when the limits of the process cannot be easily defined, infinite state spaces are often simpler. For any given realization of the process, the number of states needed is finite, but how many is not known beforehand. Hence, the model is written as if the number of states were infinite. The linear model of learning is an example. A new state is used for each trial and, although the number of trials for a particular subject is finite, there is no general maximum. As the principles that govern the transition are easily extended to an arbitrarily large state space, the infinite space makes the simpler model. The length of a queue of people waiting for something has the same property; there is no bound to the length of the queue, although of course infinite queues do not occur.

The analysis of a process with an unbounded state space is not greatly different from that of a finite-state process. The major change is that it is no longer possible to write the transitions as a closed matrix. Most of the discussion in the last chapter regarding state types applies without change. Many basic computation procedures also remain similar. However, the need to carry many of the calculations out to infinity makes them more difficult and prevents as easy an analysis as in the finite case. For example, with infinite state spaces, it is not possible to use most of the matrix methods. This makes some new mathematical methods useful.

9.1   Random Walks

A simple, but relatively general example of an infinite state space process is a random walk with one unbounded end and one at which the process is reflected. The transition rules for this process are given by Equation 2.34 (or Equations 2.33, 2.35, and 2.36) as the matrix

$$
\mathbf{T} = \begin{array}{c} S_0 \\ S_1 \\ S_2 \\ S_3 \\ \vdots \end{array}
\left[\begin{array}{ccccc}
1 - \gamma\eta & \gamma\eta & 0 & 0 & \cdots \\
\gamma(1 - \eta) & 1 - \gamma & \gamma\eta & 0 & \cdots \\
0 & \gamma(1 - \eta) & 1 - \gamma & \gamma\eta & \cdots \\
0 & 0 & \gamma(1 - \eta) & 1 - \gamma & \cdots \\
\vdots & \vdots & \vdots & \vdots & \vdots
\end{array}\right] \tag{9.1}
$$

State Probabilities

In the case of a finite chain with states numbered starting at S_0, successive state probabilities are found by

$$
P(S_{j,t}) = \sum_{i=0}^{N} P(S_{j,t}|S_{i,t-1})P(S_{i,t-1})
$$

as in Equation 3.5, or by using matrix multiplication:

$$
s_t = s_{t-1}\mathbf{T} = s_1\mathbf{T}^{t-1} \tag{9.2}
$$

as in Equation 4.4. With a countably infinite state space, the same rules apply. The only modification that needs to be made is to extend the limits of summation to infinity:

$$P(S_{j,t}) = \sum_{i=0}^{\infty} P(S_{j,t}|S_{i,t-1})P(S_{i,t-1}) \tag{9.3}$$

Equation 9.2 also works, as long as one is careful to evaluate correctly the implied infinite sums.

Of course, these infinite sums must converge to a finite value, rather than diverge. It is easy to prove that this is no problem for the state probabilities. The trick is to show that the sum is bounded by a finite number. The conditional probabilities in Equation 9.3 cannot be larger than 1; so $P(S_{j,t})$ is bounded by the sum obtained by replacing them with 1. Thus,

$$P(S_{j,t}) \leq \sum_{i=0}^{\infty} P(S_{i,t-1}) = 1$$

and so converges.

The transient behavior of the random-walk model is found by applying Equation 9.2 to Matrix 9.1. If the process starts out in state S_0, repeated multiplication of

$$s_0 = [1, 0, 0, 0, 0, \ldots]$$

by **T** gives

$$s_1 = [1 - \gamma\eta, \gamma\eta, 0, 0, 0, \ldots]$$
$$s_2 = [1 - 2\gamma\eta + \gamma^2\eta, \gamma\eta(2 - \gamma - \gamma\eta), \gamma^2\eta^2, 0, 0, \ldots]$$

and so forth. Because there is only a finite number of nonzero terms in any row or column of Matrix 9.1, the infinite sums reduce to finite sums. Some methods for finding more general solutions are treated in special cases of the random walk below.

Asymptotic Behavior

For many Markov processes, the long-term behavior is of as much interest as the transient behavior. Again, the basic results are the same as in the finite case. For large t, the state probabilities converge to a single set of probabilities

$$\mathbf{s}_\infty = [p_0, p_1, p_2, \ldots]$$

that is independent of the initial state.† The transition operation leaves the stable distribution unchanged, so

$$\mathbf{s}_\infty = \mathbf{s}_\infty \mathbf{T}$$

or, denoting elements of $\mathbf{T}$ by p_{ij}:

$$p_j = \sum_{i=0}^{\infty} p_{ij} p_i \qquad j = 0, 1, \ldots$$

For the random-walk model, substitution of transition probabilities into this equation gives

$$p_0 = (1 - \gamma\eta)p_0 + \gamma(1 - \eta)p_1$$
$$p_i = \gamma\eta p_{i-1} + (1 - \gamma)p_i + \gamma(1 - \eta)p_{i+1} \qquad i > 0 \tag{9.4}$$

As in the finite case, these equations are not sufficient to solve for the p_j. The fact that they are a probability distribution and sum to 1 is also needed:

$$\sum_{i=0}^{\infty} p_i = 1 \tag{9.5}$$

Equations 9.4 are a set of homogeneous difference equations, although not in the standard form of Appendix B (Equation B.4). After rearranging terms, renumbering the subscripts, and dividing by the coefficient of the highest indexed term, they become

$$p_1 - \frac{\eta}{1 - \eta} p_0 = 0$$
$$p_i - \frac{1}{1 - \eta} p_{i-1} + \frac{\eta}{1 - \eta} p_{i-2} = 0 \qquad i > 1 \tag{9.6}$$

Notice that the quantity γ has vanished from Equation 9.6 (as it did in Problem 8.8). This disappearance seems a bit surprising at first, but is

---

† If the chain is periodic, this is not quite correct. For a chain of period p, it is the p-step transitions $\mathbf{T}^{(p)}$ that converge. The periodic case is a simple generalization of the aperiodic case and need not be discussed further.

actually quite sensible. The probability that the process moves from an original state to another state is determined by γ (with large values, the rate of movement is rapid; with small values, it is slow) but γ is not involved in determining where the process goes when it does move. Because the rate at which the process converges to its asymptotic distribution is unrelated to the shape of the distribution, γ drops out of the asymptotic expression.

Equations 9.6 are solved by the methods of Appendix B to give

$$p_i = p_0 \left(\frac{\eta}{1 - \eta} \right)^i$$

This still depends on p_0. By Equation 9.5, the sum

$$\sum_{i=0}^{\infty} p_i = p_0 \sum_{i=0}^{\infty} \left(\frac{\eta}{1 - \eta} \right)^i \tag{9.7}$$

$$= p_0 \frac{1}{1 - \eta/(1 - \eta)}$$

must equal 1 for the p_i to be a probability distribution. Thus, $p_0 = 1 - \eta/(1 - \eta)$ and

$$p_i = \left(1 - \frac{\eta}{1 - \eta} \right) \left(\frac{\eta}{1 - \eta} \right)^i \tag{9.8}$$

The asymptotic state probabilities have a geometric distribution starting from $i = 0$.

With any infinite sum, one must be somewhat careful. The sum in Equation 9.7 converges only when $\eta/(1 - \eta) < 1$, which happens when $\eta < \frac{1}{2}$. If $\eta \geq \frac{1}{2}$, the sum diverges to infinity and Equation 9.7 makes sense only if p_0 is 0. Hence, all the p_i values are 0. These results have a sensible interpretation. When $\eta < \frac{1}{2}$, the process is more likely to move to lower-numbered states than to higher, that is, to the left in Matrix 9.1 rather than to the right. The states of the chain are all ergodic, and the asymptotic distribution piles up against S_0 in the geometric form of Equation 9.8. When $\eta > \frac{1}{2}$, the process moves to the right more often than to the left. Eventually, it surely passes to the right of any given state, leaving $p_i = 0$. Thus, all the states of the chain are transient. Leaving each state, there is less than a unit probability of ever returning.

This example illustrates one respect in which infinite chains differ from finite ones. In a finite state space it is not possible for a chain to consist entirely of transient states, but here, when $\eta > \frac{1}{2}$, all the states are transient. The special case of $\eta = \frac{1}{2}$ is slightly different from that of any other η. The sum in Equation 9.7 diverges; yet there is no net tendency for the process to move in one direction more than the other. It can be shown that the states of this chain are persistent, even though every p_i is 0. It is an example of a new type of state, which is discussed further in the next section.

State Types and Recurrence Probabilities

Most of the discussion of the renewal properties of a Markov chain in the preceding chapter applies also to chains with unbounded state spaces. The probability of first return to a state after t trials, $f_i^{(t)}$, is calculated by Equation 8.20:

$$f_i^{(t)} = p_{ii}^{(t)} - \sum_{u=1}^{t-1} f_i^{(u)} p_{ii}^{(t-u)} \tag{9.9}$$

The probability of eventual return is the sum of these probabilities (Equation 8.25):

$$f_i = \sum_{t=1}^{\infty} f_i^{(t)} \tag{9.10}$$

This quantity rigorously distinguishes between transient and persistent states: when $f_i = 1$, a state is persistent; when $f_i < 1$, it is transient.

The rule relating p_i to the mean recurrence time (Equations 8.29 and 8.30) holds for infinite-state processes,

$$\mu_i = \sum_{t=1}^{\infty} t f_i^{(t)} = \frac{1}{p_i}$$

For ergodic states, $p_i > 0$, and the mean time has a finite value. For transient states, $p_i = 0$; so μ_i is undefined, or, in effect, infinite. For the random walk when $\eta < \frac{1}{2}$, substituting the asymptotic probabilities from Equation 9.8:

$$\mu_i = \frac{1}{\left(1 - \dfrac{\eta}{1 - \eta}\right)\left(\dfrac{\eta}{1 - \eta}\right)^i} = \left(\frac{1 - \eta}{1 - 2\eta}\right)\left(\frac{1 - \eta}{\eta}\right)^i$$

This increases with i, indicating that returns are rare for states far from S_0.

Determining the persistence or transience of a state is more complicated when there is an infinite number of states than when the state
space is finite. With a finite state space, one can determine how each
state behaves by checking which transitions are possible and which are
not. With an infinite state space this is not enough; indeed, as the
random-walk example shows, states can be persistent or transient depending on the value of a parameter. The rule based on the value of f_i
ultimately determines the type of state. If a general formula for $f_i^{(t)}$ can
be found from Equation 9.9, then the sum in Equation 9.10 can be
evaluated and checked to see whether or not it equals 1.

Unfortunately, Equation 9.9 is often difficult to evaluate, and it is
helpful to have other criteria for determining the transience or persistence of a state. One such rule is based on the sum of the $p_{ii}^{(t)}$ and
another rule will be given in Section 9.4. If the $p_{ii}^{(t)}$ sum (over t) to a finite
value, then S_i is transient; while if the sum is infinite, then S_i is persistent. A demonstration of this fact is not elementary, so is deferred until
some new mathematical tools are available in Section 9.4. When a
stable distribution, s_∞, can be found, as in the random-walk example,
this rule makes it easy to identify many of the persistent states. Clearly,
as t gets large, $p_{ii}^{(t)}$ approaches p_i. If $p_i > 0$, then the sum of an infinite
number of terms roughly equal to p_i is infinite and S_i is persistent. As
any state that communicates with a persistent state is also persistent, so
showing persistence for one state in a chain like Matrix 9.1 is equivalent
to showing it for all states.

Demonstrating transience by this rule is not so easy. The fact that
$p_{ii}^{(t)} \to 0$ as $t \to \infty$ is not sufficient to make the sum of $p_{ii}^{(t)}$ finite. There
are many series whose terms go to 0, but whose sum is infinite; the
harmonic series, $1, \frac{1}{2}, \frac{1}{3}, \frac{1}{4}, \ldots$, is an example. Thus, $p_{ii}^{(t)}$ may go to 0,
even though S_i is persistent. However, such a situation is relatively
rare. Most commonly, $p_i = 0$ implies a transient state.

A persistent state for which $p_{ii}^{(t)} \to 0$ also has a divergent value of the
mean

$$\mu_i = \sum_{t=1}^{\infty} t f_i^{(t)}$$

This result is consistent with an attempt to substitute 0 for p_i in the
formula relating μ_i to p_i (Equation 9.10). The situation defines a new
class of states (and explains why the conditions on return time are
included in the definition of an ergodic state given in Chapter 8):

Null states are nonperiodic, persistent states for which the mean
time to return to the state after leaving it is infinite.

Null states occur only in infinite chains, usually as special cases, poised between situations where the states are ergodic and where they are transient. In the case of the random walk, when $\eta = \frac{1}{2}$, the process is just as likely to move left as right, so the states are null. Returns to any state always take place, but the distribution of waiting times includes many extremely long waits for a return. Because of these long waits, the expected waiting time is infinite. The special position of null states between ergodic and transient states makes them uncommon. Where the state type depends on a parameter value, null states usually occur for one exact parameter value only. Thus, they are quite unlikely to appear as a result of that particular value being estimated from data. When they do occur, it is usually because of constraints placed on the parameter values as a model is constructed.

9.2   A Queuing Example

Another example of an infinite-state process, often adaptable to psychological models, comes from queuing theory. Consider a simple queue in discrete time. A number of people arrive at a service facility and wait for service. The states of the system indicate the length of the waiting queue, including the person currently being served. In state S_0 the facility is empty and nobody is waiting; in S_1 there is one person, who is currently in the process of being served; in S_2 there are two persons, one being served and one waiting; and so forth. Although any particular queue is of finite length, there is no natural limit beyond which the queue cannot grow. So it is easiest to allow an unbounded state space.

The dynamics of the queue—the way in which it grows or shrinks— are yet to be defined. Obviously, there are many ways to do this. The simplest is to combine a homogeneous arrival process with a homogeneous departure process. Consider a queue in state S_i, $i > 0$. During each interval of time, one of three things may happen:

1. A new person may arrive, making the queue one longer. This changes the state to S_{i+1}. Let the probability of this event be α.

2. A person from the queue may be serviced and then depart. This reduces the state to S_{i-1}; let this probability be δ.

3. Either nobody may arrive or depart, or one person may arrive and one be served. In either case the queue remains in state S_i. The probability of this event is one minus the other two probabilities, or $1 - \alpha - \delta$.

Assume that there is no chance that two or more arrivals or services take place during the interval. When the queue is empty—in S_0—departures do not occur, so only events 1 and 3 are possible.

These rules describe a Markov chain. More formally, the transition probabilities are

$$P(S_{0,t+1}) = (1 - \alpha)P(S_{0,t}) + \delta P(S_{1,t})$$
$$P(S_{j,t+1}) = \alpha P(S_{j-1,t}) + (1 - \alpha - \delta)P(S_{j,t}) + \delta P(S_{j,t+1}) \quad j > 0 \tag{9.11}$$

or, in matrix form,

$$\mathbf{T} = \begin{bmatrix} 1 - \alpha & \alpha & 0 & 0 & \cdots \\ \delta & 1 - \alpha - \delta & \alpha & 0 & \cdots \\ 0 & \delta & 1 - \alpha - \delta & \alpha & \cdots \\ 0 & 0 & \delta & 1 - \alpha - \delta & \cdots \\ \vdots & \vdots & \vdots & \vdots & \end{bmatrix} \tag{9.12}$$

There are many things one may want to ask about this queue, such as whether there is a stable distribution and if so what it is, how often the server is free, what the average length of the queue is, and so forth.

Most of the analysis has already been done. A comparison of Matrix 9.12 with the transitions for the random-walk model, Matrix 9.1, shows that they are identical, except for the letters chosen to represent the parameters. If $\alpha = \gamma\eta$ and $\delta = \gamma(1 - \eta)$, they are exactly the same. The results from the random-walk model carry over to the queuing model. Once again, different physical situations lead to models that are mathematically identical.

The parameter correspondence gives $\eta = \alpha/(\alpha + \delta)$, and substitution of this into Equation 9.8 gives the asymptotic state distribution:

$$p_i = \left(1 - \frac{\alpha}{\delta}\right)\left(\frac{\alpha}{\delta}\right)^i \tag{9.13}$$

The distribution in Equation 9.8 is valid only when $\eta < \frac{1}{2}$, which here means that $\alpha < \delta$. Thus, only when the rate of arrival is less than the rate of service are the states ergodic. When $\alpha > \delta$, people arrive in the queue faster, on the average, than they are serviced, and the queue grows indefinitely. In that case, the chance that the queue is of any given length, $P(S_{i,t})$, becomes arbitrarily close to 0 for sufficiently large t. When the arrival and departure rates are the same, the states are null; so a queue once started eventually empties itself, returning to S_0, although the time required to do so is infinite.

The asymptotic distribution depends only on the ratio α/δ, not on the particular values of α and δ, just as the random-walk results depend on η and not on γ. This correctly suggests that α/δ plays a fundamental role in the queuing process. In queuing theory this ratio—here the probability of arrival divided by the probability of departure, but more generally the mean time to service each "customer" divided by the mean time between arrivals of "customers"—is known as the *traffic intensity* and denoted by ρ. With this substitution, the asymptotic distribution is

$$p_i = (1 - \rho)\rho^i \qquad (9.14)$$

With the asymptotic solution in hand, the other questions posed above can easily be answered. The server is free when the queue is in S_0; the probability of this is, asymptotically, $p_0 = 1 - \rho$. The average length of the queue is the mean of the geometric distribution in Equation 9.14, or $\rho/(1 - \rho)$. The variance of the queue length is $\rho/(1 - \rho)^2$.

Obviously, there are many more questions that might be asked about this queue, particularly concerning such things as waiting time for service and the like. Other types of arrival and service patterns than Matrix 9.12 could be treated. However, in many ways, queuing operations are more realistic when conceived of as processes in continuous time, so further discussion of queuing theory is deferred until Chapter 10.

9.3 Learning Models

Both the linear model and the RTI model are special cases of an infinite-state random walk. The addition of the response process, with responses defined as functions of the Markov states, adds a level of complexity.

Consider the linear model first. It has the trivial Markov chain

$$\mathbf{T} = \begin{array}{c} S_0 \\ S_1 \\ S_2 \\ \vdots \end{array} \left[\begin{array}{ccccc} 0 & 1 & 0 & 0 & \cdots \\ 0 & 0 & 1 & 0 & \cdots \\ 0 & 0 & 0 & 1 & \cdots \\ \vdots & \vdots & \vdots & \vdots & \end{array} \right] \qquad (9.15)$$

(see Matrix 2.9). Starting in S_0, the state probabilities are

$$P(S_{i,t}) = \begin{cases} 1 & i = t - 1 \\ 0 & \text{otherwise} \end{cases}$$

The response mapping (Equations 2.10 and 2.11) is

$$P(E|S_i) = e_i = \theta e_{i-1} = \epsilon\theta^i$$

Thus, the learning curve is

$$P(E_t) = e_{t-1} = \epsilon\theta^{t-1}$$

Note that this function is identical to the learning curve of the all-or-none model (Equation 3.12). For both models, the curve depends on one guessing-rate parameter (ϵ in the linear model, g in the all-or-none model) and one learning-rate parameter (θ or α).

The expected number of errors in acquisition is found by summing the learning curve, in the same manner as was done with the all-or-none model in Equation 3.16:

$$E(T) = \sum_{t=1}^{\infty} P(E_t) = \frac{\epsilon}{1 - \theta}$$

The finiteness of this result is reassuring. The linear model is never absorbed in a state where errors are impossible, the way that the finite-state models are. Hence, it is possible that there would never be an end to the string of errors, that every error would eventually be followed by another one. The finite expectation of T indicates that this is not the case and that each subject eventually ceases to make errors with probability 1.

If the initial error rate, ϵ, is taken from the task to be the reciprocal of the number of response alternatives, or $1 - g$, only the parameter θ needs to be estimated. The method-of-moments estimator based on $E(T)$ is

$$\hat{\theta} = 1 - \frac{1 - g}{M_T}$$

The form of the result is exactly the same as the estimator of $1 - \alpha$ for the all-or-none model (Equation 5.2), and thus, the predicted learning curve is the same.

Identical learning curves do not make the models otherwise identical. In fact, the learning curve is often a very poor discriminator of the models, for it reflects mainly the acquisition principles built into every learning model. Many other statistics discriminate better. One statistic that contrasts the small and large state spaces of the models particularly well is the conditional error probability, $P(E_{t+1}|E_t)$. For the all-or-none model, because there is only one error state, this statistic has the value

$(1 - \alpha)(1 - g)$, which is independent of t (see Equation 3.22). For the linear model, responses are independent from trial to trial, so

$$P(E_{t+1}|E_t) = P(E|S_t) = \epsilon\theta^t$$

This declines with t, unlike the predictions of the all-or-none model. Similarly, other statistics based on sequential properties differ between the models.

The Markov chain in Matrix 9.15 underlying the linear model is quite trivial, but easily generalizes to that of the RTI model. The result is an ascending random walk with probability α:

$$\mathbf{T} = \begin{bmatrix} 1 - \alpha & \alpha & 0 & \cdots \\ 0 & 1 - \alpha & \alpha & \cdots \\ 0 & 0 & 1 - \alpha & \cdots \\ \vdots & \vdots & \vdots & \end{bmatrix}$$

The states of this chain are all transient, as the discussion of the general random walk indicates.

The state distribution on trial t is easier to obtain for the RTI model than for an arbitrary random walk. The fact that movement is only rightward helps considerably. Prior to trial t there have been $t - 1$ opportunities for a state transition to have taken place, each with probability α. These events are independent, so the number of transitions that actually take place has a binomial distribution with parameters $t - 1$ and α. Hence,

$$P(S_{i,t}) = \begin{cases} \binom{t-1}{i} \alpha^i(1 - \alpha)^{t-1-i} & 0 \le i < t \\ 0 & i \ge t \end{cases} \tag{9.16}$$

The error probability on trial t follows from this distribution. Using the law of total probability (Equation A.4), then evaluating the resulting sum with the binomial theorem (Equation A.34) gives

$$\begin{aligned} P(E_t) &= \sum_{i=0}^{t-1} P(E|S_i)P(S_{i,t}) \\ &= \sum_{i=0}^{t-1} (\epsilon\theta^i) \binom{t-1}{i} \alpha^i(1 - \alpha)^{t-1-i} \\ &= \epsilon \sum_{i=0}^{t-1} \binom{t-1}{i} (\alpha\theta)^i(1 - \alpha)^{t-1-i} \\ &= \epsilon(\alpha\theta + 1 - \alpha)^{t-1} = \epsilon[1 - \alpha(1 - \theta)]^{t-1} \end{aligned} \tag{9.17}$$

As might be expected, the probability of an error falls off exponentially with t, just as it did for the all-or-none model and the linear model. By setting $\theta = 0$ or $\alpha = 1$, Equation 9.17 reduces to the corresponding formula for these models. Again, the learning curve fails to discriminate between models.

Probabilities of events that depend on a finite string of trials—for example, the sequential statistics or $P(E_{t+1}|E_t)$—are found in this manner. However, the infinite state space makes calculation of other statistics quite hard. Properties like the trial of last error or the total number of errors, where calculations extend over both the infinitude of states and of trials, are difficult to find. Calculations that involve the fundamental matrix for the finite chains (as in Section 4.2) no longer work, for the infinite state sets produce matrices that cannot be inverted. Recourse to other mathematical techniques is required. Some of these techniques are discussed in the next section.

9.4 Generating Functions

Many of the calculations in this book involve infinite series of terms. A number of mathematical tools have been developed to work with such series. One of the most useful of these is the generating function. Generating functions often allow difficult calculations, such as infinite sums or convolutions to be replaced by simpler operations, such as substitution or multiplication. For this reason, generating functions are almost essential to the more advanced analysis of statistical models. In this section, a brief introduction to these methods is presented. A more complete treatment is given in Feller, 1968; most texts on transform methods in engineering include discussions of generating functions.

The basic idea of a generating function is to use the members of a series to create a function of a new variable, but one from which the original series can be recovered. Then, instead of calculating with the original series, the new function is used. For many series, this calculation is easier than working with the original series. At the end, the result can be converted back to a series again. In this sense, a generating function is simply a computational aid.

Generating functions are members of a larger class of mathematical techniques known as *transform methods*. Generating functions are used only with discrete series, but there are similar techniques that apply to continuous functions (Laplace transforms and Fourier transforms) and probability distributions (characteristic functions and moment generating functions). The principles behind all of these are similar. Only generating functions are covered in this book.

Consider an infinite series of numbers such as probabilities, p_0, p_1, p_2, ... , that are absolutely bounded, so that $|p_i|$ is less than some maximum value, A. As a shorthand, let the symbol $\{p_i\}$ refer to this series. Now multiply each p_i by the ith power of a new variable z; then sum the result to yield a new function:

$$P(z) = p_0 + p_1 z + p_2 z^2 + p_3 z^3 + \cdots = \sum_{i=0}^{\infty} p_i z^i \qquad (9.18)$$

The variable z has no particular interpretation; it simply aids in putting the p_i together.† The function $P(z)$ is known as a *generating function* (or *probability generating function*) or sometimes as the z *transform* of the series $\{p_i\}$. It is as though each p_i is "tagged" by the power z^i, then all the terms combined together. Although combined in $P(z)$, the power of z that marks each term allows p_i to be recovered later.

Where the terms of $\{p_i\}$ are probabilities forming the distribution of a random variable X, the definition in Equation 9.18 has an additional interpretation. It is the expectation

$$E(z^X) = \sum_{i=0}^{\infty} z^i P(X = i)$$

Where only distributions are involved, the generating function is sometimes defined as this expectation.

For the definition of $P(z)$ to work properly, the sum in Equation 9.18 must converge to a finite value. This is the reason for putting the bound on p_i. The geometric series Σz^i converges to $1/(1 - z)$ in the range $|z| < 1$; and if $|p_i| \le A$, then $|P(z)|$ cannot exceed $A/(1 - z)$ in this range. Hence, the generating function exists, at least for some range of z. What happens outside the interval $|z| < 1$ depends on the series $\{p_i\}$.

For Markov processes, the geometric distribution is clearly going to be important. So consider the series

$$p_i = (1 - \alpha)\alpha^i \qquad i = 0, 1, 2, \ldots$$

Applying Equation 9.18, one finds the generating function to be

$$P(z) = \sum_{i=0}^{\infty} (1 - \alpha)\alpha^i z^i$$

$$= (1 - \alpha) \sum_{i=0}^{\infty} (\alpha z)^i$$

$$= \frac{1 - \alpha}{1 - \alpha z} \qquad (9.19)$$

---

† The letter s or ζ is frequently used instead of z.

If one has $\{p_i\}$, one can find $P(z)$ by evaluating Equation 9.18. It is also important to be able to go the other way: to start with $P(z)$ and recover $\{p_i\}$. This is always possible, although not always easy. Taylor's theorem from elementary calculus states that any function $P(z)$ that is well behaved near zero (as the generating function always is) can be written uniquely as a power series of the form in Equation 9.18, in which

$$p_i = \frac{1}{i!} \frac{d^i P(z)}{(dz)^i} \bigg|_{z=0} \tag{9.20}$$

The uniqueness part of the theorem is important. There is only one way to write a series for a given $P(z)$, and so if $P(z)$ is formed from $\{p_i\}$ by Equation 9.18, this must be the series that is recovered. It is not possible to begin with one $\{p_i\}$, transform it to $P(z)$, and then transform it back to get a different series.

It is fairly easy to use Equation 9.20 to recover the first few terms of the geometric series from Equation 9.19. First,

$$P(0) = 1 - \alpha = p_0$$

Then, using Equation D.13 and D.7 to find the derivative gives

$$P'(z) = \frac{(1 - \alpha)\alpha}{(1 - \alpha z)^2}$$

$$P'(0) = (1 - \alpha)\alpha = p_1$$

Continued differentiation gives higher-order terms.

In practice, the transformation from $P(z)$ to $\{p_i\}$ is frequently much harder than going the other way. Given $P(z)$, one can reconstruct the series by taking derivatives and calculating terms using Equation 9.20, but this is quite a lot of work and may not lead to a general formula for p_i. Often, it is possible to recognize $\{p_i\}$ when one sees $P(z)$. For example, geometric series of terms occur frequently and can be recognized because their generating functions look like Equation 9.19. Generalizing this formula slightly, the generating function

$$P(z) = \frac{A z^K}{1 - Bz} \tag{9.21}$$

implies the series

$$p_i = AB^{K+i} \qquad i = 0, 1, 2, \ldots$$

Similarly, the generating function

$$P(z) = (Az + B)^N \tag{9.22}$$

arises from the binomial series

$$p_i = \binom{N}{i} A^i B^{N-i} \qquad i = 0, 1, \ldots, N$$

(see Problem 9.6). To aid in recognizing generating functions, tables of $\{p_i\}-P(z)$ pairs are given in many mathematical handbooks (e.g., Beyer, 1978).

Properties of Generating Functions

So far, the usefulness of generating functions may not be apparent. Seemingly, they change a series to a less transparent form, while introducing a new and uninterpretable variable. Their usefulness comes from the fact that several important operations with $\{p_i\}$ are simpler when done on the generating function. Accordingly, this section examines how some common operations on $\{p_i\}$ affect the corresponding generating functions.

First consider what happens when z is set to 1. Putting $z = 1$ in Equation 9.18 gives

$$P(1) = \sum_{i=0}^{\infty} p_i 1^i = \sum_{i=0}^{\infty} p_i \tag{9.23}$$

that is, the sum of the series. For the geometric distribution, setting z to 1 in Equation 9.19 gives

$$P(1) = \frac{1 - \alpha}{1 - \alpha 1} = 1$$

which is as it should be for a probability distribution. The operation is easier than finding the corresponding sum of the original series, even for so simple a series as the geometric.

The first derivative of $P(z)$ gives a different sum:

$$P'(z) = \frac{d}{dz} \sum_{i=0}^{\infty} p_i z^i$$

$$= \sum_{i=0}^{\infty} \frac{d}{dz} p_i z^i = \sum_{i=0}^{\infty} i p_i z^{i-1}$$

$$P'(1) = \sum_{i=1}^{\infty} i p_i$$

Thus, when $\{p_i\}$ is a probability distribution of a random variable X,

$$P'(1) = \mu_X \qquad (9.24)$$

Again using the geometric distribution as an example gives

$$P'(z) = \frac{\alpha(1 - \alpha)}{(1 - \alpha z)^2}$$

$$P'(1) = \frac{\alpha}{(1 - \alpha)}$$

The importance of Equation 9.24 is that it permits the mean of a distribution to be found without knowing the individual terms. Often the moments of a distribution may be important when the terms are not.

A similar calculation (see Problem 9.11) shows that

$$\sigma_P^2 = P''(1) - P'(1)[1 - P'(1)] \qquad (9.25)$$

where $P''(z)$ is the second derivative of $P(z)$. Higher derivatives can be used to find the higher moments.

The real value of generating functions becomes apparent when several series are combined. The next two identities give rules for such combinations. The first shows that the formation of generating functions preserves linear combinations. Let $\{p_i\}$, $\{q_i\}$, and $\{r_i\}$ be series with generating functions $P(z)$, $Q(z)$, and $R(z)$, respectively. Suppose that the terms of $\{r_i\}$ are linear functions of $\{p_i\}$ and $\{q_i\}$:

$$r_i = ap_i + bq_i$$

for constants a and b. When transformed to generating functions, the same relationship holds:

$$R(z) = aP(z) + bQ(z) \qquad (9.26)$$

This is easily proved by substitution:

$$R(z) = \sum_{i=0}^{\infty} (ap_i + bq_i)z^i$$

$$= a \sum_{i=0}^{\infty} p_i z^i + b \sum_{i=0}^{\infty} q_i z^i = aP(z) + bQ(z)$$

The second identity concerns the *convolution* of the series $\{p_i\}$ and

$\{q_i\}$. Suppose that $\{t_i\}$ is defined by the convolution relationship

$$t_i = \sum_{j=0}^{i} p_j q_{i-j} \tag{9.27}$$

Then the generating function $T(z)$ of $\{t_i\}$ is the product of the component generating functions:

$$T(z) = P(z)Q(z) \tag{9.28}$$

To prove Equation 9.28, write out the product and collect terms with the same power of z:

$$P(z)Q(z) = [p_0 + p_1 z + p_2 z^2 + \cdots][q_0 + q_1 z + q_2 z^2 + \cdots]$$

$$= p_0 q_0 + p_0 q_1 z + p_0 q_2 z^2 + p_0 q_3 z^3 + \cdots$$
$$+ p_1 q_0 z + p_1 q_1 z^2 + p_1 q_2 z^3 + \cdots$$
$$+ p_2 q_0 z^2 + p_2 q_1 z^3 + \cdots$$
$$+ p_3 q_0 z^3 + \cdots$$
$$+ \cdots$$

$$= p_0 q_0 + (p_0 q_1 + p_1 q_0)z + (p_0 q_2 + p_1 q_1 + p_2 q_0)z^2 + \cdots$$
$$= t_0 + t_1 z + t_2 z^2 + \cdots = T(z)$$

Convolutions are very common in probability calculations because of their relationship to sums of random variables. If $\{p_i\}$ and $\{q_i\}$ are probability distributions of random variables X and Y, then Equation 9.27 is the distribution of the sum

$$T = X + Y$$

Unfortunately, the convolution (Equation 9.27) is often hard to compute. Clearly, the product (Equation 9.28) is much simpler. Indeed, at times the generating function is one of the few good ways to find information about the distribution of a sum.

The final rule needed here gives the generating function of a series that is offset from another series by k steps. Let

$$q_0 = q_1 = \cdots = q_{k-1} = 0, \; q_k = p_0, \; q_{k+1} = p_1, \cdots, q_{t+k} = p_t, \cdots$$

Then

$$Q(z) = \sum_{t=0}^{\infty} q_t z^t$$

$$= \sum_{t=0}^{\infty} p_t z^{t+k}$$

$$= z^k P(z) \tag{9.29}$$

Thus, multiplying (or dividing) a generating function by a power of z shifts the series one way or the other.

Difference Equations and State Probabilities

Generating functions can be used to find the state probabilities for some of the models treated above. First consider the asymptotic state probabilities for an infinite-state chain. Equations 9.6, which gave the relationships among the asymptotic probabilities for the states of the random-walk model, are difference equations and are solved by the methods of Appendix B. The same result can be obtained with generating functions, using yet another way to solve difference equations.

The general member of Equation 9.6, adjusted to remove fractions, is

$$\eta p_{i-2} - p_{i-1} + (1 - \eta)p_i = 0 \qquad i \geq 2$$

The strategy is to turn this into an equation involving the generating function of $\{p_i\}$ by introducing powers of z and summing over i. The first step is to multiply by z^i (note that i is the largest subscript of p) to give

$$\eta p_{i-2} z^i - p_{i-1} z^i + (1 - \eta)p_i z^i = 0 \qquad i \geq 2$$

This really represents an infinite set of equations, one for each value of i. Summing them over the permissible range of i gives

$$\eta \sum_{i=2}^{\infty} p_{i-2} z^i - \sum_{i=2}^{\infty} p_{i-1} z^i + (1 - \eta) \sum_{i=2}^{\infty} p_i z^i = 0$$

The sums here are not yet generating functions, for they either have the wrong power of z or are missing terms. These defects are overcome either by factoring out the unnecessary powers of z or by adding the missing terms. For example, in the middle sum, the power of z is one too high and the term p_0 is missing. Removing a z and adding and subtracting p_0 give

$$\sum_{i=2}^{\infty} p_{i-1}z^i = z\left(\sum_{i=2}^{\infty} p_{i-1}z^{i-1} + p_0 - p_0\right)$$

$$= z\left(\sum_{i=0}^{\infty} p_i z^i - p_0\right) = z[P(z) - p_0]$$

A similar reduction of the other two terms produces

$$\eta z^2 P(z) - z[P(z) - p_0] + (1 - \eta)[P(z) - p_0 - p_1 z] = 0$$

This equation is readily solved to give

$$P(z) = \frac{(1 - \eta)p_0 + [(1 - \eta)p_1 - p_0]z}{\eta z^2 - z + (1 - \eta)}$$

The next step is to clean up this expression, removing the unknown probabilities p_0 and p_1. One of these can be eliminated by using the first of the original difference equations. From Equations 9.6, when $i = 1$,

$$(1 - \eta)p_1 = \eta p_0$$

Using this to replace p_1 gives

$$P(z) = \frac{(1 - \eta)p_0(1 - z)}{\eta z^2 - z + (1 - \eta)}$$

Both numerator and denominator contain a common factor of $1 - z$. Removing this gives

$$P(z) = \frac{(1 - \eta)p_0}{1 - \eta - \eta z} = \frac{p_0}{1 - \dfrac{\eta}{1 - \eta}z}$$

The remaining constant is found by using the fact that the terms of $\{p_i\}$ are a probability distribution. Because of this, $\Sigma p_i = 1$. Setting $z = 1$ gives the sum (see Equation 9.23)

$$1 = P(1) = \frac{p_0}{1 - \dfrac{\eta}{1 - \eta}}$$

Thus, $p_0 = 1 - \eta/(1 - \eta)$ and

$$P(z) = \frac{1 - \dfrac{\eta}{1 - \eta}}{1 - \dfrac{\eta}{1 - \eta} z} \qquad (9.30)$$

The final step is to recover the distribution. It is relatively easy to do this, for Equation 9.30 can be recognized as having the form of Equation 9.21. More particularly, Equation 9.30 is the generating function of the geometric distribution in Equation 9.19 with $\alpha = \eta/(1 - \eta)$. So

$$p_i = \left(1 - \frac{\eta}{1 - \eta}\right)\left(\frac{\eta}{1 - \eta}\right)^i$$

This is identical to Equation 9.8.

This derivation found nothing that could not be found by more conventional methods. However, had the connections among the states been more complicated, it would have been much harder to solve the difference equations and, once solved, to find summary statistics such as means and variances. Generating functions might then be preferred. It is not always as easy to get back to the state probabilities as it was from Equation 9.30, but the task is not impossible. State probabilities for Markov chains are determined by systems of linear difference equations, so are usually sums of geometric terms. However complicated the generating function for such a sum looks, the fact that a generating function preserves linear combinations (see Equation 9.26) means that it can be resolved into a sum of terms like Equation 9.21. A partial-fraction decomposition (discussed in any calculus book) can be used to put $P(z)$ into the form of a sum, then the geometric terms read off from it. Where one or two of the first terms are all that are needed, the inversion formula, Equation 9.20, can also be used.

The RTI Model

Generating functions are more valuable with models like the RTI model, where the calculations are complicated. To illustrate how they are used, several results are rederived here, starting with the state distribution.

Let Y_t be a random variable indicating the state number on trial t; thus, $P(S_{i,t}) = P(Y_t = i)$. Clearly, Y_t is the sum of the steps taken on the

$t - 1$ trials preceding trial t. Let X_u be a random variable that counts the number of steps taken on trial u (it is either 0 or 1); then

$$Y_t = \sum_{u=1}^{t-1} X_u$$

Because Y_t is the sum of independent random variables, its generating function is the product of the generating functions of its parts (see Equation 9.28):

$$Y_t(z) = \prod_{u=1}^{t-1} X_u(z)$$

Let the series $\{x_i\}$ be the distribution of X_u. As the process is homogeneous, this distribution need not be indexed by u. From the definition of the RTI model, $x_0 = 1 - \alpha$, $x_1 = \alpha$, and all other x_i values are 0. Thus, the generating function of $\{x_i\}$ is

$$X(z) = (1 - \alpha)z^0 + \alpha z^1 = 1 - \alpha + \alpha z$$

and

$$Y_t(z) = [X(z)]^{t-1} = (1 - \alpha + \alpha z)^{t-1} \tag{9.31}$$

This generating function may be recognized as having the form of Equation 9.22, whence Y_t has a binomial distribution (given in Equation 9.16).

The error probability, $P(E_t)$, is obtained from the state-probability distribution by applying the response mapping

$$P(E_t) = \sum_{t=0}^{\infty} P(E|S_i)P(S_{i,t})$$

Define q_i to be a term of this sum:

$$q_i = P(E|S_i)P(S_{i,t})$$

and let $Q_t(z)$ be the corresponding generating function. Then the sum giving $P(E_t)$ is $Q_t(1)$. By definition,

$$Q_t(z) = \sum_{i=0}^{\infty} P(E|S_i)P(S_{i,t}) z^i$$

$$= \sum_{i=0}^{\infty} \epsilon \theta^i P(S_{i,t}) z^i = \epsilon \sum_{i=0}^{\infty} P(S_{i,t})(\theta z)^i$$

Except for the use of θz, this sum looks like the definition of the generating function $Y_t(z)$. So, substituting in Equation 9.31 gives

$$Q_t(z) = \epsilon\, Y_t(\theta z) = \epsilon(1 - \alpha + \alpha\theta z)^{t-1}$$

Setting $z = 1$ to sum:

$$P(E_t) = Q_t(1) = \epsilon(1 - \alpha + \alpha\theta)^{t-1}$$

which agrees with Equation 9.17. The use of generating functions and the relatively simple form of $P(E|S_i)$ make it unnecessary to explicitly find any state probability or to calculate any sums.

Recurrence Probabilities

The final example of the use of generating functions is drawn from the renewal properties treated in Section 8.3. Fundamental to these calculations is the probability that state S_i first recurs after t trials, or $f_i^{(t)}$. This is related to the i-step transition probabilities $p_{ii}^{(t)}$ by Equation 8.20:

$$f_i^{(t)} = p_{ii}^{(t)} - \sum_{u=1}^{t-1} f_i^{(u)} p_{ii}^{(t-u)} \tag{9.32}$$

This equation is somewhat difficult to evaluate directly.

The recurrence equation has a remarkably simple form when expressed with generating functions. Let $P_i(z)$ and $F_i(z)$ be the generating functions of $\{p_{ii}^{(t)}\}$ and $\{f_i^{(t)}\}$, respectively. Reordering the terms, Equation 9.32 is

$$p_{ii}^{(t)} = f_i^{(t)} + \sum_{u=1}^{t-1} f_i^{(u)} p_{ii}^{(t-u)}$$

If $p_{ii}^{(0)}$ is taken as 1 and $f_i^{(0)}$ as 0, which are both reasonable and conventional definitions, this equation is a convolution:

$$p_{ii}^{(t)} = \sum_{u=0}^{t} f_i^{(u)} p_{ii}^{(t-u)} \qquad t > 0 \tag{9.33}$$

The convolution form suggests applying Equation 9.28, writing the generating functions on the left as the product of those on the right. This would work if Equation 9.33 were true for all t. Unfortunately, it is not correct in the somewhat artificial case of $t = 0$, for $p_{ii}^{(0)}$ (which is 1) is not the same as $f_i^{(0)} p_{ii}^{(0)}$ (which is 0). To express Equation 9.33 in generating functions, the missing term for $t = 0$ is subtracted from the left-hand side:

$$P_i(z) - p_{ii}^{(0)}z^0 = F_i(z)P_i(z)$$

By definition, $p_{ii}^{(0)}z^0$ is 1, so

$$P_i(z) - 1 = F_i(z)P_i(z)$$

or

$$F_i(z) = 1 - \frac{1}{P_i(z)} \tag{9.34}$$

This simple equation expresses the same relationship as Equation 9.32.

The probability of eventual return to S_i is the sum of the $f_i^{(t)}$ (Equations 8.25 and 9.10). This sum is $F_i(1)$. From Equation 9.34, it is clear that $F_i(1)$ is 1 only when $1/P_i(1)$ is 0. This is the basis for the remark, left unproved earlier in this chapter, that a state is recurrent only when the sum of the $p_{ii}^{(t)}$ is infinite.

For a recurrent state, the expected return times are of interest. Once again, these follow directly from the generating functions, for then, by Equation 9.24,

$$\mu_i = \sum_{t=1}^{\infty} tf_i^{(t)} = F_i'(1)$$

Consider an example. For the all-or-none model,

$$p_{EE}^{(t)} = (1 - \gamma)(1 - \alpha)^t$$

(see Equation 8.22). Remembering that by definition $p_{EE}^{(0)} = 1$, the generating function for this series is

$$P_E(z) = 1 + \sum_{t=1}^{\infty} (1 - \gamma)(1 - \alpha)^t z^t$$

$$= 1 + \sum_{t=0}^{\infty} (1 - \gamma)(1 - \alpha)^t z^t - (1 - \gamma)(1 - \alpha)^0 z^0$$

$$= \gamma + (1 - \gamma) \sum_{t=0}^{\infty} [(1 - \alpha)z]^t$$

$$= \gamma + \frac{(1 - \gamma)}{1 - (1 - \alpha)z} = \frac{1 - (1 - \alpha)\gamma z}{1 - (1 - \alpha)z}$$

Applying Equation 9.34, one finds the generating function for the recurrence times to be

$$F_E(z) = 1 - \frac{1}{\left(\dfrac{1 - (1 - \alpha)\gamma z}{1 - (1 - \alpha)z}\right)} = \frac{(1 - \alpha)(1 - \gamma)z}{1 - (1 - \alpha)\gamma z} \qquad (9.35)$$

Equation 9.35 is readily identified as an example of Equation 9.21, so it is the generating function of the geometric series

$$f_E^{(t)} = (1 - \alpha)(1 - \gamma)[(1 - \alpha)\gamma]^{t-1}$$

This result was found less easily in Equation 8.23 by conventional algebra. The approach with generating functions is substantially more systematic.

The sum of this series is the probability of any eventual error, f_E. Setting $z = 1$ in Equation 9.35 gives

$$f_E = F_E(1) = \frac{(1 - \alpha)(1 - \gamma)}{1 - (1 - \alpha)\gamma}$$

replicating Equation 8.26.

Problems

9.1. Consider the queuing model of Section 9.2 and suppose that arrivals take place in pairs. When an arrival event takes place (with probability λ), this moves the process from S_i to S_{i+2}. Keep the service process the same.

  a. Draw a state diagram for the process.

  b. Write a transition matrix and a set of difference equations for this process.

  c. What is the traffic intensity for this queue?

  d. Under what conditions would you expect the states to be transient? ergodic? null?

  e. Asymptotically, what is the probability that the server is not occupied? *Hint:* One root of the auxiliary equation for the state probabilities is $m = 1$. Appreciable algebra is involved.

  f. What is the asymptotic mean length of the queue?

  g. Generalize the scheme in part a to the case where a proportion ϕ of the arrivals are single and a proportion $1 - \phi$ are double.

9.2. For the RTI model, find $P(E_{t+1}|E_t)$. Show that this reduces under appropriate conditions to the values for the linear model and the all-or-none model.

9.3. Suppose that changes in response probabilities in the RTI model took place only following errors. Specify an appropriate state space, draw a state diagram, and define the transition probabilities.

9.4. Consider a random walk in which both ends are open; that is, the states extend from S_0 both up through S_1, S_2, ... , and down through S_{-1}, S_{-2}, ... The process starts in S_0 at $t = 0$ and moves according to probabilities analogous to Equation 9.1. What is the state distribution on trial t? What happens for t very large? *Hint:* Extend the binomial-analysis procedure used with the RTI model. Do not evaluate the sum that results.

9.5. What is the generating function of the constant series $c_i = C$, $i = 0, 1, ...$.

9.6. Verify the generating functions
a. Of the geometric series in Equation 9.21.
b. Of the binomial series in Equation 9.22.

9.7. Find the generating function of the linear series $p_t = a + bt$, $t \geq 0$.

9.8. Use generating functions to solve the difference equation in Equation B.9.

9.9. Use generating functions (including the results of Problem 9.7) to solve the difference equation in Equation B.13.

9.10. Differentiate Equation 9.18 twice and set $z = 1$ to find $P''(1)$. Then show that Equation 9.25 holds.

9.11. From the generating function (Equation 9.31), obtain the mean and variance of the state number on trial t for the RTI model. Check the results, using the fact that the distribution is binomial.

9.12. Consider the double-arrival queue from Problem 9.1.
a. Using the difference equations in part b, find the generating function for the state probabilities. *Hint:* Remember that $\Sigma P(S_{i,t}) = 1$.
b. Use this generating function to answer parts e and f, without solving for the state-probability distribution.

9.13. Consider states S_4 and S_5 of Matrix 8.5. Define $P(S_{4,t}) = p_t$ and $P(S_{5,t}) = q_t$. Note that for a process starting in S_4 (i.e., $p_0 = 1$ and $q_0 = 0$), $p_t = p_{44}^{(t)}$.
a. Write the simultaneous difference equations expressing p_{t+1} and q_{t+1} in terms of p_t and q_t. Multiply these equations by z^{t+1}

and sum over t to get simultaneous equations in the generating functions $P(z)$ and $Q(z)$. Solve for $P(z)$.

b. Find the generating function for the recurrence probabilities of S_4, $F(z)$. Find the probability of eventual return to S_4. Note that this solves Problem 8.17 in a much more general way.

c. Correct the generating function in part b to condition on eventual return to S_4. What is the mean return time to S_4 given that a return takes place.

9.14. Use the method of Problem 9.13 to find the generating function for the recurrence probabilities of state A in the two-choice model in Equation 8.1. Compare with Equation 8.24. Show that state A is persistent and find the mean recurrence time.

Chapter 10

Continuous-Time
Markov Processes

In the models considered thus far, both the state space and the time (or trial) space are discrete. Finite steps in the state space are possible only at fixed time steps. However, the discreteness of the trial and state spaces is not necessary, for Markov processes over continuous structures can be defined. In this chapter, one class of such processes is considered: those with a discrete state space, but with transitions that take place in continuous time.

The most obvious application of a continuous-time space is to latencies. In particular, consider a simple reaction-time task. At an appropriate signal, the subject makes a response as rapidly as possible. To model this situation, let state S correspond to presentation of the signal and state R to production of the final response. Then the response latency is measured by the interval from the time the process is started in S until entry into R. In the simplest model, only these two states are needed; more commonly, one or more intermediate states are required, through which the subject must pass before the response. Such states could represent intermediate cognitive stages.

Continuous-time, discrete-state processes also serve as models for the arrival and processing of a series of events, in a branch of stochastic-process theory known as *queuing theory*. As its name suggests, queuing theory concerns the properties of "customers" arriving and lining up for "service." Both the way in which arrivals take place and the nature of the service can be studied, the ultimate goal being to find such things as the length of the queue or the distribution of time until a customer is served. A queuing model was introduced in discrete-time form in Section 9.2; in this chapter continuous-time queues are treated more extensively. For a deeper, but not too difficult treatment of queues and queuing theory, see Cox and Smith (1961); for a more complete discussion, see Kleinrock (1975).

Of course, the interpretation of a "customer" and of "service" in a queuing model is quite flexible. As parts of a psychological model, they may correspond to psychological processes and events. For example, in the reaction-time model, the arrival of a customer is the onset of the stimulus, the service operation is the psychological processing of the stimulus, and the completion of service is the production of the eventual response. As another example, a model for the extraction of features from a stimulus as it is perceived can be constructed by likening the features to customers and their extraction to service. The presentation of a complicated stimulus, with many features, is like the arrival of a crowd of customers. A piece of information lost because not all features are processed sufficiently rapidly is like an impatient customer who waits for only a limited time before giving up and leaving. Finally, a processing task requiring several stages, such as in a memory-scanning experiment (Sternberg, 1969), corresponds to a multistep service regimen. The process starts with the arrival of a customer, who must be processed, serially or in parallel, by a number of servers before departing.

10.1 The Poisson Process

The simplest of the discrete-state, continuous-time Markov processes is the *Poisson process*. It requires minimal assumptions and is easy to work with. Its properties are simple and it leads to common and well-known distributions. Like the all-or-none model in the discrete case, it is a good model from which to look for deviations and is the basis for many more complicated models.

The Poisson process is essentially a counting process, that is, a process in which events take place and are tallied. The process is started at a time $t = 0$, with no events having taken place. After some time an event occurs and is counted as 1. This single count is the basic unit of the process. For the simplest process, this is all that happens. However, in general, the events do not stop with the first one. Sooner or later a second event takes place, is counted, and so the process continues. In effect, the process starts in state S_0, when no events have taken place, moves to S_1 after the first event, then to S_2, and so forth, being in state S_i after the ith event. In a simple Poisson process, the rate at which these events take place is assumed to be constant. To emphasize the continuous nature of the time space and to differentiate the process from the discrete-time processes, the event of being in S_i at time t is denoted here by $S_i(t)$ rather than $S_{i,t}$. A process of this sort is, more generally, known as a *birth process,* as it involves the occurrence of new events. If S_i indicates a population of size i, then each new event is the birth of a new population member. The Poisson process is one example of a birth process; other examples appear later in the chapter.

The Poisson process is a good model for any process where events occur and are counted more or less independently of each other. The arrival of independent people at some location or of photons at the receptors of the eye are examples. Each person is, by assumption, acting without reference to the others; a photon strikes or does not strike a receptor without regard to what happens to other photons. Where events take place in a number of more or less independent channels, the combined effect is often well approximated by a Poisson process, even when the Poisson assumptions are not strictly satisfied. This makes it a reasonable model for such physical events as nerve impulses arriving over several input fibers. By extension, it may be appropriate for conceptually parallel events, such as the extraction of features from a stimulus by several processors. The important point is that each source of events is more or less autonomous.

Definition of a Poisson Process

A close parallel exists between the all-or-none model and a single Poisson event, for the assumptions that underlie both are very similar. Fundamental to the all-or-none model is the fixed and unchanging probability of passage from the guessing to the learned state on a particular trial, without regard to past events. The fundamental assumption of the Poisson process is similar, but expressed in continuous time. In essence, the probability of an event taking place at any time is constant and does not depend on what events have happened in the past.

The all-or-none model involves only one transition, whereas a Poisson process passes through a series of states. In this sense, the Poisson process is closer to the random walks treated in the preceding chapter. Consider the random walk of Matrix 9.1 with $\eta = 1$. This defines a process that moves only to the right, with the transition matrix

$$\mathbf{T} = \begin{array}{c} S_0 \\ S_1 \\ S_2 \\ S_3 \\ \vdots \end{array} \begin{bmatrix} 1 - \gamma & \gamma & 0 & 0 & \cdots \\ 0 & 1 - \gamma & \gamma & 0 & \cdots \\ 0 & 0 & 1 - \gamma & \gamma & \cdots \\ 0 & 0 & 0 & 1 - \gamma & \cdots \\ \vdots & \vdots & \vdots & \vdots & \vdots \end{bmatrix} \qquad (10.1)$$

This process advances through its state space at a probabilistically constant rate. Thus, except for being in discrete time, it embodies the ideas behind the Poisson process, as expressed informally above.

Passage from this model to continuous time is made by a limit operation. Suppose that Matrix 10.1 is used as an approximation to a continuous-time birth process. Each discrete step in Matrix 10.1 represents some short interval of time. Now let the size of the unit represented by the discrete-time step be made smaller and smaller. If one discrete step represents, say, two seconds of real time, change it to one second, to half a second, and so forth. If the process is not to pass more and more rapidly through the states as this is done, the transition probability γ must simultaneously become small, halved at each step in the example. In particular, to keep the average rate constant, for time steps of size Δt let $\gamma = \lambda \Delta t$, with λ constant. Now passage to the limit as $\Delta t \to 0$ creates the continuous-time Poisson process. The more formal definition of a Poisson process, given in the next few paragraphs, treats the properties of a single transition, but the parallel to the random walk should remain apparent.

Several assumptions characterize the Poisson process. The first is the Markov assumption translated into continuous time, as given in Equation 1.4. Using the notation of the current chapter, for any times $u_1 < u_2 < \ldots < u_k < t$, interval Δt, and state numbers $j, i, i_1, \ldots, i_k$:

$$P[S_j(t + \Delta t)|S_i(t), S_{i_k}(u_k), \ldots, S_{i_1}(u_1)] = P[S_j(t + \Delta t)|S_i(t)] \quad (10.2)$$

This assumption is very basic and applies to all the processes considered in this chapter.

Because of the continuous time space, it does not make sense to talk about the probability of an event taking place at a particular point in time. There is an infinity of time points between any two other points, and if a nonzero probability is placed at each of these points, the collection sums to an infinite, hence absurd, total. Events take place at particular times, but exact probabilities cannot be assigned to these time points. Just as continuous random variables are represented differently from discrete random variables (with density functions rather than discrete probabilities), the representation of the likelihood of an event must be different than in the finite time case.

The trick in representing event probabilities in continuous time is to use a limiting operation, like that just described for a random-walk approximation. Instead of looking at points of time, consider the probability of events taking place in intervals. Take a very short interval of time of length Δt, stretching between any time t and the time $t + \Delta t$. Denote this interval by $[t, t + \Delta t)$. Because $[t, t + \Delta t)$ is a finite span of time, albeit a short one, the probability of a transition from S_i to S_{i+1}

during the interval, which is $P[S_{i+1}(t + \Delta t)|S_i(t)]$, can have a nonzero value. What to do with the endpoints of this interval is not critical, as the probability of a transition exactly at the endpoint is zero. To make successive intervals nest together neatly, they are taken here to include the lower endpoint—indicated by a left bracket, [—and to exclude the upper endpoint—indicated by a right parenthesis,).

The meat of the Poisson-process definition concerns what happens in this short interval. There are two assumptions, which, together with Equation 10.2, define the process:

1. The probability of a single event in a short interval is proportional to the length of the interval. Thus,

$$P(\text{one event in } [t, t + \Delta t)) = \lambda \Delta t$$

   or

$$P[S_{i+1}(t + \Delta t)|S_i(t)] = \lambda \Delta t \qquad (10.3)$$

   for a constant λ.

2. The probability of more than one event in a short interval goes to 0 faster than the size of the interval; that is

$$\lim_{\Delta t \to 0} \frac{P(\text{two or more events in } [t, t + \Delta t))}{\Delta t} = 0$$

   or

$$\lim_{\Delta t \to 0} \frac{P[S_j(t + \Delta t)|S_i(t)]}{\Delta t} = 0 \qquad j > i + 1 \qquad (10.4)$$

Assumption 1 defines λ to be the instantaneous rate of transition from S_i to S_{i+1} and asserts that it is constant. To see what this constancy means, consider what λ is not a function of. First, λ does not depend on the current state number, i. Thus, the rate of events is the same regardless of how many events have already occurred. This is not a difficult feature to change, as is done later in the chapter. Second, λ does not depend on the time, t. This makes the process homogeneous. It would be possible to change this without violating the Markov property—Equation 10.2 would still hold—but to simplify this presentation, only homogeneous processes are treated. Third, λ does not depend on the time since the last transition took place. This is a very fundamental property. Changing it violates the Markov assumption. It strongly characterizes Poisson processes; for example, it severely limits the nature of the distribution of waiting time between events. To change this aspect of the process goes beyond the scope of this book.

Assumption 2 makes it possible to ignore the chance of two or more events happening at once. This is quite sensible when the events are generated by independent processes. By Equation 10.3 the probability of one event in $[t, t + \Delta t)$ is $\lambda \Delta t$, so the probability of two independent events in the interval is $(\lambda \Delta t)^2$. This satisfies Equation 10.4, for

$$\frac{P[S_{i+2}(t + \Delta t)|S_i(t)]}{\Delta t} = \frac{(\lambda \Delta t)^2}{\Delta t} = \lambda^2 \Delta t \to 0 \qquad (10.5)$$

as $\Delta t \to 0$. The same result applies to the probability of three or more events in $[t, t + \Delta t)$.

In one respect, the two Poisson-process assumptions are much less restrictive than they seem at first. An important theorem demonstrates that Poisson processes often arise from the combination of other processes. Suppose that a series of events is observed, generated by many different independent processes, which are not necessarily Poisson. When any individual event takes place, it is recorded as coming from the combined, or summed, process, but not otherwise identified. It can be proved (e.g., Cox, 1962) that in a very wide range of circumstances the behavior of the pooled process comes to obey both Poisson axioms (Equations 10.3 and 10.4) as the number of components increases. Thus, a Poisson process is useful as a summary or an average, without the necessity of arguing that the components are Poisson. For example, one need not postulate that the response of individual nerve fibers are Poisson events in order for the net excitation from a pool of nerves to have Poisson properties. It is the independence of the combined events that is the dominating property, not their individual character.

A function of Δt that goes to 0 as Δt goes to 0 in the manner of Equation 10.4 is frequently denoted by $o(\Delta t)$. Using this notation, Assumption 2 can be written as

$$P(\text{two or more events in } [t, t + \Delta t)) = o(\Delta t) \qquad (10.6)$$

In general, $o(x)$ is used to represent any function that goes to 0 faster than the argument x does, so that

$$\frac{o(x)}{x} \to 0 \quad \text{as} \quad x \to 0 \qquad (10.7)$$

When written this way, the exact form of the function is not relevant, and the symbol $o(x)$ may be used to stand for several different functions at the same time, as long as Equation 10.7 holds for all of them. The important thing about any o function is that it goes to 0 and vanishes from the final result.

The most common violation of Assumption 2 occurs when the events are tied together and so not independent. To take a queuing and service example, Equation 10.4 is inappropriate as a description of customers arriving at a restaurant, where individual people often appear in groups. However, Equation 10.4 might still be appropriate if an "event" is defined to be the arrival of a party rather than a single person. As always, the proper definition of an event makes the process simpler. In fact, it is not difficult to accommodate groups of events, and a model of this sort is presented later.

To complete specification of the process, an initial condition is necessary. The simplest thing is to start the process in S_0 at $t = 0$. Formally,

$$P[S_i(0)] = \begin{cases} 1 & \text{if } i = 0 \\ 0 & \text{otherwise} \end{cases} \tag{10.8}$$

The State Distribution

The state-probability distribution at a particular time $T > 0$ is clearly of fundamental importance to the analysis of a Poisson process. Finding this distribution amounts to counting how many events take place in the interval between time 0 and time T. To make this count, first approximate the process by the random walk of Matrix 10.1. For a fixed, finite number of steps in the random walk, it is not hard to find the state distribution (e.g., this was done in the analysis of the RTI model in Equation 9.16). Then this solution is taken to the limit as the number of steps gets very large and the probability of an event in each step very small.

More formally, pick a number N and break the time interval from 0 to T into N shorter intervals of length:

$$\Delta t = T/N \tag{10.9}$$

By Assumption 1 (Equation 10.3), the probability of a single event in each of these short intervals is $\lambda \Delta t$; and by the Markov property and the homogeneity of λ, what happens in each interval is independent of what happens in the others. Thus, the number of intervals that contain single events equals the number of successes in N independent events with probability $\lambda \Delta t$ and has a binomial distribution,

$$P(\text{one event in each of } i \text{ intervals}) = \binom{N}{i} (\lambda \Delta t)^i (1 - \lambda \Delta t)^{N-i}$$

$$= \binom{N}{i} \left(\frac{\lambda T}{N}\right)^i \left(1 - \frac{\lambda T}{N}\right)^{N-i} \tag{10.10}$$

To this quantity must be added any events from intervals containing more than one event. However, these turn out to be unimportant. The number of such intervals is also binomially distributed, but Assumption 2 assures that, when $\Delta t \rightarrow 0$, the probability of finding more than one event in an interval goes to 0 faster than N gets large. In the limit, multiple events make no contribution to this total. For example, the mean number of intervals with two or more events equals the number of intervals times the probability of two or more events, and using Equations 10.9 and 10.6, this mean is

$$NP(\text{two events in } [t, t + \Delta t)) = T\frac{P(\text{two events in } [t, t + \Delta t))}{\Delta t} = \frac{To(\Delta t)}{\Delta t}$$

As $\Delta t \rightarrow 0$, this vanishes.

The final step is to make the passage to the limit as $N \rightarrow \infty$ and $\Delta t \rightarrow 0$, removing from Equation 10.10 the fictitious variables N and Δt. An important theorem of probability theory (see Equation A.38) states that, as the events in a binomial situation become very rare and the number of opportunities for an event very large, the distribution approaches a Poisson distribution that depends only on the mean number of events. This is exactly the situation here. The mean of Equation 10.10 is the product of the number of intervals, $T/\Delta t$, and the probability of an event in each interval, $\lambda \Delta t$:

$$\left(\frac{T}{\Delta t}\right)(\lambda \Delta t) = \lambda T$$

This does not depend on the size of the interval. Hence, in the limit, the distribution of the number of events is Poisson:

$$P(i \text{ events in } [t, t + T)) = \frac{e^{-\lambda T}(\lambda T)^i}{i!}$$

This distribution gives the process its name.

This result is easily converted into a state distribution. By the initial-state assumption in Equation 10.8, the process starts in S_0 at $t = 0$. To be in S_i at time t means that i events occur in $[0, T)$, so

$$P[S_i(T)] = \frac{e^{-\lambda T}(\lambda T)^i}{i!} \tag{10.11}$$

The mean state number at time T in Equation 10.11 is λt (see Equation A.43), so the mean number of events per unit time is λ. This makes λ the *rate* at which events take place.

Waiting Times

The distribution in Equation 10.11 is constructed for a fixed interval of length T, but the argument does not change if S_i is fixed and T is allowed to vary. For fixed i, $P[S_i(t)]$ rises to a maximum as t increases, then falls off to 0, except for $i = 0$, when the mode is at 0. However, $P[S_i(t)]$ is not the most useful measure of the temporal behavior, for there is no indication of whether a small value of $P[S_i(t)]$ is caused by the process not having reached S_i yet or by its having reached S_i and departed. A more useful quantity is the time until S_i is first reached, rather than the probability of being there. The waiting time until the ith event is a continuous random variable, with a probability density function $f_i(t)$ and a cumulative distribution function $F_i(t)$. There are a number of ways to determine these functions, one of which follows.

Start with a single event. Setting $i = 0$ in Equation 10.11 gives $P[S_0(t)]$, the probability that no event has taken place by time t. The complement of this is the probability that at least one event has taken place—in other words, that the first event occurred before time t. This is the cumulative distribution of the waiting time for the first event, $F_1(t)$. Thus,

$$F_1(t) = 1 - P[S_0(t)]$$
$$= 1 - e^{-\lambda t}$$

To get a density function, differentiate $F_1(t)$ to give

$$f_1(t) = \frac{dF_1(t)}{dt} = \lambda e^{-\lambda t} \tag{10.12}$$

This is the exponential distribution, discussed in Section A.4 (see Equation A.46). Its mean is $1/\lambda$; quite logically, the average time to wait for an event is the reciprocal of the rate. The mode is 0, which means that short waiting times are more likely than longer ones.

The exponential distribution of waiting times characterizes Poisson events. Its occurrence follows from the fact that the rate of arrival is constant throughout the interval and independent from event to event. In fact, any homogeneous Markov process in continuous time has exponential distributions of waiting times for single events. In this sense, the exponential has the same role as the geometric distributions that turned up consistently in discrete Markov chains. The prevalence of the exponential distribution limits the applicability of the pure Poisson process. Many events that one wishes to model do not have exponential distributions of waiting times, but have modes well different from 0. Clearly, the Poisson process—or any Markov process—is not satisfactory as a direct representation of these events.

It is the memory-less character of the Markov assumption that is reflected in the exponential distribution. Although noted in Appendix A, the point is sufficiently important to warrant discussion here. The shape of the tail of an exponential distribution is exactly the same as the shape of the whole distribution. If no event has taken place for some period of time, say, up to $t = t_0$, then the conditional distribution of waiting times after t_0 is no different from the original distribution. Formally,

$$f_1(t|t > t_0) = \frac{f_1(t)}{P(t > t_0)}$$

$$= \frac{\lambda e^{-\lambda t}}{e^{-\lambda t_0}} = \lambda e^{-\lambda(t-t_0)}$$

This equation describes the same shape as Equation 10.12. The starting point is shifted, but the distribution is otherwise unchanged (see Figure 10.1). It can be shown that the exponential is the only distribution with this property. This is a highly distinctive property of a Markovian process: whenever one starts looking at a Poisson process, the process looks the same. Regardless of the amount of time that has passed without an event, the future looks just as it did at the start.

The waiting time until an event other than the first does not have an exponential distribution. The process now is a multistage one: when waiting to get to S_3, say, there is (probably) less time to wait if one has already reached S_2 than if one is starting from S_0. The waiting time to reach S_i is the sum of the waiting times for each of i steps, and the combined distribution can be found in that way. Because of the inde-

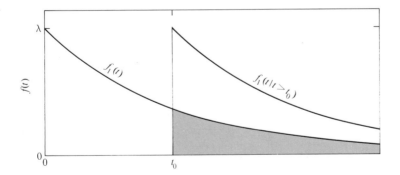

Figure 10.1   The exponential distribution of waiting times for a Poisson process and the distribution conditional on $t > t_0$. The shaded portion of $f_1(t)$ is renormalized by the conditionalization to give $f_1(t|t > t_0)$.

pendence of events and the stationarity of λ, the i exponential distributions that make up the waiting time for S_i are independent and identical. The sum of exponentials is a gamma distribution (described in Appendix A.4), in this context often called an *Erlang distribution*. From Equation A.49, the density until S_i is reached is

$$f_i(t) = \frac{\lambda^i}{(i-1)!} \, t^{i-1} e^{-\lambda t} \qquad (10.13)$$

This distribution has a mode at $(i-1)/\lambda$, which is nonzero when $i > 1$.

Erlang Processes

The appearance of the gamma distribution in Equation 10.13 gives a way to model processes that do not have exponential waiting times without losing the advantages of a Markovian model. The trick is to think of the nonexponential waiting time as composed of a series of r shorter stages, each of which is a Poisson event and has an exponential waiting time. One of the nonexponential events takes place every time r Poisson events have been counted. More formally, denote the states of the process that is to be modeled by R_0, R_1, R_2, ... , and define an underlying Poisson process with state space S_0, S_1, S_2, ... The process starts out simultaneously in S_0 and R_0 and advances to S_1, S_2, and so forth. When it reaches S_r, the first of the modeled events takes place and the R state changes from R_0 to R_1 (see Figure 10.2). The transition from R_1 to R_2 takes place when the S process moves into S_{2r}, and so forth.

This scheme is similar to the way that response processes are defined in the discrete models of the earlier chapters, that is, by letting the responses be functions of underlying Markovian states (recall Figure 2.1). The S_i values are Markovian states, and the R_j are observable responses. States S_0, S_1, ... , S_{r-1} map to R_0; states from S_r to S_{2r-1} map to R_1; and so forth. Once again, functions of a Markov chain need

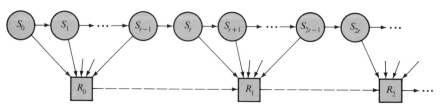

Figure 10.2   The relationship between the non-Markovian states R_j of an Erlang process and the underlying Poisson states S_i.

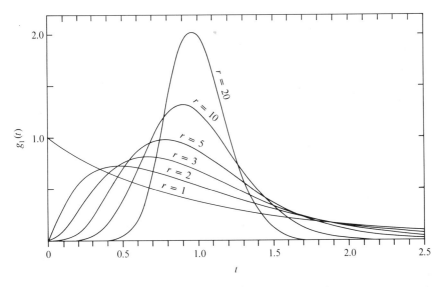

Figure 10.3 Waiting-time distribution for a process with rate $\mu = 1$ composed of r Poisson stages (Equation 10.14). When $r = 1$, the distribution is exponential.

not be Markovian; waiting times for steps in the S process are exponential, while waiting times for the R process are not.

As the sum of the exponential steps of the S process, waiting times for the R process have the gamma distributions given in Equation 10.13. However, it is often more useful to parameterize this function in terms of the overall rate, rather than the rate of the component Poisson process. The mean time in one Poisson stage is $1/\lambda$; so for r stages, it is r/λ. If the mean waiting time for an R event is $1/\mu$, then set $1/\mu = r/\lambda$, or

$$\lambda = r\mu$$

In other words, the underlying Poisson process has a rate parameter r times that of the observable process. Substituting this into the density, Equation 10.13, gives the S process density. As the waiting time until the jth event for the R process is the waiting time until the rjth event in the S process, the density for the wait until entry to R_j, $g_j(t)$, is

$$g_j(t) = f_{rj}(t) = \frac{r\mu(r\mu t)^{rj-1}e^{-r\mu t}}{(rj-1)!} \tag{10.14}$$

Distributions for the first event, $g_1(t)$, are shown in Figure 10.3 for $\mu = 1$ and for several values of r. This figure is a rescaling of the gamma distributions in Figure A.6 to fix the means at 1.

The modes of the scaled gamma distributions in Figure 10.3 lie at

$(r - 1)/r$. As r increases, this mode approaches 1, while the shape of the distribution becomes more symmetric and (as might be expected from the fact that it is the sum of independent and identical components) approaches a normal distribution in form. The variance is $1/r$, decreasing as r increases. More generally, for a rate other than 1, the mean of Equation 10.14 is $1/\mu$, the mode is $(r - 1)/r\mu$, and the variance is $1/r\mu^2$. These statistics give a method of approximating r for an actual distribution. Given an observed distribution of waiting times, μ can be estimated from the mean, after which an integral value of r can be selected by looking at either the mode or the variance.

This procedure for writing a complicated process as a series of simpler ones is very powerful. Indeed, it can be shown that any waiting-time distribution can be approximated by a suitable combination of Poisson states, although combinations more complicated than those considered here are sometimes needed (Kleinrock, 1975). However, as empirical fits to distributions are usually of less interest than theoretical models, this point is not pursued.

10.2   Birth Processes with State-Dependent Rates

The pure Poisson process is simple and easy to analyze, but this simplicity limits its usefulness. For one thing, the rate at which events take place is constant. In many situations this is not realistic. In some way, one wants to modify the basic assumptions to allow λ to vary. As discussed with the first Poisson-process assumption, this can be done in several ways. First, one may index λ with the current state number. The dynamics of any single event are the same as those of a homogeneous Poisson process, but the rate changes from event to event. This retains the structure of a Poisson process, including its Markov character. Interevent times still have exponential distributions. Models of this sort are the topic of this section.

Another way to vary the rate is to let λ depend on the time parameter. There are two ways to do this. If λ is replaced by $\lambda(t)$, where t refers to the absolute time, the process is Markovian, although no longer homogeneous. Although the Markov property holds, the waiting-time distributions are not necessarily exponential. However, because there are not many situations where changes in rate occur without regard for the state of the process, models in which λ depends only on t are not common as psychological models (although see Norman and Rummelhart, 1970, or Rummelhart, 1970, in which a nonhomogeneous Poisson process is used for a single event).

Rather than depending on absolute time, it is attractive to let λ be a function of the time since the last event. Unfortunately, this is a very fundamental modification and destroys the Markovian nature of the process. Equation 10.2 no longer holds. Waiting-time distributions other than the exponential are possible, but the cost is much greater complexity in the analysis. At a minimum, transform methods such as those described in Section 9.4, but applied to continuous variables (e.g., Laplace transforms), must be used. These models are well beyond the scope of this text. The use of a response mapping from a set of latent Markovian states, as in the Erlang process, is usually a preferable way to obtain nonexponential distributions.

Allowing the rate parameter to depend on the state makes only a small change in the Poisson assumptions. All that is required is to introduce a dependence on state into Assumption 1. The parameter λ is replaced by λ_i, and Equation 10.3 becomes

$$P[S_{i+1}(t + \Delta t)|S_i(t)] = \lambda_i \Delta t$$

Clearly, the character of this process is very similar to that of a simple Poisson process. Any particular event looks like a simple Poisson event; only when one looks over several events do differences appear. Thus, the waiting time between any two events is exponential, just as it is for the pure Poisson process. However, as different events have different exponential waiting times, the waiting time for several events may not have a gamma distribution.

A process of this sort can be developed very naturally as the limit of a random walk. In the random walk approximating a pure Poisson process, the probability of transition between each pair of states is the same. These rates may vary, replacing Matrix 10.1 by

$$\mathbf{T} = \begin{bmatrix} 1 - \gamma_0 & \gamma_0 & 0 & 0 & \cdots \\ 0 & 1 - \gamma_1 & \gamma_1 & 0 & \cdots \\ 0 & 0 & 1 - \gamma_2 & \gamma_2 & \cdots \\ 0 & 0 & 0 & 1 - \gamma_3 & \cdots \\ \vdots & \vdots & \vdots & \vdots & \end{bmatrix}$$

The limiting operation remains unchanged. One lets $\gamma_i = \lambda_i \Delta t$ and passes to the limit as $\Delta t \to 0$ to give the continuous-time process.

Because rates may change from event to event, the number of events in a series of short intervals no longer has the binomial distribution of Equation 10.10. If, say, λ_i decreases with i, the number of events at the start of an interval almost surely is greater than the number at the end. Thus, a more general method of analysis is needed. One way to do this is to express the rate at which the probability of being in S_i changes as a differential equation. The probability that the process is in S_i at time t

changes with time due to two opposing influences. First, events can take place that move the process from S_{i-1} into S_i, thereby increasing $P[S_i(t)]$. The rate at which these events occur is the product of the probability that the process is in S_{i-1}, or $P[S_{i-1}(t)]$, and the event rate in S_{i-1}, or λ_{i-1}. Second, $P[S_i(t)]$ decreases as events occur that take processes from S_i to S_{i+1}. The rate of these events is the product $\lambda_i P[S_i(t)]$. The composite rate of change of $P[S_i(t)]$, its derivative, sums these tendencies:

$$\frac{dP[S_i(t)]}{dt} = \lambda_{i-1} P[S_{i-1}(t)] - \lambda_i P[S_i(t)]$$

This equation applies for each $i \geq 1$, but not for $i = 0$. It is possible only to depart from S_0, not to arrive, so only the second term on the right-hand side appears. In full,

$$\frac{dP[S_i(t)]}{dt} = \begin{cases} -\lambda_0 P[S_0(t)] & i = 0 \\ \lambda_{i-1} P[S_{i-1}(t)] - \lambda_i P[S_i(t)] & i > 0 \end{cases} \tag{10.15}$$

Using the same initial (or "boundary") conditions as in Equation 10.8:

$$P[S_i(0)] = \begin{cases} 1 & i = 0 \\ 0 & \text{otherwise} \end{cases}$$

gives a system of differential equations that can be solved for the probabilities.

Equation 10.15 can be derived more formally. Express the probability of being in S_i at $t + \Delta t$ in terms of the probabilities at time t as

$$\begin{aligned} P[S_i(t + \Delta t)] &= P(\text{in } S_{i-1} \text{ at time } t)P(\text{go to } S_i \text{ during } \Delta t) \\ &\quad + P(\text{in } S_i \text{ at time } t)P(\text{stay in } S_i \text{ for } \Delta t) \\ &\quad + P(\text{all other ways to get to } S_i) \\ &= P[S_{i-1}(t)]\lambda_{i-1}\Delta t + P[S_i(t)](1 - \lambda_i\Delta t) + o(\Delta t) \end{aligned}$$

Rearranging terms gives

$$P[S_i(t + \Delta t)] - P[S_i(t)] = \lambda_{i-1} P[S_{i-1}(t)]\Delta t - \lambda_i P[S_i(t)]\Delta t + o(\Delta t)$$

or

$$\frac{P[S_i(t + \Delta t)] - P[S_i(t)]}{\Delta t} = \lambda_{i-1} P[S_{i-1}(t)] - \lambda_i P[S_i(t)] + \frac{o(\Delta t)}{\Delta t}$$

By definition, the derivative is the ratio on the left in the limit as $\Delta t \to 0$ (see Equation D.1). When this limit is taken, $o(\Delta t)/\Delta t \to 0$, giving

$$\frac{dP[S_i(t)]}{dt} = \lim_{\Delta t \to 0} \frac{P[S_i(t + \Delta t)] - P[S_i(t)]}{\Delta t}$$

$$= \lambda_{i-1}P[S_{i-1}(t)] - \lambda_i P[S_i(t)]$$

which is the $i > 0$ case of Equation 10.15. The same logic applies to $P[S_0(t)]$ (see Problem 10.1).

The system of equations of Equation 10.15 is similar to the systems of simultaneous difference equations obtained for the discrete-time models in the earlier chapters, but with time derivatives substituted for the differences between probabilities on successive trials. This combination of difference (in i) and differential (in t) aspects can make the system difficult to solve. Of course, one does not solve Equation 10.15 in general, for the solution depends on the particular way in which λ_i is related to i. This relationship is determined by the particular situation that is being modeled. Many assignments lead to simple solutions that parallel results in the discrete-time situations. In the following sections, several specific examples are considered.

Yule Processes

One natural form of birth process treats a population of independent individuals, each of whom gives birth to further members of the population. If each event represents the birth of a new individual, then S_i is the population size. The larger the state number, the faster the population grows. If the rate of production of new individuals by each member of the population is λ, then

$$\lambda_i = i\lambda \tag{10.16}$$

Because Equation 10.16 implies that $\lambda_0 = 0$ (a population with no members has no births), the process must start out in an initial state other than S_0. Thus, the initial conditions must be altered to start the process in S_K, with $K > 0$:

$$P[S_i(0)] = \begin{cases} 1 & i = K \\ 0 & \text{otherwise} \end{cases} \tag{10.17}$$

Such a process is known as a *Yule process*. Substituting Equation 10.16

into Equation 10.15 gives the system of differential equations:

$$\frac{dP[S_i(t)]}{dt} = \begin{cases} -K\lambda P[S_K(t)] & i = K \\ (i-1)\lambda P[S_{i-1}(t)] - i\lambda P[S_i(t)] & i > K \end{cases} \quad (10.18)$$

There are general methods for solving systems of simultaneous differential equations such as Equation 10.18, which can be found in most texts on differential equations. Here a simpler method is possible. Each equation of Equation 10.18 depends only on terms with the same or lower values of i, and so the system can be solved by successive steps, starting with the case of $i = K$. The first equation is very simple:

$$\frac{dP[S_K(t)]}{dt} = -K\lambda P[S_K(t)]$$

This equation is solved as an example in Section D.3 (Equation D.29). Using that solution gives

$$P[S_K(t)] = Ae^{-K\lambda t}$$

The value of the constant A is found from the initial conditions. Setting $t = 0$ gives

$$P[S_K(0)] = Ae^{-K\lambda 0} = A$$

By Equation 10.17, $P[S_K(0)] = 1$; so $A = 1$ and

$$P[S_K(t)] = e^{-K\lambda t}$$

When $i = K + 1$, Equation 10.18 is

$$\begin{aligned}\frac{dP[S_{K+1}(t)]}{dt} &= K\lambda P[S_K(t)] - (K+1)\lambda P[S_{K+1}(t)] \\ &= -(K+1)\lambda P[S_{K+1}(t)] + K\lambda e^{-K\lambda t}\end{aligned}$$

This equation is only slightly more complicated than when $i = K$ and is solved by

$$P[S_{K+1}(t)] = Ke^{-K\lambda t}(1 - e^{-\lambda t})$$

as can easily be verified. In turn, this is substituted into Equation 10.18 to get the third equation, which is solved in the same manner. A pattern is soon established with

$$P[S_i(t)] = \binom{i - 1}{i - K} e^{-K\lambda t} (1 - e^{-\lambda t})^{i-K} \qquad (10.19)$$

This is the general solution (as verified in Problem 10.3).

When viewed as a distribution in i for a particular value of t, Equation 10.19 is a negative binomial with parameters $e^{-\lambda t}$ and K (in contrast to the Poisson distribution for a process with state-independent rates). There is a fairly simple interpretation for this distribution. Like any negative binomial, Equation 10.19 is the sum of K independent, geometrically distributed variables, here with parameter $e^{-\lambda t}$ (see the discussion of the negative binomial distribution in Section A.3). Thinking of the process as a series of births, one sees that each of these geometric variables corresponds to one original member of the population with its progeny. Each of the K "families" grows independently of the others; together their sizes sum to the total population.

Death Processes

Consider a fixed set of N entities that must be processed. The extraction of N features from a stimulus is an example, as are the comparison of a stimulus to N standards and the service of N customers waiting in a queue. In such situations, the "reaction time" until the last process is complete is of principal importance. How long this takes depends on how the processing of the N events are related to each other. Where the N events are generated in series by a single processor, the result is a Poisson process of the form discussed above, and the time until all N entities have completed processing is the time for N Poisson events, given by Equation 10.13 with $i = N$.

A different case occurs when the N entities are acted upon simultaneously by independent processes working in parallel. Each process operates until it produces an event, then stops. As in the Yule process, this introduces a change of rate with the state changes, but here the rate becomes slower as the state increases. As time passes, the number of uncompleted entities declines, and with it the probability of the next event. When N events have taken place, all activity is finished and the system stops. A process of this type can be thought of as representing the death of the N individuals as the population moves toward extinction. For this reason, processes of this sort are sometimes called *death processes*.

The simplest form of death process, and the only one to be treated here, occurs when the N entities are independent and identical Poisson

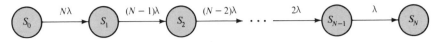

Figure 10.4   State-transition diagram for a death process produced by N identical Poisson processes operating in parallel. Paths are labeled with the rate at which the transitions take place.

processes. Let the rate of the process be λ and let state S_i indicate that i events (deaths) have taken place. Thus, the state space is $\{S_0, S_1, \ldots, S_N\}$ and the process starts in S_0. When the overall process is in S_i, there are $N - i$ individual, independent Poisson processes operating, each with rate λ. As with the equivalent assumption for the Poisson process (Equation 10.5), the chance of two entities producing an event in the same Δt is $o(\Delta t)$; so the overall rate is the sum of the individual rates, or

$$\lambda_i = (N - i)\lambda \tag{10.20}$$

for $i = 0, 1, \ldots, N$. These rates are shown in the state diagram in Figure 10.4. When $i = N$, all the individual processes are complete, $\lambda_N = 0$, and the combined process is absorbed in S_N.

Either of the arguments used to get Equation 10.15 leads to a finite system of differential equations for the state probabilities:

$$\frac{dP[S_i(t)]}{dt} = \begin{cases} -N\lambda P[S_0(t)] & i = 0 \\ (N - i + 1)\lambda P[S_{i-1}(t)] \\ \qquad - (N - i)\lambda P[S_i(t)] & 0 < i < N \\ \lambda P[S_{N-1}(t)] & i = N \end{cases} \tag{10.21}$$

(see Problem 10.6). Both the initial state, S_0, and the final state, S_N, are special cases.

Systems of equations such as Equation 10.21 are sometimes represented by a matrix, rather like a transition-probability matrix for a discrete-time chain, except that its entries are rate parameters. For Equation 10.21,

$$\begin{bmatrix} -n\lambda & n\lambda & 0 & \cdots & 0 & 0 \\ 0 & -(n-1)\lambda & (n-1)\lambda & \cdots & 0 & 0 \\ 0 & 0 & -(n-2)\lambda & \cdots & 0 & 0 \\ \vdots & \vdots & \vdots & & \vdots & \vdots \\ 0 & 0 & 0 & \cdots & -\lambda & \lambda \\ 0 & 0 & 0 & \cdots & 0 & 0 \end{bmatrix} \tag{10.22}$$

Rows in Matrix 10.22 indicate sources; columns, destinations. The principal difference between Matrix 10.22 and a transition-probability matrix is in the diagonal entries. A transition from S_i to S_j appears both as a rate of increase in $P(S_j)$ and as a rate of decrease in $P(S_i)$. Thus, the diagonal entries are negative (unless 0), reflecting loss of probability. An analogy to the flow of a fluid is helpful here: the rate at which the fluid (probability) flows from S_i exactly equals the rate at which it appears in the neighboring states. This "conservation of probability" principle implies that the rows of a rate matrix sum to 0. The last line of Matrix 10.22 is entirely 0's, indicating that there is no flow away from the absorbing state S_N.

Equations 10.21 can be solved step by step, starting with $P[S_0(t)]$, in the same way that the equivalent equations were solved for the Yule process. However, another method of solution is simpler here. Because each component process is a simple Poisson process, the probability that a particular entity has not produced an event by time t is given by the Poisson probability of zero events, $e^{-\lambda t}$. Thus, the probability that an entity has produced an event is $1 - e^{-\lambda t}$. When the full process is in state S_i, i of the entities have had an event take place, while $N - i$ have not. As the N sources are independent and identical, the binomial distribution applies and

$$P[S_i(t)] = \binom{N}{i}(1 - e^{-\lambda t})^i(e^{-\lambda t})^{N-i} \tag{10.23}$$

If the death process is to be used as a reaction-time model, the most interesting event is the entry into S_N, which completes processing. Denote the density function for the distribution of the waiting time until this event by $g_N(t)$ and the cumulative distribution function by $G_N(t)$. Because S_N is absorbing, $P[S_N(t)]$ is the probability that the waiting time is less than t, or $G_N(t)$. Substituting $i = N$ into Equation 10.23:

$$G_N(t) = (1 - e^{-\lambda t})^N$$

Differentiation gives the density:

$$g_N(t) = \frac{dG_N(t)}{dt} = N\lambda(1 - e^{-\lambda t})^{N-1}e^{-\lambda t} \tag{10.24}$$

The first two moments of this distribution are fairly simple:

$$E(T_N) = \frac{1}{\lambda}\sum_{i=1}^{N}\frac{1}{i} \qquad \text{var}(T_N) = \frac{1}{\lambda^2}\sum_{i=1}^{N}\frac{1}{i^2}$$

The relationship between these quantities and the number of processes is quite attractive: adding another process, operating in parallel, increases the mean time to completion by the reciprocal of the total number of processes and increases the variance by the square of this increment. As with the Erlang processes (Equation 10.14), the relationship between the mean and the standard deviation provides a way to estimate N based on the moments of T.

10.3   Processes with Arrivals and Departures

In essense, the processes discussed so far in this chapter count sequences of events; any transitions are always upward from state S_i to state S_{i+1}. This unidirectionality is not necessary. More complicated processes can be defined that allow movement both up and down. In effect, such processes allow both births and deaths of individuals. A common example of this is a real queue. Customers arrive in the queue according to the properties of one process; they are serviced and depart according to the properties of another. The state number indicates the number of customers currently in the system.

A bidirectional process can be constructed from two independent unidirectional processes. The first of these processes governs arrivals to the system (or births) and results in transitions from state S_i to state S_{i+1}; let α_i be the rate parameter of this process. Departures (or deaths) are governed by the second process, with parameter δ_i, which moves the state from S_i down to S_{i-1}. Together these two component processes define the overall process.

Analysis of this process, like that of the simpler processes, starts with the short interval $[t, t + \Delta t)$, then passes to the limit. Assume once again that the chance of more than one action (either several steps up or down or some up and some down) in the short interval Δt is $o(\Delta t)$. Thus, three things can happen to a process in S_i during $[t, t + \Delta t)$. With probability $\alpha_i \Delta t$, it moves to S_{i+1}; with probability $\delta_i \Delta t$, it moves to S_{i-1}; and with probability $1 - \alpha_i \Delta t - \delta_i \Delta t$, it stays in S_i. Using these three probabilities:

$$P[S_i(t + \Delta t)] = \alpha_{i-1} \Delta t P[S_{i-1}(t)] + (1 - \alpha_i \Delta t - \delta_i \Delta t) P[S_i(t)]$$
$$+ \delta_{i+1} \Delta t P[S_{i+1}(t)] + o(\Delta t)$$

Arranging terms, dividing by Δt, and passing to the limit as $\Delta t \to 0$ lead to the differential equations

$$\frac{dP[S_i(t)]}{dt} = \begin{cases} -\alpha_0 P[S_0(t)] + \delta_1 P[S_1(t)] & i = 0 \\ \alpha_{i-1}P[S_{i-1}(t)] - (\alpha_i + \delta_i)P[S_i(t)] & \\ \qquad + \delta_{i+1}P[S_{i+1}(t)] & i > 0 \end{cases} \quad (10.25)$$

The first of these equations is different from the others, reflecting the fact that the process cannot enter S_0 from below.

The system of equations in Equation 10.25 is far more difficult to solve than any encountered so far. It combines difference equations (in the dependence on i) with differential equations (in the dependence on t), and no one equation is independent of the others. Where only unidirectional transitions are involved, it is possible to start with one of the equations, solve it, then use it to set up another equation, and continue from there. In Equation 10.25, however, there is no equation that depends on only a single state probability. The full system of equations must be solved at once. Even for simple versions of the process, this is quite difficult. In the simplest case, when α_i and δ_i are constant, the transient behavior is beyond the scope of this book.

Fortunately, for most applications, the transient solutions are not of great interest. More important is the state distribution that the process eventually reaches. Just as with the chains in discrete time, $P[S_i(t)]$ either goes to 0 or converges to a form that does not depend either on t or on the starting configuration. This long-term behavior is much easier to determine.

A Simple Queue

Consider a service queue in which "customers" arrive according to a Poisson process at a constant rate of α per unit time and are served according to another Poisson process with rate δ. Let state S_i, $i > 0$, indicate that i customers are in service, including one currently being served and $i - 1$ waiting. In S_0, the queue is empty and the server is idle. This process is described by Equation 10.25 with constant $\alpha_i = \alpha$ and constant $\delta_i = \delta$. Making these substitutions, the equations governing the state probabilities are

$$\frac{dP[S_i(t)]}{dt} = \begin{cases} -\alpha P[S_0(t)] + \delta P[S_1(t)] & i = 0 \\ \alpha P[S_{i-1}(t)] - (\alpha + \delta)P[S_i(t)] & \\ \qquad + \delta P[S_{i+1}(t)] & i > 0 \end{cases} \quad (10.26)$$

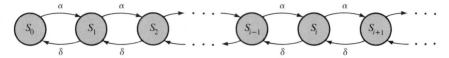

Figure 10.5 State-transition diagram for a process with constant birth and death rates.

with initial conditions appropriate to the situation. A state-transition diagram is shown in Figure 10.5.

As noted above, a general solution to Equation 10.26 is quite complicated (it contains what are called *Bessel functions*), but the stable distribution is easy to find. By its nature, a stable solution to Equation 10.26 does not depend on t, and so $P[S_i(t)]$ can be replaced by p_i, following the analogous notation in Chapters 8 and 9. Because p_i does not change, its derivative with respect to time, the left-hand side of Equation 10.26, is 0, and so

$$0 = -\alpha p_0 + \delta p_1$$
$$0 = \alpha p_{i-1} - (\alpha + \delta)p_i + \delta p_{i+1} \qquad i > 0$$

(10.27)

These are straightforward difference equations, identical to those for a discrete-time queuing chain of the sort discussed in Section 9.2. Indeed, Equations 10.27 are the limiting form of Equations 9.11 for large t. The models are the same, except for the fact that the model in this chapter is expressed in continuous time. The solution to Equations 10.27 is given by Equations 9.13 and 9.14:

$$p_i = \left(1 - \frac{\alpha}{\delta}\right)\left(\frac{\alpha}{\delta}\right)^i = (1 - \rho)\rho^i$$

(10.28)

where $\rho = \alpha/\delta$ is the traffic intensity.

As in Chapter 9, the traffic intensity, defined as the ratio of the expected number of arrivals per unit time to the expected number of departures, determines the stability of the queue. Equation 10.28 applies only as long as the traffic intensity is less than 1, or $\alpha < \delta$, so that the rate of arrival is less than the rate of service. In such case, a stable distribution is obtained. If $\alpha > \delta$, customers arrive in the queue more rapidly, on the average, than they can be serviced, the queue expands without limit, and all states are transient. When $\alpha = \delta$, the states are all null, and a return to any state is certain, but only after an average infinite waiting time.

It is easy to write the asymptotic state-probability equations directly from the state diagram in Figure 10.5, using the "conservation of probability'' principle mentioned above. For example, consider S_1. The arrow labeled by α from S_0 to S_1 indicates that the probability in S_1 is increasing (in the absence of other tendencies) at a rate $\alpha P[S_0(t)]$. The value of $P[S_1(t)]$ is also increasing because of transitions from S_2 to S_1 and decreasing because of transitions from S_1 to S_0 and S_2. At asymptote, there is no net change in the state probability, so $P[S_i(t)] = p_i$ and the two rates,

$$\text{rate entering } S_1 = \alpha p_0 + \delta p_2$$

and

$$\text{rate leaving } S_1 = (\alpha + \delta)p_1$$

must balance each other. Hence,

$$(\alpha + \delta)p_1 = \alpha p_0 + \delta p_2$$

which, in a different organization, is the equation from Equations 10.27 for $i = 1$. A similar argument can be made for any other state to complete Equations 10.27.

State Proportional Rates

In both the Yule process and the simple death process, the transition rate is proportional to the population size (see Equations 10.16 and 10.20). These actions can be combined. Suppose that, in the interval $[t, t + \Delta t)$, each member of the population either can produce an offspring with probability $\alpha \Delta t$ or can cease to exist with probability $\delta \Delta t$. In S_i, there are i active individuals, so a process with $\alpha_i = i\alpha$ and $\delta_i = i\delta$ results. The state-transition diagram for this process is shown in Figure 10.6.

The differential equations for this process can be written directly by inspection of Figure 10.6. They are

$$\frac{dP[S_i(t)]}{dt} = \begin{cases} \delta P[S_1(t)] & i = 0 \\ (i-1)\alpha P[S_{i-1}(t)] - i(\alpha + \delta)P[S_i(t)] \\ \qquad\qquad + (i+1)\delta P[S_{i+1}(t)] & i > 0 \end{cases}$$

Once again, transient behavior is complex, but the ultimate destination is the most interesting. The state S_0 is an absorbing state, for when the population has reached extinction there can be neither births nor deaths. If the process ever reaches this state, it ceases to evolve. Ex-

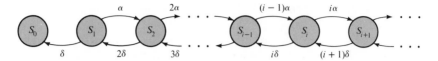

Figure 10.6   State-transition diagram for a process with birth and death rates proportional to population size.

actly how likely this is to happen depends on the starting state and on the relative values of α and δ. As long as $\alpha \leq \delta$, so that the probability of a death is at least as large as that of a birth, the process reaches S_0 with probability 1 and terminates. When births are more likely than deaths—that is, $\alpha > \delta$—there is a chance that the process never reaches S_0 and grows without bounds.

The probability of extinction is of considerable importance. Let e_i denote this probability for a process starting in S_i. Extinction from S_i can come about either by moving to S_{i-1} and eventually to S_0 or by moving to S_{i+1} and then to S_0. The relative rates of arrivals and departures determine the direction of exit; the probability that exit is to S_{i-1} is $i\delta/(i\alpha + i\delta)$ or $\delta/(\alpha + \delta)$, that it is to S_{i+1} is $\alpha/(\alpha + \delta)$. This relationship is expressed in the difference equation

$$e_i = \frac{\delta}{\alpha + \delta} e_{i-1} + \frac{\alpha}{\alpha + \delta} e_{i+1}$$

which has the solution

$$e_i = A + B\left(\frac{\delta}{\alpha}\right)^i$$

To evaluate the constants, note first that $e_0 = 1$, and second that, for $i \neq 0$, e_i is 0 when $\delta = 0$. Using these facts, $A = 0$, $B = 1$, and so

$$e_i = \left(\frac{\delta}{\alpha}\right)^i$$

When $\delta > \alpha$, e_i is not a proper probability, reflecting the certainty of extinction.

Multiple-Step Transitions

It should be apparent that the procedures in the preceding few sections can be used with processes that allow transitions to other than neigh-

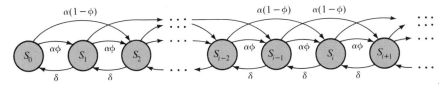

Figure 10.7   State-transition diagram for a process with multiple arrivals.

boring states. The trick is to avoid violating the Poisson nature of the process, but to allow Poisson-type events to take the process to states other than S_{i+1} or S_{i-1}. For example, consider a queuing situation where the arrivals are not independent. As in Problem 9.1g, suppose that a proportion ϕ of the arrivals are single events, but a proportion $1 - \phi$ are double and result in transitions from S_i to S_{i+2}. A situation like this could arise if people arrived at a queue sometimes singly and sometimes in couples. In an interval of length Δt, a single arrival takes place with probability $\phi\alpha\Delta t$, and a double arrival with probability $(1 - \phi)\alpha\Delta t$. For simplicity, assume that the departure process is still Poisson with parameter δ.

A state diagram for this process is shown in Figure 10.7. There are now two ascending transitions from each state, with rates $\phi\alpha$ and $(1 - \phi)\alpha$. Asymptotic state-probability equations are written from this diagram by balancing the flow into and out of the states. Writing the flow in on the left and the flow out on the right yields the three equations

$$\delta p_1 = \alpha p_0$$

$$\phi\alpha p_0 + \delta p_2 = (\alpha + \delta)p_1 \qquad (10.29)$$

$$(1 - \phi)\alpha p_{i-2} + \phi\alpha p_{i-1} + \delta p_{i+1} = (\alpha + \delta)p_i$$

These are second-order difference equations, which, with the constraint $\Sigma_i p_i = 1$, can be solved for the asymptotic probabilities (see Problem 10.8). Schemes of this sort generalize readily to model more complicated conditions for arrival and departure.

Problems

10.1. Derive the $P[S_0(t)]$ case of Equation 10.15 by taking the limit as a finite time increment Δt goes to 0.

10.2. Specialize Equation 10.15 for the simple Poisson process of Section 10.1 and show that it is solved by Equation 10.11.

10.3. Verify that Equation 10.19 is the solution to Equation 10.18.

10.4. Suppose that two Poisson processes are operating, with rates λ_1 and λ_2, but that their events are not distinguishable. Consider what happens in the interval $[t, t + \Delta t)$ and find the properties of the combined output. Generalize the result to N processes.

10.5. A birth process is observed for which the waiting-time distribution between events has a mean of M, a variance of V, and a mode away from 0.

    a. Find method-of-moments estimators of the parameters of an Erlang-process model for these events.

    b. Suppose that the mean is 8 seconds and the standard deviation is 4 seconds. According to this model, what is the distribution of time until the third event?

10.6. Find the probability of an event in time Δt for the death process discussed in Section 10.2. Pass to the limit as $\Delta t \to 0$ to derive Equations 10.21.

10.7. Suppose that a stimulus must be compared to N standards before a response is made. Consider two models for the comparisons:

    (1) The comparisons are made serially, with the completion of each comparison marked by Poisson events with parameter λ_s.

    (2) The comparisons are made in parallel by a set of independent and identical Poisson processes with parameter λ_p.

    a. Let $N = 4$ and $M = 1$. Plot the predicted response-time distributions under the two models.

    b. Suppose that N is unknown and that a mean of 15.8 seconds and a standard deviation of 9.1 seconds is observed. What is the best choice for N under the two models? Plot the response-time distributions.

10.8. Consider the multiple-arrival model at the end of this chapter (see also Problems 9.1 and 9.12).

    a. Find the traffic intensity.

    b. Solve Equations 10.29 to find the asymptotic state distribution. For what conditions on α and δ does this result apply?

10.9. Suppose that a queue is started with N people in it (i.e., it is in S_N) and operates with a Poisson arrival rate α and a Poisson departure rate δ. When the queue becomes empty (i.e., enters state S_0), the server quits work and no more arrivals are permitted.

    a. What is the transition-rate matrix for such a queue?

    b. What is the probability that the queue ever closes?

10.10. Suppose that arrivals in a queuing situation come from many independent sources, so are well modeled by a Poisson process. Let the rate of this process be λ. The service distribution has a nonzero mode and is better approximated by a gamma distribution with parameters $r = 3$ and mean service time τ. How might this process be represented? Write a state diagram and a set of asymptotic equations for the process. *Hint:* Consider the way that the Erlang process was represented.

10.11. Consider the following model for the search of a memory store during free recall (adapted from Shiffrin, 1970). The subject initially is presented with a set of N items, and later tries to recall them. To retrieve an item for recall, the subject must search a part of memory that contains representations both of the N items and of M irrelevant items. Items that are recovered in this search are generated as responses if they are list members that have not been recovered before. The subject's problem is to retrieve as many of the N list items as possible while avoiding the M distracting items. Assume that recovery of each item occurs according to a Poisson process with a rate inversely proportional to the size of the pool that is being searched. Hence, for a single item, the rate of recovery is $\alpha/(N + M)$ for some constant α. When there are N list members, the rate of recovery of any item on the list is $N\alpha/(N + M)$. After the first item is recovered, the subject continues to search, but the recovered item is now irrelevant; so there are now $N - 1$ target items and $M + 1$ distracting items, changing the recovery rate.
   a. Formalize this model.
   b. Suppose that the subject is given a time period of length T to recover items. What is the distribution of the number of items that are recovered, R?
   c. Suppose that instead of a fixed period, the subject is allowed to continue until giving up. The subject gives up when a time period τ has elapsed without recovery of a new item. Again, find the distribution of R.

Appendix A

Summary of Probability Theory

The models that are discussed in this book are probabilistic in nature. They represent psychological processes using uncertain events and describe the probabilistic structure of these events. This appendix summarizes the results from probability theory needed for these models. It is principally a review; the reader should have had some contact with the concept of probability before (such as the introduction in Hays, 1981).

A.1 Fundamental Definitions

Probability is a numerical measure of the chance that an event takes place. It is defined on the subsets of a basic set of *elementary events*, called the *sample space*. These subsets are called *events*. The *probability*, $P(A)$, of any event A is a number between 0 and 1 denoting how likely A is to occur.† Probabilities obey the fundamental rule that, for

---

† For some sample spaces (e.g., the real line), it is not possible to define probability for every possible subset. This poses no practical problems for the models in this book.

events A and B with no elements in common (i.e., $A \cap B = \emptyset$),

$$P(A \cup B) = P(A) + P(B) \tag{A.1}$$

Recall that the *intersection* of two sets, $A \cup B$, is the set of elements contained simultaneously in both A and B, the *union*, $A \cup B$, is the set of elements in A and B or both, and that $\emptyset$ is the *empty set* containing no elements at all; where events without set representation are involved, logical *and*, $\wedge$, and *or*, $\vee$, can be used. Any assignment of numbers to events obeying Equation A.1 and with the probability of the complete sample space equal to 1 is a satisfactory probability rule. A pair of events that has an empty intersection is said to be *mutually exclusive*. If, mutually exclusive or not, the union of the events is the full sample space, the events are said to be *exhaustive*.

It is often necessary to work with probabilities when the space of possible events is restricted to a subset of the sample space. The *conditional probability* of an event A given restriction to the event B is defined by looking at how likely it is for both A and B to happen and at the probability of B alone:

$$P(A|B) = \frac{P(A \cap B)}{P(B)} \tag{A.2}$$

or, rearranging Equation A.2,

$$P(A \cap B) = P(A|B)P(B) \tag{A.3}$$

There are many cases where conditionalization of this sort is carried on for several steps, in expressions such as

$$P(A \cap B \cap C) = P(A|B \cap C)P(B|C)P(C)$$

Sometimes it is possible to break down an event A according to which of a series of mutually exclusive and exhaustive categories it falls into. Let $B_1, B_2, \ldots , B_n$ be a collection of categories; then $P(A)$ is the sum of the intersections of A with each of the B_i:

$$P(A) = \sum_{i=1}^{n} P(A \cap B_i)$$

Applying Equation A.3 gives

$$P(A) = \sum_{i=1}^{n} P(A|B_i)P(B_i) \tag{A.4}$$

This relationship, sometimes called the *law of total probability,* is used very frequently.

The law of total probability can be used to calculate the denominator of Equation A.2 (after reversing the roles of A and B) to give the relationship

$$P(B_j|A) = \frac{P(A \cap B_j)}{P(A)}$$

$$= \frac{P(A|B_j)P(B_j)}{\Sigma_i P(A|B_i)P(B_i)} \tag{A.5}$$

This formula, known as *Bayes' theorem,* serves to change a conditionalization on the B_i to one on A.

The conditional probability $P(A|B)$ can take any value from 0 to 1, depending on the relationship between A and B. One particularly important value occurs when knowing B provides no information about A. Then

$$P(A|B) = P(A) \tag{A.6}$$

and A and B are said to be *independent.* It is easily shown, using Equation A.2, that Equation A.6 also implies $P(B|A) = P(B)$. Under independence, Equation A.3 becomes

$$P(A \cap B) = P(A)P(B) \tag{A.7}$$

Because it is much easier to find simple probabilities than conditional ones, independence is an important part of many models.

A.2   Random Variables

A *random variable* is, in essence, a numerical variable that takes values according to a probabilistic rule. Generally in this book, capital letters are used for random variables; and lowercase letters, for their values. One speaks of the probability that a random variable X takes some particular value a, $P(X = a)$, or of the probability that it takes a value somewhere in a range, $P(X \leq a)$ or $P(a < X \leq b)$. Although a random variable takes a particular value, or *realization,* in a particular instance, the value usually differs from realization to realization. The full description of a random variable includes the rule that relates values to probabilities, or the *distribution* of the random variable.

It is necessary to distinguish the case where X can take only a countable number of values from the case where it draws values from a dense range on the real line. In the former case, X is a *discrete* random variable, and it makes sense to describe the *distribution function* of X by listing probabilities $P(X = a)$. These completely specify the distribution. Another way to describe the random variable is with the *cumulative distribution function* (or *cdf*):

$$F(a) = P(X \le a) \qquad (A.8)$$

This starts at 0 when a is a very large negative number and goes to 1 when a is a very large positive number, making a jump at each point where $P(X = a) > 0$.

When X takes values from the real numbers, it is said to be *continuous*. For a pure, continuous random variable, it no longer makes sense to talk of the probability $P(X = a)$. For any a, the probability of an exact match, to an infinite number of decimal places, is 0. Instead, the distribution of X is represented in one of two ways. First, a cumulative distribution function (Equation A.8) can be defined just as in the discrete case. The second representation is the *probability density function* (or *pdf*), $f(x)$, which is defined so that the probability that X falls between a and b is given by the area under the graph of $f(x)$ between the two points:

$$P(a < X \le b) = \int_a^b f(x)\,dx \qquad (A.9)$$

(see Section D.2 for this use of the integral). The fact that b is included in the interval and a is excluded results from the fact that it is convenient to have

$$P(a < X \le b) = F(b) - F(a)$$

and this means that the endpoint can be included on one side only. For continuous distributions, both $P(X = a)$ and $P(X = b)$ are 0, so inclusion or exclusion of the endpoints is not of practical importance.

The relationship between the probability density function and the cumulative distribution function is shown in Figure A.1. The density $f(x)$ measures how fast the cumulative distribution $F(x)$ increases with x. The density is always positive, rising from 0 when x is a very large negative number and returning to 0 when x is a very large positive number. It is related to the cumulative distribution function by

$$f(x) = \frac{d}{dx} F(x) \qquad (A.10)$$

or

$$F(a) = \int_{-\infty}^a f(x)\,dx \qquad (A.11)$$

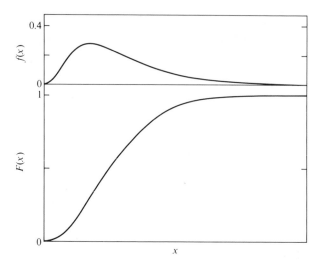

Figure A.1   Probability density function and cumulative distribution function for the same continuous random variable.

Of course, Equations A.10 and A.11 apply only when the distribution is continuous, so that a well-defined density function exists.

A random variable always takes some value, so $P(-\infty < X < \infty) = 1$. In terms of the distributions, this means that

$$\sum_{\text{all } a} P(X = a) = 1 \tag{A.12}$$

for discrete distributions, or

$$\int_{-\infty}^{\infty} f(x) \, dx = 1 \tag{A.13}$$

for continuous ones. Equations A.12 and A.13 often provide good ways to check calculations. In most cases, if they do not hold, the distribution has been derived incorrectly.

However, there are cases where Equations A.12 and A.13 truly have values less than 1. Distributions of this sort are called *defective*. They appear when the random variable is not defined over the full sample space of possible events. A random variable representing the number of trials to learn a problem is an example: it is defective if some subjects are unable to learn the problem at all.

It is possible for distributions to be neither completely discrete nor continuous. A random variable X that takes a range of real variables, yet for which $P(X = a) > 0$ for certain a, is an example. Consider the waiting time for service in a store. With some probability (greater than 0), a clerk is free at the moment of arrival and the waiting time is 0. Otherwise, the wait until service has a continuous distribution on $t > 0$. In a sense, the distribution is a combination of a discrete and a continuous part, each of which, by itself, is defective. *Hybrid distributions* of this sort have cumulative distribution functions, defined by Equation A.8, and work with these distributions is usually based on this function. Integrals analogous to Equation A.9, A.11, or A.13, but employing what are called *Lebesgue–Stieltjes integrals,* can be used.

Expected Values

The *expected value* or *expectation* of a random variable is the sum (or integral) of its values weighted by their probabilities. It is denoted by $E(X)$ and calculated by

$$E(X) = \sum_{\text{all } a} aP(X = a) \qquad (A.14)$$

for a discrete distribution and

$$E(X) = \int_{-\infty}^{\infty} xf(x)\, dx \qquad (A.15)$$

for a continuous one. The expected value of a random variable X is its *mean* and is frequently denoted by μ_X or simply μ. For example, if X has the simple distribution

$$P(X = a) = \begin{cases} 0.2 & \text{if } a = 1 \\ 0.5 & \text{if } a = 2 \\ 0.3 & \text{if } a = 3 \end{cases}$$

then, by Equation A.14,

$$E(X) = (1)(0.2) + (2)(0.5) + (3)(0.3) = 2.1$$

It is easy to define the expectation of a function of a random variable as well. Consider an arbitrary function of X, $g(X)$. Its average value is obtained by replacing a [or x] with $g(a)$ [or $g(x)$] in Equation A.14 [or A.15], to give

$$E[g(X)] = \sum_{\text{all } a} g(a)P(X = a) \qquad (A.16)$$

$$E[g(X)] = \int_{-\infty}^{\infty} g(x)f(x)\,dx \tag{A.17}$$

The expectation is a linear operator. A little manipulation of the sums or integrals in Equation A.16 or A.17 shows, for two random variables X and Y (or functions of random variables) and constants, a, b, and c, that

$$E(aX + bY + c) = aE(X) + bE(Y) + c \tag{A.18}$$

This equation is often useful, for the actual distribution of the sum may be quite difficult to find.

Of particular importance are the expectations of the powers of X, known as the *moments* of the distribution, the power $E(X^k)$ being called the *kth moment of X about* 0. The *moments about the means*, or *central moments*, $E[(X - \mu_X)^k]$, are even more important. In particular, the second central moment is the *variance* of the distribution, denoted $\mathrm{var}(X)$ or σ_X^2. It is usually easier to calculate moments about 0 than moments about the mean, so it pays to express the latter in terms of the former. For the variance, expanding the square, then using Equation A.18 gives

$$\sigma_X^2 = E[(X - \mu_X)^2] = E(X^2) - \mu_X^2 \tag{A.19}$$

Similar formulas can be derived for higher central moments.

A linear property, such as Equation A.18, also holds for the moments about 0, but does not, in general, hold for central moments. In particular, the variance of the sum of two random variables does not equal the sum of the individual variances unless the variables being summed are independent. When they are, the analog to Equation A.18 is

$$\mathrm{var}(aX + bY + c) = a^2\sigma_X^2 + b^2\sigma_Y^2 \tag{A.20}$$

More commonly, the variance of a sum must be obtained by using Equation A.19.

A distribution that takes values all the way out to infinity can have means, variances, or higher moments that are infinite in size, yet still be a proper distribution. For example, if X has the distribution

$$P(X = k) = \frac{6}{\pi^2 k^2} \qquad k = 1, 2, 3, \ldots$$

then $\sum_{k=1}^{\infty} P(X = k) = 1$; yet none of its expectations exist. For example,

$$E(X^2) = \sum_{k=1}^{\infty} k^2 P(X = k) = \sum_{k=1}^{\infty} \frac{6}{\pi^2}$$

which is clearly infinite. The mean of this distribution is also infinite, although the fact is less obvious.

A.3 Some Discrete Distributions

Several discrete distributions appear frequently in this book. Most of these distributions can be interpreted using random variables measured on a series of identical two-alternative events, each of which is independent of the others. Such events are known as *Bernoulli events*. A good physical example of a Bernoulli event is the flip of a possibly biased coin. Each of a series of flips has the same P(heads), and each flip is independent of the flips before it. For convenience, one outcome of a Bernoulli event is usually called a "success"; the other, a "failure" (reflecting the gambling origin of some of the distributions). The probability of a success will be denoted by α.

The Geometric Distribution

The most frequently encountered distribution in the study of Markov chains is the *geometric distribution*. This can be thought of as the number of trials required to obtain a success in the series of independent Bernoulli events. If X is a random variable with this distribution,

$$P(X = 1) = P(\text{success}) = \alpha$$
$$P(X = 2) = P(\text{failure})P(\text{success}) = (1 - \alpha)\alpha$$
$$P(X = 3) = P(\text{failure})P(\text{failure})P(\text{success}) = (1 - \alpha)^2\alpha$$

or, in general,

$$P(X = k) = (1 - \alpha)^{k-1}\alpha \qquad k = 1, 2, 3, \ldots \qquad (A.21)$$

Geometric distributions have a mode at 1 and fall off toward infinity. The nearer α is to 1, the more rapid is this fall. Two examples are shown in Figure A.2.

The moments of the geometric distribution are found by direct evaluation of their definitions, Equations A.14 and A.16, using the methods

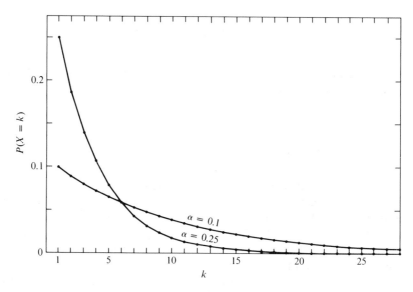

Figure A.2   Geometric distributions drawn for $\alpha = 0.25$ and $\alpha = 0.1$.

discussed in the next section. Starting from the definition of the mean,

$$\mu = E(X) = \sum_{k=1}^{\infty} k(1 - \alpha)^{k-1}\alpha \qquad (A.22)$$

$$= \alpha \sum_{k=1}^{\infty} k(1 - \alpha)^{k-1} = \frac{1}{\alpha} \qquad (A.23)$$

(using Equation A.30, below, to find the value of the sum). Likewise,

$$E(X^2) = \sum_{k=1}^{\infty} k^2(1 - \alpha)^{k-1}\alpha = \frac{2 - \alpha}{\alpha^2}$$

Then, by Equation A.19,

$$\sigma^2 = \frac{2 - \alpha}{\alpha^2} - \left(\frac{1}{\alpha}\right)^2 = \frac{1 - \alpha}{\alpha^2} \qquad (A.24)$$

Distributions like the geometric are often started at points other than 1. Suppose, for example, that Y is the number of failures before the first success in the Bernoulli sequence. It has a distribution similar to X, but is always smaller by 1, starting at 0 rather than 1:

$$P(Y = k) = (1 - \alpha)^k\alpha \qquad k = 0, 1, 2, \ldots \qquad (A.25)$$

This changes the mean slightly:

$$E(Y) = \frac{1 - \alpha}{\alpha}$$

but does not alter the central moments. Such changes in the origin of counting are common and do not change the names of the distributions involved—both Equation A.21 and Equation A.25 are said to be geometric distributions. Because of this, one must be careful about applying formulas such as Equation A.23 for the mean without checking to see that the correct distribution is involved.

The geometric distribution has a very important property that sets it apart from any of the other discrete distributions: the distribution of X, conditional on X being at least as large as a number x_0, has the same form as the original unconditional distribution. This fact is important enough to warrant both an illustration (see Figure A.3) and a proof. First,

$$P(X = k|X > x_0) = \frac{P(X = k)}{P(X > x_0)} \qquad k > x_0$$

In this,

$$P(X > x_0) = 1 - P(X \leq x_0)$$

$$= 1 - \sum_{j=1}^{x_0} P(X = j)$$

$$= 1 - \alpha \sum_{j=1}^{x_0} (1 - \alpha)^{j-1}$$

$$= 1 - \alpha \left[\frac{1 - (1 - \alpha)^{x_0}}{1 - (1 - \alpha)} \right] = (1 - \alpha)^{x_0}$$

(using Equation A.29, below, to evaluate the sum). So

$$P(X = k|X > x_0) = \frac{\alpha(1 - \alpha)^{k-1}}{(1 - \alpha)^{x_0}}$$

$$= \alpha(1 - \alpha)^{(k-x_0)-1} = P(X = k - x_0) \qquad \text{(A.26)}$$

This is a geometric distribution, but started at x_0 instead of at 1. In terms of the Bernoulli-events interpretation of the geometric distribution, it means that the fact that x_0 failures have been observed while waiting for a success has no effect on the distribution of trials still to

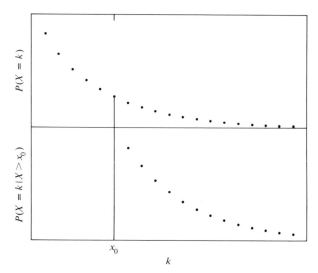

Figure A.3   Illustration of the result $P(X = k|X > x_0) = P(X = k - x_0)$ for the geometric distribution.

wait. The geometric distribution is the only discrete distribution to have this memory-less property. This meshes with the memory-less characteristics of the Markov chains, and is responsible for the prevalence of geometric terms throughout this book.

Sums of Geometric Series

The importance of the geometric distribution makes it essential to be able to sum a finite or an infinite number of geometric terms. This section presents formulas for evaluating sums involving series in which each term is a higher power of x:

$$x^0 = 1, \ x^1 = x, \ x^2, \ x^3, \ x^4, \ \ldots$$

Such series are known as *geometric series*.

First consider the sum

$$S = 1 + x + x^2 + x^3 + \cdots = \sum_{i=1}^{\infty} x^{i-1} \tag{A.27}$$

As long as $|x| \geq 1$, each power of x is at least as large as the preceding one, and S has no finite or stable value. When $|x| < 1$, large powers of x approach 0 fast enough to give the sum a finite value. A simple way to evaluate Equation A.27 is to subtract x times the sum from itself:

$$\begin{array}{rcccccccccc} S &=& 1 &+& x &+& x^2 &+& x^3 &+& x^4 &+& \cdots \\ xS &=& & & x &+& x^2 &+& x^3 &+& x^4 &+& \cdots \\ \hline S - xS &=& 1 &+& (x - x) &+& (x^2 - x^2) &+& (x^3 - x^3) &+& (x^4 - x^4) &+& \cdots \\ &=& 1 \end{array}$$

Thus, $S - xS = 1$, which is easily solved to give

$$S = \sum_{i=1}^{\infty} x^{i-1} = \frac{1}{1 - x} \tag{A.28}$$

An equivalent route to the same end is to note that S can be rewritten in terms of itself:

$$S = 1 + x(1 + x + x^2 + \cdots) = 1 + xS$$

again giving Equation A.28.

When the series is finite in length, the same techniques can be used, but a term is left over on the right-hand end. For example, if

$$S_n = \sum_{i=1}^{n} x^{i-1}$$

then

$$\begin{array}{rcl} S_n &=& 1 + x + x^2 + x^3 + \cdots + x^{n-1} \\ xS_n &=& \phantom{1 + {}} x + x^2 + x^3 + \cdots + x^{n-1} + x^n \\ \hline S_n - xS_n &=& 1 \phantom{+ x + x^2 + x^3 + \cdots + x^{n-1} + {}} - x^n \end{array}$$

Solving for S_n gives

$$S_n = \frac{1 - x^n}{1 - x} \tag{A.29}$$

Frequently a sum is almost in the form to use Equation A.28 or A.29, but has extra terms, is missing terms, or is multiplied by a constant. To sum such a series, one need only make adjustments until a known form is reached. Thus, faced with

$$y + \sum_{i=3}^{\infty} 5x^{i+1}$$

note that y and 5 are constants, that the limits of summation start at 3, and that the exponent is $i + 1$. Nevertheless, it is easy to recognize Equation A.27 within the sum when a few terms are written out:

$$y + 5x^4 + 5x^5 + 5x^6 + \cdots = y + 5x^4(1 + x + x^2 + \cdots)$$

$$= y + 5x^4S = y + \frac{5x^4}{1 - x}$$

This sum could also be evaluated directly by the subtraction method.

In some series, the part represented by x in Equation A.27 is not simple. For example, the sum

$$a + \frac{a}{b + c} + \frac{a}{(b + c)^2} + \frac{a}{(b + c)^3} + \cdots$$

is Equation A.27 multiplied by a and with $x = (b + c)^{-1}$. Its value is

$$\frac{a}{1 - (b + c)^{-1}} = \frac{a(b + c)}{b + c - 1}$$

In order for this sum to have a finite value, $|b + c|$ must be greater than 1.

Equation A.27 lets one total the terms of a geometric distribution, but is not enough to evaluate the mean or variance. In sums like Equation A.22, each geometric term is multiplied by a number from an arithmetic series. For example, consider

$$T = \sum_{i=1}^{\infty} ix^{i-1} = 1 + 2x + 3x^2 + 4x^3 + \cdots$$

There are several ways to evaluate this sum. The subtraction method is not so simple as it was before, as it gives an infinite sum:

$$\begin{array}{rl} T = & 1 + 2x + 3x^2 + 4x^3 + 5x^4 + \cdots \\ xT = & x + 2x^2 + 3x^3 + 4x^4 + \cdots \\ \hline T - xT = & 1 + x + x^2 + x^3 + x^4 + \cdots \end{array}$$

The sum on the right-hand side is given in Equation A.28 to be $(1 - x)^{-1}$, whence

$$T = \sum_{i=1}^{\infty} ix^{i-1} = \frac{1}{(1 - x)^2} \qquad (A.30)$$

The value of Equation A.30 can also be found by differentiating the known sum S. Differentiating the left-hand side of Equation A.28 gives

$$\frac{dS}{dx} = \frac{d}{dx}(1 + x + x^2 + x^3 + \cdots)$$

$$= \frac{d1}{dx} + \frac{dx}{dx} + \frac{dx^2}{dx} + \frac{dx^3}{dx} + \cdots$$

$$= 0 + 1 + 2x + 3x^2 + \cdots = T$$

(using Equations D.6 and D.7). Direct differentiation of the right-hand side of Equation A.28 must equal the same result:

$$\frac{dS}{dx} = \frac{d}{dx}(1 - x)^{-1}$$

$$= (-1)(1 - x)^{-2}\frac{d(1 - x)}{dx} = (1 - x)^{-2}$$

which gives Equation A.30 again.

Again, it may be necessary to factor out constants or to add or subtract terms in order to put the sum into the form of Equation A.30. For example,

$$\sum_{i=1}^{\infty} ix^i = x + 2x^2 + 3x^3 + \cdots$$

$$= x(1 + 2x + 3x^2 + \cdots) = \frac{x}{(1 - x)^2}$$

Either the subtraction or the differentiation procedure can be used with sums containing higher powers of i. For example, a subtraction to give T or a second differentiation of Equation A.30 gives

$$\sum_{i=1}^{\infty} i^2 x^{i-1} = \frac{1 + x}{(1 - x)^3} \tag{A.31}$$

which appears in expressions for the variance. Further operations can get higher powers of i; in general, the subtraction operation expresses a sum where i^m multiplies x^i as a series where the multiplier is i^{m-1}, and the differentiation operation converts a formula in i^{m-1} to one in i^m.

The Binomial Distribution

Like the geometric distribution, the *binomial distribution* can be related to a set of Bernoulli events. In N independent and identical events, count the number of successes. This random variable, call it X, has the distribution

$$P(X = k) = \binom{N}{k} \alpha^k (1 - \alpha)^{N-k} \tag{A.32}$$

where

$$\binom{N}{k} = \frac{N!}{k!(N-k)!} \tag{A.33}$$

Equation A.32 applies only when k is between 0 and N (inclusive); for values outside this range, $P(X = k) = 0$. This distribution function can be interpreted as the product of three terms. First, the coefficient in Equation A.33 gives the number of ways to choose the k successes from the N events; second, α^k is the probability of k successes; and third, $(1 - \alpha)^{N-k}$ is the probability of $N - k$ failures.

The coefficient in Equation A.33, called a *binomial coefficient*, appears frequently in probability theory.[†] It equals the number of different ways to select a sample of k items from a larger set of N, without regard to the order in which they are selected. It also appears in the expansion of the product:

$$(y + z)^N = y^N + Ny^{N-1}z + \frac{N(N-1)}{2} y^{N-2}z^2 + \cdots + Nyz^{N-1} + z^N$$

$$= \sum_{i=0}^{N} \binom{N}{i} y^i z^{N-i} \tag{A.34}$$

This relationship is known as the *binomial theorem*. When $y = \alpha$ and $z = 1 - \alpha$, the terms of Equation A.34 are the probabilities in a binomial distribution, which gives the distribution its name.

The mean of the binomial distribution is

$$\mu = N\alpha \tag{A.35}$$

[†] The binomial coefficient is sometimes denoted by C_k^N, $_NC_k$, $C(N, k)$, or the like.

and the variance is

$$\sigma^2 = N\alpha(1 - \alpha) \qquad (A.36)$$

The binomial distribution has two limiting forms of considerable importance. First, as N gets large with α constant, the distribution becomes more and more symmetric and bell-shaped, and is approximated by a normal distribution with mean $N\alpha$ and variance $N\alpha(1 - \alpha)$. More exactly, the standardized value of X,

$$z = \frac{X - N\alpha}{\sqrt{N\alpha(1 - \alpha)}} \qquad (A.37)$$

approaches a standard normal distribution with zero mean and unit variance.

The second limiting form applies in cases where N gets large, but where the mean, $\mu = N\alpha$, remains fixed by virtue of α simultaneously becoming 0. In this case it can be shown that the distribution takes the form

$$P(X = k) \rightarrow \frac{e^{-\mu}\mu^k}{k!} \qquad \text{as } N \rightarrow \infty \qquad (A.38)$$

This distribution, called the *Poisson distribution,* is discussed below.

As approximations, the two limiting forms are applicable in somewhat different situations. The normal approximation is most realistic when N is large, the mean is also large, and α takes values that are neither close to 0 nor close to 1. The Poisson approximation is more accurate when α is very small and the mean is not large. In cases where α is small, yet μ is rather large, either approximation is fairly accurate.

The Negative Binomial Distribution

The notion of counting the number of Bernoulli events until the first success, which was the basis of the geometric distribution, can be extended to counts of the number of events until the rth success. The resulting random variable has a *negative binomial distribution,* sometimes called a *Pascal distribution.* Its distribution function is constructed from the binomial as follows. For a negative binomial random variable X to have value k, there must be $r - 1$ successes and $k - r$ failures in the first $k - 1$ trials, then a success on the kth trial. The first probability is a binomial with parameters $k - 1$ and α; the second is just α. Thus, multiplying these gives

$$P(X = k) = \binom{k-1}{r-1} \alpha^k (1 - \alpha)^{r-k} \tag{A.39}$$

The moments of this distribution are

$$\mu = r/\alpha \tag{A.40}$$

$$\sigma^2 = \frac{r(1 - \alpha)}{\alpha^2} \tag{A.41}$$

The negative binomial random variable can also be thought of as the sum of r independent geometric random variables, that is, as the number of trials to the first success, plus the number to the second, and so forth, or

$$X = Y_1 + Y_2 + \cdots + Y_r$$

where the Y_i are exponential random variables. The form of the distribution function is not obvious from this fact—the distribution of a sum of random variables is rarely easy to find—but the expected value, Equation A.40, is r times the expected value for a geometric distribution (Equation A.23), as the additive property of random variables, Equation A.18, shows. Because of the independence of the Y_i, the variances also sum (see Equation A.20); thus, Equation A.41 is r times Equation A.24.

The Poisson Distribution

The distribution encountered in Equation A.38 as the limit of the binomial is important in its own right and is known as the *Poisson distribution*. Its distribution function is usually written with parameter λ, as

$$P(X = k) = \frac{e^{-\lambda} \lambda^k}{k!} \tag{A.42}$$

The Poisson distribution is a good model for the frequency of relatively rare events, either as the limit of the binomial, as described above, or through the continuous-time stochastic processes that are discussed in Chapter 10. The rationale behind the distribution is developed more fully in that chapter.

Several examples of Poisson distributions are shown in Figure A.4.

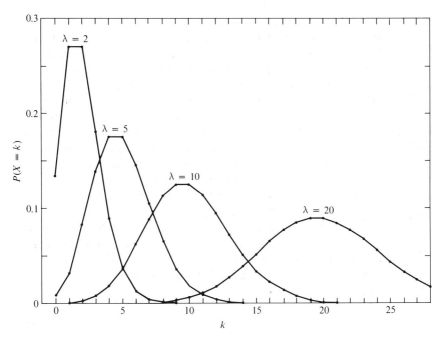

Figure A.4   Poisson distributions plotted for several values of the parameter λ.

As is apparent from that figure, when λ is large, the Poisson distribution is well approximated by a normal distribution.

The moments of the Poisson distribution are quite simple; both the mean and the variance equal the parameter λ:

$$\mu = \sigma^2 = \lambda \qquad\qquad (A.43)$$

A.4   Some Continuous Distributions

The discrete nature of the processes discussed in the bulk of this book means that continuous random variables play a smaller role than do discrete distributions. Nevertheless, several appear fairly often.

Distributions from Statistics: The Chi-Square and the Normal

Most of the distributions familiar from conventional statistical testing are not used in this book. In particular, the *t* distribution and the *F* do not appear at all. However, two distributions, the chi-square and the normal, make limited appearances.

The statistical testing of Markov models, presented in Chapter 6, generates test statistics that measure the discrepancy between data and a model. These are compared to a *chi-square distribution* to indicate whether a discrepancy is larger than could be expected by chance. Large values of the statistic lead to rejection of the model.

The chi-square distribution depends on a single, integer-valued parameter, known as the number of *degrees of freedom*. This number equals the difference between the number of observations used to calculate the statistic and the number of constraints that are put on the model: the greater the number of observations and the fewer the constraints, the more the degrees of freedom. In essence, the number of degrees of freedom equals the number of unconstrained dimensions along which the observations can vary.

Chi-square random variables have an important reproductive property: the sum of two independent chi-square random variables is also distributed as chi-square. More formally, let the independent random variables X_1 and X_2 have chi-square distributions with f_1 and f_2 degrees of freedom, respectively. Then

$$Y = X_1 + X_2 \qquad (A.44)$$

has a chi-square distribution with $f_1 + f_2$ degrees of freedom. The same rule does not hold for subtraction: in general, $X_1 - X_2$ does not have a chi-square distribution, even though its independent parts do. However, there are several practical situations in which the conditions of Equation A.44 are satisfied, but only the values of X_1 and Y are known (note that they are not independent). Then $Y - X_1$ gives the value of X_2 and has a chi-square distribution.

The actual form of the chi-square density function is not important here. It is used only to test for discrepancies, and for this purpose, it suffices to list values of a such that $P(X > a)$ takes certain standard values. A table of these values is given in Appendix F for degrees of freedom from 1 to 25. For larger values of the degrees of freedom, the values of X are approximated by referring to a normal distribution. With f degrees of freedom,

$$z = \sqrt{2X} - \sqrt{2f - 1} \qquad (A.45)$$

has approximately a standard normal distribution. The chi-square distribution increases about as rapidly as its degrees of freedom, which means that it is not roughly equal to any particular value. However, it is handy to remember that chi-square is unlikely to be greatly larger than its degrees of freedom: when $f > 7$, the 5% level is less than twice f; and when $f > 25$, it is less than $1.5f$.

The second important statistical distribution is the *normal distribution*. It appears here primarily as the limit of other distributions, such as the binomial, the Poisson, or the chi-square (for example, Equation A.37 or A.45). The distribution depends on two parameters: its mean and its variance. However, because the shape of the distribution is the same for any mean and any variance, only the standard form, with mean 0 and variance 1, need be given. For any other μ and σ, the variable

$$z = \frac{X - \mu}{\sigma}$$

has the standard form. Some standard values of the normal distribution are shown in Appendix F.

The importance of the normal distribution stems largely from the *central limit theorem*, which asserts that any random variable Y formed from the sum of n independent and identical random variables,

$$Y = X_1 + X_2 + \cdots + X_n$$

tends to be normal. As n gets large,

$$z = \frac{Y - \mu_Y}{\sigma_Y}$$
$$= \frac{Y - n\mu_X}{\sqrt{n}\,\sigma_X}$$

comes to have a standard normal distribution. Many of the distributions discussed here, such as the binomial or the chi-square, can be written as sums of independent parts, so the central limit theorem applies. It is often easy to spot these sums. For example, the negative binomial is a sum of independent geometric variables, so is roughly normal for large r.

The Exponential Distribution

The *exponential distribution* plays a fundamental role in continuous-time Markov processes, similar to the role of the geometric distribution with discrete-time processes. The distribution depends on the single parameter $\alpha > 0$ and has the density function

$$f(x) = \alpha e^{-\alpha x} \tag{A.46}$$

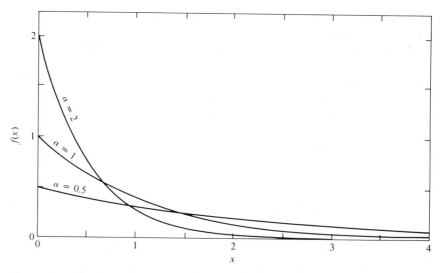

Figure A.5   Exponential distributions drawn for $\alpha = 0.5$, 1, and 2.

for $x \geq 0$. It is not defined for negative x. Some examples are shown in Figure A.5. The moments of the exponential distribution are

$$\mu = 1/\alpha \qquad (A.47)$$

and

$$\sigma^2 = 1/\alpha^2 \qquad (A.48)$$

The most significant property of an exponential distribution is its memory-less character as a waiting-time distribution. The conditional distribution of an exponential variable, given that it has exceeded any particular constant, looks just like the original distribution. A proof of this is similar to that of the same property for the geometric distribution, leading to Equation A.26. For any positive x_0, the conditional density of X given $X \geq x_0$ is

$$f(x|X \geq x_0) = f(x - x_0) = \alpha e^{-\alpha(x-x_0)}$$

The right-hand side of this equation is identical to Equation A.46, except shifted to start at x_0. The exponential distribution is unique among continuous distributions in having this characteristic, which makes it closely related to the Markov assumption. This point is discussed in more detail in Chapter 10 (see Figure 10.1).

The Gamma Distribution

Just as the sum of a number of geometric random variables has a negative binomial distribution, the sum of a series of independent and identical exponential random variables has what is known as a *gamma distribution*. When r exponentials are added together, the result has the density function

$$f(x) = \frac{\alpha^r}{(r-1)!} x^{r-1} e^{-\alpha x} \qquad (A.49)$$

for positive x. When $r = 1$, Equation A.49 reduces to the exponential density, Equation A.46.

The parameter r in Equation A.49 must be integral for the factorials to be meaningful. However, there is a generalization to nonintegers. The *gamma function*,

$$\Gamma(r) = \int_0^\infty x^{r-1} e^{-x} \, dx \qquad (A.50)$$

has $\Gamma(1) = 1$ and

$$\Gamma(r) = (r-1)\Gamma(r-1) \qquad (A.51)$$

Thus, for integral r,

$$\Gamma(r) = (r-1)!$$

Substituting this into Equation A.49 gives the general gamma distribution:

$$f(x) = \frac{\alpha^r}{\Gamma(r)} x^{r-1} e^{-\alpha x} \qquad (A.52)$$

In this form, nonintegral values of r are acceptable.

The similarity between the gamma function, Equation A.50, and the distribution function, Equation A.52, gives the gamma distribution its name. The cumulative distribution function for a gamma distribution looks like the integral in Equation A.50, but with limits 0 and a rather than 0 and infinity; for this reason the gamma cumulative distribution function is sometimes called the *incomplete gamma function*.

The gamma distribution has a single mode that shifts away from 0 as r increases (see Figure A.6). Its construction as the sum of independent parts means that the central limit theorem applies and the form tends toward the normal distribution when r is large. The mean and the vari-

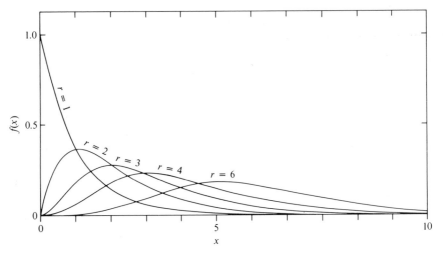

Figure A.6 Gamma distributions for $\alpha = 1$ and several values of r.

ance follow from this summation; they are r times the corresponding quantities for an exponential distribution. Using the moments of that distribution from Equations A.47 and A.48 gives

$$\mu = r/\alpha \qquad\qquad\qquad (A.53)$$

$$\sigma^2 = r/\alpha^2 \qquad\qquad\qquad (A.54)$$

The fact that the gamma distribution is a sum of independent exponentials gives it several important properties. First, like the chi-square, the gamma has a reproductive property. If X_1 and X_2 have independent gamma distributions with parameters r_1, r_2 and the same α, then their sum also has a gamma distribution, with parameters $r_1 + r_2$ and α. In effect, the combination of X_1 and X_2 is just the sum of $r_1 + r_2$ independent exponentials.

There is a relationship between the gamma distribution and the Poisson distribution that links them in several applications. When $\alpha = 1$ (the standard form of the gamma distribution), then Equation A.49 becomes

$$f(x) = \frac{x^{r-1}e^{-x}}{(r - 1)!}$$

If x is treated as the parameter and r as the variable, this is the distribution function for a Poisson random variable, Equation A.42. In other words, the value of a series of gamma densities, such as the ones shown in Figure A.6, when selected at a particular value of x, are terms of a Poisson distribution. This connection is exploited in Chapter 10 in the discussion of the Poisson process.

The Beta Distribution

The final distribution considered here stands in a similar relationship to the binomial as the gamma distribution does to the Poisson. A random variable X on the interval [0, 1] has a *beta distribution* when its density function is

$$f(x) = \frac{1}{B(\alpha,\beta)} x^{\alpha-1}(1 - x)^{\beta-1} \tag{A.55}$$

where α, $\beta > 0$.† The normalization constant, known as a *beta function,* is

$$B(a,b) = \int_0^1 x^{a-1}(1 - x)^{b-1}dx \tag{A.56}$$

(the B in $B(a,b)$ is a capital beta). The similarity between Equation A.55 and Equation A.56 leads the cumulative beta distribution function to sometimes be called the *incomplete beta function.*

The mean of the beta distribution,

$$\mu = \frac{\alpha}{\alpha + \beta} \tag{A.57}$$

can lie anywhere in the interval [0, 1]. Subject to this mean, the size of the parameters indicates the spread of the distribution between 0 and 1. The variance is

$$\sigma^2 = \frac{\alpha\beta}{(\alpha + \beta)^2(\alpha + \beta + 1)} \tag{A.58}$$

---

† The parameters are sometimes one smaller than given here, in which case Equation A.55 is written

$$f(x) = \frac{1}{B(\alpha + 1, \beta + 1)} x^\alpha(1 - x)^\beta$$

for α, $\beta > -1$. There is no fundamental difference between the two forms, but it is important to know which one a particular author is using.

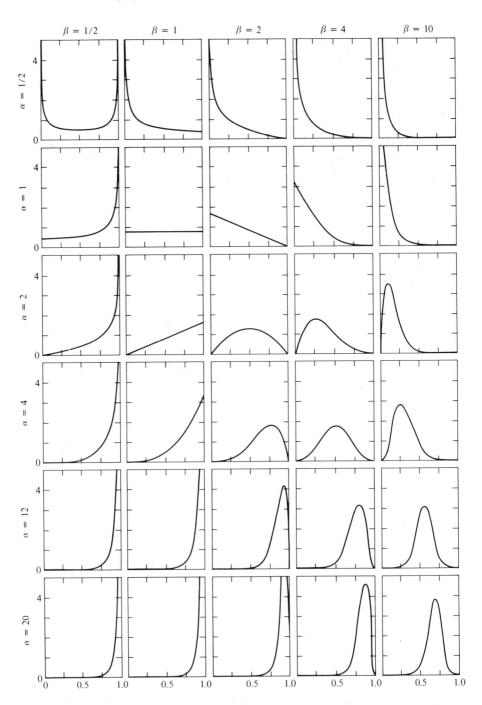

Figure A.7 Beta distributions for a variety of parameter values.

so the larger the α and β, the tighter the distribution clusters about μ. Several examples are shown in Figure A.7. Note that when either parameter is less than 1, the distribution rises to infinity at the low (α) or high (β) end of the distribution. When the parameter exceeds 1, the density function falls to 0 at that end.

The beta function, Equation A.56, can be expressed in terms of the gamma function as

$$B(a,b) = \frac{\Gamma(a)\Gamma(b)}{\Gamma(a + b)} \qquad (A.59)$$

When a and b are integral, the factorials can be used:

$$B(a,b) = \frac{(a - 1)!(b - 1)!}{(a + b - 1)!} \qquad (A.60)$$

Thus, $B(a,b)$ is quite similar to the binomial coefficients of Equation A.33 (although not identical to them). This, along with the basic form of the density function, gives the beta distribution a parallel to the binomial distribution.

Appendix B

Difference Equations

In the construction of a model for an evolving process, quantities occurring at one time are often described in terms of the same quantities at earlier times. For example, in the all-or-none paired-associate model (see Chapter 2), the probability that an item has not been learned by trial t is expressed as a proportion $1 - \alpha$ of the probability that it has not been learned by trial $t - 1$:

$$P(G_t) = (1 - \alpha)P(G_{t-1}) \tag{B.1}$$

In this equation, one member of a series is described as a function of earlier values. It can be rewritten to express the difference between two successive terms as a function of the earlier terms:

$$P(G_t) - P(G_{t-1}) = -\alpha P(G_{t-1})$$

Equations such as these, known as *difference equations*, appear frequently throughout this book.

The solution to a difference equation is an expression written as a function of t, without reference to other terms of the series. For example, Equation B.1 has the solution

$$P(G_t) = (1 - \alpha)^{t-1} \tag{B.2}$$

as is easily verified by substitution.

A difference equation cannot be solved in isolation; it is also necessary to know how the series starts out. The solution to Equation B.1 is different when $P(G_1) = 1$ (as was assumed in finding Equation B.2) than when $P(G_1) = \frac{1}{2}$. A number of initial terms must be supplied along with the difference equation in order to get the series started.

Simple difference equations can often be solved by calculating successive terms of the series until a pattern becomes evident, then verifying a surmise about the general solution by substituting it into the original equation. With simple equations, such as Equation B.1, this method is satisfactory; but with more complicated equations, a general procedure is necessary. This appendix describes solution procedures for a limited, but very useful class of difference equations. A more extensive discussion can be found in Goldberg (1958).

More formally, a *difference equation* is a function on a series of quantities $x_1, x_2, x_3, \ldots, x_{t-1}, x_t, \ldots$, that relates the values of the terms x_{t-k}, $x_{t-k+1}, \ldots, x_{t-1}$, and x_t. Where only the preceding value of x is needed, so that the equation contains only x_t and x_{t-1}, the equation is of the *first order*. Where the equation reaches back k terms, it is of the *kth order*. Equation B.1 is a first-order difference equation.

The order of the difference equation determines how many values of x_t are needed to start the series out. First-order equations require a single term, second-order equations require two terms, and in general, a difference equation of the kth order requires k terms.

The difference equation that relates the terms of the series to each other can take many mathematical forms, leading to many sorts of solutions and many solution methods. Fortunately, only a relatively few types occur with Markov models and these are simple to work with. Generally, the function relating $x_{t-k}, x_{t-k+1}, \ldots$, and x_t is linear and has coefficients that do not depend on t. Such an equation is known as a *linear difference equation* with *constant coefficients* and is written in standard form as

$$x_t + a_1 x_{t-1} + a_2 x_{t-2} + \cdots + a_k x_{t-k} = b_t \tag{B.3}$$

In Equation B.3, any terms that do not involve one of the x_i values (but that may depend on t) have been brought over to the right-hand side and denoted by b_t. If b_t is 0, the difference equation is called a *homogeneous equation*. A nonhomogeneous equation gives rise to a homogeneous one when b_t is replaced by 0. The solution to this homogeneous equation forms part of the solution to the nonhomogeneous equation, so homogeneous equations are covered first.

B.1   Homogeneous Difference Equations

Homogeneous linear difference equations are written in general as

$$x_t + a_1 x_{t-1} + a_2 x_{t-2} + \cdots + a_k x_{t-k} = 0 \qquad \text{(B.4)}$$

In this form, Equation B.1 is

$$P(G_t) - (1 - \alpha)P(G_{t-1}) = 0$$

As is demonstrated below, one solution to Equation B.4 is

$$x_t = Am^{t-1} \qquad \text{(B.5)}$$

for the appropriate choice of the constants A and m. In fact, with the exception noted below, every solution to a homogeneous linear difference equation is a linear combination of terms like Equation B.5.

In the case of first-order equations such as Equation B.1, it is easy to show that Equation B.5 is a solution. Writing out a few terms, starting with $x_1 = A$, makes this obvious. For kth-order equations, some more work is required. If Equation B.5 is to solve Equation B.4, the correct values of A and m must be found. The value of m comes first. Substituting the potential solution into the original equation gives

$$Am^{t-1} + a_1 Am^{t-2} + a_2 Am^{t-3} + \cdots + a_k Am^{t-k-1} = 0$$

Every term contains the common factor Am^{t-k-1}, and if this is divided out, a simple polynomial in m remains:

$$m^k + a_1 m^{k-1} + a_2 m^{k-2} + \cdots + a_{k-1} m + a_k = 0 \qquad \text{(B.6)}$$

To make Equation B.5 fit Equation B.4, m must be chosen to satisfy Equation B.6, known as the *auxiliary equation* or *characteristic equation*. Any one of the k roots of Equation B.6 provides a solution to Equation B.4 of the form in Equation B.5, giving k different solutions in all. Because of the linearity of the original equation, if $A_1 m_1^{t-1}$ and $A_2 m_2^{t-1}$ solve the difference equation, so also does their sum. Thus, for the appropriate constants A_i and the k roots of the auxiliary equation, a general solution to the difference equation (Equation B.4) is the sum of

k terms:

$$x_t = A_1 m_1^{t-1} + A_2 m_2^{t-1} + \cdots + A_k m_k^{t-1} \tag{B.7}$$

The constants $A_1, A_2, \ldots, A_k$ remain to be determined. The auxiliary equation (Equation B.6) gives no help in finding them. For this, the initial conditions are necessary. As many initial values as there are constants are equated to their values from Equation B.7, and the result is solved for $A_1, A_2, \ldots, A_k$. Specifically, consider a special case of Equation B.4, a second-order equation. The solution, Equation B.7,

$$x_t = A_1 m_1^{t-1} + A_2 m_2^{t-1} \tag{B.8}$$

contains two unknown constants, A_1 and A_2. To find them, two initial values, x_1 and x_2, are needed. Setting these values equal to Equation B.8 with $t = 1$ and $t = 2$:

$$x_1 = A_1 + A_2$$
$$x_2 = A_1 m_1 + A_2 m_2$$

These are readily solved for A_1 and A_2.

For example, suppose that the original difference equation is

$$x_t = 6x_{t-1} - 8x_{t-2} \tag{B.9}$$

with $x_1 = 4$ and $x_2 = 6$. In standard form, this equation is

$$x_t - 6x_{t-1} + 8x_{t-2} = 0$$

Replacing x_{t-2} by 1, x_{t-1} by m, and x_t by m^2, as in Equation B.6, gives the auxiliary equation

$$m^2 - 6m + 8 = 0$$

This has roots $m_1 = 2$ and $m_2 = 4$. Substituting these into Equation B.8 (or, in general, into Equation B.7) gives

$$x_t = A_1 2^{t-1} + A_2 4^{t-1}$$

To find A_1 and A_2, set $t = 1$ and $t = 2$ so as to apply the initial conditions. These give

$$A_1 + A_2 = x_1 = 4$$
$$2A_1 + 4A_2 = x_2 = 6$$

which solve to give $A_1 = 5$ and $A_2 = -1$. Thus, the full solution of Equation B.9 is

$$x_t = (5)(2^{t-1}) - 4^{t-1}$$

It is advisable to verify the solution by substituting it into the original equation, Equation B.9, and showing that it fits.

Equation B.7 is correct as long as the k roots of Equation B.6 are distinct. When two or more roots of the auxiliary equation are the same, the solution is slightly different. Suppose that there are two roots equal to m. There is no need to put Am^{t-1} in the equation twice. Instead, both $A_1 m^{t-1}$ and $A_2 t m^{t-1}$ can be shown to solve the original difference equation. A third identical root adds a term with t^2 in it and, in general, if there are r identical roots, the solution contains

$$A_1 m^{t-1} + A_2 t m^{t-1} + A_3 t^2 m^{t-1} + \cdots + A_r t^{r-1} m^{t-1} \qquad (B.10)$$

For an example showing this, take the equation

$$x_t - (2\alpha + \beta)x_{t-1} + \alpha(\alpha + 2\beta)x_{t-2} - \alpha^2\beta x_{t-3} = 0$$

for some constants α and β. This is a third-order equation, and its auxiliary equation,

$$m^3 - (2\alpha + \beta)m^2 + \alpha(\alpha + 2\beta)m - \alpha^2\beta = 0$$

factors into

$$(m - \alpha)(m - \alpha)(m - \beta) = 0$$

There are two identical roots here and one unique root. Thus, the full solution is

$$x_t = A_1\alpha^{t-1} + A_2 t\alpha^{t-1} + A_3\beta^{t-1}$$

The A_i are determined by the first three values of x.

In some cases, the roots of the auxiliary equation are complex, that is, of the form $m = a + ib$, where $i = \sqrt{-1}$. This sounds disturbing, but it is not so bad as it seems. The methods of the preceding few paragraphs remain correct, but the complex roots do not actually produce a complex value for x_t. Complex roots always appear in conjugate pairs, so that, for every root $m = a + ib$, there is another root $\bar{m} = a - ib$ in which the sign of the imaginary term is changed. These conjugate roots give rise to conjugate values of the constant A, so the solution contains $Am^{t-1} + \bar{A}\bar{m}^{t-1}$. In every case this sum is real, equaling $Cr^{t-1}\cos(\theta t + D)$, where $r = \sqrt{a^2 + b^2}$, $\theta = \cos^{-1}(a/r)$, and the two constants C and D are determined from initial conditions. Complex roots do not turn up in psychological models very often.

B.2 Nonhomogeneous Difference Equations

A nonhomogeneous or *complete difference equation* of the form in Equation B.3 is like a homogeneous equation, but contains an additional term that does not depend on the x series, although it may depend on t. The solution to Equation B.3 is closely related to the solution of the homogeneous equation created by deleting b_t from Equation B.3. Suppose that $x_t^{(1)}$ and $x_t^{(2)}$ are any two different solutions to Equation B.3— the (1) and (2) identify the solutions; they are not exponents. Subtracting two copies of Equation B.3—one for $x_t^{(1)}$ and one for $x_t^{(2)}$—shows that the difference $x_t^{(1)} - x_t^{(2)}$ satisfies the homogeneous equation, Equation B.4. So $x_t^{(2)}$ can be found from $x_t^{(1)}$ by adding a solution to the homogeneous equation. Any solution to Equation B.3 has this property, so in general

$$x_t = x_t^{(h)} + x_t^{(p)} \tag{B.11}$$

where $x_t^{(h)}$ is the general solution to the homogeneous equation, Equation B.4, and $x_t^{(p)}$ is any solution, no matter how trivial, to the full nonhomogeneous equation (including b_t). The solution $x_t^{(p)}$ is known as a *particular solution*.

For example, consider the first-order equation

$$x_t - \alpha x_{t-1} = c^t \tag{B.12}$$

The homogeneous form of the equation, obtained by replacing c^t with 0,

$$x_t^{(h)} - \alpha x_{t-1}^{(h)} = 0$$

has the general solution

$$x_t^{(h)} = A\alpha^{t-1}$$

with the constant A to be determined. For a particular solution, anything that fits Equation B.12 can be used. If $\alpha \neq c$, a geometric series works. Let

$$x_t^{(p)} = Bc^{t-1}$$

for some B. Substituting this equation into Equation B.12 gives

$$Bc^{t-1} - \alpha Bc^{t-2} = c^t$$

and solving for B gives

$$B = \frac{c^2}{c - \alpha}$$

The fact that this value of B does not depend on t indicates that the exponential is a satisfactory choice for the particular solution to Equation B.12. Thus,

$$x_t^{(p)} = \frac{c^{t+1}}{c - \alpha}$$

The general solution to Equation B.12 combines $x_t^{(h)}$ and $x_t^{(p)}$ in Equation B.11:

$$x_t = A\alpha^{t-1} + \frac{c^{t+1}}{c - \alpha}$$

The initial conditions are used to find A.

The only trick to solving a complete difference equation is to know the form of the particular solution. This depends on the form of b_t, but fortunately, there are only a limited number of cases that appear with any frequency. The particular solutions usually have the same form as b_t, so are easy to remember. For most Markov models, the most useful case has just been covered in the example: when the b_t are a geometric series, $b_t = c^t$, then the particular solution is also a geometric series. If c is the same as one of the roots of the auxiliary equation, the solution must be multiplied by t, just as in the case of identical roots of the auxiliary equation in Equation B.10.

The other common nonhomogeneous term b_t is a polynomial in t:

$$b_t = a_0 + a_1 t + a_2 t^2 + \cdots + a_k t^k$$

Then, the particular solution is a polynomial of the same degree with unknown coefficients. The case where b_t is a constant is included as a zero-degree polynomial; its particular solution is also a constant.

As another example, combining several of the principles discussed so far, consider the equation

$$x_t - 4x_{t-1} + 4x_{t-2} = 2t - 1 \tag{B.13}$$

with the initial conditions $x_1 = 13$ and $x_2 = 25$. The solution is conveniently broken into five steps:

1. Write and solve the homogeneous equation. This is

$$x_t^{(h)} - 4x_{t-1}^{(h)} + 4x_{t-2}^{(h)} = 0$$

The corresponding auxiliary equation,

$$m^2 - 4m + 4 = 0$$

has a duplicate root at $m = 2$, and so the general solution to the homogeneous equation is

$$x_t^{(h)} = (At + B)2^{t-1}$$

2. Find a particular solution. Since $b_t = 2t - 1$ is a first-degree polynomial, the particular solution is also a polynomial of degree 1:

$$x_t^{(p)} = Ct + D$$

The constants C and D are chosen so that this satisfies the original difference equation. Substituting $x_t^{(p)}$ into the left-hand side of Equation B.13 gives

$$(Ct + D) - 4[C(t - 1) + D] + 4[C(t - 2) + D]$$
$$= Ct + D - 4C$$

This must equal $2t - 1$ for every value of t, which happens when the coefficients of corresponding powers of t are the same:

$$Ct = 2t$$
$$D - 4C = -1$$

This pair of equations has the solution $C = 2$ and $D = 7$, and thus,

$$x_t^{(p)} = 2t + 7$$

3. Combine the homogeneous and the particular solutions in Equation B.11 to find a general solution for the complete equation. Here,

$$x_t = x_t^{(h)} + x_t^{(p)} = (At + B)2^{t-1} + 2t + 7$$

4. Use the initial conditions to solve for the constants. Letting $t = 1$ gives

$$13 = x_1 = A + B + 2 + 7$$

while from $t = 2$,

$$25 = x_2 = (2A + B)2 + 4 + 7$$

These have solutions $A = 3$ and $B = 1$, and so

$$x_t = (3t + 1)2^{t-1} + 2t + 7$$

5. Check the solution by substituting in the original equation. Here this means showing that

$$(3t + 1)2^{t-1} + 2t + 7 - 4\{[3(t - 1) + 1]2^{t-2} + 2(t - 1) + 7\}$$
$$+ 4\{[3(t - 2) + 1]2^{t-3} + 2(t - 2) + 7\} = 2t - 1$$

which it does.

B.3   Simultaneous Difference Equations

Models sometimes give rise to sets of difference equations that express terms from two or more series as functions of each other. Consider, for example, the pair of equations

$$x_t + ax_{t-1} + by_{t-1} = 0 \qquad \text{(B.14)}$$

$$y_t + cx_{t-1} + dy_{t-1} = 0 \qquad \text{(B.15)}$$

The terms of the x_t series and the y_t series are given as functions of the preceding terms of both series. Neither Equation B.14 nor Equation B.15 can be solved by itself.

Solving a system of linear difference equations such as these requires little beyond the methods that have already been introduced. Sets of simultaneous difference equations are equivalent to simple difference equations of a higher order, which can be solved by the methods above. For example, the two equations B.14 and B.15 combine to form a second-order equation. Using Equation B.15 to replace the value of y_{t-1} in Equation B.14 gives

$$x_t + ax_{t-1} - b(cx_{t-2} + dy_{t-2}) = 0$$

This still depends on y_{t-2}, but Equation B.14 can be solved for y_{t-1} and this used (with t replaced by $t - 1$) to remove y:

$$x_t + ax_{t-1} - bcx_{t-2} - d(-x_{t-1} - ax_{t-2})$$
$$= x_t + (a + d)x_{t-1} + (ad - bc)x_{t-2} = 0$$

This second-order equation gives rise to the auxiliary equation

$$m^2 + (a + d)m + (ad - bc) = 0 \qquad \text{(B.16)}$$

and is readily solved.

Following the same procedure with y_t yields Equation B.16 again. The roots are the same; so, for every term Am^{t-1} in the solution for x_t, there is a term in the solution for y_t that differs only in the constant and can be written as Afm^{t-1} for some f. This fact can be used to solve the simultaneous equations without combining them into a higher-order equation. Substituting $x_t = Am^{t-1}$ and $y_t = Afm^{t-1}$ into Equations B.14 and B.15, then dividing out the common factor of Am^{t-2}, produces the pair of auxiliary equations

$$m + a + bf = 0$$
$$fm + c + df = 0 \qquad \text{(B.17)}$$

These are not linear equations in m and f (the two unknowns appear as a product in the second equation); and when f is eliminated from them, the quadratic equation, Equation B.16, results. Thus, the two solutions of Equations B.17, m_1, f_1 and m_2, f_2, include the roots of Equation B.16. The solution to the original set of difference equations is

$$x_t = A_1 m_1^{t-1} + A_2 m_2^{t-1}$$
$$y_t = A_1 f_1 m_1^{t-1} + A_2 f_2 m_2^{t-1}$$

The two unknown constants, A_1 and A_2, are obtained from the initial values of x_1 and y_1. It is often easier to forget about solving for the f_i by using the original difference equations to get x_2 and y_2 from x_1 and y_1, then finding A_1 and A_2 from the two values of x and $(f_1 A_1)$ and $(f_2 A_2)$ from the two values of y.

When a set of simultaneous difference equations is not homogeneous, the solution procedure is exactly analogous to the corresponding single-equation procedure. First the homogeneous equations are solved; then a particular solution, appropriate in form to the nonhomogeneous part, is added. Constants are determined from the initial conditions as usual.

In practice, one rarely needs to completely solve a set of simultaneous difference equations in this way. The equations can be written in matrix form (see Appendix C) as

$$\mathbf{x}_t = [x_t, y_t] = \mathbf{x}_{t-1}\mathbf{A} \tag{B.18}$$

This brings the machinery of matrix algebra to bear. From Equation B.18, it follows that

$$\mathbf{x}_t = \mathbf{x}_1\mathbf{A}^{t-1}$$

For many purposes, simply writing this equation may be enough. It also opens the way to the more advanced solution methods discussed in Section C.6. In particular, the combined auxiliary equation for a set of simultaneous difference equations (such as Equation B.16) is the same as the characteristic equation of the coefficient matrix $\mathbf{A}$ (see Equation C.38). Thus, the roots m_i are eigenvalues of $\mathbf{A}$. With the eigenvalues and a set of initial conditions, a solution to the original system of equations is readily obtained.

Another method for solving difference equations uses the mathematical entities known as generating functions. This procedure, which often yields the solution most rapidly, is discussed in Chapter 9 (see the discussion leading to Equation 9.30; see also Problem 9.13a).

Appendix C

Introduction to Linear Algebra

The mathematical methods presented in this book make frequent use of linear combinations. These combine two series by taking the product of corresponding terms, then summing the products; thus, the series a_1, a_2, ... , a_n and x_1, x_2, ... , x_n, combine in the sum

$$\sum_{i=1}^{n} a_i x_i \qquad (C.1)$$

The law of total probability, Equation A.4, exemplifies this operation, as does the "dot product" that may be familiar from physics or engineering. Since expressions like Equation C.1 appear so often in the analysis of Markov models, it vastly simplifies the formulas to have a notation that makes the combinations easy to write and to manipulate. Matrix algebra fills this need.

This appendix describes some useful results from matrix theory and linear algebra. The coverage is largely limited to those procedures that are specifically used in this book. More detail can be found in most texts on linear algebra.

C.1 Basic Definitions

As a purely descriptive device, matrix notation allows a number of quantities to be referred to by a single symbol. For example, suppose that one was working with a set of n probabilities, $p_1, p_2, \ldots, p_n$. Rather than writing the individual p_i, the full set of probabilities can be represented by the single symbol $\mathbf{p}$, where

$$\mathbf{p} = [p_1, p_2, p_3, \ldots, p_n]$$

This array is called a *row vector*. Had the items been written vertically rather than horizontally,

$$\mathbf{q} = \begin{bmatrix} p_1 \\ p_2 \\ p_3 \\ \vdots \\ p_n \end{bmatrix}$$

a *column vector* would have resulted. A *vector*, then, is just a row or a column of numbers. In this book, vectors are written as boldface lowercase letters to distinguish them from simple numbers.

Geometrically, a vector is a point in n-dimensional space or a line segment of a direction and length equal to that of a line from the origin to the point (see Figure C.1). Although this geometric picture is not necessary to vector algebra, it often simplifies thinking about vectors.

Clearly, the same information is available from a row vector and a column vector, and one can be changed to the other by turning it on its end. This operation of turning row vectors into column vectors and vice versa is called taking the *transpose* of the vector and is denoted by a prime. In the example just given, $\mathbf{q} = \mathbf{p}'$ and $\mathbf{p} = \mathbf{q}'$. The transpose of a transpose gets the original vector back again: $(\mathbf{p}')' = \mathbf{p}$. To save confusion, all vectors in this book represented by single symbols are row vectors.† Where column vectors are needed, they are written as the transpose of row vectors.

A *matrix* is an extension of this idea to a two-dimensional array. For example, with quantities denoted by x arrayed along two sets of sub-

---

† There is no standard convention here. In general, a symbol may stand for either a row vector or a column vector. In multivariate statistics, it is more common to use column vectors; while in stochastic-process theory, row vectors are slightly more common. Many authors represent both row and column vectors by unprimed symbols.

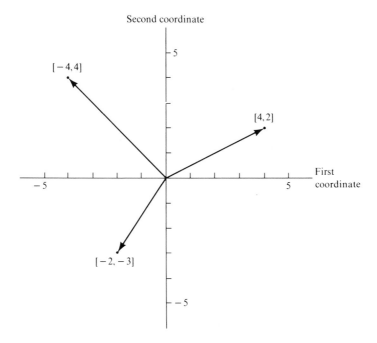

Figure C.1   Some examples of vectors interpreted as directed line segments in two-dimensional space.

scripts, a matrix is

$$
\mathbf{X} = \begin{bmatrix}
x_{11} & x_{12} & x_{13} & \cdots & x_{1n} \\
x_{21} & x_{22} & x_{23} & \cdots & x_{2n} \\
x_{31} & x_{32} & x_{33} & \cdots & x_{3n} \\
\vdots & \vdots & \vdots & & \vdots \\
x_{m1} & x_{m2} & x_{m3} & \cdots & x_{mn}
\end{bmatrix}
$$

In this matrix there are m rows and n columns, so it is said to be an $m \times n$ *matrix* (read as "m by n" not "m times n"). Note the way in which the items are organized, with the first subscript indicating the row and the second the column. This is the most normal organization and has the mnemonic property that the subscripts count across the rows in ordinary numerical order, 11, 12, 13, ...† In this book matrices are denoted by boldface capital letters.

---

† Certain computer languages, such as FORTRAN, define their subscript operations in such a way that it is more natural to number the elements in the opposite manner. Be wary!

A matrix can be thought of as a collection of vectors. So X could be a set of m row vectors, each with n elements, or a set of n column vectors with m elements each.

One can also view a vector as a matrix in which one of the coordinates takes only a single value, so a row vector of n elements is just an $n \times 1$ matrix and a column vector a $1 \times n$ matrix. This allows operations that apply to matrices to be applied to vectors as well. For this reason the word "matrix" is often used to refer to both matrices and vectors. An ordinary number can at times be thought of as a 1×1 matrix or as a vector of length 1. In the terminology of matrix notation, a single number, when not viewed as a matrix or a vector, is called a *scalar*.

The idea of a *transpose* applies to matrices as well as to vectors. The principle is the same: rows are turned into columns, and columns into rows. This is equivalent to exchanging the subscripts, so the i,jth element of X becomes the j,ith element of X'. For example,

$$X = \begin{bmatrix} 1 & 2 & 3 \\ 4 & 5 & 6 \end{bmatrix} \quad \text{becomes} \quad X' = \begin{bmatrix} 1 & 4 \\ 2 & 5 \\ 3 & 6 \end{bmatrix}$$

Again, the transpose operation is its own inverse:

$$(X')' = X$$

C.2   Fundamental Operations

The principal importance of matrix notation is not descriptive, but as a way to summarize arithmetic operations. This is done by defining arithmetic operations directly on matrix symbols.

The easiest of these is *addition*. This is defined only when two matrices (or vectors) have exactly the same dimensions. The sum is found by simply adding corresponding elements together:

$$\begin{bmatrix} a_{11} & a_{12} & \cdots \\ a_{21} & a_{22} & \cdots \\ \vdots & \vdots & \end{bmatrix} + \begin{bmatrix} b_{11} & b_{12} & \cdots \\ b_{21} & b_{22} & \cdots \\ \vdots & \vdots & \end{bmatrix} = \begin{bmatrix} a_{11} + b_{11} & a_{12} + b_{12} & \cdots \\ a_{21} + b_{21} & a_{22} + b_{22} & \cdots \\ \vdots & \vdots & \end{bmatrix}$$

(C.2)

For example,

$$\begin{bmatrix} 2 & 5 & 8 \\ 7 & 1 & 3 \end{bmatrix} + \begin{bmatrix} 3 & 1 & 9 \\ 6 & 1 & 10 \end{bmatrix} = \begin{bmatrix} 5 & 6 & 17 \\ 13 & 2 & 13 \end{bmatrix}$$

If the matrices are of the wrong size, addition is not defined:

$$\begin{bmatrix} 3 & 6 \\ 1 & 4 \end{bmatrix} + \begin{bmatrix} 1 \\ 2 \\ 3 \end{bmatrix} = \text{meaningless!}$$

Matrix addition obeys the usual rules of addition. It is both *commutative*:

$$\mathbf{A} + \mathbf{B} = \mathbf{B} + \mathbf{A} \qquad \text{(C.3)}$$

and *associative*:

$$(\mathbf{A} + \mathbf{B}) + \mathbf{C} = \mathbf{A} + (\mathbf{B} + \mathbf{C}) \qquad \text{(C.4)}$$

Thus, it does not matter in which order the matrices of a sum are written, nor which of three matrices are added together first. Furthermore, transposition can occur either before or after addition:

$$(\mathbf{A} + \mathbf{B})' = \mathbf{A}' + \mathbf{B}' \qquad \text{(C.5)}$$

Subtraction of matrices works the same way as addition. For example,

$$\begin{bmatrix} 2 & 5 & 8 \\ 7 & 1 & 3 \end{bmatrix} - \begin{bmatrix} 3 & 1 & 9 \\ 6 & 1 & 10 \end{bmatrix} = \begin{bmatrix} -1 & 4 & -1 \\ 1 & 0 & -7 \end{bmatrix}$$

There are two forms of matrix *multiplication*. The simple form is multiplication of a matrix by a scalar, appropriately called *scalar multiplication*. This is done by multiplying each element of the matrix by the scalar; for example,

$$5 \begin{bmatrix} 2 & 3 \\ 5 & -7 \\ 9 & 1 \end{bmatrix} = \begin{bmatrix} 10 & 15 \\ 25 & -35 \\ 45 & 5 \end{bmatrix}$$

Of course, scalar multiplication can be done to vectors as well as to matrices.

One might expect that multiplication of two matrices would be similar to matrix addition, and the product formed by multiplying corresponding elements together, but this is not so.† The definition is both more complicated and more useful. In the type of linear systems to

---

† Except for some computer languages, e.g., APL.

which matrix algebra is applied, linear combinations of the form in Equation C.1 are far more common than element-wise multiplication, and the definition of *matrix multiplication* reflects this. The simplest case is the product of a row vector and a column vector. This is defined to be the combination, Equation C.1:

$$\mathbf{ax'} = [a_1, a_2, \ldots, a_n] \begin{bmatrix} x_1 \\ x_2 \\ \vdots \\ x_n \end{bmatrix} = \sum_{i=1}^{n} a_i x_i \qquad (C.6)$$

One goes across the first vector and down the second, forming products, then sums them. The result is a scalar.

The product of two full matrices is an extension of this idea. One takes a row from the first matrix and a column from the second and forms a linear combination of them to create an element of the result. Thus, the i,jth element of the product is formed by going across the ith row of the first matrix and down the jth column of the second, multiplying and summing them just as with the two vectors in Equation C.6. This is illustrated by

$$\begin{bmatrix} a_1 & a_2 & a_3 & \cdots & a_n \\ b_1 & b_2 & b_3 & \cdots & b_n \\ c_1 & c_2 & c_3 & \cdots & c_n \end{bmatrix} \begin{bmatrix} x_1 & y_1 \\ x_2 & y_2 \\ x_3 & y_3 \\ \vdots & \vdots \\ x_n & y_n \end{bmatrix} = \begin{bmatrix} \Sigma a_i x_i & \Sigma a_i y_i \\ \Sigma b_i x_i & \Sigma b_i y_i \\ \Sigma c_i x_i & \Sigma c_i y_i \end{bmatrix} \qquad (C.7)$$

where the sums run from $i = 1$ to $i = n$. In order for this to work, the number of columns in the first matrix must be equal to the number of rows in the second. If the left matrix is $p \times n$, the right matrix must have exactly n rows, so be $n \times q$. The numbers p and q can be different, but n is the same in both matrices. The product of these matrices is a $p \times q$ matrix. As a mnemonic for this, think of canceling out the letters n in the middle:

$$(p \times n)(n \times q) = (p \times q)$$

A numerical example of matrix multiplication is

$$\begin{bmatrix} 1 & 2 & 4 & 7 \\ 3 & 4 & 6 & 8 \\ 4 & 9 & 1 & 1 \end{bmatrix} \begin{bmatrix} 1 & 2 \\ 3 & 6 \\ 5 & 1 \\ 7 & 0 \end{bmatrix} = \begin{bmatrix} 76 & 18 \\ 101 & 36 \\ 43 & 63 \end{bmatrix} \qquad (C.8)$$

This follows the formula in Equation C.7, with $p = 3$, $m = 4$, and $q = 2$. The first entry, in position 1,1 of the product, is

$$1 \times 1 + 2 \times 3 + 4 \times 5 + 7 \times 7 = 76$$

and so on.

Matrix multiplication obeys some of the rules of conventional multiplication, although not all of them. The *associative law* still holds:

$$(AB)C = A(BC) \qquad (C.9)$$

Similarly, matrix multiplication can be *distributed* with respect to addition:

$$A(B + C) = AB + AC \qquad (C.10)$$

and

$$(A + B)C = AC + BC \qquad (C.11)$$

However, it is not the case that matrix multiplication is *commutative*; that is, the relationship

$$AB = BA$$

does not hold except in a few special cases. Indeed, frequently one of these products is not even defined. In the numerical example of Equation C.8, the matrices could not be multiplied in the opposite order, since the number of columns in the first no longer equals the number of rows in the second. Even when both products are defined, they usually don't give the same answer; for example,

$$\begin{bmatrix} 1 & 2 \\ 3 & 4 \end{bmatrix} \begin{bmatrix} 1 & 3 \\ 5 & 0 \end{bmatrix} \neq \begin{bmatrix} 1 & 3 \\ 5 & 0 \end{bmatrix} \begin{bmatrix} 1 & 2 \\ 3 & 4 \end{bmatrix}$$

One more rule is useful: the transpose of a product equals the product of the transpose, but in the opposite order:

$$(AB)' = B'A' \qquad (C.12)$$

The importance of the matrix multiplication notation is that it lets many mathematical expressions be written much more compactly and allows operations to be chunked into larger units. To take a simple example, think of the set of simultaneous linear equations

$$3x_1 + 2x_2 = 7$$
$$4x_1 - x_2 = 3$$

(C.13)

This is equivalent to either the matrix expression

$$\begin{bmatrix} 3 & 2 \\ 4 & -1 \end{bmatrix} \begin{bmatrix} x_1 \\ x_2 \end{bmatrix} = \begin{bmatrix} 7 \\ 3 \end{bmatrix}$$

or

$$[x_1, x_2] \begin{bmatrix} 3 & 4 \\ 2 & -1 \end{bmatrix} = [7, 3]$$

In general, consider the set of equations

$$a_{11}x_1 + a_{12}x_2 + \cdots + a_{1n}x_n = b_1$$
$$a_{21}x_1 + a_{22}x_2 + \cdots + a_{2n}x_n = b_2$$
$$\vdots$$
$$a_{n1}x_1 + a_{n2}x_2 + \cdots + a_{nn}x_n = b_n$$

(C.14)

If the matrix of coefficients is denoted by $\mathbf{A}$, the row vector of x values by $\mathbf{x}$, and the row vector of constants by $\mathbf{b}$, then Equation C.14 becomes

$$\mathbf{Ax}' = \mathbf{b}'$$

(C.15)

This is a great deal easier to write and leads, in the next section, to a systematic way to solve the equations.

The form of Equation C.15 should be noted. On the left-hand side of this equation a matrix is multiplied on the right by a column vector to create another column vector:

[matrix][column vector] = [column vector]

A similar thing occurs with multiplication on the left by a row vector:

[row vector][matrix] = [row vector]

Thus, multiplication by an appropriate vector serves to turn matrices to vectors. When a matrix is multiplied by a vector on both sides, it becomes a scalar:

$$[\text{row vector}][\text{matrix}][\text{column vector}] = [\text{scalar}]$$

Keeping patterns like this in mind helps in reading matrix equations. Of course, the part marked [matrix] in these relationships may consist of several matrices added or multiplied together; the important point is that the presence of the vectors on the end reduces the result to a vector or a scalar.

The special properties of one particular matrix should be noted. Just as the number 1 serves as an identity for ordinary multiplication (i.e., $1 \times a = a \times 1 = a$), the *identity matrix*,

$$\mathbf{I} = \begin{bmatrix} 1 & 0 & 0 & \cdots & 0 \\ 0 & 1 & 0 & \cdots & 0 \\ 0 & 0 & 1 & \cdots & 0 \\ \vdots & \vdots & \vdots & & \vdots \\ 0 & 0 & 0 & \cdots & 1 \end{bmatrix}$$

acts as an identity for multiplication. This matrix is 0 everywhere except on the diagonal, where it is 1. Multiplication of any matrix by **I** leaves the matrix unchanged:

$$\mathbf{AI} = \mathbf{IA} = \mathbf{A}$$

If **A** is not square, the size of **I** needed for the left and right multiplications differs.

C.3 Matrix Inversion

There is no matrix division to go with matrix multiplication. One cannot write **A/B**, unless **B** is really a scalar and division of each element, analogous to scalar multiplication, is intended. There is, however, a concept rather similar to division: the matrix inverse. Any scalar $a \neq 0$ has associated with it a multiplicative inverse a^{-1} such that multiplication of a by the inverse gives the multiplicative identity:

$$a \times a^{-1} = a^{-1} \times a = 1 \tag{C.16}$$

For example, if $a = 5$, the inverse is $a^{-1} = 0.2$, since $(5)(0.2) = 1$. Division by a is the same as multiplication by a^{-1}; to divide by 5 is to multiply by 0.2. This idea generalizes to matrices.

Suppose that **A** is a square matrix. Its *inverse* is defined to be a matrix **A**$^{-1}$, if one exists, such that

$$\mathbf{AA}^{-1} = \mathbf{I} \tag{C.17}$$

This parallels the scalar inverse of Equation C.16. It can be shown that, when an inverse matrix exists, it is commutative, so that

$$\mathbf{A}^{-1}\mathbf{A} = \mathbf{I} \tag{C.18}$$

Of course, it is not enough to assert the existence of an inverse; a procedure is needed to find it. Calculation of the inverse is complicated and so is not covered in general here. For matrices of large size, considerable calculation is needed. Texts on linear algebra (for mathematical methods) or computer algorithms (for computational techniques) should be consulted as needed. Most computer systems have procedures for matrix inversion readily available. Fortunately, no general inversion procedures are needed in this book. For simple calculation, it suffices to give formulas for the inverses for 2 × 2 and 3 × 3 matrices. As can be verified by calculation, if

$$\mathbf{A} = \begin{bmatrix} a & b \\ c & d \end{bmatrix}$$

then

$$\mathbf{A}^{-1} = \frac{1}{D} \begin{bmatrix} d & -b \\ -c & a \end{bmatrix} \tag{C.19}$$

where

$$D = ad - bc \tag{C.20}$$

For 3 × 3 matrices, if

$$\mathbf{A} = \begin{bmatrix} a & b & c \\ d & e & f \\ g & h & i \end{bmatrix}$$

then

$$\mathbf{A}^{-1} = \frac{1}{D} \begin{bmatrix} ei - fh & ch - bi & bf - ce \\ fg - di & ai - cg & cd - af \\ dh - eg & bg - ah & ae - bd \end{bmatrix} \tag{C.21}$$

where

$$D = aei + bfg + cdh - afh - bdi - ceg \qquad \text{(C.22)}$$

The scalar D, known as the *determinant* of the matrix, is an important quantity in its own right, denoted by $|A|$ or by det(A). There is not much need to use the determinant in this book, except for its relationship to singular matrices, discussed below. Hence, its properties are not pursued.

For example, suppose that

$$A = \begin{bmatrix} 1 & 2 \\ 3 & 4 \end{bmatrix}$$

Then, by Equations C.19 and C.20, $D = -2$ and A has the inverse

$$A^{-1} = \begin{bmatrix} -2 & 1 \\ 3/2 & -1/2 \end{bmatrix}$$

The inverse can be used to solve problems where division by a matrix is apparently needed. The system of simultaneous equations in Equation C.14 is an example of this. In matrix form, Equation C.15, this is

$$Ax' = b'$$

Since the goal is to solve for x, one would like to divide by A. Instead, multiplying on the left by A^{-1} gives

$$A^{-1}(Ax') = A^{-1}b'$$

Using the associative law, then the definition of A^{-1}:

$$(A^{-1}A)x' = A^{-1}b'$$

$$Ix' = A^{-1}b'$$

$$x' = A^{-1}b' \qquad \text{(C.23)}$$

The last line gives the unknown x. Throughout this derivation, it is essential to be careful with the order of the terms because of the lack of multiplicative commutativity. In the numerical example above, Equation C.13,

$$A = \begin{bmatrix} 3 & 2 \\ 4 & -1 \end{bmatrix} \quad \text{and} \quad b' = \begin{bmatrix} 7 \\ -3 \end{bmatrix}$$

So, by Equation C.19,

$$\mathbf{A}^{-1} = \begin{bmatrix} 1/11 & 2/11 \\ 4/11 & -3/11 \end{bmatrix}$$

and using Equation C.23 gives

$$\mathbf{x}' = \begin{bmatrix} 1/11 & 2/11 \\ 4/11 & -3/11 \end{bmatrix} \begin{bmatrix} 7 \\ 3 \end{bmatrix} = \begin{bmatrix} 13/11 \\ 19/11 \end{bmatrix}$$

Equation C.23 gives a method to solve for **x** in any set of linear equations. Of course, calculation of $\mathbf{A}^{-1}$ is still needed and this is not trivial with larger sets of equations, but at least that problem is well defined and need not be of concern while one is worrying about manipulating the equations for other purposes. The computation is compartmentalized and separated from the theory (and perhaps given to a computer to solve).

Unfortunately, there are matrices that have no inverse, just as with scalars there is no multiplicative inverse for the number 0. The inverse of both 2 × 2 and 3 × 3 matrices (Equations C.19 and C.21) require division by the determinant. If this is 0, which is quite possible, calculation must stop. In that case there is no inverse; that is, no matrix $\mathbf{A}^{-1}$ can be found that fits the definition of the inverse, Equations C.17 and C.18. The matrix

$$\mathbf{S} = \begin{bmatrix} 1 & 2 \\ 4 & 8 \end{bmatrix}$$

has this property. Such a matrix is said to be a *singular matrix*. Singular matrices always have a 0 determinant and can be identified in that way. Conversely, when $|\mathbf{A}| \neq 0$, an inverse always exists and the matrix is said to be a *nonsingular matrix*.

Notice that one row of **S** is a scalar multiple of the other row. Something like this is always the case with singular matrices. Whenever a matrix is singular, it is possible to write at least one row (or column— either can be used) as a linear combination of the other rows (or columns). The application of matrix multiplication to simultaneous equations suggests the same thing. A pair of equations corresponding to **S**,

$$x_1 + 2x_2 = 3$$
$$4x_1 + 8x_2 = 6$$

cannot be solved since one equation is a multiple of the other. The second equation gives no information that is not in the first. Another interpretation of singularity appears in Section C.5.

The above discussion of inverses applies only to square matrices. When the matrix **A** is not square, things are quite a bit more complicated. Inverses may not exist and, when they do, they are not unique. Furthermore, even if a matrix **B** can be found such that $\mathbf{AB} = \mathbf{I}$, usually $\mathbf{BA} \neq \mathbf{I}$. Thus, one must treat left and right inverses separately. Fortunately, there is only occasional need for inverses of other than square matrices in this book.

C.4   Partitioned Matrices

There are often cases where the rows and columns of a matrix fall naturally into groups with some common property. For example, when the rows or columns are associated with the responses of an experiment, one may wish to distinguish between those tied to correct responses and those tied to errors. In these cases the matrix can appropriately be divided into a number of *submatrices*, represented by single symbols. For example, one might divide a matrix **A** into four parts, as

$$\mathbf{A} = \begin{bmatrix} \mathbf{C} & \mathbf{D} \\ \mathbf{E} & \mathbf{F} \end{bmatrix}$$

where **C**, **D**, **E**, and **F** are themselves matrices. Such a matrix is called a *partitioned matrix*.

The importance of partitioned matrices comes from the fact that matrix operations on them can be expressed in terms of matrix operations on the submatrices, which are often considerably simpler. Applications of this appear elsewhere; for the moment it is enough to display for reference the relevant formulas. All of these derive directly from the definitions of the operations on simple matrices.

Addition and subtraction. For a matrix **A** partitioned as above and for

$$\mathbf{B} = \begin{bmatrix} \mathbf{G} & \mathbf{H} \\ \mathbf{J} & \mathbf{K} \end{bmatrix}$$

of identical size partitioned in an identical manner,

$$\mathbf{A} + \mathbf{B} = \begin{bmatrix} \mathbf{C} + \mathbf{G} & \mathbf{D} + \mathbf{H} \\ \mathbf{E} + \mathbf{J} & \mathbf{F} + \mathbf{K} \end{bmatrix} \tag{C.24}$$

Subtraction is similar.

Multiplication. When **A** and **B** are partitioned in such a way that the partitioning of the columns of **A** is the same as the partitioning of the rows of **B**, then

$$\mathbf{AB} = \begin{bmatrix} \mathbf{CG + DJ} & \mathbf{CH + DK} \\ \mathbf{EG + FJ} & \mathbf{EH + FK} \end{bmatrix} \tag{C.25}$$

As with regular matrix multiplication, the partitioning of the rows of **A** and the columns of **B** need not conform with each other. This formula is easy to remember if one realizes that it is the same as the formula for multiplication of a pair of 2×2 matrices, but using submatrices rather than scalars as elements.

Inversion. In order for $\mathbf{A}^{-1}$ to exist, both **C** and **F** must be nonsingular. Then

$$\mathbf{A}^{-1} = \begin{bmatrix} \mathbf{X} & -\mathbf{C}^{-1}\mathbf{DY} \\ -\mathbf{F}^{-1}\mathbf{EX} & \mathbf{Y} \end{bmatrix} \tag{C.26}$$

where

$$\mathbf{X} = (\mathbf{C} - \mathbf{DF}^{-1}\mathbf{E})^{-1}$$

$$\mathbf{Y} = (\mathbf{F} - \mathbf{EC}^{-1}\mathbf{D})^{-1}$$

There are several equivalent, but superficially different, versions of this formula. In a pinch, Equation C.26 can be used to reduce the inverse of a large matrix to smaller matrices for which Equation C.19 or Equation C.21 applies.

C.5   *Vector Spaces, Bases, and Transformations*

Throughout this book it is common to encounter cases where a vector y is formed by the application of a linear operator to a vector x:

$$\mathbf{y} = \mathbf{xA} \tag{C.27}$$

This operation has a direct geometric interpretation. Each vector is represented as an arrow from the origin to a point in space with coordinates given by the components of the vector, as in Figure C.1. The transformation takes this arrow into another one. For example, the matrix

$$\mathbf{A} = \begin{bmatrix} 1 & 3 \\ 2 & 0 \end{bmatrix} \tag{C.28}$$

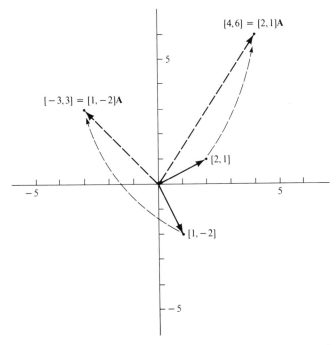

Figure C.2   Transformation of vectors (from solid to dashed)
by Matrix C.28.

serves to transform the vector $x = [2, 1]$ to $y = [4, 6]$, the vector
$x = [1, -2]$ to $y = [-3, 3]$, and the vector $x = [1, 1]$ to $y = [3, 3]$. The
first two of these transformations are shown in Figure C.2. In this way
every point in the plane is transformed into another point.

It helps here to introduce the concept of a space of vectors. Roughly,
a *vector space*, $\mathcal{V}$, is a set of vectors that is complete in the sense that it
is *closed* under linear combination. Any linear combination of vectors
in the set yields another vector in the set. Thus, for any $x_1, x_2 \in \mathcal{V}$ and
any real numbers a_1 and a_2,

$$x = a_1 x_1 + a_2 x_2 \in \mathcal{V}$$

By taking linear combinations, it is always possible to build a vector
space up from a small set of vectors in the space. Such a set is said to
span the space. For example, any vector in the plane (which is a vector
space) can be formed from a linear combination of the two vectors
$[1, 0]$ and $[0, 1]$, which lie along the axes. For example, the vector
$[1, -2]$ is obtained as

$$[1, -2] = (1)[1, 0] + (-2)[0, 1]$$

Spanning sets are not unique. The plane could equally well be formed from any set of vectors that are not all in the same line. Thus, from [1, 1] and [3, 2],

$$[1, -2] = (-8)[1, 1] + (3)[3, 2]$$

Although the vectors needed to generate a vector space are not unique, the number of vectors in the smallest generating set is constant. A minimal generating set is called a *basis* for the space, and the number of vectors in it is the *dimension* of the space. The plane, for example, has dimension 2, and either of the sets above is a basis for it. As another example, the two vectors [1, 3, 4] and [2, −1, 1] are the basis of a vector space of dimension 2. All vectors in this space can be written as

$$\mathbf{x} = a_1[1, 3, 4] + a_2[2, -1, 1] \tag{C.29}$$

Although there are three coordinates to these vectors, not every part of ordinary three-dimensional space can be reached by Equation C.29. In fact, if one plotted the space of points formed by Equation C.29, choosing all values for a_1 and a_2, one would obtain a plane passing through three-dimensional space. Formed from a basis of two vectors, the vector space has dimension 2. Clearly, the dimensionality of a space is one of its most fundamental properties.

By selecting different bases, one may write the vectors of a vector space in different ways. Thus, the example above shows that the vector [1, −2] written with respect to the basis {[1, 0], [0, 1]} becomes [−8, 3] when written with respect to the basis {[1, 1], [3, 2]}.

When a basis change is made, the matrix that represents a particular linear transformation is also changed. Matrix C.28 represents the transformation in Figure C.2 when vectors are written with respect to the basis {[1, 0], [0, 1]}. If a point is written with respect to a different basis, the matrix must also be changed in order for the geometric picture shown in Figure C.2 to stay the same. For example, Matrix C.28 took $\mathbf{x} = [1, -2]$ to $\mathbf{y} = [-3, 3]$ in the basis {[1, 0], [0, 1]}. In the basis {[1, 1], [3, 2]}, exactly the same transformation takes $\mathbf{x} = [-8, 3]$ to $\mathbf{y} = [15, -6]$. The coefficients of Matrix C.28 do not perform the transformation in the new basis. Rather,

$$[15, -6] = [-8, 3] \begin{bmatrix} 3 & 0 \\ 13 & -2 \end{bmatrix}$$

The mapping of the one point is not enough to determine the new transformation, which must correctly map every point under the new basis. In fact, the new form of the transformation matrix is

$$\mathbf{A}_{new} = \mathbf{B}\mathbf{A}_{old}\mathbf{B}^{-1} \tag{C.30}$$

where **B** is the matrix whose rows are the new basis vectors expressed in terms of the old basis. Here the new basis is $\{[1, 1], [3, 2]\}$, so

$$\mathbf{B} = \begin{bmatrix} 1 & 1 \\ 3 & 2 \end{bmatrix} \quad \text{and} \quad \mathbf{B}^{-1} = \begin{bmatrix} -2 & 1 \\ 3 & -1 \end{bmatrix}$$

Applying Equation C.30 gives

$$\mathbf{A}_{new} = \begin{bmatrix} 1 & 1 \\ 3 & 2 \end{bmatrix} \begin{bmatrix} 1 & 3 \\ 2 & 0 \end{bmatrix} \begin{bmatrix} -2 & 1 \\ 3 & -1 \end{bmatrix} = \begin{bmatrix} 3 & 0 \\ 13 & -2 \end{bmatrix}$$

Solving for $\mathbf{A}_{old}$ in Equation C.30, then applying the result to Equation C.27 gives

$$\mathbf{y} = \mathbf{x}\mathbf{A}_{old} = \mathbf{x}\mathbf{B}^{-1}\mathbf{A}_{new}\mathbf{B}$$

In effect, multiplication of **x** by $\mathbf{B}^{-1}$ converts it to the new basis, $\mathbf{A}_{new}$ transforms it, and **B** returns the result to the original basis again.

Vector spaces provide a larger view of what happens when a transformation like Equation C.27 is applied. Members of the vector space containing **x** are carried by Equation C.27 into a new vector space containing **y**. At times, as with Matrix C.28, the complete space is mapped into a space just like itself. In other cases, the second space is different from the first. The dimensionality of the transformed space depends both on the original space and on the nature of the transformation. Most fundamentally, there is no way for the new space to have a larger dimension than that of the original space. No transformation can create complexity that was not in the space to begin with.

A second limit on the dimensionality of the resultant space of a transformation is the capacity of the transformation to preserve the original space. This is embodied in a quantity known as the *rank* of the transformation. The rank is the maximum number of dimensions that are preserved by the transformation. So a vector space of dimension d transformed by a transformation of rank r results in a space with dimension no larger than the smaller of d and r. The rank is equal to the maximum number of linearly independent rows or columns that can be found in the matrix of the transformation. Thus, a matrix cannot have a larger rank than its smaller dimension. A 3×5 matrix, for example, has a rank no greater than 3.

The concept of rank allows another interpretation of the singularity of a square matrix. A singular matrix is one that has a rank less than its size. An $n \times n$ matrix potentially can preserve a full n-dimensional space, but if singular, some of this complexity is lost. The absence of an inverse for such a matrix makes sense. If A defines a transformation from space $\mathcal{V}_1$ to space $\mathcal{V}_2$, then A^{-1} defines the inverse transformation from $\mathcal{V}_2$ back to $\mathcal{V}_1$. But if the rank of A is less than its size, then $\mathcal{V}_2$ is of smaller dimension than $\mathcal{V}_1$. Since no linear transformation can increase the dimensionality of a space, there is no way to recover the lost dimensionality, hence no way to get back to $\mathcal{V}_1$ and no A^{-1}.

C.6   Eigenvalues and Eigenvectors

The variety of bases that can be chosen for a vector space creates a proliferation of matrices to represent a transformation. From among these bases and matrices, it is useful to identify those that characterize the transformation in ways that are particularly simple or convenient. This section presents one such form. In addition to conceptual simplicity, some useful computational procedures also appear.

Consider again the transformation with Matrix C.28. The vector $e = [1, 1]$ is transformed by Matrix C.28 into the vector $[3, 3]$, which is in the same direction as e, but three times as long. That is,

$$eA = \lambda e \qquad \qquad (C.31)$$

where λ is the scalar 3. This is a rather special property: the vector e is stretched by A, but its direction is not changed. When viewed in terms of the geometry (see Figure C.3), this property does not depend on the basis in which the transformation is expressed. There are only a small number of vectors for which Equation C.31 holds, and it can be shown that they completely characterize the transformation. Vectors with the property of Equation C.31 are known as *eigenvectors* (or *characteristic vectors* or *latent vectors; eigen* means "*characteristic*" in German) and the scalar multiplies as *eigenvalues* (or *characteristic values, latent values, characteristic roots,* or *latent roots*). A matrix has as many eigenvalues as it has rows or columns and no more eigenvectors than eigenvalues (sometimes fewer). The eigenvalues are unique, and the eigenvectors are unique up to multiplication by a scalar. For example, although $[1, 1]$ (with $\lambda = 3$) is an eigenvector of the matrix A in Matrix C.28, so also is $[2, 2]$ since it is transformed into $[6, 6]$. The matrix A has a second eigenvector–eigenvalue pair with $\lambda_2 = -2$ and, for example, $e_2 = [2, -3]$.

In Equation C.31, the eigenvectors are row vectors and multiply A on

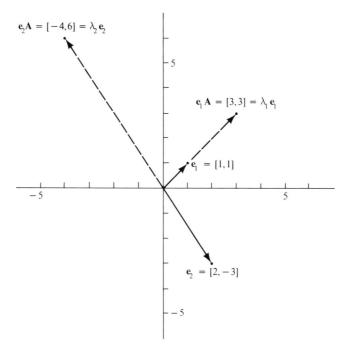

Figure C.3   Transformation of the eigenvectors of Matrix C.28.

the left. So they are called *left eigenvectors*. Similarly, *right eigenvectors* are formed by multiplication of A by a column vector on the right:

$$Af' = \lambda f' \tag{C.32}$$

Eigenvectors come in left–right pairs with (it can be shown) the same eigenvalue. For the matrix A in Matrix C.28, right eigenvectors are

$$f_1' = \begin{bmatrix} 3 \\ 2 \end{bmatrix} \quad \text{and} \quad f_2' = \begin{bmatrix} 1 \\ -1 \end{bmatrix}$$

for $\lambda_1 = 3$ and $\lambda_2 = -2$, respectively. When the matrix is symmetric, that is, when $A = A'$, the left and right eigenvectors are transposes of each other. With stochastic models (unlike much of statistics), the matrices are rarely symmetric; so the left–right distinction must be maintained.

The importance of the eigenvectors and eigenvalues of A comes from the fact that they embody information about A as a transformation in a very simple way. Geometrically, the transformation stretches or shrinks vectors in the direction of the eigenvectors by an amount indicated by the eigenvalues, but does not change their direction (Figure C.3).† For example, using the value of A given in Matrix C.28, the transformation $y = xA$ changes any component in the direction $e_1 = [1, 1]$ to one three times as long ($\lambda_1 = 3$) and any component in the direction $e_2 = [2, -3]$ to one twice as long and in the reverse direction ($\lambda_2 = -2$), but does not mix them up. If x is written in terms of the eigenvectors as (in two dimensions)

$$x = a_1 e_1 + a_2 e_2$$

then the transformation in Equation C.27 is

$$y = xA = a_1 e_1 A + a_2 e_2 A$$
$$= (a_1 \lambda_1) e_1 + (a_2 \lambda_2) e_2$$

In effect, the transformation is accomplished by using nothing more than scalar multiplication.

The last result makes the eigenvectors a natural basis in which to express the transformation. The component of x along e_i is multiplied by λ_i, but is not otherwise changed. So in a basis of eigenvectors, the transformation has a diagonal matrix:

$$\Lambda = \begin{bmatrix} \lambda_1 & 0 & \cdots & 0 \\ 0 & \lambda_2 & \cdots & 0 \\ \vdots & \vdots & & \vdots \\ 0 & 0 & \cdots & \lambda_n \end{bmatrix} \tag{C.33}$$

More formally, let $e_1, e_2, \ldots, e_n$ be the left eigenvectors of A with associated eigenvalues $\lambda_1, \lambda_2, \ldots, \lambda_n$. Then the matrix with eigenvectors as rows,

$$E = \begin{bmatrix} e_1 \\ e_2 \\ \vdots \\ e_n \end{bmatrix}$$

acts by Equation C.30 to change the transformation to a basis of eigenvectors:

$$\Lambda = EAE^{-1}$$

---

† This is not always the case when there are several identical eigenvalues. A text on linear algebra should be consulted for details.

Solving for **A** gives

$$\mathbf{A} = \mathbf{E}^{-1}\mathbf{\Lambda}\mathbf{E} \tag{C.34}$$

The matrix $\mathbf{E}^{-1}$ is actually the matrix of right eigenvectors, although this is not important to the calculation. The result, Equation C.34, is sometimes called the *spectral decomposition* of **A**. For example, using the eigenvectors of the 2×2 example Matrix C.28 gives

$$\mathbf{E} = \begin{bmatrix} 1 & 1 \\ 2 & -3 \end{bmatrix} \quad \text{and} \quad \mathbf{E}^{-1} = \begin{bmatrix} 0.6 & 0.2 \\ 0.4 & -0.2 \end{bmatrix}$$

Applying these matrices to the eigenvalues, using Equation C.34, gives **A** again:

$$\mathbf{A} = \begin{bmatrix} 0.6 & 0.2 \\ 0.4 & -0.2 \end{bmatrix} \begin{bmatrix} 3 & 0 \\ 0 & -2 \end{bmatrix} \begin{bmatrix} 1 & 1 \\ 2 & -3 \end{bmatrix} = \begin{bmatrix} 1 & 3 \\ 2 & 0 \end{bmatrix}$$

The usefulness of the eigenvector basis becomes apparent when the transformation is applied many times. Using Equation C.34 gives

$$\mathbf{A}^k = (\mathbf{E}^{-1}\mathbf{\Lambda}\mathbf{E})(\mathbf{E}^{-1}\mathbf{\Lambda}\mathbf{E}) \cdots (\mathbf{E}^{-1}\mathbf{\Lambda}\mathbf{E})$$

$$= \mathbf{E}^{-1}\mathbf{\Lambda}\mathbf{I}\mathbf{\Lambda}\mathbf{I} \cdots \mathbf{I}\mathbf{\Lambda}\mathbf{E}$$

$$= \mathbf{E}^{-1}\mathbf{\Lambda}^k\mathbf{E} \tag{C.35}$$

The diagonal form of $\mathbf{\Lambda}$ makes $\mathbf{\Lambda}^k$ easy to find:

$$\mathbf{\Lambda}^k = \begin{bmatrix} \lambda_1^k & 0 & \cdots & 0 \\ 0 & \lambda_2^k & \cdots & 0 \\ \vdots & \vdots & & \vdots \\ 0 & 0 & \cdots & \lambda_n^k \end{bmatrix} \tag{C.36}$$

Thus, finding $\mathbf{A}^k$ requires only two matrix multiplications using Equation C.35, rather than $k - 1$.

With eigenvectors, some problems involving the raising of matrices to powers are almost trivial. For example, the solution to a set of simultaneous difference equations, treated in Section B.3, is obtained almost for free. Consider a pair of equations analogous to Equations B.14 and B.15:

$$x_t = ax_{t-1} + by_{t-1}$$

$$y_t = cx_{t-1} + dy_{t-1}$$

Let

$$\mathbf{x}_t = [x_t, y_t] \quad \text{and} \quad \mathbf{A} = \begin{bmatrix} a & c \\ b & d \end{bmatrix}$$

Then, in matrix form, using Equation C.35:

$$\mathbf{x}_t = \mathbf{x}_{t-1}\mathbf{A} = \mathbf{x}_1\mathbf{A}^{t-1}$$
$$= \mathbf{x}_1\mathbf{E}^{-1}\mathbf{\Lambda}^{t-1}\mathbf{E} \tag{C.37}$$

The power $\mathbf{\Lambda}^{t-1}$ is found from Matrix C.36, and a solution is obtained with three matrix multiplications. If desired, an algebraic solution is not hard to obtain from this result. The eigenvalues here are the same as the roots of the auxiliary equation in Equation B.16.

Computation by these methods is easy only when the eigenvectors and eigenvalues are known, however, and finding them involves some work. There are several methods, of which the most straightforward is to work from the definitions.† One starts by finding the eigenvalues. It can be shown that if λ is an eigenvalue of the matrix $\mathbf{A}$, then the matrix $\mathbf{A} - \lambda\mathbf{I}$ is singular, and therefore

$$|\mathbf{A} - \lambda\mathbf{I}| = 0 \tag{C.38}$$

For small matrices this determinant can be found using Equation C.20 or Equation C.22. The resulting equation, called the *characteristic equation*, is solved for λ. As an example, let $\mathbf{A}$ be the matrix

$$\mathbf{A} = \begin{bmatrix} 1 & 4 \\ 1 & 1 \end{bmatrix}$$

Then, using Equations C.38 and C.20 gives

$$\begin{bmatrix} 1-\lambda & 4 \\ 1 & 1-\lambda \end{bmatrix} = \lambda^2 - 2\lambda - 3 = 0$$

This equation is a quadratic, with the two roots $\lambda_1 = -1$ and $\lambda_2 = 3$.

With the eigenvalues in hand, the set of equations implied by the definitional equations, Equations C.31 and C.32, are solved for the eigenvectors. For example, to find the left eigenvector for $\lambda_2 = 3$, ap-

---

† For a purely numerical solution, there are better procedures; see a text on numeral algorithms.

plying Equation C.31:

$$[e_1, e_2] \begin{bmatrix} 1 & 4 \\ 1 & 1 \end{bmatrix} = 3[e_1, e_2]$$

This matrix equation is equivalent to the two simple equations

$$e_1 + e_2 = 3e_1$$
$$4e_1 + e_2 = 3e_2$$

both of which reduce to

$$e_2 = 2e_1$$

The eigenvector is determined only up to a scalar multiple, so any vector of the form $e = [x, 2x]$ is an eigenvector. The quantity x may be chosen to give numerical simplicity or to set the length of e to some value. The corresponding right eigenvector, obtained from Equation C.32, has the form $f = [2y, y]$. Conventionally, y is chosen so that $ef' = 1$. The complete set of eigenvectors and eigenvalues for this example are

$$\lambda_1 = -1 \qquad e_1 = [1, -2] \qquad f'_1 = \begin{bmatrix} 0.50 \\ -0.25 \end{bmatrix}$$

$$\lambda_2 = 3 \qquad e_2 = [1, 2] \qquad f'_2 = \begin{bmatrix} 0.50 \\ 0.25 \end{bmatrix}$$

Appendix D

Some Concepts from Calculus

Some of the analysis in this book uses calculus. Derivation of some predictions are greatly simplified by its use, and for certain calculations it is almost essential. Avoiding calculus makes these models more complex rather than simpler. However, some readers may find calculus only dimly (if at all) familiar. Hence, this appendix reviews some of the most useful techniques. Obviously, it is impossible to treat in an appendix material that often forms the better part of a year's course work. All that is provided here is enough information to make it possible to follow most of the derivations used in this book. Anyone desiring to learn calculus properly (particularly the computational procedures) should go to one of the many introductory books on the subject.

In essence, calculus deals with continuous quantities and the way in which functions of continuous variables change; a continuous variable being one whose change takes place gradually, rather than by steps. Except in its more general forms, calculus does not apply to quantities that vary by discrete steps. Thus, the methods of calculus are less frequently required to work with models involving discrete sample spaces and quantized time. However, there is a close parallel between discrete methods and continuous methods. Many techniques that apply to discrete functions are analogous to techniques for continuous functions. This similarity is noted in many places below.

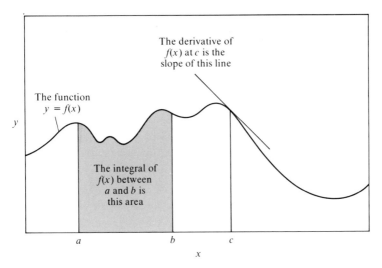

The derivative of
$f(x)$ at c is the
slope of this line

The function
$y = f(x)$

y

The integral of
$f(x)$ between
a and b is
this area

a b c

x

Figure D.1   The derivative and the integral of the function $y = f(x)$.

Most of calculus concerns the properties of two complementary operations: the derivative and the integral. These are operations that are applied to a continuous function to make new functions. The *derivative* of a continuous function of a continuous variable at a point is the slope of the function at that point or its rate of change. The *integral* of the function between two points is the area under a graph of the function between the points. These relationships are illustrated in Figure D.1.

D.1   The Derivative

The *derivative* of a continuous function, $y = f(x)$, is the slope of the function at any point, that is, the slope of a straight line tangent to the function at that point. Finding this value is analogous to taking the difference between successive terms of a discrete series $y_1, y_2, y_3, \ldots$. The difference

$$\Delta y_x = y_{x+1} - y_x$$

gives the rate at which y_x changes with a change of one unit in x. With a continuous function, this difference cannot be taken quite so simply. Since x is a continuous variable, values of $f(x)$ can be found at any separation, and the size of the difference between them depends on the size of the difference between the two x points. If the two points are x

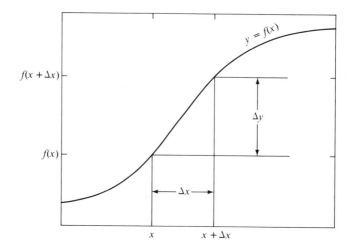

Figure D.2   Calculation of the derivative.

and $x + \Delta x$, the difference is

$$\Delta y = f(x + \Delta x) - f(x)$$

This is shown in Figure D.2. To get the slope, or rate of change per unit step between x and $x + \Delta x$, one needs to divide Δy by Δx:

$$\text{slope} \approx \frac{\Delta y}{\Delta x} = \frac{f(x + \Delta x) - f(x)}{\Delta x}$$

This is only an approximate value of the slope of $f(x)$ at x. An exact value is obtained only when Δx becomes infinitesimally small:

$$\text{slope} = \lim_{\Delta x \to 0} \frac{f(x + \Delta x) - f(x)}{\Delta x} \tag{D.1}$$

Equation D.1 can be used as the definition of the derivative. An example of a function with derivatives indicated at several points is shown in Figure D.3.

The derivative can be found at any point x, so it is really a new function of x. It is denoted by placing a prime on y or on $f(x)$, as y' or $f'(x)$, or, exploiting the similarity to $\frac{\Delta y}{\Delta x}$, by $\frac{dy}{dx}$ or $\frac{df(x)}{dx}$ or $\frac{d}{dx} f(x)$. Symbols such as dx in this notation are the limit of finite quantities such as Δx as they go to 0, but not ordinary numbers in their own right.

The derivative $f'(x)$ is itself a function of x, and so can be differen-

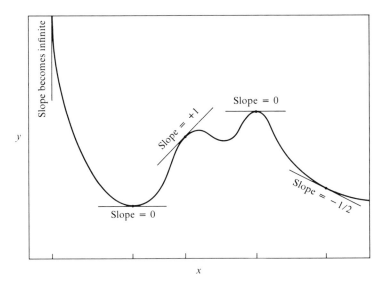

Figure D.3   A function with the derivative at several points indicated.

tiated. The resulting *second derivative* measures the curvature of the function, called its *acceleration*. The second derivative is denoted by any of the equivalent representations

$$y'' = f''(x) = \frac{d}{dx}\frac{df(x)}{dx} = \frac{d^2y}{(dx)^2} = \frac{d^2f(x)}{(dx)^2}$$

More generally, the *nth derivative* is obtained by differentiating $f(x)$ n times, and is written

$$\frac{d^ny}{(dx)^n} \quad \text{or} \quad \frac{d^nf(x)}{(dx)^n}$$

When f is a function of several variables, the derivative with respect to one of them is referred to as a *partial derivative,* and the symbol ∂ is used rather than d. Thus, with respect to the variable x,

$$\frac{\partial f(x,y,z)}{\partial x} = \lim_{\Delta x \to 0} \frac{f(x + \Delta x, y, z) - f(x,y,z)}{\Delta x}$$

In terms of the mechanics of calculation, partial derivatives do not differ from simple derivatives.

There are two common uses of the derivative in stochastic-process theory. First, derivatives can be used to find the extrema of functions, that is, their largest or smallest values. This is discussed in the next section. Second, in some models it is easier to describe the rate of change of a quantity than the quantity itself. This leads to equations that contain both quantities and their derivatives, called *differential equations*. A discussion of differential equations is deferred until the integral has been presented.

Finding Extrema of Functions

There are occasions where it is necessary to find the value of a variable x that makes the function $f(x)$ take its largest or its smallest value. This occurs often in problems of estimation, where the parameters of a model must be chosen to maximize some measure of goodness of fit to the data or to minimize some measure of deviation. The principle involved in finding such points is quite straightforward. Suppose that the function is continuous and smooth (i.e., without jumps, kinks, or angles). At the point where the function reaches an extremum, it becomes at least momentarily flat (see, e.g., the points in Figure D.3 with slopes of 0). Thus, finding the points where the slope is 0 locates the extrema. One need only differentiate $f(x)$, set the result equal to 0,

$$\frac{df(x)}{dx} = 0 \tag{D.2}$$

and then solve this equation for x. Not all solutions to Equation D.2 are true extrema, but every finite extremum is a solution.

As an example, suppose that the minimum of the function

$$f(x) = (x - 1)^2 e^{1-x} + 2 \tag{D.3}$$

is to be found. This can be approached by drawing a good graph, such as Figure D.4, which suggests a minimum near $x = 1$. A graph, however, is not highly accurate. Using methods that are explained in the next section, the derivative of Equation D.3 is

$$f'(x) = -(x - 1)(x - 3)e^{1-x} \tag{D.4}$$

At an extremum this is 0; so, by Equation D.2,

$$-(x - 1)(x - 3)e^{1-x} = 0$$

This holds whenever one of the three multiplicative factors is 0, that is, whenever $x - 1 = 0$, $x - 3 = 0$, or $e^{1-x} = 0$. These equations are easily solved: the first two by $x = 1$ and $x = 3$, the last as $x \to \infty$. Thus,

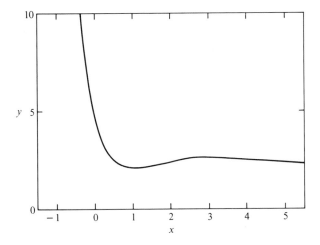

Figure D.4   The function $f(x) = (x - 1)^2 e^{1-x} + 2$.

the "near 1" extremum is in fact exactly at 1. Some knowledge of the function is needed to know that a minimum lies at $x = 1$ and a maximum at $x = 3$ (rather than, say, the other way around). This is where the graph is useful. There are also more precise ways based on the second derivative (the derivative of the derivative), to decide which points are minima, which maxima, and which neither. In practice, with simple models, it is usually obvious what is going on. A second minimum of Equation D.3 is approached as $x \to \infty$. How important this solution is depends on whether infinite (or very large) values of x are meaningful or not.

When the function depends on two variables, an extreme point corresponds to the top of a hill or the bottom of a valley. At this point the function is flat in all directions and has zero derivative with respect to both of its variables. This idea can be generalized to any number of dimensions: for the function $f(x,y,z)$ at the extremum, the three equations

$$\frac{\partial f(x,y,z)}{\partial x} = 0 \qquad \frac{\partial f(x,y,z)}{\partial y} = 0 \qquad \frac{\partial f(x,y,z)}{\partial z} = 0 \qquad (D.5)$$

hold. To find the extrema, these three equations are solved simultaneously for x, y, and z.

Finding Derivatives

The actual process of differentiation is fairly easy, and a few rules carry one quite far. To start with, most elementary functions have simple derivatives. The most useful of these, for the work here, are

$$\frac{da}{dx} = 0 \qquad \text{(where } a \text{ is a constant)} \qquad \text{(D.6)}$$

$$\frac{dx^n}{dx} = nx^{n-1} \qquad n \neq 0 \qquad \text{(D.7)}$$

$$\frac{de^{ax}}{dx} = ae^{ax} \qquad \text{(D.8)}$$

$$\frac{d \log(ax)}{dx} = \frac{1}{x} \qquad \text{(D.9)}$$

The logarithm in Equation D.9 is a natural logarithm, that is, to the base e. Other formulas, particularly those related to the trigonometric functions, can be found in any calculus book.

The simple functions differentiated in Equations D.6 to D.9 can be combined to form more complicated expressions. For example, the function $(x - 1)^2 e^{1-x}$ is formed from the product of two functions, $(x - 1)^2$ and e^{1-x}; while the first of these parts is formed from the composition of the function $u = x - 1$ and the function u^2. The simplicity of differentiation comes from the fact that there are rules for calculating the derivative of combinations of functions of this sort. In the following rules, $f(x)$ and $g(x)$ are functions, $f'(x)$ and $g'(x)$ are their derivatives, and a and b are constants. Then

$$\frac{d}{dx} [af(x)] = af'(x) \qquad \text{(D.10)}$$

$$\frac{d}{dx} [af(x) + bg(x)] = af'(x) + bg'(x) \qquad \text{(D.11)}$$

$$\frac{d}{dx} [f(x)g(x)] = f(x)g'(x) + f'(x)g(x) \qquad \text{(D.12)}$$

$$\frac{d}{dx} \left(\frac{f(x)}{g(x)} \right) = \frac{g(x)f'(x) - f(x)g'(x)}{[g(x)]^2} \qquad \text{(D.13)}$$

$$\frac{d}{dx} [f(g(x))] = f'(g(x))g'(x) \qquad \text{(D.14)}$$

The last of these is known as the *chain rule*.

As an example, consider the function in Equation D.3 that was minimized above:

$$f(x) = (x - 1)^2 e^{1-x} + 2$$

By the addition rule, Equation D.11, and the fact that the derivative of a constant is zero, Equation D.6,

$$\frac{df(x)}{dx} = \frac{d}{dx}(x - 1)^2 e^{1-x} + \frac{d2}{dx}$$

$$= \frac{d}{dx}(x - 1)^2 e^{1-x}$$

This leaves the product of $(x - 1)^2$ and e^{1-x} to be differentiated; so, by Equation D.12,

$$\frac{df(x)}{dx} = (x - 1)^2 \frac{de^{1-x}}{dx} + \frac{d(x - 1)^2}{dx} e^{1-x} \qquad \text{(D.15)}$$

Both the terms to be differentiated contain the simple function $u = x - 1$. Hence, the chain rule, Equation D.14, applies. For example,

$$\frac{d(x - 1)^2}{dx} = \frac{du^2}{du} \frac{du}{dx}$$

$$= 2u \frac{du}{dx}$$

$$= 2(x - 1) \frac{d(x - 1)}{dx}$$

$$= 2(x - 1)$$

using Equation D.7 twice in the process. Likewise,

$$\frac{de^{1-x}}{dx} = \frac{de^{-u}}{du} \frac{du}{dx} = -e^{1-x}$$

Putting these into Equation D.15, then simplifying gives

$$f'(x) = -(x - 1)(x - 3)e^{1-x}$$

the result in Equation D.4 above.

D.2 Integration

The integral is the continuous analog of a sum, just as the derivative is the analog of a difference. The easiest geometric picture of the integral is as an area. Suppose that $x_1, x_2, \ldots$, are points on the x axis of a

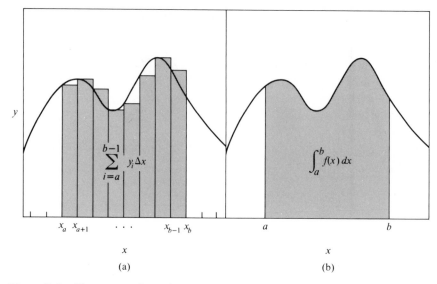

Figure D.5   The area under a function as a sum (part a) and an integral (part b).

function $f(x)$ separated by the distance Δx (i.e., $x_i - x_{i-1} = \Delta x$) and that $f(x_1)$, $f(x_2)$, ... , are values of the function at these points (see Figure D.5a). The sum

$$A = \sum_{i=a}^{b-1} f(x_i)\, \Delta x \tag{D.16}$$

is the area under the series of bars each having the height $f(x_i)$ and the width Δx. This sum approximates the area under a smooth graph of the function (Figure D.5b). Now let the distance between the x_i get very small; then the area under the smooth function becomes better and better approximated by the sum in Equation D.16. In the limit as $\Delta x \to 0$, the area is exact. The result of this limit is defined to be the integral of the function.

The symbol for integration is closely parallel to the symbol for the corresponding finite sum. The operation of integrating is denoted by the symbol $\int$ (originally an old-style, tall S), with the limits placed above and below. The symbol dx replaces Δx. Thus, the analog to Equation D.16 is

$$A = \int_a^b f(x)\, dx \tag{D.17}$$

The most important use of the integral in this book is in the calculation of probabilities for continuous random variables. These variables are represented by probability density functions; and the probabilities, by areas below the functions (as in Figure A.1 and Equation A.9). Thus, if $f(x)$ is the density function of a random variable X,

$$P(a < X \le b) = \int_a^b f(x) \, dx$$

Integrals as Weighted Combinations

Another use of integrals is to combine a quantity across the range of a continuous variable according to some weighting. In the work here, the weighting function is usually a probability density function, and the combination involves averaging across this distribution. Again, it is easiest to understand this by starting with the finite equivalent. Suppose that members of the disjoint set of events $E_1, E_2, \ldots, E_n$ take place with probability $P(E_i)$. Now suppose that a quantity Q_i can be measured for each of the E_i values. Thus, the E_i might represent the possible states of the subject at a point in an experiment, $P(E_i)$ the probability of being in a particular one of those states, and Q_i the mean latency for a response in that state. Then the average or expected value of the Q_i—the average latency in the example—is

$$\mu_Q = \sum_{i=1}^n Q_i P(E_i) \tag{D.18}$$

(cf. Equation A.16). The Q_i are the things that are to be combined, and the probabilities weight them for combination.

If the division into events is not into discrete possibilities, but depends on a continuous variable x, then the number of terms in Equation D.18 is infinite, although the contribution of each one is infinitesimal in size. This corresponds to passing from the sum to an integral, exactly as was done in going from Equation D.16 to D.17. Suppose that X is a continuous random variable with density $f(x)$ and that $Q(x)$ is another function defined over x. Then the average or expected value is

$$\mu_Q = \int Q(x) f(x) \, dx \tag{D.19}$$

(cf. Equation A.17). The range of the integral is over the values that x may permissibly take.

Weighted integrals also appear in the continuous analogue of the law of total probability. For a mutually exclusive and exhaustive set of events $B_1, B_2, \ldots, B_n$ and the additional event A, the law of total probability (Equation A.4) states that

$$P(A) = \sum_{i=1}^n P(A|B_i) P(B_i)$$

When the set of conditionalizing events is a continuous random variable with density $f(x)$, then the sum becomes an integral:

$$P(A) = \int P(A|X = x)f(x) \, dx \qquad \text{(D.20)}$$

By using a slightly different definition of the integral, Equation D.19 or D.20 may be rewritten in a form based on the cumulative distribution function $F(x)$, rather than the density function $f(x)$. In essence, the product $f(x) \, dx$ is replaced by a small increment in the cumulative distribution function, denoted $dF(x)$. In this notation, Equation D.19 becomes

$$\mu_Q = \int Q(x) \, dF(x)$$

This integral, known as a *Lebesgue–Stieltjes integral,* is more general than the ordinary or *Riemann integral* used earlier. It subsumes both Riemann integration and summation (as well as mixed forms) in a common operation; thus, both Equation D.18 and Equation D.19 have the identical expression. In theoretical work, the Lebesgue–Stieltjes form has advantages, since results need be stated and proved only once. Hence, it is frequently found in more mathematical treatments of probability theory. In actual calculations, one must treat the discrete and continuous parts separately, using ordinary summation and integration; so the two simpler forms are used throughout this book.

The Relation of the Integral to the Derivative

The integral and the derivative are inverse operations. This is a very important result, known as the *fundamental theorem of calculus.* Suppose that $f(x)$ is a function and $F(x)$ the cumulative area under it from the point a up to the point x:

$$F(x) = \int_a^x f(z) \, dz \qquad \text{(D.21)}$$

The letter z has been used in this equation as the variable of integration to keep it from getting confused with the upper limit of the integral, which is x. The total area under the function $f(x)$ is $F(x)$, and the rate at which $F(x)$ increases with x equals the size of the $f(z)$ at $z = x$. Where $f(x)$ is small, $F(x)$ grows slowly; where $f(x)$ is large, it grows rapidly (see Figure D.6). In more mathematical terms,

$$\frac{d}{dx} F(x) = f(x) \qquad \text{(D.22)}$$

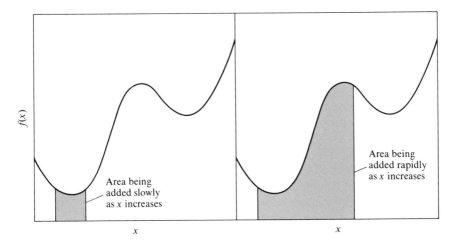

Figure D.6 The relationship between the integral and the derivative.

This relationship goes the other way as well. If the derivative is integrated, the original function is obtained again. However, one qualification must be added. The exact value of an integral depends on both of its limits: where one starts to find the area and where one ends. Because the starting limit—the constant a in Equation D.21—may be anywhere, the recovered function may differ from the original by an additive constant. If $F'(x)$ is the derivative of $F(x)$, then

$$\int_a^x F'(z)\, dz = F(x) + C \qquad (D.23)$$

where C is a constant depending on a. The relationships in Equations D.22 and D.23 express essentially the same result. When Equation D.23 is differentiated, the constant term vanishes (recall Equation D.6) and $F'(x)$ is obtained.

The fundamental theorem of calculus is very important, both in giving a way to organize and interpret the calculus and in giving methods of calculation. For example, in the next section it is used to convert differentiation formulas into integration formulas.

Calculation of Integrals

Finding the integral of a function is a great deal more difficult than finding its derivative. Much of the difficulty can be attributed to the lack of a rule comparable to the chain rule for differentiation (Equation D.14), which allowed the derivative of the composition of two functions to be found. It is frequently impossible to write the integral of a combined expression as a simple combination of the integrals of simpler expressions. This problem is reflected in the sizes of the tables of formulas that have been prepared to aid calculations and can be found in many handbooks. A typical table may contain a few dozen derivative relationships and many hundreds of integrals. Indeed, there are a number of apparently simple functions whose exact integrals cannot be written in a finite number of terms. A familiar example of such a function is e^{-x^2}, which is part of the density function for the normal distribution. Such integrals can be evaluated only by approximations.

The rules for the evaluation of integrals go well beyond the scope of this appendix. Fortunately, a few simple integrals suffice for most of the actual calculations in the book. These can be obtained by application of the fundamental theorem of calculus. Since the integral is the inverse of the derivative, a differentiation rule translates into an integral rule. Thus, Equation D.7,

$$\frac{d}{dx} x^n = nx^{n-1}$$

when substituted into Equation D.23, gives

$$\int nx^{n-1} \, dx = x^n + C$$

It is more convenient to rewrite this expression so that the integrand is a simple power function. Dividing both sides by n, then replacing $n - 1$ by the single letter m, gives

$$\int x^m \, dx = \frac{x^{m+1}}{m + 1} + C \tag{D.24}$$

The value of C is not the same here as in the previous expression.

The original formula, Equation D.7, held only for $n \neq 0$; hence Equation D.24 holds only when $m \neq 1$, leaving the integral of $1/x$ undetermined. This integral is obtained from another derivative formula, that for $\log x$, Equation D.9. This gives the important relationship

$$\int \frac{dx}{x} = \log x + C \tag{D.26}$$

One more integration formula is easily obtained from the derivatives given above, that of e^{ax}. Using Equation D.8 gives

$$\int e^{ax} \, dx = \frac{1}{a} e^{ax} \tag{D.26}$$

Although general rules for the integration of a combination of functions do not exist, there are some specific exceptions. Most important is the fact that integration (like summation) is a linear operation. So the integral of a linear combination is the same linear combination of the integrals:

$$\int [af(x) + bg(x)]dx = a\int f(x)\ dx + b\int g(x)\ dx \qquad (D.27)$$

When $g(x)$ is 0, this reduces to the simpler formula

$$\int af(x)\ dx = a\int f(x)\ dx \qquad (D.28)$$

which says that a term unrelated to the variable of integration can be placed either inside or outside the integral sign.

D.3   Differential Equations

Models expressed in a discrete-time space can often be described as differences between quantities at successive points in time. This gives rise to the difference equations, which are analyzed by the methods discussed in Appendix B. With models in continuous space, a similar logic often applies, except that what results is a relationship between a quantity and its rate of change. Such relationships are known as *differential equations* since they contain derivatives. For example, consider a pure growth process in continuous time. Suppose that the size of a population at time t is $s(t)$. If the old members add to the population by "giving birth" to new members, the rate at which the population increases is proportional to the size of the population. Thus,

$$\frac{ds(t)}{dt} = \gamma s(t) \qquad (D.29)$$

where γ is the growth rate. This equation is similar to a difference equation, except that it contains a derivative rather than a difference between s at two values of time.

From Equation D.29 it is apparent that $s(t)$ and its derivative are similar in form, differing only by the multiplicative constant γ. An examination of the differentiation formulas shows that the exponential function, Equation D.8, has this property. If

$$s(t) = Se^{\gamma t} \qquad (D.30)$$

for some constant S, then

$$\frac{ds(t)}{dt} = S\gamma e^{\gamma t} = \gamma s(t)$$

This exactly matches Equation D.29. Thus, Equation D.30 is a solution to Equation D.29; in fact, it is the only solution. This sort of exponential function is characteristic of populations with uncontrolled growth.

Of course, few differential equations can be solved by guessing the solution. Solving the equation amounts to undoing the derivative, which presents difficulties of greater magnitude than those encountered in calculating integrals. There are numerous texts on the subject, and the topic cannot be covered here. However, once again, it is interesting to note the similarity between the solutions to discrete equations and those to continuous equations. The method for solving linear differential equations with constant coefficients is almost exactly the same as the method for solving linear difference equations with constant coefficients, presented in Appendix B. The derivative plays the same role as the difference did there; and e^{mt}, the same role in the solution as m^t (compare, e.g., Equations D.30 and B.5). To solve a homogeneous differential equation, one sets up an auxiliary polynomial, uses its solutions to get a sum of exponential terms, then determines the constants from the initial conditions. For nonhomogeneous equations, an appropriate particular solution is added to the homogeneous solution.

Appendix E

The Greek Alphabet

Name	Lowercase	Uppercase
alpha	α	A
beta	β	B
gamma	γ	Γ
delta	δ	Δ
epsilon	ϵ	E
zeta	ζ	Z
eta	η	H
theta	θ	Θ
iota	ι	I
kappa	κ	K
lambda	λ	Λ
mu	μ	M
nu	ν	N
xi	ξ	Ξ
omicron	o	O
pi	π	Π
rho	ρ	P
sigma	σ	Σ
tau	τ	T
upsilon	υ	Υ
phi	ϕ	Φ
chi	χ	X
psi	ψ	Ψ
omega	ω	Ω

Appendix F

Chi-Square and Normal Distributions

This table shows the values of a such that the upper-tail probability, $P(X > a)$, equals the values at the top of the table. See the discussion of these distributions in Section A.4.

	0.95	0.9	0.7	0.5	0.3	0.2	0.1	0.05	0.01	0.001
d.f.					Chi-square distributions					
1	0.00	0.02	0.15	0.45	1.07	1.64	2.71	3.84	6.63	10.83
2	0.10	0.21	0.71	1.39	2.41	3.22	4.61	5.99	9.21	13.82
3	0.35	0.58	1.42	2.37	3.66	4.64	6.25	7.81	11.34	16.27
4	0.71	1.06	2.19	3.36	4.88	5.99	7.78	9.49	13.28	18.47
5	1.15	1.61	3.00	4.35	6.06	7.29	9.24	11.07	15.09	20.52
6	1.64	2.20	3.83	5.35	7.23	8.56	10.64	12.59	16.81	22.46
7	2.17	2.83	4.67	6.35	8.38	9.80	12.02	14.07	18.48	24.32
8	2.73	3.49	5.53	7.34	9.52	11.03	13.36	15.51	20.09	26.12
9	3.32	4.17	6.39	8.34	10.66	12.24	14.68	16.92	21.67	27.88
10	3.94	4.87	7.27	9.34	11.78	13.44	15.99	18.31	23.21	29.59
11	4.57	5.58	8.15	10.34	12.90	14.63	17.28	19.68	24.72	31.26
12	5.23	6.30	9.03	11.34	14.01	15.81	18.55	21.03	26.22	32.91
13	5.89	7.04	9.93	12.34	15.12	16.98	19.81	22.36	27.69	34.53
14	6.57	7.79	10.82	13.34	16.22	18.15	21.06	23.68	29.14	36.12
15	7.26	8.55	11.72	14.34	17.32	19.31	22.31	25.00	30.58	37.70
16	7.96	9.31	12.62	15.34	18.42	20.47	23.54	26.30	32.00	39.25
17	8.67	10.09	13.53	16.34	19.51	21.61	24.77	27.59	33.41	40.79
18	9.39	10.86	14.44	17.34	20.60	22.76	25.99	28.87	34.81	42.31
19	10.12	11.65	15.35	18.34	21.69	23.90	27.20	30.14	36.19	43.82
20	10.85	12.44	16.27	19.34	22.77	25.04	28.41	31.41	37.57	45.31
21	11.59	13.24	17.18	20.34	23.86	26.17	29.62	32.67	38.93	46.80
22	12.34	14.04	18.10	21.34	24.94	27.30	30.81	33.92	40.29	48.27
23	13.09	14.85	19.02	22.34	26.02	28.43	32.01	35.17	41.64	49.73
24	13.85	15.66	19.94	23.34	27.10	29.55	33.20	36.42	42.98	51.18
25	14.61	16.47	20.87	24.34	28.17	30.68	34.38	37.65	44.31	52.62
				Normal distribution						
	−1.64	−1.28	−0.52	0.00	0.52	0.84	1.28	1.64	2.33	3.09

Solutions to Problems

Chapter 2

2.1.

	L	G
L	1	0
G	α	$1 - \alpha$

	C	E
L	$1 - \epsilon$	ϵ
G	g	$1 - g$

2.2.

	L	G
L	$1 - \delta$	δ
G	α	$1 - \alpha$

	C	E
L	1	0
G	g	$1 - g$

2.3. a.

	X	Y	GC	GE
X	1	0	0	0
Y	0	1	0	0
GC	0	0	g	$1 - g$
GE	$\alpha\xi$	$\alpha(1 - \xi)$	$(1 - \alpha)g$	$(1 - \alpha)(1 - g)$

b. A third absorbing state XY is needed. The transition probabilities from GE are now $\xi(1 - \psi)$, $(1 - \xi)\psi$, $\xi\psi$, $(1 - \xi)(1 - \psi)g$, and $(1 - \xi)(1 - \psi)(1 - g)$ for states X, Y, XY, GC, and GE, respectively.

2.4. Let $p_c = n_c/N$, $p_i = n_i/N$, and $p_p = n_p/N$. Indicate the state by the selected hypothesis, C, P, or I and the response C or E. Then

	C	PC	PE	IC	IE
C	1	0	0	0	0
PC	0	π	$1 - \pi$	0	0
PE	p_c	πp_p	$(1 - \pi)p_p$	$g p_i$	$(1 - g)p_i$
IC	0	0	0	g	$1 - g$
IE	p_c	πp_p	$(1 - \pi)p_p$	$g p_i$	$(1 - g)p_i$

	C	E
C	1	0
PC	1	0
PE	0	1
IC	1	0
IE	0	1

2.5.

	L	IC	IE	GC	GE
L	1	0	0	0	0
IC	0	π	$1 - \pi$	0	0
IE	δ	$(1 - \delta)\pi$	$(1 - \delta)(1 - \pi)$	0	0
GC	0	0	0	g	$1 - g$
GE	$\alpha\beta$	$\alpha(1 - \beta)\pi$	$\alpha(1 - \beta)(1 - \pi)$	$(1 - \alpha)g$	$(1 - \alpha)(1 - g)$

2.6. a.

	L	I	G
L	1	0	0
I	λ	$1 - \lambda$	0
G	λ^2	$2\lambda(1 - \lambda)$	$(1 - \lambda)^2$

b.

	L	I	G
L	1	0	0
I	λ	$1 - \lambda$	0
G	0	λ	$1 - \lambda$

2.7. Divide state I to include the choice of viewpoint: let IL indicate that the chosen way has been learned, IU that it has not. If each element is selected with probability $\frac{1}{2}$, then

	L	IL	IU	G
L	1	0	0	0
IL	0	$\frac{1}{2}$	$\frac{1}{2}$	0
IU	α	$(1 - \alpha)/2$	$(1 - \alpha)/2$	0
G	0	$\alpha/2$	$\alpha/2$	$1 - \alpha$

	C	E
L	1	0
IL	1	0
IU	g	$1 - g$
G	g	$1 - g$

2.8. Let α, β, and γ be the selection probabilities, with $\gamma = 1 - \alpha - \beta$. Then for Equation 2.21:

	A	B	C	U
A	1	0	0	0
B	0	1	0	0
C	0	0	1	0
U	$\delta\alpha$	$\delta\beta$	$\delta\gamma$	$1 - \delta$

For Equation 2.22:

	A	A_1	B	B_1	C	C_1	U
A	1	0	0	0	0	0	0
A_1	$\delta\alpha$	$1 - \delta$	0	0	0	0	$\delta(1 - \alpha)$
B	0	0	1	0	0	0	0
B_1	0	0	$\delta\beta$	$1 - \delta$	0	0	$\delta(1 - \beta)$
C	0	0	0	0	1	0	0
C_1	0	0	0	0	$\delta\gamma$	$1 - \delta$	$\delta(1 - \gamma)$
U	0	$\delta\alpha$	0	$\delta\beta$	0	$\delta\gamma$	$1 - \delta$

Other definitions of the probabilities can be used, but the pattern of the entries will be the same.

2.9. The result is an 8-state chain with a matrix composed of four blocks, each of which is Matrix 2.29 or Matrix 2.30 multiplied by π or $1 - \pi$:

$$\begin{bmatrix} \pi(2.29) & (1 - \pi)(2.29) \\ \pi(2.30) & (1 - \pi)(2.30) \end{bmatrix}$$

2.10. For example, introduce unobservable states A_1, A_2, B_1, and B_2, which are mapped onto the responses R_1 and R_2. Equation 2.26 is replaced by

	A_2	A_1	B_1	B_2
A_2	1	0	0	0
A_1	α	$1 - \alpha$	0	0
B_1	0	σ	$1 - \sigma$	0
B_2	0	σ	0	$1 - \sigma$

	R_1	R_2
A_2	ϵ	$1 - \epsilon$
A_1	1	0
B_1	0	1
B_2	$1 - \epsilon$	ϵ

where $\epsilon < 1$. A similar matrix replaces Matrix 2.27.

2.11. A single-matrix form of the model (such as Matrix 2.28) must be used:

	R_1E_1	R_2E_1	R_1E_2	R_2E_2
R_1E_1	δ_1	0	$1 - \delta_1$	0
R_2E_1	$\sigma\delta_1$	$(1 - \sigma)\delta_2$	$\sigma(1 - \delta_1)$	$(1 - \sigma)(1 - \delta_2)$
R_1E_2	$(1 - \sigma)\delta_1$	$\sigma\delta_2$	$(1 - \sigma)(1 - \delta_1)$	$\sigma(1 - \delta_2)$
R_2E_2	0	δ_2	0	$1 - \delta_2$

2.12. The model in Problem 2.6b.

2.13.

	S_0	S_1	S_2	S_3
S_0	1	0	0	0
S_1	$\gamma(1 - \eta)$	$1 - \gamma$	$\gamma\eta$	0
S_2	0	$\gamma(1 - \eta)$	$1 - \gamma$	$\gamma\eta$
S_3	0	0	$\gamma(1 - \eta)$	$1 - \gamma(1 - \eta)$

Chapter 3

3.2. a,b. $P(U_t) = (1 - \delta)^{t-1} \to 0$, $P(A_t) = \alpha[1 - (1 - \delta)^{t-1}] \to \alpha$,
$P(B_t) = (1 - \alpha)[1 - (1 - \delta)^{t-1}] \to 1 - \alpha$
c. $\delta(1 - \delta)^{t-1}$

3.3. a. $\alpha + (1 - \alpha)g$

b. $$\frac{(1 - \pi)[\delta + (1 - \delta)\pi]P(I_t) + (1 - g)[\alpha\beta + \alpha(1 - \beta)\pi + (1 - \alpha)g]P(G_t)}{(1 - \pi)P(I_t) + (1 - g)P(G_t)}$$

3.4. $$\frac{1 - \{1 - [\alpha + (1 - \alpha)g]g\}(1 - \alpha)^{t-1}}{1 - (1 - g)(1 - \alpha)^{t-1}}$$

A correct response does not determine the item's state.

3.6. $1/\delta$

3.8. $[1 - (1 - \alpha)^m](1 - g)/\alpha \to (1 - g)/\alpha$

3.9. $P(L = 0) = gb$; $P(L = k) = (1 - g)b(1 - \alpha)^{k-1}$, $k > 0$;
$E(L) = (1 - g)b/\alpha^2 = (1 - g)/\alpha[1 - (1 - \alpha)g]$

3.10. a. $\sigma + (1 - \sigma)gb$
b. $(1 - \sigma)(1 - g)/\alpha$
c. $(1 - \sigma)(1 - g)/\alpha[1 - (1 - \alpha)g]$

3.11. a. $P(GC_t) = (1 - \tau)g[1 - \beta(1 - g)]^{t-1}$, etc.
  b. $P(E_t) = P(GE_t) = (1 - \tau)(1 - g)[1 - \beta(1 - g)]^{t-1}$
  c. $(1 - \tau)/\beta$
  d. $P(T = 0) = \tau$; $P(T = k) = (1 - \tau)\beta(1 - \beta)^{k-1}$, $k > 0$
  e. $P(L = 0) = \tau$;
    $P(L = k) = (1 - \tau)\beta(1 - g)[1 - \beta(1 - g)]^{k-1}$, $k > 0$
  f. $(1 - \beta)(1 - g)$

3.12. $\dfrac{\delta(1 - \pi)P(I_k)}{1 - (1 - \delta)\pi} + \dfrac{[\beta(1 - \pi) + \delta\pi]\alpha(1 - g)P(G_k)}{[1 - (1 - \alpha)g][1 - (1 - \delta)\pi]}$, $k > 0$

3.13. a. $P(F = 0) = g$;
    $P(F = k) = (1 - g)[\alpha + (1 - \alpha)g][(1 - \alpha)(1 - g)]^{k-1}$,
    $k > 0$; $E(F) = (1 - g)/[\alpha + (1 - \alpha)g]$
  b. $P(R = 0) = gb$;
    $P(R = k) = (1 - gb)[\alpha + (1 - \alpha)g][(1 - \alpha)(1 - g)]^{k-1}$,
    $k > 0$; $E(R) = (1 - gb)/[\alpha + (1 - \alpha)g]$

3.14. $P(G_t) = (1 - \lambda)^{t-1}$, $P(I_t) = (t - 1)\lambda(1 - \lambda)^{t-2}$
  Both roots of the auxiliary equation are the same.

3.15. $P(G_t) = (1 - \alpha)^{t-1}$,
  $P(IL_t) = P(IU_t) = (1 - \alpha/2)^{t-1} - (1 - \alpha)^{t-1}$,
  $P(E_t) = (1 - g)(1 - \alpha/2)^{t-1}$

3.16. a. See Equations 5.14.
  b. $P(C_tE_{t+1}) = \pi(1 - \delta)(1 - \pi)P(I_t)$
    $+ g[\alpha(1 - \beta)(1 - \pi) + (1 - \alpha)(1 - g)]P(U_t)$, etc.

3.17. See Figure 6.2.

3.18. a. $P(R_1) \to 1$, $P(R_2) \to 0$; $P(R_1) \to 0$, $P(R_2) \to 1$
  c. $\mu_{t+1} = (1 - \theta)\mu_t + \pi\theta$,
    whence $\mu_t = \pi + (p_1 - \pi)(1 - \theta)^{t-1} \to \pi$

3.19. Fixed: $P(C_{t+1}|E_t) = \alpha + (1 - \alpha)g$
  Variable: $P(C_{t+1}|E_t) = [\gamma + g(\delta + t - 1)]/(\gamma + \delta + t - 1)$,
  $P(C_2|E_1) = \mu_\alpha + (1 - \mu_\alpha)g$, $P(C_\infty|E_\infty) = g$

3.20. $\operatorname{var}(T) = E(T)\left[g + \dfrac{\gamma\delta(1 - g)}{(\gamma - 1)(\gamma - 2)} \right]$

Chapter 4

4.1.

	L	IL	IUC	GC	IUE	GE
L	1	0	0	0	0	0
IL	0	$1/2$	$g/2$	0	$(1-g)/2$	0
IUC	α	$(1-\alpha)/2$	$(1-\alpha)g/2$	0	$(1-\alpha)(1-g)/2$	0
GC	0	$\alpha/2$	$\alpha g/2$	$(1-\alpha)g$	$\alpha(1-g)/2$	$(1-\alpha)(1-g)$
IUE	α	$(1-\alpha)/2$	$(1-\alpha)g/2$	0	$(1-\alpha)(1-g)/2$	0
GE	0	$\alpha/2$	$\alpha g/2$	$(1-\alpha)g$	$\alpha(1-g)/2$	$(1-\alpha)(1-g)$

	L	IHC	ILC	GC	IHE	ILE	GE
L	1	0	0	0	0	0	0
IHC	δ	$(1-\delta)\eta\pi$	$(1-\delta)(1-\eta)\pi$	0	$(1-\delta)\eta(1-\pi)$	$(1-\delta)(1-\eta)(1-\pi)$	0
ILC	δ	$(1-\delta)\eta\pi$	$(1-\delta)(1-\eta)\pi$	0	$(1-\delta)\eta(1-\pi)$	$(1-\delta)(1-\eta)(1-\pi)$	0
GC	$\alpha\beta$	$\alpha(1-\beta)\eta\pi$	$\alpha(1-\beta)(1-\eta)\pi$	$(1-\alpha)g$	$\alpha(1-\beta)\eta(1-\pi)$	$\alpha(1-\beta)(1-\eta)(1-\pi)$	$(1-\alpha)(1-g)$
IHE	δ	$(1-\delta)\eta\pi$	$(1-\delta)(1-\eta)\pi$	0	$(1-\delta)\eta(1-\pi)$	$(1-\delta)(1-\eta)(1-\pi)$	0
ILE	δ	$(1-\delta)\eta\pi$	$(1-\delta)(1-\eta)\pi$	0	$(1-\delta)\eta(1-\pi)$	$(1-\delta)(1-\eta)(1-\pi)$	0
GE	$\alpha\beta$	$\alpha(1-\beta)\eta\pi$	$\alpha(1-\beta)(1-\eta)\pi$	$(1-\alpha)g$	$\alpha(1-\beta)\eta(1-\pi)$	$\alpha(1-\beta)(1-\eta)(1-\pi)$	$(1-\alpha)(1-g)$

4.4. a. $\mathbf{S} = (\mathbf{I} + \mathbf{X})(\mathbf{I} - \mathbf{X})^{-3}$

b. $\mathrm{var}(\mathbf{T}) = \mathbf{f}[(\mathbf{I} + \mathbf{D})(\mathbf{I} - \mathbf{D})^{-1} - (\mathbf{I} - \mathbf{D})^{-1}\mathbf{1}'\mathbf{f}](\mathbf{I} - \mathbf{D})^{-1}\mathbf{1}'$

$\quad = \mathbf{f}(\mathbf{I} - \mathbf{D})^{-1}(\mathbf{I} + \mathbf{D} - \mathbf{1}'\mathbf{f})(\mathbf{I} - \mathbf{D})^{-1}\mathbf{1}'$

4.7. a. $P(F = 0) = s_{1,a} + s_{1,c}\mathbf{1}'_c$

$\quad P(F = k) = \mathbf{s}_{1,e}\mathbf{Q}_{ee}^{k-1}[\mathbf{a}'_e + \mathbf{Q}_{ec}\mathbf{1}'_c], \; k > 0$

$\quad E(F) = \mathbf{s}_{1,e}(\mathbf{I} - \mathbf{Q}_{ee})^{-2}[\mathbf{a}'_e + \mathbf{Q}_{ec}\mathbf{1}'_c]$

$\quad E(F^2) = \mathbf{s}_{1,e}(\mathbf{I} + \mathbf{Q}_{ee})(\mathbf{I} - \mathbf{Q}_{ee})^{-3}[\mathbf{a}'_e + \mathbf{Q}_{ec}\mathbf{1}'_c]$

b. $P(R = 0) = s_{1,a} + \mathbf{s}_{1,c}\mathbf{N}_{cc}\mathbf{a}'_c$

$\quad P(R = k) = [\mathbf{s}_{1,e} + \mathbf{s}_{1,c}\mathbf{N}_{cc}\mathbf{Q}_{ce}]\mathbf{Q}_{ee}^{k-1}[\mathbf{a}'_e + \mathbf{Q}_{ec}\mathbf{1}'_c], \; \text{etc.}$

4.8. a. $P(H = 0) = [s_{1,L}, s_{1,HC}, s_{1,HE}]\mathbf{1}'_3$

$$P(H = k) = [\mathbf{s}_{1,LC}, \mathbf{s}_{1,LE}]\begin{bmatrix} \mathbf{Q}_{LC,LC} & \mathbf{Q}_{LC,LE} \\ \mathbf{Q}_{LE,LC} & \mathbf{Q}_{LE,LE} \end{bmatrix}^{k-1}\left\{ \begin{bmatrix} \mathbf{Q}_{LC,HE} \\ \mathbf{Q}_{LE,HE} \end{bmatrix} \right.$$

$$\left. + \begin{bmatrix} \mathbf{Q}_{LC,HC} \\ \mathbf{Q}_{LE,HC} \end{bmatrix} + \begin{bmatrix} \mathbf{a}'_{LC} \\ \mathbf{a}'_{LE} \end{bmatrix} \right\}$$

b. $s_{1,HE} + [s_{1,HC}, s_{1,LC}, s_{1,LE}]$

$$\left\{ \mathbf{I} - \begin{bmatrix} \mathbf{Q}_{HC,HC} & \mathbf{Q}_{HC,LC} & \mathbf{Q}_{HC,LE} \\ \mathbf{Q}_{LC,HC} & \mathbf{Q}_{LC,LC} & \mathbf{Q}_{LC,LE} \\ \mathbf{Q}_{LE,HC} & \mathbf{Q}_{LE,LC} & \mathbf{Q}_{LE,LE} \end{bmatrix} \right\}^{-1}\begin{bmatrix} \mathbf{Q}_{HC,HE} \\ \mathbf{Q}_{LC,HE} \\ \mathbf{Q}_{LE,HE} \end{bmatrix}$$

4.10. a. $\mathbf{b}' = (\mathbf{I} - \mathbf{TW}_c)^{-1}\mathbf{TW}_a\mathbf{1}'$, where $\mathbf{W}_c$ selects transient-correct states and $\mathbf{W}_a$ selects absorbing states.

c. $P(L = 0) = \mathbf{s}_1(\mathbf{W}_c + \mathbf{W}_a)\mathbf{b}'$; $P(L = k) = \mathbf{s}_1\mathbf{T}^{k-1}\mathbf{W}_E\mathbf{b}'$, $k > 0$

d. $P(T = 0) = \mathbf{s}_1(\mathbf{W}_c + \mathbf{W}_a)\mathbf{b}'$;

$\quad P(T = k) = \mathbf{s}_1(\mathbf{I} + \mathbf{W}_c\mathbf{N}_c)\mathbf{W}_E[\mathbf{T}(\mathbf{I} + \mathbf{W}_c\mathbf{N}_c)\mathbf{W}_E]^{k-1}\mathbf{b}'$, $k > 0$,

$\quad$ where $\mathbf{N}_c = (\mathbf{I} - \mathbf{TW}_c)^{-1}\mathbf{T}$.

4.11. $P(E_{F+t}) = (s_{1,c} + s_{1,e}N_{ee}Q_{ec})[I_{cc}, 0_{ce}]Q^{t-1} \begin{bmatrix} 0_{ce} \\ I_{ee} \end{bmatrix} 1'_e$

4.12. a. $E(\mathscr{L}_{L+t}) = \dfrac{1}{E} [s_{1,c}, s_{1,e}]N \begin{bmatrix} 0_{ce} \\ I_{ee} \end{bmatrix} [a'_e \quad Q_{ec}] \begin{bmatrix} 1 & 0 \\ a'_c & Q_{cc} \end{bmatrix}^{t-1} M \begin{bmatrix} 1 \\ b'_c \end{bmatrix}$,

where $E = 1 - P$(no errors) and M is a diagonal matrix containing the expected latencies of the absorbing and correct states.

b. $\mu + \delta[(1 - \alpha)g]^t; \mu$

Chapter 5

5.1. $\hat{\alpha} = \frac{2}{3}/3.4 = 0.196$

5.2. $\hat{\alpha} = \dfrac{\sqrt{(1 - g)^2 + 4g(1 - g)/M_L} - (1 - g)}{2g} = 0.180$

5.3. $\hat{\alpha} = e_1/M_T = 0.162, \hat{\sigma} = 1 - e_1/(1 - g) = 0.175$

5.4. $\hat{\gamma} = \dfrac{2(V_T - gM_T)}{V_T + M_T(1 - 2g) - M_T^2}$

$\hat{\delta} = \dfrac{(V_T - M_T + M_T^2)(M_T - 1 + g)}{(1 - g)[V_T + M_T(1 - 2g) - M_T^2]}$

5.5. $\hat{\alpha} = 0.0885$

5.6. $\hat{\alpha} = 0.176$

5.7. c. $\hat{\alpha} = 0.157, \hat{\sigma} = 0.137$

5.8. See Equation 6.8; $\hat{\alpha} = 0.157, \hat{\sigma} = 0.118, \hat{\gamma} = 0.395$.

5.9. a. $L(\alpha) = \begin{pmatrix} N \\ A \end{pmatrix} \dfrac{\alpha^{2A}(1 - \alpha)^{2(N-A)}}{[1 - 2\alpha(1 - \alpha)]^N}$

b. $\hat{\alpha} = \dfrac{\sqrt{A(N - A)} - A}{N - 2A}$

5.10. a. $\hat{\beta} = 1/M_T$

b. $\hat{\beta} = 1/M_T$

c. $\hat{\beta} = 1/M_T^*$, where M_T^* is calculated using only items for which at least one error is made, $M_T^* = E/N(1 - z)$.

d. $\hat{\beta} = 1/M_T^*, \hat{\tau} = z, \hat{\epsilon} = 1 - M_T/M_L$

Chapter 6

6.1. $P(C_3C_4C_5) = 0.282$, $P(C_3C_4E_5) = 0.030$, etc.; $\chi^2 = 2.12$, $df = 1$, retain H_0, all-or-none model fits

6.2. $\log L(\omega^*) = -112.757$, $\log L(\omega) = -112.033$; $\chi^2 = 1.45$, $df = 1$, retain H_0

6.3. $\chi^2 = 1.12$, $df = 1$, retain all-or-none model

6.4. a. $\chi^2 = 58.72$, $df = 4$, reject H_0
   b. $\chi^2 = 26.90$, $df = 2$, reject H_0
   c. $\chi^2 = 1.04$, $df = 1$, retain H_0

6.5.
$$H_0: \beta = \beta_0: \chi^2 = 2 \left[N(1-z) \log \frac{N(1-z)}{E\beta_0} \right.$$
$$\left. + [E - N(1-z)] \log \frac{E - N(1-z)}{E(1-\beta_0)} \right]$$

$$H_0: \sigma = \sigma_0: \chi^2 = 2 \left[Nz \log \frac{z}{\sigma_0} + N(1-z) \log \frac{1-z}{1-\sigma_0} \right]$$

$$H_0: \gamma = \gamma_0: \chi^2 = 2 \left[C \log \frac{M_L - M_T}{M_L\gamma_0} + E \log \frac{M_T}{M_L(1-\gamma_0)} \right]$$

6.6. $\hat{\beta} = 0.116$, $\chi^2 = 6.93$, $df = 1$, reject $\beta = 0.2$
   $\hat{\sigma} = 0.200$, $\chi^2 = 0$, $df = 1$, retain $\sigma = 0.2$
   $\hat{\gamma} = 0.473$, $\chi^2 = 0.75$, $df = 1$, retain $\gamma = 0.5$

6.7. a. $\hat{\alpha}_A = 0.047$, $\hat{\alpha}_B = 0.073$
   b. $\hat{\alpha}_{AB} = 0.057$
   c. $\chi^2 = 19.83$, $df = 1$; conclude items have different difficulty, type B being easier

Chapter 7

7.2
$$\beta = \frac{\alpha}{1 - (1-\alpha)\gamma}, \epsilon = (1-\alpha)\gamma, \tau = 1 - \frac{(1-\sigma)(1-\gamma)}{1 - (1-\alpha)\gamma}$$

$$\alpha = \beta(1-\epsilon), \gamma = \frac{\epsilon}{1 - \beta(1-\epsilon)}, \sigma = \frac{\tau[1 - \beta(1-\epsilon)] - \epsilon\beta}{1 - \beta}$$

7.4. a. $\omega = [\alpha_{11}, \alpha_{12}, \alpha_{13}, \alpha_{21}, \alpha_{22}, \alpha_{23}, \alpha_{31}, \alpha_{32}, \alpha_{33}, \tau]$, $\omega^* = [\kappa_1, \kappa_2, \kappa_3, \sigma_1, \sigma_2, \sigma_3, \tau]$ with a constraint such as $\kappa_1 = 1$ to make the parameters of ω^* identifiable; $df = 10 - 6 = 4$
   b. $\omega = [1, \kappa_2, \kappa_3, \sigma_1, \sigma_2, \sigma_3, \tau]$, $\omega^* = [1, 1, 1, \sigma_1, \sigma_2, \sigma_3, \tau]$ (if $\kappa_1 = 1$ is used to identify parameters); $df = 2$

c. $\boldsymbol{\omega} = [1, \kappa_2, \kappa_3, \sigma_1, \sigma_2, \sigma_3, \tau]$, $\boldsymbol{\omega}^* = [1, \kappa_2, \kappa_3, \sigma, \sigma, \sigma, \tau]$; $df = 2$

d. All tests are based on the assumption that study time acts only through σ, obscuring any effects on κ.

7.5. $\lambda_1 = 1$, $\lambda_2 = 1 - \alpha(1 - \delta) - \beta\delta$, $\lambda_3 = \lambda_4 = 0$; so $\alpha_{AON} = \alpha(1 - \delta) + \beta\delta$

7.6. $\lambda_1 = 1$, $\lambda_2 = 1 - \alpha\delta - \beta(1 - \delta)$, $\lambda_3 = 1 - \epsilon$, $\lambda_4 = 0$; cannot match the all-or-none model, need at least two stages

7.7. $\alpha = \phi\epsilon + \psi(1 - \epsilon)$, $\delta = \zeta\pi + \eta(1 - \pi)$

Chapter 8

8.1. a. 1 absorbing; 2 transient
   b. 1–2 ergodic
   c. 1–3 ergodic
   d. 1, 3 ergodic; 2 transient
   e. 2 absorbing; 1, 3 transient
   f. 1–4 persistent and periodic ($p = 2$)
   g. 1, 3–4 persistent and periodic ($p = 2$); 2 transient
   h. 2, 4 ergodic; 1, 3, 5 transient and periodic ($p = 2$)

8.4. $(0.1143)(0.8857)^{k-1}$

8.5. $(1 + 2\eta^2)/\gamma\eta^3$

8.7. a. $[1, 0]$
   b. $[7/9, 2/9]$
   c. $[6/51, 10/51, 35/51]$
   d. $[4/7, 0, 5/7]$
   e. $[0, 1, 0]$
   f. $[10/76, 0, 0, 66/76]$ and $[0, 1/19, 18/19, 0]$
   g. $[0, 0, 1, 0]$ and $[\alpha, 0, 0, 1 - \alpha]$
   h. $[0, 7/12, 0, 5/12, 0]$

8.8. $\{(2\eta - 1)/[\eta^4 - (1 - \eta)^4]\}[(1 - \eta)^3, (1 - \eta)^2\eta, (1 - \eta)\eta^2, \eta^3]$

8.9. $(1 - g)\delta/(\alpha + \delta)$

8.10. a. $\pi, 1 - \pi, 1 - 2\pi(1 - \pi), 2\pi(1 - \pi)$
   b. $0.7, 0.7, 0.64, 0.592, \ldots, 0.4$

8.11. a. $\delta_2/(1 - \delta_1 + \delta_2)$, $\delta_2/(1 - \delta_1 + \delta_2)$,
      $1 - 2(1 - \delta_1)\delta_2/(1 - \delta_1 + \delta_2)$
   b. $P(E_1)$ and $P(R_1)$ go from 0.7 to 0.8; $P(C)$ goes from 0.58 to 0.84

8.13. $0.3, 0.2, 0.12, 0.072, 0.0432, \ldots$

8.14. $f_B^{(1)} = 1 - \beta$; $f_B^{(t)} = \alpha\beta(1 - \alpha)^{t-2}$, $t > 1$

8.15. $\dfrac{\eta^4 - (1 - \eta)^4}{(2\eta - 1)(1 - \eta)^3}$, $\dfrac{\eta^4 - (1 - \eta)^4}{(2\eta - 1)\eta(1 - \eta)^2}$, etc.

8.16. a. $1/(1 - \pi)$
   b. $\pi/(1 - \pi)$

8.17. 0.375, 0.25, 0.15, 0.09, 0.054, ...

8.18. $1/[1 - (1 - \alpha)\gamma]$

Chapter 9

9.1. b.
$$\begin{bmatrix} 1 - \alpha & 0 & \alpha & 0 & 0 & \cdots \\ \delta & 1 - \alpha - \delta & 0 & \alpha & 0 & \cdots \\ 0 & \delta & 1 - \alpha - \delta & 0 & \alpha & \cdots \\ \vdots & \vdots & \vdots & \vdots & \vdots \end{bmatrix}$$

c. $\rho = 2\alpha/\delta$

d. Transient: $\rho > 1$, $2\alpha > \delta$; null: $\rho = 1$; ergodic: $\rho < 1$

e. $1 - \rho$

f. $3\rho/2(1 - \rho)$

g.
$$\begin{bmatrix} 1 - \alpha & \phi\alpha & (1 - \phi)\alpha & 0 & 0 & \cdots \\ \delta & 1 - \alpha - \delta & \phi\alpha & (1 - \phi)\alpha & 0 & \cdots \\ 0 & \delta & 1 - \alpha - \delta & \phi\alpha & (1 - \phi)\alpha & \cdots \\ \vdots & \vdots & \vdots & \vdots & \vdots \end{bmatrix}$$

9.2. $\epsilon(\alpha\theta + 1 - \alpha)[(\alpha\theta^2 + 1 - \alpha)/(\alpha\theta + 1 - \alpha)]^{t-1}$

9.3. Divide each S_i into correct response and error states C_i and E_i. Let $e_i = \epsilon\theta^i$. Then

	C_0	E_0	C_1	E_1	C_2	E_2	...
C_0	$1 - e_0$	e_0	0	0	0	0	...
E_0	$(1 - \beta)(1 - e_0)$	$(1 - \beta)e_0$	$\beta(1 - e_1)$	βe_1	0	0	...
C_1	0	0	$1 - e_1$	e_1	0	0	...
E_1	0	0	$(1 - \beta)(1 - e_1)$	$(1 - \beta)e_1$	$\beta(1 - e_2)$	βe_2	...
C_2	0	0	0	0	$1 - e_2$	e_2	...
E_2	0	0	0	0	$(1 - \beta)(1 - e_2)$	$(1 - \beta)e_2$	...
$\vdots$	$\vdots$	$\vdots$	$\vdots$	$\vdots$	$\vdots$	$\vdots$	

9.4. To be in S_i, $i \geq 0$, there must be i, or $i + 2$, or $i + 4$, and so on movements, of which $i, i + 1, i + 2, \ldots$, are to the right. If L is the greatest integer less than $(t - 1 - i)/2$, then

$$P(S_{i,t}) = \sum_{k=0}^{L} \binom{t-1}{i+2k} \binom{i+2k}{i} \gamma^{i+2k}(1 - \gamma)^{t-1-i-2k} \alpha^{i+k}(1 - \alpha)^k$$

A similar equation holds for $i \le 0$. If $\alpha > \frac{1}{2}$, the process vanishes to the right; if $\alpha < \frac{1}{2}$, to the left; if $\alpha = \frac{1}{2}$, states are null.

9.5. $C/(1 - z)$

9.7. $[(b - a)z + a]/(1 - z)^2$

9.12. a. $P(z) = \dfrac{\delta p_0}{\delta - \alpha z - \alpha z^2} = \dfrac{2(1 - \rho)}{2 - \rho z - \rho z^2}$

9.13. a. $P(z) = \dfrac{1 - 0.6z}{1 - 0.9z - 0.02z^2}$

b. $F(z) = (0.3 + 0.02 z)z/(1 - 0.6 z)$

c. 2.5625

9.14. $F(z) = (1 - \alpha)z + \alpha\beta z^2/[1 - (1 - \beta)z]$

Chapter 10

10.4. Poisson process with $\lambda_{\text{comb}} = \Sigma\lambda_i$

10.5. a. $\hat{\mu} = 1/M$, $\hat{r}$ is nearest integer to M^2/V

b. $g_3(t) = \frac{1}{2}(t/2)^{11}e^{-t/2}/11!$

10.7. a. Serial: $128t^3e^{-4t}/3$

Parallel: $25(1 - e^{-25t/12})^3 e^{-25t/12}/3$

b. Serial: $N = 3$; Parallel: $N = 4$

10.8. a. $\rho = (2 - \phi)\alpha/\delta$

b. $p_i = (1 - \rho)(m_1^{t+1} - m_2^{t+1})/(m_1 - m_2)$,

where $m_1, m_2 = [\alpha \pm \sqrt{\alpha^2 + 4\alpha\delta(1 - \phi)}]/2\delta$.

Alternatively, $P(z) = [\delta - \alpha(2 - \phi)]/[\delta - \alpha z - \alpha(1 - \phi)z^2]$.

The result applies for $0 \le \rho < 1$; i.e., $(2 - \phi)\alpha < \delta$.

10.9. a.
$$\begin{bmatrix} 0 & 0 & 0 & 0 & \cdots \\ \delta & -\alpha - \delta & \alpha & 0 & \cdots \\ 0 & \delta & -\alpha - \delta & \alpha & \cdots \\ \vdots & \vdots & \vdots & \vdots & \end{bmatrix}$$

b. $e_i = (\delta/\alpha)^i$, $\alpha > \delta$; $e_i = 1$, $\alpha \le \delta$

10.10. Let S_0 indicate a queue of length 0; S_1, S_2, and S_3, a queue of length 1, etc. Then $\lambda\tau p_0 = 3p_1$; $(\lambda\tau + 3)p_i = 3p_{i+1}$, $i = 1, 2$; $(\lambda\tau + 3)p_i = \lambda\tau p_{i-3} + 3p_{i+1}$, $i > 2$.

10.11. a. A death process (see Equation 10.20) with $\lambda = \alpha/(N + M)$

b. Binomial with parameters N and $1 - e^{-\alpha T/(N+M)}$

c. $P(R = r) = e^{-K(N-r)} \prod_{i=0}^{r-1} [1 - e^{-K(N-i)}]$, where

$K = \alpha\tau/(N + M)$.

References

The number(s) or letter(s) in brackets following a reference indicates the chapter(s) or appendix(es) in which that reference is cited.

Atkinson, R. C., Bower, G. H., and Crothers, E. J. *An introduction to mathematical learning theory.* New York: Wiley, 1965. [2, 3]

Atkinson, R. C., and Crothers, E. J. A comparison of paired-associate learning models having different acquisition and retention axioms. *Journal of Mathematical Psychology,* 1964, *1,* 285–315. [2, 3]

Bernbach, H. A. Derivation of learning process statistics for a general Markov model. *Psychometrika,* 1966, *31,* 225–234. [4]

Beyer, W. H. *CRC standard mathematical tables,* 25th ed. Boca Raton, FL: CRC Press, 1978. [9]

Bower, G. H. Application of a model to paired-associate learning. *Psychometrika,* 1961, *26,* 255–280. (Reprinted in Neimark and Estes, 1967.) [2, 3]

Bower, G. H., and Trabasso, T. R. Concept identification. In R. C. Atkinson, ed., *Studies in mathematical psychology.* Stanford, CA: Stanford University Press, 1964. (Partially reprinted in Neimark and Estes, 1967.) [2, 8]

Bush, R. R., and Mosteller, F. *Stochastic models for learning.* New York: Wiley, 1955. [2]

Bush, R. R., and Sternberg, S. H. A single operator model. In R. R. Bush and W. K. Estes, eds., *Studies in mathematical learning theory.* Stanford CA: Stanford University Press, 1959. [2]

Calfee, R. C., and Atkinson, R. C. Paired-associate models and the effect of list length. *Journal of Mathematical Psychology,* 1965, *2,* 254–265. [2]

Coombs, C. H., Dawes, R. M., and Tversky, A. *Mathematical psychology: An elementary introduction.* Englewood Cliffs, NJ: Prentice-Hall, 1970. [2]

Cox, D. R. *Renewal theory.* London: Methuen, 1962. [8, 10]

Cox, D. R., and Smith, W. L. *Queues.* London: Methuen, 1961. [10]

Daniels, R. W. *An introduction to numerical methods and optimization techniques.* New York: Elsevier–North Holland, 1978. [5]

Estes, W. K. Probability learning. In A. W. Melton, ed., *Categories of human learning.* New York: Academic Press, 1964. [2]

Feller, W. *An introduction to probability theory and its applications.* Vol. I, 3rd ed. New York: Wiley, 1968. [9]

Goldberg, S. *Introduction to difference equations.* New York: Wiley, 1958. [B]

Green, D. M., and Swets, J. A. *Signal detection theory and psychophysics.* New York: Wiley, 1966. (Reprinted: New York: Krieger, 1974.) [1]

Greeno, J. G. Paired-associate learning with short-term retention: Mathematical analysis and data regarding identification of parameters. *Journal of Mathematical Psychology,* 1967, *4,* 430–472. [2, 7]

Greeno, J. G. Identifiability and statistical properties of two-stage learning with no successes in the initial state. *Psychometrika,* 1968, *33,* 173–215. [2, 7]

Greeno, J. G. Representation of learning as discrete transition in a finite state space. In D. H. Krantz, R. C. Atkinson, R. D. Luce, and P. Suppes, eds., *Contemporary developments in mathematical psychology.* Vol. 1: *Learning, memory, and thinking.* San Francisco: W. H. Freeman and Company, 1974. [2]

Greeno, J. G., James, C. T., DaPolito, F., and Polson, P. G. *Associative learning: A cognitive analysis.* Englewood Cliffs, NJ: Prentice-Hall, 1978. [1]

Greeno, J. G., Millward, R. B., and Merryman, C. T. Matrix analysis of identifiability of some finite Markov models. *Psychometrika,* 1971, *36,* 389–408. [7]

Greeno, J. G., and Steiner, T. E. Markovian processes with identifiable states: General considerations and application to all-or-none learning. *Psychometrika,* 1964, *29,* 309–333. [7]

Hays, W. L. *Statistics,* 3rd ed. New York: Holt, Rinehart, and Winston, 1981. [5, 6, A]

Holland, P. W. A variation on the minimum chi-square test. *Journal of Mathematical Psychology,* 1967, *4,* 377–413. [5]

Kemeny, J. G., and Snell, J. L. *Finite markov chains.* Princeton: Van Nostrand, 1960. (Reprinted: New York: Springer-Verlag, 1976.) [4, 8]

Kendall, M., and Stewart, A. *The advanced theory of statistics.* Vol. 2: *Inference and relationship,* 4th ed. New York: Macmillan, 1979. [5, 6]

Kleinrock, L. *Queueing systems.* Vol. 1: *Theory.* New York: Wiley-Interscience, 1975. [10]

Koopmans, T. C., ed. *Statistical inference in dynamic economic models.* New York: Wiley, 1950. [7]

Kraemer, H. C. Point estimation in learning models. *Journal of Mathematical Psychology,* 1964, *1,* 28–53. [5]

Lamming, D. *Mathematical psychology.* London: Academic Press, 1973. [2]

Larkin, J. H., and Wickens, T. D. Population states and eigenstructure: A simplifying view of Markov learning models. *Journal of Mathematical Psychology,* 1980, *22,* 176–208. [7]

McNicol, D. *A primer of signal detection theory.* London: Allen and Unwin, 1971. [1]

Millward, R. B. Derivations of learning statistics from absorbing Markov chains. *Psychometrika,* 1969, *34,* 215–232. [4]

Millward, R. B. Theoretical and experimental approaches to human learning. In J. W. Kling and L. A. Riggs, eds., *Woodworth and Schlosberg's experimental psychology,* 3rd ed. New York: Holt, Rinehart, and Winston, 1971. [2]

Millward, R. B., and Wickens, T. D. Concept-identification models. In D. H. Krantz, R. C. Atkinson, R. D. Luce, and P. Suppes, eds. *Contemporary developments in mathematical psychology.* Vol. 1: *Learning, memory, and thinking.* San Francisco: W. H. Freeman and Company, 1974. [2]

Myers, J. L. Sequential choice behavior. In G. H. Bower, ed., *The psychology of learning and motivation.* Vol. 4. New York: Academic Press, 1970. [2]

Myers, J. L. Probability learning and sequence learning. In W. K. Estes, ed., *Handbook of learning and cognitive processes.* Vol. 3: *Approaches to human learning and motivation.* Hillsdale, NJ: Earlbaum, 1976. [2]

Neimark, E. D., and Estes, W. K. *Stimulus sampling theory.* San Francisco: Holden-Day, 1967. [2]

Norman, D. A., and Rummelhart, D. E. A system for perception and memory. In D. A. Norman, ed., *Models of human memory.* New York: Academic Press, 1970. [10]

Norman, M. F. Incremental learning on random trials. *Journal of Mathematical Psychology,* 1964, *1,* 336–350. [2]

Offir, J. D. Stochastic learning models with distributions of parameters. *Journal of Mathematical Psychology,* 1972, *9,* 404–417. [3]

Paz, A. *Introduction to probabilistic automata.* New York: Academic Press, 1971. [2]

Polson, P. G. Presolution performance functions for Markov models. *Psychometrika,* 1972, *37,* 453–459. [4]

Polson, P. G., and Huizinga, D. Statistical methods for absorbing Markov-chain models for learning: Estimation and identification. *Psychometrika,* 1974, *39,* 3–22. [7]

Restle, F. The selection of strategies in cue learning. *Psychological Review,* 1962, *69,* 329–343. (Reprinted in Neimark and Estes, 1967.) [2, 8]

Restle, F., and Greeno, J. G. *Introduction to mathematical psychology.* Reading, MA: Addison-Wesley, 1970. [2]

Rummelhart, D. E. A multicomponent theory of the perception of briefly exposed visual displays. *Journal of Mathematical Psychology,* 1970, *7,* 191–218. [10]

Shiffrin, R. M. Memory search. In D. A. Norman, ed., *Models of human memory.* New York: Academic Press, 1970. [10]

Steiner, T. E., and Greeno, J. G. An analysis of some conditions for representing *N* state Markov processes as general all-or-none models. *Psychometrika,* 1969, *34,* 416–487. [7]

Sternberg, S. Memory-scanning: Mental processes revealed by reaction-time experiments. *American Scientist,* 1969, *57,* 421–457. [10]

Tolman, E. C. Prediction of vicarious trial-and-error by means of the schematic sow-bug. *Psychological Review,* 1939, *46,* 318–336. [2]

Trabasso, T. R., and Bower, G. H. *Attention in learning: Theory and research.* New York: Wiley, 1968. [2]

Wandell, B. A., Greeno, J. G., and Egan, D. A. Equivalence classes of functions of finite Markov chains. *Journal of Mathematical Psychology,* 1974, *11,* 391–403. [7]

Yellot, J. I., Jr. Probability learning with noncontingent success. *Journal of Mathematical Psychology,* 1969, *6,* 541–575. [2]

Index

A boldface page number indicates the primary definition of a term; an italic page number indicates material in a problem.

Absorbing barrier, 46
Absorbing chain, **175**
Absorbing state, **26**, 52, **173**
All-or-none model, 1, **3–5**, **24–29**, *48*,
    74, *75*, *76*
  basis change, 161–162, *170*
  conditional response probability,
    65–66, *74*
  equivalent versions, 154–156,
    160–161, *169*
  errors before first success, *75*
  generating function, 222–223
  goodness-of-fit tests, 140–141, *148*
  hypothesis testing: *See* Hypothesis-
    testing all-or-none model
  item variability: *See* Variable item-
    difficulty all-or-none model
  latency, *107*, 166–167
  learning rate, 26
  likelihood, 121, *132*, 155
  likelihood-ratio tests, *145–148*, *149*
  maximum-likelihood estimators,
    119–122, *132*, 145
  method-of-moments estimators,
    113–116, *131*, *132*
  minimum chi-square estimates,
    140–141, *148*
  number of errors, 61–65, *75*

recurrence of errors, 189–192, *198*,
    222–223
response probabilities, 58–59
response-state sets, 83
runs of errors, *75*
sequential statistics, *76*, 124, 141
state probabilities, 52–54
trial of last error, *75*
variable item difficulty: *See* Variable
    item-difficulty all-or-none model
Alternative hypothesis, **136**
Associative law, **297**
Asymptotic state distribution: *See*
    Stationary distribution
ATKINSON, R. C., 35, 38, 41, 65
Automaton, 39n
Auxiliary equation, **282**

Backward latency curve, 104–105
Backward learning curve, **102**–104
Basis, **306**
  of eigenvectors, 309–311
Basis change, 306–307
  all-or-none model, 161–162, *170*
  likelihoods under, 100–102, 158–161
  model equivalence under, 158–162
  response-state sets, 86–88
Bayes' theorem, 256

BERNBACH, H. A., 82
Bernoulli event, **261**
Beta distribution, **277–279**
Beta function, **277**
BEYER, W. H., 214
Bias, **111**
Binomial coefficient, **268**
Binomial distribution, **268–269**
  generating function, 213–214, *224*
Binomial theorem, **268–269**
Birth-and-death process, **246**, 249–250
  extinction probability, 250
  multiple-step transitions, 250–251,
    253
Birth process:
  fixed rate, **228**: *See also* Poisson
    process
  variable rate, 238–246
BOWER, G. H., 27, 29, 41, *48*, 65, 187
BUSH, R. R., 30

CALFEE, R. C., 38
cdf (cumulative distribution function),
  257
Central limit theorem, **273**
Central moment, **260**
Chain rule, **320**
Change of basis: *See* Basis change
Chapman–Kolmogorov equations, 80n
Characteristic equation, **282**, **312**
Characteristic root (eigenvalue), 56n,
  308–313
Characteristic vector (eigenvector),
  308–313
  as basis vector, 309–311
Chi-square distribution, **272**
  as sampling distribution, 136
  table, 330
Chi-square statistic:
  likelihood-ratio, **139**, 144–145
  Pearson, **124**, 137
  relation between estimators, *133*
Choice model, repeated, **41–43**, *171*
  expected return time, 194
  recurrence probabilities, 190, 191,
    198
  stationary distribution, 180–181
Choice model, simple, **39–43**, *49*
  parameter estimates, 133
  state probabilities, 56, *74*
Classification of Markov states,
  172–176, *196*, 205–206
Communicating states, **172**
Commutative law, **297**
Comparison of models, 141–148
Concept identification, 28, *48*
  See also Hypothesis-testing all-or-
    none model

Conditional error probability: *See*
  Conditional response probability
Conditional probability, **255**
Conditional response probability, **65**–67
  all-or-none model, 65–66, *74*
  linear model, 209–210
  RTI model, *224*
  two-stage model, 66–67, *74*
  variable item-difficulty all-or-none
    model, 71–72, *76*
Confidence ratings, *105*, *106*
Consistent estimator, **111**
Convolution, **215–216**
COOMBS, C. H., 19
COX, D. R., 185n, 227, 231
CROTHERS, E. J., 35, 41, 65
Cumulative distribution function (cdf),
  257
Cyclic chain, 175n

DANIELS, R. W., 126
DAPOLITO, F., 8n
DAWES, R. M., 19
Death process, **243–246**, *252*
Decision rule, **136**
Defective distribution, **258**
Degrees of freedom, 137, **272**
Density function, **257**
Derivative, **315–316**, 317–321
  calculation rules, 319–321
  chain rule, 320
  partial derivative, 317
  relation to integral, 324–325
Determinant, **300–301**
Difference equation(s), **280–281**,
  282–290
  complete, **285**
  eigenvalues and, 290, 311–312
  generating function solution,
    217–218, *224–225*
  homogeneous, **281–285**
  linear, **281**
  matrix form, 290, 311–312
  nonhomogeneous, **285–288**
  order, **281**
  particular solution, **285**
  simultaneous, *224–225*, **288–290**,
    311–312
Differential equation, **327–328**
Differentiation: *See* Derivative
Diffusion process, 12
Distribution: *See* specific types
Distribution function, **257**
Distributive law, **297**

Efficiency, **112**
Efficient estimator, **112**
EGAN, D. A., 152, 158n

Eigenstructure, **308–313**
 of ergodic chain, 182–183
 relation to state probabilities, 82
 of simultaneous difference equations,
  311–312
Eigenvalue, 56n, **308**–313
Eigenvector, **308**–313
 as basis vector, 309–311
Elementary event, **254**
Empty set, **255**
Equivalent models:
 all-or-none model, 160–161, *169*
 basis change and, 158–162
 equivalence classes of, 163–164
 two-stage model, 157–158, 162, *170*
Ergodic chain, **174**, 175
 eigenstructure of, 182–183
 state probabilities, 179–183
 stationary distribution, 179–183, *197*,
  198: See also Stationary
  distribution
Erlang distribution, **236**
Erlang process, **236**–238, *253*
 parameter estimates, *252*
Errors before first success, **75**
 all-or-none model, *75*
 matrix formulation, *106*
ESTES, W. K., 19, 43
Estimable parameter, **152**
Estimates of parameters: *See* Parameter estimates
Estimator, **108**–113
 maximum-likelihood, 116–117,
  118–119, 120–123: *See also*
  Maximum-likelihood estimator
 method-of-moments, **113**–116: *See*
  also Method-of-moments
  estimator
 minimum chi-square, **123–124**,
  125–126: *See also* Minimum chi-
  square estimator
Event, **254**
Exhaustive event, **255**
Expectation, **261**
Expected recurrence time, 192–194
 all-or-none model, *198*
 choice model, 194
Expected value, **259**–261
Exponential distribution, 235, **273–274**
Extinction probability, birth-and-death
 process, 250
Extrema:
 analytical, 318–319
 numerical, 126–131, *134*

FELLER, W., 211
First-passage time, **194**
 matrix formulation, 194–196
 See also Recurrence probability

Fundamental matrix:
 ergodic chain, **196**
 transient states, **91–92**
Fundamental theorem of calculus,
 324–325

Gamma distribution, **275–277**
Gamma function, **275**
Generating function, 211, **212**–223, *224*,
 225
 binomial distribution, 213–214, *224*
 convolutions, 216
 difference equations, 217–218,
  224–225
 geometric distribution, 212, 213, *224*
 moments of distributions, 214–215
 queueing model, *224*
 recurrence probabilities, 221–223,
  225
 RTI model, 219–221
 sum of random variables, 216
 sum of series members, 214
 sum of two series, 215
Geometric distribution, **261–264**
 generating function, 212, 213, *224*
Geometric representation of state
 probabilities, 56–58
Geometric series, sums of, 264–267
Gradient, **128**
Greek alphabet, 26, **329**
GREEN, D. M., 9
GREENO, J. G., 8n, 19, 24n, 35, 152,
 158n, *170*

HAYS, W. L., 113, 135, 254
Hill climbing, 128
HOLLAND, P. W., 125n
Homogeneous difference equation,
 281–285
Homogeneous process, **23**
HUIZINGA, D., 152
Hybrid distribution, **259**
Hypothesis testing, 28, 35
Hypothesis-testing all-or-none model,
 27–29, *75*, 154
 likelihood, 155
 likelihood-ratio test, *149*
 observable-state property, 163–164
 parameter estimates, *133*, *169*

Identifiable model, **151**
Identifiable parameter, **151**
Identification of models and parame-
 ters, 151–170
Identifying restriction, 164–165
Identity matrix, **299**
Incomplete beta function, **277**
Incomplete gamma function, **275**

Independent events, **256**
Initial (state) vector, **23**, **78**
Integral, **321–322**, 323–327
  calculation rules, 325–327
  Lebesgue–Stieltjes, 324
  relation to derivative, 324–325
  Riemann, 324
Integration: *See* Integral
Intersection, **255**
Irreducible chain, **175**
Item variability, **68**–73
  See also Variable item-difficulty all-
    or-none model

JAMES, C. T., 8n

KEMENY, J. G., 82, 196
KENDALL, M., 113, 135
KLEINROCK, L., 227, 238
Knowledge-state space, **20**
KOOPMANS, T. C., 152
KRAEMER, H. C., 119n

LAMMING, D., 19
LARKIN, J. H., 152, 158n, *170*
Last error: *See* Trial of last error
Latency of response, **97–98**
  all-or-none model, *107*, 166–167
  backward, 104–105
  after last error, *106–107*
Latent value or root (eigenvalue), 56n,
  308–313
Latent vector (eigenvector), **308**–313
  as basis vector, 309–311
Law of total probability, **255–256**
Learning curve:
  backward, **102**–104
  forward, **58**–60
Lebesgue–Stieltjes integral, 324
Likelihood, **88**–91, 99–102, *106*, *107*,
  117
  all-or-none models, 121, *132*, 155
  under basis change, 100–102,
    158–161
Likelihood-ratio chi-square, *133*, **139**,
  144–145
Likelihood-ratio tests, **144**–148
  all-or-none model, 145–*148*, *149*
  hypothesis-testing all-or-none model,
    149
  two-stage model, 147–*148*, *149*
Linear model, **29–31**, 208–210
  conditional response probability,
    209–210
  number of errors, 209
  parameter estimates, 209
  state probabilities, 208–209
Long-and-short model, **35–38**
  equivalence to two-stage model, 162

McNICOL, D., 9
MARKOV, A. A., 15
Markov chain, **15**
Markov model, **9–10**, **19–23**
Markov process, 9, **15**
Markov property, 10, **15**–16
Matrix, **292**
  addition, **294**, 303
  eigenstructure of, **308–313**
  identity, **299**
  inverse, 299, **300–304**
  multiplication, 295, **296–297**, 304
  partitioned, **303–304**
  rank, **307–308**
  simultaneous difference equations,
    290, 311–312
  simultaneous equations, 298, 301–302
  singular, **302–303**, 308
  subtraction, **295**, 303
Maximum-likelihood estimator,
  116–117, **118–119**, 120–123
  all-or-none model, 119–122, *132*, 145
  choice model, *133*
  hypothesis-testing all-or-none model,
    133
  relationship to minimum chi-square
    estimator, *133*
Mean, **160**
  from generating function, 214–215
Memory search, *253*
MERRYMAN, C. T., 152, *170*
Method-of-moments estimator, **113**–116
  all-or-none model, 113–116, *131*, *132*
MILLWARD, R. B., 29, 43n, 82, 92, 152,
  170
Minimum chi-square estimator,
  123–124, 125–126
  all-or-none model, *148*
  relationship to maximum-likelihood
    estimator, *133*
Model(s), 6, **7–9**
  restricted and unrestricted, **142**
Moment (central, about zero and
  mean), **260**
MOSTELLER, F., 30
Multiplication:
  matrix, 295, **296–297**, 304
  scalar, **295**
Mutually exclusive events, **255**
MYERS, J. L., 43, 43n

Negative binomial distribution, **269–270**
NEIMARK, E. D., 19
Nonhomogeneous difference equation,
  285–288
Nonhomogeneous model, **23**
Nonsingular matrix, **302**
Nonstationary model, **23**

Normal distribution, **273**
　table, 330
NORMAN, D. A., 238
NORMAN, M. F., 32
Null hypothesis, **135**
Null states, **205**
Number of errors, 60, **61**–65
　all-or-none model, 61–65, *75*
　linear model, 209
　matrix formulation, 93–95, *105, 106*
　two-stage model, *75*
　variable item-difficulty all-or-none
　　model, 72–73, *76*
Numerical extrema, 126–131, *134*
Numerical optimization, 126–131

Observable states, **163–164**
OFFIR, J. D., 69
Order of difference equation, **281**

Parallel Poisson processes, 243, *252*
Parameter, **26**, 108
Parameter estimates:
　all-or-none model, 113–116, 119–121,
　　131, 132, 145
　choice model, *133*
　Erlang process, *252*
　hypothesis-testing all-or-none model,
　　133, 169
　linear model, 209
　variable item-difficulty all-or-none
　　model, *132*
Parameter space, **109**
Parametric restrictions, 164–165
Partial derivative, **317**
Partitioned matrix, 303–304
Pascal distribution, **269**
PAZ, A., 39n
pdf (probability density function), **257**
Pearson chi-square, **124**, *133*, 137
Period, **174**, 191
Periodic chain, **175**
Periodic state, **173**, 191
　state probabilities, 184
　stationary distribution, 184, 202n
Persistent state, **173**
Poisson distribution, 269, **270–271**
Poisson process, 227, **228–232**,
　　233–236, *251, 252, 253*
　event rate, 233
　parallel events, 243, *252*
　serial events, *252*
　state probabilities, 232–233
　waiting time, 234–236
POLSON, P. G., 8n, 82, 92, 152
Population state, **183**
Probability, **254**
　conditional, **255**

Probability density function (pdf), **257**
Probability generating function, **212**
　See also Generating function
Probability-learning model, **43–45**, *49,
　　50, 76*
　stationary distribution, *197–198*

Queuing model, **206–208**, 247–*252, 253*
　discrete time, 206–208, *223*
　multiple arrivals, *223, 224*, 250–*252*
　state probabilities, 207–208, 248
　stationary distribution, 207–208,
　　248–249
　traffic intensity, 208, *223*, 248, *252*
Queuing theory, 226

Random-trials-increment model: *See*
　RTI model
Random variable, **256**
Random walk, **46–47**, *50*, 171–172, *197*,
　　200–206, *224*
　recurrence probabilities, 204
　state classification, 204–206
　state probability, 200–201
　stationary distribution, *197*, 201–204
Rank, **307–308**
Recurrence probability, **185**–186,
　　187–196, *198*
　all-or-none model, errors in, 189–192
　choice model, 190, 191, *198*
　generating function, 221–223, *225*
　random walk, 204
Recurrent event, **185**–186
Recurrent states, 173n
Reducible chain, **175**
Reflecting barriers, 46
Regular chain, 175n
Renewal probability: *See* Recurrence
　probability
Renewal process, **185**
Response latency: *See* Latency of
　response
Response mapping, **21**, *79*
Response matrix, **22**
Response operator, **21**
Response probability, **58–60**, *107*
　all-or-none model, 58–59
　matrix formulation, 78–80
　two-stage model, 58–60
　variable item-difficulty all-or-none
　　model, 69–71
Response selection matrix, **98–102**, *106*
Response-state sets, **83–88**, *105*
　all-or-none model, 83
　with confidence ratings, *105*
　formed by basis change, 86–88
　two-stage model, 84
Response-state space, **21**

Response (probability) vector, **79**
RESTLE, F., 19, 29, 187
Restricted model, **142**
Riemann integral, 324
RTI (random-trials-increment) model, **31–32**
  conditional response probability, *224*
  state probabilities, 210–211, 219–221
RUMMELHART, D. E., 238
Runs of errors, **75**
  all-or-none model, *75*
  matrix formulation, *106*

Sample space, **254**
Sampling distribution, **110**
Scalar, **294**
Scalar multiplication, **295**
Selection matrix, **98**–102, *106*
Sequential statistics, **68**
  all-or-none model, *76*, 124, 141
  two-stage model, *76*
Serial Poisson processes, *252*
SHIFFRIN, R. M., *253*
Signal detection theory, 9
Significance level, **136**
Simultaneous difference equations, **288–290**
  eigenstructure of, 311–312
  generating-function solution, *224–225*
Singular matrix, **302–303**, 308
SMITH, W. L., 227
SNELL, J. L., 82, 196
Span, **305**
Spectral decomposition, 311
State classification, 172–176, *196*, 205–206
State occupancy:
  ergodic states, 179–183
  transient states, 177–179, *197*
State probabilities, 52–53, **54**–58, *107*
  all-or-none model, 52–54
  choice model, 56, *74*
  eigenstructure, 82
  general chain, 176–177
  generating function of, 217–219
  geometric representation, 56–58
  linear model, 208–209
  matrix formulation, 78–79
  periodic chain, 184–185
  periodic states, 184, 202n
  Poisson process, 232–233
  queueing model, 207–208, 248
  random walk, 200–201
  RTI model, 210–211, 219–221
  two-stage model, 54–55, *75*
State sets as responses, 83–88
  See also Response-state sets

State space, **10–12, 21**
  knowledge, **20**
  response, **21**
  as vector space, 56–58, 86–88
State vector, **23**
Stationarity of error probability, 66
Stationary distribution, **179**–183, *197, 198*
  choice model, 180–181
  as eigenvector, 182–183
  periodic states, 184, 202n
  probability-learning model, *197–198*
  queuing model, 207–208, 248–249
  random walk, *197*, 201–204
  relation to recurrence time, 193–194
Stationary model, **23**
Statistical testing, 135–150
STEINER, T. E., 152
STERNBERG, S., 30, 227
STEWART, A., 113, 135
Stimulus sampling theory, 19
Stochastic automaton or machine, 39n
Stochastic process, **9**
Submatrix, **303**
Sufficient estimator, **111**
Sums:
  geometric series, 264–267
  random variables, 216
  series using generating functions, 214
SWETS, J. A., 9
System state, **183**

Test statistic, **135**
Theory, **6–9**
TLE: *See* Trial of last error
TNE (total number of errors): *See* Number of errors
TOLMAN, E. C., 41
Total probability, law of, **255–256**
TRABASSO, T. R., 29, *48*, 187
Traffic intensity, **208**, *223*, **248**, *252*
Transient state, **26**, 52, **173**
  occupancy, 177–179, *197*
Transition matrix, **22**, **78**
Transition operator, 21
  multiple, 38–39
Transition probability, **13**, **22**
  multiple-step, 81
  two-step, 80–81, 85
Transition-rate matrix, **224–245**, *252*
Transpose, **292**, **294**
Trial of last error, **75**
  all-or-none model, *75*
  matrix formulation, 95–96, *105, 106*
TVERSKY, A., 19
Two-element model, **32**, *49*
  See also Two-stage model

Two-stage model, **32–39**, *48, 49*
  conditional response probability,
    66–67, *75*
  equivalent versions, 157–158, 162,
    170
  with forgetting, 81
  likelihood-ratio tests, 147–*148, 149*
  number of errors, *75*
  response probabilities, 58–60
  response-state sets, 84
  sequential statistics, *76*
  state probabilities, 54–55, *75*

Unbiased estimator, **111**
Union, **255**
Unrestricted model, **142**

Variability of items, **68**–73
Variable item-difficulty all-or-none
    model, **69**, 73, *76*
  conditional response probability,
    71–72

number of errors, 72–73, *76*
parameter estimates, *132*
response probability, 69–71
Variance, **260**
  from generating function, 215, *224*
Vector, **292**
Vector space, 304, **305**–306
  equivalent models, 158–162
  state probabilities, 56–58, 86–88

Waiting times for Poisson process,
    234–236
WANDELL, B. A., 152, 158n
WICKENS, T. D., 29, 152, 158n, *170*

YELLOT, J. I., JR., *50*
Yule process, **241–243**

z-Transform, **212**
  See also Generating function